THE NAKED MOLE-RAT
AND THE
CONSERVATIVE WORLDVIEW

BY JUSTIN BOND

The Naked Mole-Rat and the Conservative Worldview

Copyright © 2024 by Justin Bond
(Defiance Press & Publishing, LLC)

Printed in the United States of America

10 9 8 7 6 5 4 3 2 1

All rights reserved. No part of this publication may be reproduced, distributed, or transmitted in any form or by any means, including photocopying, recording, or other electronic or mechanical methods, without the prior written permission of the publisher, except in the case of brief quotations embodied in critical reviews and certain other noncommercial uses permitted by copyright law.

This book is a work of non-fiction. The author has made every effort to ensure that the accuracy of the information in this book was correct at the time of the publication. Neither the author nor the publisher nor any other person(s) associated with this book may be held liable for any damages that may result from any of the ideas made by the author in this book.

ISBN-13: 978-1-963102-40-6 (Paperback)
ISBN-13: 978-1-963102-39-0 (eBook)
ISBN-13: 978-1-963102-41-3 (Hardcover)

Published by Defiance Press & Publishing, LLC

Bulk orders of this book may be obtained by contacting Defiance Press & Publishing, LLC. www.defiancepress.com.

Public Relations Dept. – Defiance Press & Publishing, LLC
281-581-9300

Defiance Press & Publishing, LLC
281-581-9300
info@defiancepress.com

For Kristen, Edras, and Zemanesh

Table of Contents

Three Revolutions 5
The Case for Free Markets 29
Imperfect Competition 51
Social Norms 71
Woke Postmodernism 85
The Free Rider Problem 103
Jack Welch and the Fall of Boeing 119
Social Status 143
Government Failure 157
Evolutionary Psychology 171
The Philosophy (and Abuse) of Science 207
Cultural Rationality 233
Peer Socialization 253
Strategic Behavior 269
The Hobbesian Problem 283
The Rise of the West 309
The Soft Bigotry of Low Expectations 319
How Does a Dream Die? 347

Further Reading 371
Appendix: Behavioral Genetics and GWAS 375
Endnotes 385
Bibliography 407

Three Revolutions

> Oh Liberty, what crimes are committed in thy name!
>
> – the final words of Madame Roland

The purpose of this book is to explain and defend the conservative worldview. By that I mean the power of ordinary people when socialized by the right norms, values, and culture. This book is about more than history or economics, so don't let the opening chapters fool you. It's about unraveling puzzles of human nature and the lessons they reveal when understood.

Why were the bros right and the scientists wrong about how much protein bodybuilders need? Why do children get their accents from their peers and not their parents? How does a coffee mug predict the fall of communism? Why is science like smoking cigarettes and math like touching a hot stove? What can peasant farmers sharing an irrigation system teach Fortune 500 CEOs? What do naked mole-rats teach us about the downstream consequences of "hookup" culture? And how does the faulty O-ring that caused the space shuttle *Challenger* to explode explain the rise of Western civilization?

These are just a few of the many puzzles in this book, and they all teach a different lesson. Bodybuilders practice their sport in an ecology that produces rational outcomes. Ideas that work spread and become standard. Ideas that fail are weeded out of the crucible of competition. That's why there aren't any Mr. Olympia winners who eat a low-protein diet. Bodybuilders are muscular and hardworking, but other than that, they're ordinary people with ordinary gifts. They aren't scientists with advanced degrees, but they didn't have to be in order to figure out what worked.

In fact, scientists had gone down a dead end chasing nitrogen balance studies.[1] I picked up an old copy of Arnold Schwarzenegger's *Encyclopedia of Modern Bodybuilding* from 1985, and in the nutrition section he was desperately trying to justify high protein diets without sounding like a flat-Earther.[2] Eventually scientists thought to test high protein diets on trained athletes in randomized controlled trials, and the wisdom of bodybuilders like Arnold was proven right.[3] The story has a happy ending, and these days exercise scientists work cooperatively with athletes. Many of them mine folk wisdom and "bro science" for research topics the same way economists mine the writings of Adam Smith.

That's what the conservative worldview is all about—unlocking the power of ordinary people.

The American Revolution

The Founding Fathers did not plan to start a revolution. That was plan B when asserting their rights as Englishmen fell on deaf ears. So in 1776, they gathered in Philadelphia, and Thomas Jefferson created a beautiful summary of natural rights philosophy in the Declaration of Independence.

> We hold these Truths to be self-evident, that all Men are created equal, that they are endowed by their Creator with certain unalienable Rights, that among these are Life, Liberty, and the Pursuit of Happiness—That to secure these Rights, Governments are instituted among Men, deriving their just Powers from the Consent of the Governed, that whenever any Form of Government becomes destructive of these Ends, it is the Right of the People to alter or to abolish it, and to institute new Government

The Declaration of Independence is America's national creed. Other nations are founded on shared ethnicity or accidents of history, but America is founded on a shared belief in these ideals. The original source of these ideals was the philosopher John Locke. He believed that God created a set of moral principles called the *natural law*. Since natural law comes from God, it has a higher authority than any man-made law. Therefore, the proper role of government is to secure and defend these God-given *natural rights*.

John Locke was a philosopher of the *Enlightenment*, which was a period of history known for its emphasis on reason, science, and individual rights. It began in the 1600s, although it has roots that stretch back to the Middle Ages,[4] and it is traditionally considered to end with the French Revolution. The Enlightenment was a period of great intellectual and religious diversity, although it was evolving in a secular direction.

Since this is a book about the power of ordinary people, let's focus on the American colonists asserting their rights as Englishmen. These rights came from English common law, which had been limiting the power of the government since 1215, when the Magna Carta was originally signed. England at that time was ruled by King John—the same King John who was the main villain in the legend of Robin Hood. He was known for high taxes, losing wars, and arbitrarily imprisoning anyone who disagreed with him. Needless to say, he was not a popular king. That much of the legend is true.

A group of angry barons launched a rebellion and forced him to sign a seemingly inconsequential document. It contained a list of grievances about inheritance laws, fishing traps in the river Thames, and the serving size of ale. It wasn't until clauses 38 to 40 that it became clear why the document would become timeless. They established the right of *due process*. That protected most ordinary people from arbitrary arrest and imprisonment. It also granted them the right to a jury trial by their equals. But above and beyond due process, the Magna Carta established something even more important: a legal limit on the power of the king. Before the Magna Carta, the king had absolute power to do whatever he wanted.

King John promptly rescinded the Magna Carta, so the barons promptly resumed their rebellion. However, the war did not last long because John would soon die of natural causes. It was at this point that the Magna Carta became important. John's son, Henry III, was still a boy, and the track record of boy kings was pretty dismal. Luckily Henry had a good regent who realized that the best option was to make peace with the warring barons. He reissued the Magna Carta as part of the reconciliation process, and it's been with the English in some form or another ever since.

The Magna Carta, much like the U.S. Constitution, has an inner logic within its language of rights. This inner logic led to the gradual expansion of the classes of people protected, and of the rights that were included. 800 years later and the document itself is obsolete. The original grievances are no longer relevant and the important principles like due process were affirmed by subsequent laws. But its spirit is deeply infused into English common law and every modern declaration of rights. That includes both the Bill of Rights to the U.S. Constitution and the United Nations Declaration of Human Rights. The Magna Carta was invoked by leaders of both the American and French revolutions.

The upshot of this common law tradition is that the revolutionaries did not see themselves as forming a radical new society, but as asserting their rights as Englishmen against the crown. At least, that was their original plan before it became clear that war with Britain could not be settled with negotiations. That's when they went with plan B: John Locke and a new social contract.

Conservatives have practically canonized Locke because of his full-throated defense of natural rights. But I'll take an 800-year-old tradition of people securing their rights against tyranny over the ideas that sprang out of one man's head, no matter how penetrating and insightful. Locke's two treatises on government are unquestionably works of philosophical genius. Very few human beings before or after Locke could have produced works of that quality.

The Magna Carta was not a work of genius. It was just a list of things that angered a few rich barons. That's why due process was all the way down at numbers 38 to 40 on their list of grievances. There were 37 other things that irritated the barons more than King John's arbitrary arrests. However, over the following years and decades, clauses 38 to 40 were repeatedly invoked even as the other clauses gradually became forgotten. Their repeated use made them grow in importance over time.

No human being could have anticipated the profound downstream consequences of the Magna Carta. It evolved into the document it is today as ordinary people used it to defend their rights. King Henry III would reissue the Magna Carta when he became an adult, and later kings would follow his lead. Then it became a tradition to read it aloud twice each year.[5] This was a time when literacy was rare, so the reading ensured that even uneducated commoners would know their rights.

Sometimes people try to recast the barons as the Founding Fathers of a free and democratic England. Don't let them do it. The barons had no interest in defending the rights of commoners. The credit belongs to the countless numbers of ordinary English people who pounced on these obscure clauses in order to defend their own rights.

The final legacy of the Magna Carta is that, as people became self-aware of how important it was, it helped give rise to our modern understanding of rights. This self-awareness is part of the inner logic of the document. Once people got used to invoking their rights against tyranny in one aspect of their lives, they started doing it in others, even if it wasn't in the Magna Carta. This self-understanding slowly dissolved into English culture and English common law. In fact, Locke himself could never have conceived of his philosophy of natural law if he didn't live in a world that had a Magna Carta in it.

Conservatism is a *bottom-up* movement based on the actions of ordinary people. Liberalism is a *top-down* movement based on the ideas of elite intellectuals. The main thesis of this book is that bottom-up processes are more flexible, powerful, and truth-seeking. The Magna Carta is one example of this phenomenon. The bodybuilders who quickly and accurately figured out the protein needs of athletes, while scientists were fumbling down dead ends, is another.

The French Revolution

Now let's look at what is unquestionably the first truly liberal movement in history: the French Revolution. It started with modest yet admirable goals. French peasants were forced to pay high taxes and fees so that the nobility could afford basic necessities like silver asparagus tongs and diamond-encrusted snuff boxes. The original revolutionaries wanted a reduction in these fees as well as greater rights. It was only later that radicals who wanted a republic like the United States emerged. It wouldn't be long before many of these radicals would be executed as traitors during the Reign of Terror.

The British politician Edmund Burke saw where the revolution was headed long before it got ugly. He predicted in his book, *Reflections on the Revolution in France*, that it would end in chaos, violence, and tyranny. Burke was a lifelong reformer and a member of the Whig party, not the Tory party that supported the king. Burke was a frequent critic of King George III, and he had defended the American colonists.

In fact, Burke had made another successful prediction: that if Britain denied the colonists their rights as Englishmen, then they would assert their rights as Englishmen and start a revolution.

Given Burke's background, many people were shocked when he came out against the French Revolution, and his criticisms marked the beginning of the modern conservative movement. In that sense the French Revolution gave birth to both modern liberalism and conservatism. The idea of conservative reform still surprises many on the left, who often assume that any reform is liberal, and any defense of historical injustice is conservative. So here's a parable to understand how Burkeans view reform.

The California gold rush of 1849 has become famous, but there was also a less well-known "fur rush." Sea otters in California and the North Pacific were hunted for their fur, which was unusually warm and soft. This had profound downstream consequences because sea otters are a keystone species. Sea urchins are one of the primary food sources of sea otters, so as the sea otter population declined, the sea urchin population exploded. The sea urchins eat kelp, so the kelp forests off the coast of California and the North Pacific were decimated. These kelp forests play a vital role in the lives of many marine species, and overhunting sea otters almost destroyed them.

Conservatives see social norms, traditions, and institutions as existing in an equally delicate ecosystem. That doesn't mean they can't be changed, but it does mean that the best way to change society is through a series of small incremental steps. The evolution of the Magna Carta is a textbook example, as is the inner logic of the Constitution, which would invariably lead to universal suffrage and the abolition of slavery. Here's a basic conservative principle: Don't assume whatever norm, tradition, or institution you want to alter or abolish is not a sea otter. The French would learn this lesson the hard way.

A good way to get a handle on the French Revolution is through the influence of the two leading philosophers who inspired it: Voltaire and Jean-Jacques Rousseau. Voltaire was the biggest influence on the revolution during the early moderate stage. He did not have an overriding philosophy but was instead a lifelong critic of religion, nobility, corruption, and hypocrisy. He could best be summarized by one of his most famous quotes: "I have never made but one prayer to God, a very short one: Oh Lord, make my enemies ridiculous. And God granted it."

Voltaire's defining principle was religious tolerance. That might seem odd for someone who was a lifelong critic of religion, but Voltaire knew enough about human nature to understand that only bad things would happen if leaders had the power to choose their people's religion. The revolution's leaders, inspired by Voltaire, included freedom of religion in The Declaration of the Rights of Man and Citizen. It was basically the French version of the Bill of Rights.

It did not take long before the revolution's commitment to tolerance was tested. Although the French people now had freedom of religion, Catholicism remained the official state faith. If the leaders of the revolution had really learned from Voltaire, they would not have done this, and keeping Catholicism as the state religion came back to haunt them. It's sea otters all the way down.

The French leaders subordinated the Catholic Church to the French government. They confiscated Church property, made priests and bishops an elected position, and forced clergy members to swear an oath to the new government that transcended their loyalty to their faith. This took John Locke's principle that natural law was higher than man-made law and turned it upside down. Almost half of all priests refused to swear this oath, and they would be increasingly persecuted. Many of them would be executed for their beliefs.

The next step that widened the rift with Catholics was the growing momentum behind forming a republic, like in the United States. Many Catholics still loved both their religion and their king, so they were increasingly opposed to the direction the revolution was taking. They supported it when it meant a reduction in the fees peasants were forced to pay and constitutional limits to the power of the king. But now they weren't so sure.

This created a timeless dilemma that we still face today: What do you do if you have power and believe yourself to be on the right side of history, but much of the population disagrees with you? Do you patiently set out to win their hearts and minds? Or do you force your beliefs on others? The revolution's leaders chose the second option. That's when the influence of Voltaire gave way to the philosophy of Jean-Jacques Rousseau.

Until the Enlightenment, most Medieval and Modern philosophers felt that human nature was naturally bad, a belief that came from the Christian doctrine of original sin. This negative vision of human nature had been eroding over the course of the Enlightenment, but it took Rousseau to make the final break. He made his fame when he heard about an essay contest on whether or not science and the arts had improved the moral character of society. In a flash of insight, he decided the answer was *no*. In this essay and other works, he developed his radical philosophy that people are naturally good but corrupted by civilization.

Rousseau explained how this works with the parable of the *noble savage*.[6] In an imagined history of primitive life, people lived together in peace and harmony. Everyone took what they needed by hunting and foraging, and the Earth provided plenty of food and other resources to keep people happy. There was no need to fight or wage war because there was nothing to fight about.

Rousseau may have rejected the Christian doctrine, but all

philosophical systems have a concept of original sin and Rousseau's was no different. That sin was private property. Rousseau wrote:

> The first man who, having fenced in a piece of land, said 'This is mine,' and found people naïve enough to believe him, that man was the true founder of civil society. From how many crimes, wars, and murders, from how many horrors and misfortunes might not any one have saved mankind, by pulling up the stakes, or filling up the ditch, and crying to his fellows: Beware of listening to this impostor; you are undone if you once forget that the fruits of the earth belong to us all, and the earth itself to nobody.

The idea was that as soon as someone claimed the land, they could start accumulating more stuff than everyone else. This would lead to envy, and then other people would start hoarding more wealth and possessions than they needed too. The race would be on, and some people would become wealthy and others would be paupers. This is when envy leads to conflict as people try to steal from others. Governments had to be formed to protect the private property of the citizens, which only escalated the level of violence and conflict as nations warred on other nations.

Rousseau said it was too late to go back to these simpler times, but it was possible to recreate their spirit. The people could form a new social contract organized around the *general will*, which is what's good for the people as a whole. If everyone submits to the general will, then you get three things: liberty, equality, and fraternity (community). Thus, Rousseau gave the French Revolution its famous slogan of Liberté, Égalité, Fraternité. You still see this slogan in French documents, public buildings, and schools.

The darkness lurking in Rousseau's philosophy emerged when he discussed what to do with people who refused to submit to the general will. Rousseau said they should be "forced to be free." Those four short words would be the cause of untold violence and misery for centuries.

Rousseau was an important intellectual influence on virtually every major totalitarian movement that would come after him. Although Rousseau himself was not opposed to all private property, Marx and the communists would take the logical next step. The *Black Book of Communism* estimates that communism caused 100 million deaths during the twentieth century. Rousseau would also inspire Nazism. In *The History of Western Philosophy*, Bertrand Russell wrote, "At the present time, Hitler is an outcome of Rousseau; Roosevelt and Churchill, of Locke."[7] The philosopher Paul Strathern agrees, "Rousseau's ideas were to inspire both the glories and the excesses of the French Revolution, and continued to play a similar role in the twentieth century. His ideas are recognizable in both fascism and communism, as well as in the underlying drift towards self-expression and liberalism."[8]

The more you read about Rousseau, the more you see his ghost haunting modern liberalism. To paraphrase (or butcher) John Maynard Keynes, "Modern liberals, who believe themselves to be quite exempt from any intellectual influence, are usually the slaves of Jean-Jacques Rousseau." Rousseau was a product of the Enlightenment, but his writings marked a sharp break from that tradition, so he is often considered the first philosopher of the *Romantic Age*, which began after the Enlightenment.

If the Enlightenment was about reason, science, and individual rights, then the Romantic Age was about emotion, nature, and self-expression. When the conservative Ben Shapiro says, "the facts don't care about your feelings," he's invoking Enlightenment reason against Romantic passions. The quasi-religious undertones of the modern environmental movement are also straight out of the Romantic period, as is the idea that everyone is a unique and special "snowflake."

The excesses of the French Revolution could be seen most clearly with the program of *dechristianization*. It escalated in intensity after a republic was formed and King Louis XVI was put on trial and executed. Monasteries and convents were closed, and the revolution auctioned off the remaining Church property. The priests and monks were usually able to find new careers, but it was a cruel transition for elderly nuns. Many of them had outlived any family that they knew, so they were cast out onto the streets and became homeless.

The French made a couple attempts to create new secular state religions to replace Catholicism, although they never really gained much traction. Nevertheless, it was made illegal for priests to perform the Catholic mass and to give communion. Priests who refused to swear the loyalty oath continued these now-illegal practices, and they were heavily persecuted. Many of them would be executed during the Reign of Terror. The old Gregorian calendar with its seven-day week was replaced with a new calendar that had a ten-day week. That was not a smart move because ordinary French people went from having a day off every seven days to a day off every ten days.

Conscription was the last straw for many Catholics. France had declared war on several nations, which meant that soldiers were needed. When it became clear that there weren't enough volunteers, the revolution's leaders passed laws for conscription. That gave Catholics a choice: they could fight for the revolution that oppressed them, or they could fight back. Many chose to fight back, particularly in the Vendée region of France.

Women were active participants in the counter-revolution. They had been some of the earliest advocates for the revolution in its early days, and events like the bread riots and the Women's March on Versailles were crucial turning points. But when the revolution became oppressive, women were also the first to criticize.

One reason women opposed the revolution is that they were worried, correctly, that they would lose their hard-won rights if the revolution grew too radical and failed. The male leaders of the revolution were fighting for their legacy; the women were fighting for their rights. Many of these women, like Olympe de Gouges, who wrote *The Declaration of the Rights of Woman and of the Female Citizen*, were executed by the guillotine because of their criticisms. Another was Madame Roland, whose final words before her execution form the epigraph of this chapter: "Oh Liberty, what crimes are committed in thy name!" The other reason women opposed the revolution was that they were more devout than men, so they were particularly upset at the persecution of the Catholic Church. Women in the Vendée served as nurses, spies, and messengers. Some of these women even fought and died alongside the men in battle.

The war in the Vendée was extremely brutal, although in fairness, all wars back then were extremely brutal. There were no Geneva Conventions, so tactics like killing civilians, burning houses, killing livestock, and destroying farmlands were common. The goal was to literally starve the population into submission. The war may also have been a genocide depending on how you untangle dechristianization from the revolution's political goals. The most notable atrocity was the Drownings at Nantes, where the desire to kill captive counter-revolutionaries more efficiently led to loading thousands of non-combatants, including women and children, onto barges and then sinking them.

I've been focusing on the top-down aspects of the French Revolution, but it's important to realize that many turning points were achieved by a lawless mob using extra-legal methods. This continued to be true even after the French had a constitution. In the beginning, it led to a virtuous cycle between the leaders and the French peasants. Events like the Storming of the Bastille and the Women's March on Versailles paved the way for major reforms. The leaders empowered the peasants who empowered the leaders, which created an unstoppable momentum.

However, as the revolution progressed, that momentum became a curse. A good example is the Insurrection of May 31 to June 2, when the French mob stormed the revolutionary government and forced them to arrest and later execute the moderate members of the National Convention. This put the French government under the control of far-left radicals and paved the way for the Reign of Terror, at which point power was shifted once more to Maximilien Robespierre and the Committee of Public Safety. They used Terror against the nobility, Catholic clergy, counter-revolutionaries, ultra-radicals who wanted the revolution to go even further, and moderates who wanted to curb its excesses. In the process, they exposed the major design flaw of the guillotine: the rivers of blood that were created when it was used to behead people repeatedly.

The final tally of the Reign of Terror was 35,000 political prisoners executed, about half of them by the guillotine. When the Reign of Terror finally ended, the government was too weak and too illegitimate to hold power. The brilliant young general Napoleon stepped in to become dictator and rolled back many of the revolution's reforms, although he did keep others. Edmund Burke's criticism was proven right. In a letter to a member of the National Assembly he had warned: "It is ordained in the eternal constitution of things, that men of intemperate minds cannot be free. Their passions forge their fetters."[9] The revolution proved that the French people had intemperate minds.

The thesis of this book is a defense of the power of ordinary people—but only when socialized by the right norms, values, and culture. The French people were not ready for democracy. France would bounce around between kings, dictators, and republics until 1870 with the start of the Third Republic. But even that didn't last, and France wouldn't have a truly stable government until the Fifth Republic began in 1958.

The English Revolution

Liberals sometimes argue that the modern left-right terminology dates back to the French Revolution. The liberals who wanted a republic sat on the left in the National Assembly, and the conservatives who wanted a constitutional monarchy sat on the right. In other words, the left believes in freedom and equality whereas the right believes that some people are inherently better than others, and they deserve to rule over their inferiors.

This argument takes a lot of moxie, given that the people on the left side would go on to execute both their enemies and their friends during the Reign of Terror. The hierarchy between the executioner and his victim is the most rigid and extreme of all hierarchies. Moreover, American conservatives are not trying to conserve the monarchy, but the classical liberalism of John Locke and the Founding Fathers. Unlike the left, conservatives never progressed to Rousseau, Karl Marx, and postmodernists like Michel Foucault.

However, I do want to defend Burke and his belief in incremental change, and in his case, the argument is not without merit. Both Burke and his moderate liberal counterpart Voltaire supported a constitutional monarchy. Burke's belief in incremental change would prove timeless, as would Voltaire's defense of religious tolerance. But when it comes to opposing the monarchy, Rousseau was on the right side of history.

So let's engage the hierarchy argument. It's tempting for Burkeans to respond with the American Revolution, but that has two problems. The first is that both sides can lay claim to it. Mapping modern politics onto the past is hard, and it's easy to cherry-pick with the benefit of hindsight. This is compounded by the problem that liberals tend to assume any reform is automatically liberal and any defense of tradition is automatically conservative.

The second problem is that the Americans had a much easier job. They didn't have to worry about dismantling a thousand years of feudalism. The French revolutionaries themselves were well aware of this problem, and it was one of the main arguments for sticking with a constitutional monarchy. If we want a fair comparison, then we need a revolution in a conservative nation with a feudal tradition. Then we don't have to untangle the threads of which party did what.

And it just so happens that 140 years before the French beheaded their king, dabbled in a republic, and then collapsed into the dictatorship of a brilliant military leader, the British had done the exact same thing. Let's compare and contrast the conservative revolution in England with the liberal revolution in France. We'll see that England was taking a Burkean path of incremental change towards democracy, and that they did it without a Reign of Terror.

Historically the French kings shared power with the clergy, nobility, and the people. These three groups formed a body called the Estates-General. They didn't meet regularly, but the king did have to call them when he wanted to raise taxes for a war or an economic crisis. Then the members of the Estates-General would draw up grievance lists and a negotiation with the king would begin. How many of their grievances would the king take care of for how much of a tax increase?

In the centuries prior to the French Revolution, the balance of power had been shifting towards the king. Armored knights on horseback used to dominate the battlefield, but the invention of the musket made them obsolete. (Henry V would make the same claim about the English longbow.) Instead, wars were fought by a mix of conscripts, mercenaries, and standing armies. That was expensive. Knights were members of the nobility who owed military service to their king, but armies had to be paid. As Europe grew wealthy and powerful, merchants began filling in the gap left by the increasingly useless nobles. They were a good source of taxable wealth, and the king could make even more money by selling them noble titles and royal offices.

In 1614 the French King Louis XIII called the Estates-General to meet for what would be the last time for 175 years. After that, the king's chief minister, Cardinal Richelieu, had the fortified castles of the French nobility destroyed. Between that and a variety of other measures, they were able to weaken the French nobility enough for French kings to claim absolute power, including the power to levy new taxes. This process culminated with King Louis XIV, the "Sun King", who was the greatest of Europe's absolute monarchs.

The French nobility hated Cardinal Richelieu after that, and he was the main villain in Alexandre Dumas' classic *The Three Musketeers*. The lesson, as always, is that powerful men can defeat their enemies, but they can't defeat the novelists. Dumas was the grandson of a Haitian slave named Marie-Cessette Dumas (one guess as to who his grandfather was). His father, Thomas-Alexandre Dumas, rose to the rank of general in the French army during the revolution, and his life provided the inspiration and background for many of Dumas' stories. As a conservative, I'm obliged to be a critic of the French Revolution, but it really is astonishing how much opportunity they created—before it all fell apart.

On the other side of the English Channel, King James was trying to do the exact same thing: dissolve Parliament and take absolute power. The Tudor kings and queens before James had already done the hard work of weakening the nobility, but James didn't have a Cardinal Richelieu on his side. Instead, religion was working against him. After England became a Protestant nation, the Bible could be freely translated into English and read by the literate population. It didn't take long before a group called the *Puritans* emerged and began to make a nuisance of themselves. They were determined to reform the Anglican church, including dismantling the church's hierarchy and getting rid of the position of bishop.

King James' doctrine of "no bishop, no king" shows that he clearly understood the potential for conflict. If the Puritans were allowed to bring bishops down to the level of ordinary people, then it wouldn't be long before they did the same thing to the king. This was over 150 years before Jean-Jacques Rousseau inspired philosophers of the French Enlightenment with his iconic work, *The Social Contract.* But the Puritans didn't get their ideas by reading esoteric philosophies beyond the reach of ordinary minds. They did it by reading the Bible, where they found passages like "There is neither Jew nor Greek, there is neither bond nor free, there is neither male nor female: for ye are all one in Christ Jesus." (Galatians 3:28, KJV) These passages upholding the equality of all people resonated deeply with the Puritans and began to dissolve more broadly throughout British culture. (We'll see more of how religion dissolves through culture in the chapter on the Hobbesian Problem, which is where we'll see how the West became WEIRD.)

The Puritans believed that the Bible is the divinely inspired word of God, but here is a secular way to think about it: The Bible is like the Magna Carta with a longer track record. If the Magna Carta didn't have clauses 38 to 40, then it would never have passed the test of time. It would be a minor footnote to a minor rebellion, of interest only to a few medieval historians. And if the Bible didn't have passages like Galatians 3:28, then it too wouldn't have passed the test of time. It would be a minor footnote to a minor desert religion, of interest only to a few Near East Roman historians.

One particularly radical Puritan group was called the *Levellers.* Like many groups, their name was originally a slur. They were accused of wanting to break down hierarchy and level society. It can be hard to get inside the minds of people who lived in the past, and understanding why Leveller was a slur is a good example. Medieval society was organized around a divinely ordained hierarchy called *The Great Chain of Being*. It ranked society from God down to the lowliest creatures. This hierarchy was taught in universities and from the pulpits of the Catholic and Anglican churches on Sundays. Everyone embraced their role in this hierarchy because it was the source of order and stability. When plagues and economic hardships happened, it was often thought this was because people had stopped respecting The Great Chain of Being. Nevertheless, the Levellers embraced the name and took it to heart.

The Levellers originated from the rank-and-file of England's first professional standing army—the *New Model Army*. It had a large contingent of Puritans, and in many ways this army was the first true power block of ordinary people in English history. One of the ways the 2 percent were able to rule the 98 percent was by only sparingly giving military power to ordinary people, but the need for a higher quality and better trained army changed that.

This group of ordinary soldiers who lived 150 years before the French Revolution had many surprisingly modern ideas. In a time when only the wealthiest 2 percent of men could vote, they supported universal male suffrage. Some even supported women's suffrage. They wanted to abolish the House of Lords and have the House of Commons elected by this universal vote. They wanted to get rid of the king and institute a republic. They believed in both religious tolerance and freedom of speech. More generally, they wanted equal treatment of all people before the law. Some of the Levellers even wanted a welfare state that would provide for widows and orphans.

These modern ideas have meant that the Levellers have been claimed by such diverse groups as Marxists and libertarians. The Marxists claimed the Levellers because their name particularly refers to the fact that their opponents accused them of wanting to "level" society so that there would be no rich and no poor. That's not quite what the Levellers themselves believed. Their ideas could be summarized with this quote by the Leveller leader John Liburne: "All and every particular and individual man and woman, that ever breathed in the world, are by nature all equal and alike in their power, dignity, authority and majesty, none of them having (by nature) any authority, dominion or magisterial power one over or above another."[10] The Marxist historians saw the origins of a class consciousness in these ideas. And libertarians have claimed the Levellers because of their staunch defense of individual rights, their opposition to government tyranny, and their full-throated defense of English common law such as the Magna Carta.

The historian Richard Ashcroft argued that the Levellers inspired the natural rights philosopher, John Locke.[11] They shared many of the same ideas and Locke's father served in the New Model Army, so he would have been exposed to the Levellers. It's an intriguing theory and difficult to prove, but in the end, I hope it is wrong. I'd rather believe that there was something in the water that kept leading the British to the cause of freedom.

King James' fears over a conflict with the Puritans were prescient, but it didn't happen until his son, Charles I, became king. The brilliant military leader turned dictator was the Puritan Oliver Cromwell, who led the New Model Army. The English Revolution had other similarities with the French. It too unleashed forces that had been bottled up, and their release made governing a much harder job than the revolutionaries expected when they put their respective kings on trial for treason. As with the French, the republic did not last because it did not have a broad enough base of power and support. Nevertheless, the English Revolution was much less chaotic and did not have a Reign of Terror.

In fact, many historians don't even use the term English Revolution because it wasn't a significant enough break from the past.

Cromwell proved to be one of the best rulers in British history. He dismantled the old patronage system and turned Britain's administrative state into a meritocracy. That often meant hiring relative unknowns who proved their competence in the New Model Army. He increased funding for education. He reformed the legal system to use English instead of Latin and Norman French, which was part of a push to make the law more accessible to ordinary people. He increased foreign trade and spending on naval infrastructure, which helped pave the way for Britain to become a dominant naval power.

Animal lovers will be happy to know that Cromwell banned cockfighting and bear-baiting. Unfortunately, the same moralistic impulse led to him regulating the alehouses, banning people from playing sports on Sunday, and prohibiting the celebration of Christmas. This was probably his biggest mistake because most people liked the alehouses and bear-baiting. They were on board with the Puritans when it meant helping ordinary people, but now they were starting to think that they were better off in the old days when they had a king.

Religious tolerance was the most important of Cromwell's reforms. It even extended to the Jews, who were invited back into England for the first time in centuries. This religious tolerance was also extended to Catholics, even though Cromwell had fought a brutal war with Catholic Ireland. However, the historian John Morrill spent eleven years tracking down 1,253 pieces of Cromwell's writings from libraries around the world. From this research he drew two conclusions.[12] The first was that Cromwell believed persecution is counter-productive because it radicalizes moderates. The second is that Cromwell's goal was to stop the *royalists* who wanted to put a king back on the English throne. After Charles I was put on trial and executed, many English royalists fled to

Ireland, where they formed alliances with Catholic royalists who also opposed Cromwell. Cromwell supported the freedom of individual Catholics to practice their faith—as long as they were politically loyal to him.

Cromwell ruled until he died, but when it became clear that his son was not up to the job, Parliament invited Charles II to be king of England. That must have been one of the more awkward conversations in history: "Sorry about killing your dad, but we're looking forwards to working with you." And just like that, England had a king again. French historians always wonder "what if?" about the French Revolution, and I wonder the same about the Puritan Revolution. It seemed like there was a window for democracy and they just barely missed it. If Charles I had been a better king, the Puritans would have had another generation or two to organically grow and spread. Britain might have become a republic a century before the American Revolution. We'll never know.

Cromwell's moralism alienated the common people, and the power both he and the commoners drew from the New Model Army alienated the nobility. The taxes that were needed to fund the New Model Army and other reforms alienated just about everyone. The Puritans were discredited, and the more hierarchical but less moralistic Anglican Church was restored as the official state religion. The Puritans were persecuted, but England's loss was America's gain because many of them fled to the colonies, where their descendants would have a more successful revolution.

Britain had a king again, but the long-term trends were on Parliament's side. In keeping with England's conservative nature, it's hard to say exactly when the king became a figurehead, because it was a slow and incremental process. It began in 1720 when the position of Prime Minister was formally created, and was probably completed during Queen Victoria's reign in the nineteenth century. England was still far from being a true democracy, but it was ahead of France in having elected representative government, and the British did it with much less chaos and tyranny. France has been through five different republics, and the current installment is only sixty-six years old, but Parliament has a history that stretches back 800 years. This tradition can also be attributed to the Magna Carta because clause 61 authorized a type of proto-Parliament. However, as long as we're giving credit to historical continuity, Iceland's parliament has been in existence for 1100 years.

The French Revolution might not have even happened if it weren't for the English. That takes the story back to Voltaire, because he got many of his ideas from the English. He was a frequent critic of the elite, and after insulting a French noble he was sent to the notorious Bastille prison, where he was able to negotiate an exile to England. Voltaire was astonished at how much freer England was. Commoners and the nobility might frequent the same cafes, writers could criticize the nobility and even the king (although delicately), and the nobility did not have special rights, such as exclusive hunting rights on land owned by commoners.

The rule of law was also much stronger in England, in large part because of the Magna Carta. The people had the right to a jury trial, to face their accusers, and habeas corpus, which was a crucial safeguard against arbitrary arrest and imprisonment. By contrast, France often had secret legal proceedings decided by a judge, and the French king had the power to imprison people without a trial. Finally, Voltaire devoured British thinkers like Jonathan Swift and John Locke. Voltaire wrote of his experiences in his book *Letters on the English* and inspired Jean-Jacques Rousseau and other leaders of the French Enlightenment.[13] In many ways the French Revolution was a child of what the English had already accomplished.

The most important thing Voltaire learned from the English was support for religious tolerance. Voltaire saw this as the highest pinnacle of the Enlightenment. It meant freedom of thought, freedom of conscience, and the ultimate respect for the rights of others. In the past, religious differences resulted in wars and bloodshed, but religious tolerance led to people with different beliefs living side by side as brothers and sisters. Voltaire's deep belief in religious tolerance stands in stark contrast to dechristianization and Rousseau's doctrine of "forced to be free." The battle between these two figures for the soul of liberalism began during the French Revolution and continues to this day.

The Case for Free Markets

> An economic transaction is a solved political problem. ... Economics has gained the title Queen of the Social Sciences by choosing solved political problems as its domain.
>
> —Abba Lerner, *The Economics and Politics of Consumer Sovereignty*

The opening chapter gave the view from 30,000 feet. Now it's time for the basics. This chapter will explain tools of economic reasoning, and the following chapters will build on them. Eventually we'll get back up to 30,000 feet again, but with a stronger foundation.

Economics is based on the pursuit of self-interest through free markets, which is why you can see the ghost of Rousseau in liberals who criticize economics on these grounds. But if human nature is flawed, then you have two live options. You can pretend that people are naturally good, and then create increasingly totalitarian machinery when people don't behave the way they are supposed to. That's how communism works. Or you can redirect self-interest so that it promotes the greater good. That's how free markets work.

The *invisible hand* is the economic principle that the pursuit of self-interest through free markets promotes the greater good. This is true so often in our modern world that it's almost enough to make you think that the invisible hand is a universal principle. Unfortunately, it is not. The main thesis of this book is that when the invisible hand fails, social norms and moral values are the string and duct tape holding society together. Without these norms and values, society falls apart. But for the next two chapters, we'll focus on what markets do well.

People Respond to Incentives

Parents and pet owners already know the first lesson of economics: People respond to *incentives*. Behaviors that are rewarded are done more often. Behaviors that are punished are done less often. My dog Josh likes to sneak food from the kitchen counter, but he doesn't (usually) do it, because he knows I'll scold him. And if I tell Josh to sit, he'll sit, because he knows he'll be rewarded with a scratch behind the ears. This lesson may not be familiar to cat people.

The fact that people respond to incentives is the first key to understanding how people behave. Whenever you want to predict the effects of a new law, the first thing you should ask yourself is: Which behaviors are punished, and which ones are rewarded? It's a pretty safe bet that people will do less of whatever is punished, and more of whatever is rewarded. Sometimes politicians understand this. The goal of sin taxes on cigarettes and alcohol is not to raise money for the government, but to change behavior. Smokers are punished with higher prices so they will smoke less. Conversely, we subsidize (reward) buying a house with lower taxes. Buying a home creates stability for children, and we want more of that. That's why economists say, "You get less of what you tax, and more of what you subsidize."

Unfortunately, politicians don't always appreciate the fact that people respond to incentives. And that almost invariably means that they will run afoul of *the law of unintended consequences*. This law shows up in many different ways. A good example is the prohibition of alcohol in the 1920s. The intended consequence was to eliminate drinking, but it caused a major rise in organized crime that sold bootleg alcohol on the black market.

Another example of unintended consequences is student loans for college. In the late 1990s, federal regulations for student loans were weakened. According to research by Adam Looney and Constantine Yannelis: "This led to rising enrollment of relatively disadvantaged students, but primarily at poor-performing, low-value institutions whose students systematically failed to complete a degree, struggled to repay their loans, defaulted at high rates, and foundered in the job market."[14] The unintended consequence of trying to send more students to college is creating more people who drop out of low-quality or for-profit schools. They begin their working careers with a lot of debt but no degree.

Politicians routinely run afoul of the law of unintended consequences. The economist James Gwartney has one of my favorite examples in his book *Common Sense Economics*:

> In the former Soviet Union, managers and employees of glass plants were at one time rewarded according to the tons of sheet glass they produced. Because their revenues depended on the weight of the glass, most factories produced sheet glass so thick that you could hardly see through it. The rules were changed so that managers were compensated according to the number of square meters of glass they could produce. Under these rules Soviet firms made glass so thin that it broke easily.[15]

The intended consequence was to find a fair way to pay factory workers and give them an incentive to work hard. The unintended consequence was workers making low-quality glass to maximize their salary.

There is no getting around the fact that the communists ignored the destructive incentives of their policies. Consider Karl Marx's famous slogan, "From each according to their ability, to each according to their need." That's a good way to express the spirit of communism. The intended consequence is to create a society where everyone is equal, even if they aren't as talented or gifted as someone else. Now let's think about the incentives. What is punished? Hard work, because workers wouldn't make any extra money no matter how much effort they put in. What is rewarded? Shirking, because workers would make the same wage no matter how little work they did. Economic reasoning predicts that communism destroys the work ethic and the economy along with it. Sure enough, that's exactly what happened.

The economist John McMillan explains in *Reinventing the Bazaar* that communist China put Marx's slogan into practice. Chinese peasants worked the fields collectively, and they each got an equal share of the harvest. People who worked hard got just as much food as people who shirked. Needless to say, the outcome was a lot more shirking. And since no one wants to be the only sucker, even the hard workers started shirking too. The Chinese Anhui province was known as the granary of China, but after communism, the people could not even feed themselves. Some of the people were so poor that they were forced to resort to cannibalism.

Things got so bad that in 1978 people from the Xiaogang village met in secret. They decided to divide the commune into privately owned lots, one lot for each family. In other words, they switched from communism to capitalism. One farmer explained, "You can't be lazy when you work for your family and yourself." Sure enough, their harvests skyrocketed, and the people weren't poor anymore. Neighboring villages followed suit, and their harvests skyrocketed too.[16]

Luckily the villagers began their experiment at a time when reformers were challenging the old guard of the Communist party. Otherwise, the villagers might have been imprisoned or killed. Instead, the reformers let the experiments continue, and by 1984, there were no more communes left. The lesson is that communism is the world's most powerful engine for creating poverty, and that capitalism is the world's most powerful engine for improving the lives of ordinary people.

Unintended consequences are everywhere. The Americans with Disabilities Act (ADA) was designed to boost employment for the disabled by requiring workplaces to be more accessible. Unfortunately, it had the opposite effect—it increased unemployment for people with disabilities. Research by Daren Acemoglu and Joshua Angrist shows that this drop in employment was largest in medium-sized firms. Large firms could afford to make the accommodations that the ADA required, and small firms were exempt, but medium-sized firms were stuck.[17] They simply stopped hiring disabled workers.

"Ban the Box" laws are similar. They make it illegal for employers to ask if job applicants have a criminal record. The goal is to make it easier for felons to reenter the workforce, and to reduce the gap between black and white employment. Research by Jennifer Doleac and Benjamin Hansen shows that the opposite happened. Employers simply stopped hiring black men for entry level jobs.[18]

Supply and Demand

Many people say that they support free markets, "but only if the prices are fair." That is just a roundabout way of saying that they don't support free markets at all. It's only when prices are high that the magic happens. Let's take the textbook case of unfair prices—the case of *price gouging*. Many firms raise their prices after a natural disaster like a hurricane. And yet these selfish acts promote the greater good. The economist Walter Williams explains:

> In [hurricane] Isabel's wake, private contractors from nearby states brought their heavy equipment to Virginia to clear fallen trees from people's houses. Producers and shippers of generators, plywood and other vital supplies worked overtime to increase the flow of these goods to Virginians. What was it that got these people and millions of

others to help their fellow man in time of need? Was it admonitions from George Bush? Was it conscience or love for one's fellow man? I'll tell you what it was. It was rising prices and the opportunity for people to cash in on windfall profits.[19]

The nice thing about economics is that even the most complicated lessons can be captured by a simple parable. The parable of the price gouger teaches us the three great virtues of supply and demand.

Prices increase the supply. The first virtue is that high prices create a powerful incentive to increase the *supply* of goods and services. That's because the first few contractors to get their heavy machinery to Virginia reaped windfall profits. More and more contractors followed so they could also get a share of these windfall profits. High prices also plant the seeds of their own destruction. As more and more contractors moved to the hurricane-stricken region, they began to meet the demand and prices came back down. At that point the out-of-state contractors packed up their equipment and went back home. Without price-gouging, the contractors would have stayed home, and people would have had to wait a lot longer to get their houses fixed.

What about homeowners who didn't want to pay the price-gouging rate, or who simply couldn't afford it? That takes us to the second virtue of supply and demand.

Prices ration demand. The word "ration" is usually a bad word, but the fact of the matter is that we cannot have unlimited amounts of everything we want. A global revolution to worldwide communism is not going to put more oil and steel under the ground. The essence of socialism is that the government does the rationing. The essence of free markets is that consumers do their own rationing based on prices.

Here's why prices work so well. Suppose the hurricane damaged Alicia's garage and Blake's house. Alicia doesn't want to pay the price gouging rate to fix her garage, so she decides to wait until the first rush of hurricane repairs are done. Then she can hire a roofer at the normal price. Blake is in a different situation. He doesn't want it to rain in his living room, so he swallows hard and pays the high prices. Blake has the greatest need, and price as a rationing method makes sure that he can find a contractor right away. If Virginia had laws against price-gouging, the out-of-state contractors would have stayed home, and Blake would have to go on a waiting list. He might have had to wait a year or two to get his house fixed.

Prices broadcast information. The third virtue of supply and demand is that prices broadcast information. If the price for bananas in Houston goes up, then entrepreneurs know to ship more bananas to Houston. If the price for apples in Chicago goes up, then entrepreneurs know to ship more apples to Chicago. Prices make it easy to see if supply and demand are out of whack. That's how the out-of-state contractors knew to move to Virginia. They saw the high prices people were paying to get their houses fixed and decided to get a piece of the action.

Communism does not use the price system. Instead, it relies on central planners moving goods around by monitoring inventory lists. They'd have to study apple inventories for Chicago grocery stores to determine if they needed to ship more apples to Chicago. In theory, that should work, because ultimately that's how free markets do it too. Suppose the owner of a local grocery store notices that he's almost out of apples. Then he'd place an order for the next day's delivery.

The problem is that communist central planners don't have any skin in the game. They get paid whether a grocery store has apples or not. They aren't punished when stores are missing vital products, and they aren't rewarded when they are fully stocked. The incentives of communism are so bad that stores have widespread shortages even in normal times. If you go on YouTube and search for "USSR grocery store," you can find footage of a typical grocery store during communism.[20] It was small and dirty with terrible lighting and had shelves that were almost completely empty. By contrast, when the Soviet president Boris Yeltsin was making a diplomatic visit to the United States, he demanded to see a nearby grocery store. Yeltsin spent over forty-five minutes wandering the aisles in sheer amazement. He was particularly taken with Jell-O Pudding Pops.

Maybe I'm reading too much into this one anecdote, but I think the Pudding Pops were the final proof of the superiority of capitalism. Yeltsin was perfectly well aware of the fact that the Soviet Union built *Potemkin Villages* to fool credulous journalists into thinking that the Soviet Union was wealthy. So he demanded a surprise visit, hoping to catch the Americans flat-footed. If the Soviets had built a "Potemkin Grocery Store," it would have been clean, well-lit, and beautiful. The shelves would have been stocked to the brim with fresh meat, dairy, fruits, and vegetables. There would be prepackaged snacks and treats along with candies, chocolate bars, and ice cream. But no bureaucrat in the world would think to make a sugary dessert out of frozen chocolate-flavored gelatin as a "healthy" low-fat alternative to ice cream. A fake grocery store would have wonderful products; only a real grocery store would have ridiculous products.

Communism primarily relies on top-down decision-making—a few powerful central planners in Moscow making decisions for the rest of the country. Capitalism primarily relies on bottom-up decision-making—many ordinary people who own and run their businesses and depend on them being successful for their livelihood. This distinction between top-down vs. bottom up is a key part of the conservative worldview. We've already seen one example in the opening chapter. The Magna Carta is the result of bottom-up processes, and John Locke's theory of natural rights is the result of a top-down process. We'll see more examples in the rest of the book.

Supply and Demand in Action

Virtually everything that you need to know about supply and demand is found in the parable of the price gougers. Now it's just a matter of teaching the same lesson over and over again. Let's start with the example of middlemen. No one likes middlemen, but they perform a valuable service. Suppose the price of rice is $2 per pound in North Carolina and $7 per pound in California. Enterprising middlemen could buy rice in North Carolina and ship it to California. This would drive down the price of rice in California and make it more affordable. The middlemen make money, but it's a win for consumers too. Economists call this process *arbitrage*.

One real-world example of arbitrage comes from a former slave who purchased his freedom and became a leading abolitionist. Olaudah Equiano was a Nigerian boy who was captured at age of eleven and sold into slavery. He ended up being put to work on a ship sailing from island to island in the Caribbean. He noticed that the prices of certain goods, such as fruit, were higher on some islands than on others. He was allowed to engage in his own trade and was ultimately able to make enough money to purchase his freedom and get an education. He would write *The Interesting Narrative of the Life of Olaudah Equiano or Gustavus Vassa, the African*. It was both his autobiography and a record of the cruel treatment of African slaves. It became a classic abolitionist text.

The cowboys were another example of arbitrage. After the Civil War, ranchers discovered that a longhorn steer worth $4 in Texas was worth $40 in the North. Every year, cowboys would drive hundreds of thousands of cattle north along iconic routes like the Chisolm trail to the railway stop in Abilene, Kansas. They were then transported by rail to Chicago where they were slaughtered and sold. Driving large herds across rivers and dealing with dangers like stampedes meant that skilled cowboys were in high demand. This also meant that cowboys were a racially integrated profession because ranchers couldn't afford to turn down a qualified minority ranch hand. About a quarter of all cowboys were black,[21] and many others were either Native American or Hispanic. This era of American history came to an end when railway lines were extended into Texas.

Arbitrage can even happen over time, although in that case we call it *speculation*. Suppose a speculator thinks there is going to be a shortage of wheat. Then he can buy and horde wheat when it is both cheap and plentiful (at the present time) and then sell it when it is scarce and expensive (in the future). The speculator, if he gambles correctly, makes windfall profits but he also makes a wheat famine less severe. Once again, the incentive to make windfall profits benefits consumers.

The movie *The Big Short* does an entertaining job telling the stories of speculators who bet on the collapse of the housing market. It's a grisly subject for a bet because you'll make money on people losing their homes, but supply and demand work in mysterious ways. The credit default swaps of these speculators were the early warning system of the incoming housing bust. Without them, the housing bubble could have continued to inflate for much longer. More people would have bought homes that they could not afford, and the Great Recession might have become a Great Depression.

Speculation isn't always good. The housing bubble only happened in the first place because speculators bid the value of housing above what it was worth. Libertarians sometimes object to the argument that free markets can cause speculative bubbles, and instead place the blame on the government. Rather than engage in a complicated economic debate about free markets versus government, let's consider the Tulip Bubble of 1637.

The seventeenth century was a time when the Dutch were a

worldwide economic powerhouse. Their increasing wealth led to growing demand for luxury goods such as tulips. The most valuable tulips had a disease called the Tulip Breaking Disease. It led to vivid and unique mosaic patterns on the bulbs. Tulips from prize lineages with particularly striking patterns were extraordinarily valuable and were bred like modern racehorses.

The tulip bubble was rational in the sense that there was legitimate uncertainty about the value of tulips. But a rational bubble is still a bubble, and it still causes economic hardship after it goes pop. It seems safe to say that the Tulip Bubble of 1637 was not caused by Big Government or an inflationary Federal Reserve. The lesson of the Tulip Bubble applies more generally. Ronald King and colleagues reviewed the research on experimental markets created in laboratories. He found that bubbles are an essentially universal phenomenon of markets.[22] As long as people can "flip" something for more money, you're going to get bubbles.

The price system has its virtues, but it also has one big vice. Suppose a hurricane destroyed the roof of the garage of one of Mark Zuckerberg's vacation homes. He would be perfectly willing to pay the price gouging rate even though he doesn't have much need. Even more troubling is the fact that someone who is poor probably can't afford to get the roof of his house fixed at any price. In fact, he might not even be able to afford his next meal. So far, we've been working under the assumption that everyone has more or less the same amount of money. In these cases, it seems fair to use prices as a rationing method. But prices are unfair when some people are desperately poor.

That raises the question of what can be done to help the poor. In the remainder of the chapter, we'll apply an economic analysis to the three main options. The first option is using the government to set lower prices, the second is private charity, and the third is using taxes to fund programs that help the poor.

Rent Control

Using the government to set lower prices is to give up on the free market and all the magic it can perform. The textbook example is *rent control*. Rent control is a law that makes it illegal for landlords to raise the rent. Suppose that a city attracts a lot of newcomers, so the demand for apartments increases. Since there are many renters fighting for a small number of vacant apartments, the price of rent would go up. That should be a temporary problem because windfall profits are also an incentive. Landlords would rush to build more apartments so that they could capture a larger share of the windfall profits. Soon the supply of apartments would increase, and prices would come back down. But what happens if politicians pass a law against raising the rent? We get a series of downstream consequences.

The first downstream consequence of rent control is a reduction in the supply of apartments. Landlords won't build new apartments since they can't make any money from them. They may even take existing apartments off the market. Rent control laws generally make this illegal, but there are always loopholes, such as reserving the apartment for a family member.

The second downstream consequence of rent control is an increase in the demand for apartments. The price of rent is kept low, so there is no incentive to ration. Renters will be more likely to look for a one-bedroom apartment instead of a studio, or a two-bedroom apartment instead of a one-bedroom. Empty nesters will keep the same apartment they've always rented instead of moving into a smaller place. Lower rents also make people less likely to look for a roommate. The root cause of the apartment crunch was that demand was high and the supply was low. Well, rent control just made the root cause of the problem even worse.

The outcome of rent control is shortages. Landlords get many applicants for every vacant apartment. That's a big problem, but it gets even worse when it leads to discrimination. Racist landlords can take their pick from many applicants, so they will choose to rent only to white people. Free markets don't have this problem because landlords cannot count on immediately renting a vacant apartment. Turning down a qualified black applicant may mean having to leave the apartment vacant for a month or two until a qualified white applicant comes along. There are many racists in the world, but most of them aren't willing to give up a few thousand dollars of lost rent money to indulge their racism.

Even landlords who aren't racist would prefer to rent to affluent, middle-class professionals. The data backs this up. Rolfe Goetze has found that rent-controlled apartments were concentrated among educated professionals.[23] This leads to an important point. Liberals argue that a strong government is needed to limit the power of the wealthy, and in some cases that is true. But in other cases, the government amplifies the power of the rich and politically connected. Rent control gives wealthy professionals cheaper apartments than the poor and working class. The New York Times has reported that Congressman Charles Rangel had *four* rent-controlled apartments in New York City.[24]

If the poor do not have rent-controlled apartments, then where are they? William Tucker has shown that rent control leads to higher rates of homelessness.[25] Of course, homelessness is an extreme case. Most poor and working-class renters are forced into the *gray market*, which is not governed by rent control laws. Some landlords, particularly on an informal basis, will rent apartments under the table. Examples include people who rent spare rooms, condos, and in-law apartments. Local governments usually allow these markets to exist because they are difficult to police, and besides, they help relieve the apartment shortage that was created by rent control.

The gray market also includes apartments that are given a legal exemption from rent control. Local governments sometimes grant these exemptions because it is the only way to get landlords to build new apartments. The problem with the gray market is that there isn't enough competition to drive down prices. Apartments in the gray market are more expensive than apartments in cities that do not have rent control.[26] The goal of rent control was to lower the price of rent for the poor, but the outcome was that it made their apartments more expensive. The law of unintended consequences strikes again.

A decline in quality is another consequence of rent control. Landlords may have to skimp on basics like paint and maintenance just to make a small profit. Walter Block reviews the research on rent control and finds that 29 percent of rent-controlled apartments in the United States were in a state of disrepair, compared to only 8 percent for areas without rent control.[27] If the drop in quality is minor, then affluent professionals can take care of it themselves. If the drop in quality is severe, then it can lead to slums. The paint starts peeling; broken windows get boarded up; the brickwork begins to crumble; and the graffiti doesn't get washed away. That's when the affluent professionals move out of rent-controlled apartments and into luxury apartments that are legally exempt from rent control. Then the poor and working class are pushed into the rent-controlled slums.

Charity

The second option to help the poor is private charity. Libertarians and economically minded conservatives sometimes wish to abolish the welfare state and replace it with private charity. That way we don't have to worry about the harmful downstream consequences of government interference. But charity has a different problem, and an economic analysis of charity shows why.

Supply and demand work magic for goods and services. Consider a generic product such as light bulbs. If the demand for light bulbs suddenly increases, then firms that supply light bulbs will be able to raise the price and reap windfall profits. But they'll also expand their manufacturing capacity in order to capture a larger share of these windfall profits. New firms may enter the light bulb market as well. Pretty soon the increase in supply will match the increase in demand and the price for light bulbs will go back down.

Charity is not like light bulbs. Suppose that a recession hits and the demand for charity increases. People who supply charity won't be able to "raise the price" and reap windfall profits. Other people won't enter the charity market to capture a share of these windfall profits. Supply and demand work for goods and services, but not for charity. People may be motivated to give extra money by goodwill and compassion, but goodwill and compassion can't guarantee an increase in supply the way windfall profits can.

Charity does have advantages. It is more personal than the government and does a better job of avoiding unintended consequences. It is also more flexible than the government and can rapidly adapt to changing conditions like natural disasters. Charity can also fill in gaps that are left by government programs, such as when people don't quite meet the threshold to qualify for a program. Charities can also provide innovative services like working with local food distributors to give extra inventory to the needy, or to sell it at rock-bottom prices like $5 for a bag of groceries. This flexibility means that charity will always play an essential role in the portfolio of programs that help the poor. But charity is not a magic bullet.

The Liberal Tax Argument

The third option for helping the poor is by using income taxes to raise money for the government. This money can then be used to fund various welfare state programs like food stamps and healthcare. But this option seems like it will run afoul of the law of unintended consequences just like rent control. The free market case against taxes is simple: People respond to incentives. Things that are punished are done less often, and things that are rewarded are done more often. Income taxes punish people for working, so the outcome is that people work less. Hence the economic slogan: "You get less of what you tax and more of what you subsidize."

This argument was so simple and logical that I believed it for quite a while even in the face of contradictory evidence. I'm in good company. When President Clinton raised taxes, the free market economist Martin Feldstein wrote in the Wall Street Journal that "The Clinton revenue estimates are based on the fallacy that taxpayers will not change their behavior in response to a 37% jump in their marginal tax rates."[28] Virtually everything in classical economics says that Feldstein was right, but he wasn't. Tax revenues were actually *higher* than the Congressional Budget Office's estimates predicted. Liberals point out the weakness of the free market vision of taxes all the time, but it usually falls on deaf ears. Here is a typical example from the *Washington Post*:

> When President Bill Clinton raised taxes in 1993, the unemployment rate dropped, from 6.9 to 6.1 percent, and kept falling each of the next seven years. When President Bush cut taxes in 2001, the unemployment rate rose, from 4.7 to 5.8 percent, then drifted to 6 percent last year when taxes were cut again.[29]

THE CASE FOR FREE MARKETS

If the economy is going through boom times, as it was during Clinton's presidency, then a modest tax increase isn't going to slow it down very much. And if the economy is in a recession, as it was during at the start of Bush's presidency, then a tax cut isn't going to single-handedly turn it around. But I always assumed that if economists could isolate the effect of taxes from the overall state of the economy, then we would see that income taxes are highly destructive. I was wrong. It turns out that income taxes are the exception that proves the rule.

There are two main reasons why income taxes are an exception: social norms and the income effect.

Social norms. Social norms around the forty-hour work week have a special power. The forty-hour work week is sticky. No firm is going to say, "Well, the Democrats just passed a tax increase, so there's no point working hard anymore. Go ahead and start putting in thirty-five-hour weeks." Conversely, they aren't going to say, "Well, the Republicans passed a tax cut, so we can finally keep the money we make. I expect everyone to start working forty-five-hour weeks." Well, they might try to say it, but workers aren't going to listen. Shift workers and contractors do have more flexibility, but the stickiness of the forty-hour work week is an important reason why income taxes are not as directly harmful as you might think.

Income and substitution effects. Here's a thought experiment. Suppose you are an hourly worker. Perhaps you are a carpenter or a computer programmer. You normally charge $50 per hour for your labor, but your work goes viral. Suddenly you are in heavy demand and many deep-pocketed clients have bid up the value of your work to $500 per hour. Would you:

- *Option A*: Increase the number of hours you work to maximize your new income.

- *Option B*: Decrease the number of hours you work so that you make more money *and* have more leisure time.
- *Option C*: Stay the same. You enjoy your job and have a healthy work-life balance already, so you keep working the same hours and enjoy making ten times as much money.

According to the simple free market vision of economics, everyone would choose option A. But in practice you would get a mix of all three options. The people who choose to work less would partially offset the people who choose to work more.

The same logic applies to a tax increase. Suppose taxes go up. Would you think, "Well, I guess there's no point working hard anymore since the government's just going to take even more of my money"? Or would you think, "Well that's annoying. Now I have to tighten my belt and maybe even take up a side hustle in order to make ends meet"? I suspect most people would feel closer to the second option. If that's the case, then raising taxes doesn't lower the work effort—it might even increase it.

This tradeoff between making more money and having more leisure time is an important reason why the simple free market vision of taxes breaks down. It falls under a phenomenon that economists call the *income effect* (using increased wealth to "buy" leisure time) versus *substitution effect* (the higher the wages, the higher the opportunity cost of choosing leisure over work). The slogan that "you get less of what you tax" is based purely on the substitution effect. In the real world, the income effect at least partially offsets the substitution effect.

The Backwards Bending Supply Curve

Libertarians do not dispute these liberal arguments against taxes, but they are only part of the picture.

Low-income workers tend to follow the simple economic model, as do workers for whom working at a higher pay rate is a rare windfall. That's why shift workers will often work overtime for higher pay. My son, like many New England teenagers before him, has a part-time job at Dunkin's. He will usually pick up an extra shift if his boss needs him, but he'll never turn down an extra shift with overtime pay. More money in his pocket means a greater reward for working, which translates to him working more hours. That's exactly what the simple economic model predicts.

Here's how to think about low-income workers. Imagine that for some reason you only made one penny per hour, so at the end of each week your boss would give you your weekly pay of forty cents. You'd probably just quit because your take-home pay was way too low. That's also the simple economic model: the incentive to work is simply too low to make working worthwhile.

The famous libertarian economist Milton Friedman designed a program for the poor called the *negative income tax*. Normally income taxes mean that the government takes away a percentage of a worker's income, but the negative income tax actually gives extra money back. For example, Blake might make $300, but after including the negative income tax, his take-home pay is $360. The idea is that it increases the incentive to work. Just like regular taxes, the negative income tax has brackets, and workers are phased out of the program as their income increases.

Libertarians are often criticized for not caring about the poor, but Friedman's creative thinking about real-world incentives led to one of the most successful programs in the modern welfare state: the *Earned Income Tax Credit* (EITC). Research by Nada Eissa and Jeffrey Liebman shows that this program increases the employment of low-income workers.[30] And of course, by its design, it increases their income as well. Liberals are supporters of the EITC, but it does have a libertarian twist: the reason why it works is because it relies on the simple economic model of "you get less of what you tax and more of what you subsidize." The EITC subsidizes work and thus people work more. In other words, it's an argument in favor of lower taxes.

In fact, the thought experiment of the viral contractor was a bit rigged in order to make the concept of the income effect as intuitive as possible. A wage of $500 per hour works out to a salary of $1 million for a full-time worker. This wage is so high that many people could be both rich and have lots of leisure time. Even the more reasonable example of a worker taking up a side hustle to make ends meet after a tax hike is rigged. In the short term, people don't have an option but to find a way to pay the bills. In the long run, people adapt to lower take-home pay, which will lead to them downsizing their lifestyle and then perhaps their work effort.

If you put all this together you get what economists call the *backwards bending supply curve*. I won't use a graph, but the main idea is that when wages are low the substitution effect dominates. Higher take-home pay and lower taxes induce people to work more. But as people gain more and more wealth, the income effect dominates, and they start to choose leisure time and vacations over an even larger house and fancier car.

If you are interested in a deeper dive on taxes, then head over to Google Scholar and search up Michael Keane's research article *Labor Supply and Taxes: A Survey*.[31] He's also a touch more of a tax hawk than the typical economist, which more economically minded conservatives will appreciate. The main takeaway is that income taxes are not great, they do punish working, but the income effect and social norms blunt much of the harm.

State Capacity Libertarianism

This insight leads to what the economist Tyler Cowen calls *state capacity libertarianism*.[32] It may seem like an oxymoron because libertarians want a small government and the term "state capacity" suggests a big government. And yet that's exactly what the highest functioning economies in the world do: combine free markets with big governments.

The Heritage Foundation is a conservative think tank that ranks nations based on economic freedom.[33] The more a nation embraces free markets, the higher the ranking. Like all ranking systems, they are arbitrary and have been criticized, but they do provide a good overview of general trends. What they found may be surprising. In the past, the list had been dominated by small Asian nations that focus on manufacturing, like Hong Kong and Singapore, as well as historically conservative English-speaking nations like the United States, the United Kingdom, and Australia. But over time that has changed.

Singapore is still #1 but now the top of the list features many European nations known for their generous welfare states, such as Sweden, Denmark, Norway, and Finland. By contrast, the United States has fallen all the way down to #25. Even Singapore, which is a tiny nation of just 6 million people, has mandatory savings and universal healthcare provided by a program called MediShield Life. They also have another program called MediFund to provide extra healthcare coverage for the poor. If tiny free market Singapore has universal healthcare, then the United States probably isn't going to abolish the welfare state any time soon.

These European nations have learned the main lesson of state capacity libertarianism, often the hard way: If you want a welfare state, then you need to generate a lot of wealth to fund it. The only way to generate that wealth is with free markets. You can have heavy-handed government regulations, or you can have high taxes, but you can't have both. Sweden is the textbook example. The economist Andre Bergh explains in his research paper *What are the policy lessons from Sweden? On the rise, fall and revival of a capitalist welfare state*. He points out that Sweden was stagnant for about 25 years starting in 1970 due to an over-regulated economy. So Sweden cut taxes, deregulated the economy, and emerged from their stagnation as a capitalist welfare state. The United States went a different route and decided that having somewhat lower taxes gave it the slack to monkey with the economy in other ways. That's why our ranking has fallen so low. We should learn from Sweden's lesson.

Imperfect Competition

> Even a small number of rivals may bring prices down close to the competitive level ... Competition is a tough weed, not a delicate flower.
>
> – George Stigler, *Concise Encyclopedia of Economics*

If the typical person off the street was asked why we are wealthier today than we were 200 years ago, they would probably answer that it is because of modern technology. And they would be right. Competition between firms can slash the price of consumer goods by a factor of two or three, but improvements in technology can slash the price by a factor of two or three *hundred*.

The Parable of the Pin Makers

In 1776 Adam Smith published the book that would become the foundation of modern economics: *The Wealth of Nations*. He observed on the very first page that pin makers could only make about 20 pins per day by hand. With the help of some simple machines and assembly lines, the output per worker rose to about 5,000 pins per day.[34] Economists call this the *division of labor*—taking a complex job and breaking it down into simple steps. That's how assembly lines work. If the job is simple enough, a machine can do it.

The division of labor has important downstream consequences. The first was that it became much cheaper to manufacture pins. The second was that a lot of workers lost their jobs. This story has been reenacted many times in other industries such as cars and textiles. The question is always the same: Do the benefits of cheaper products outweigh the lost jobs?

With the benefit of 250 years of hindsight, the answer is obvious. The world is much wealthier than it used to be, even for the poorest of the poor. But if you were to read through 250 years of newspapers, you would come to the opposite conclusion—that the world was on a downward spiral in which jobs were constantly being destroyed by technology. And frankly, it's hard to fault observers for getting it wrong. The historian Ernst H. Gombrich explains in *A Little History of the World* what life was like for weavers who lost their jobs to machines:

> And naturally, rather than see his family starve a person will do anything. Even work for a pittance as long as it means he has a job to keep body and soul together. So the factory owner, with his machines, could summon the hundred starving weavers and say: 'I need people to run my factory and look after my machines. What will you charge for that?' One of them might say: 'I want so much, if I am to live as comfortably as I did before.' The next would say: 'I just need enough for a loaf of bread and a kilo of potatoes a day.' And the third, seeing his last chance of survival about to disappear, would say: 'I'll see if I can manage on half a loaf'. Four others then said: 'So will we!' 'Right,' said the factory owner. 'I'll take you five. How many hours can you work in a day?' 'Ten hours.' said the first. 'Twelve,' said the second, seeing the job slipping from his grasp. 'I can do sixteen,' cried the third, for his life depended on it.[35]

This problem gave rise to the Luddite movement. These days, the word Luddite suggests people who don't like smartphones and social media. But during the Industrial Revolution, the Luddite movement was about survival. The Luddites were a group of English textile workers who broke into factories and destroyed the machines that cost them their jobs. This was common during the Industrial Revolution.

An engineer would invent a labor-saving machine, and angry workers would promptly destroy it. They didn't want their labor saved—they wanted their jobs.

Karl Marx had a more revolutionary vision. He claimed that it was futile to stop progress. Instead of destroying machines, the workers needed to take ownership of them. That way everyone could enjoy the benefits of progress rather than a few rich capitalists. But history has proven that Marx was wrong, and that socialism only produces grinding poverty and oppression. Yet Marx's analysis seems correct. Where did he go wrong?

The answer is found in the virtues of supply and demand. Remember the parable of the hurricane and the price gouging contractors. High prices work their magic just as easily after a technological advance as they do after a hurricane. The first entrepreneur to build an assembly line would be able to corner the pin market and reap windfall profits. But these profits are a signal to entrepreneurs: "Hey! Hurry up and make your own factory so you can get a share of these windfall profits!" New firms would rush into the pin market, and older firms would rush to upgrade their equipment. This competition would drive down prices. In the short run, the factory owners captured the benefits of rising technology in the form of windfall profits. In the long run, they were passed on to consumers in the form of lower prices. Lower prices effectively make consumers richer because the things they want to buy cost less money. Consumers were the long-term winners.

Creative Destruction

Unfortunately, there was also a group that clearly lost—the workers without jobs. Are the benefits of cheap pins really worth so many people losing their jobs? Once again, hindsight tells us that it is. Consumers have to do something with their extra wealth, so they buy more goods and services. Someone has to make those extra goods, so new jobs are created in other industries.

Joseph Schumpeter called this process *creative destruction*. New innovations cause inefficient firms to go out of business, and skills to become obsolete. Creative destruction can even destroy entire markets, such as the market for horse and buggies, steam engines, and COBOL programmers. The consequence is inevitably lost jobs.

In the *Concise Encyclopedia of Economics*, Richard Alm and W. Michael Cox document some of these wrenching transformations. In 1920 there were 2.1 million Americans working in the railroad industry compared to only 200,000 today. In 1910 nearly 12 million Americans worked as farmers compared to only 716,000 today.[36] Yes, the government could have stepped in and bailed out the horse and buggy industry, but in the long run, that doesn't do anyone any favors. Besides, failure is essential for the creative side of the process—creating new jobs in new industries. There are over 2.1 million engineers today compared to only 38,000 in 1910. There are over 4 million truck, taxi, and bus drivers today, but none in 1900.[37]

Creative destruction is not a gentle process, but it is a necessary one. Without it, we'd be stuck with yesterday's technology and yesterday's standard of living. In their paper, *The Greatest Century That Ever Was*, Stephen Moore and Julian L. Simon documented some of the major advances that happened during the twentieth century. Inflation-adjusted per-capita GDP increased from $4,800 to $31,000, and car ownership increased from 1 percent to 91 percent. Meanwhile the poverty rate fell from 40 percent to 12 percent and the length of the average work week fell from fifty hours to thirty-five hours.[38]

Creative destruction is not easy. It is good for society as a whole, but it causes permanent harm to the lives of some workers. What does a fifty-five-year-old horse-and-buggy maker do when Ford releases the Model T? What does someone who has a high-quality assembly line job at Ford do when he is laid off because more and more consumers start buying Japanese and Korean cars? It's easy to say, "Go learn a new trade." But how is a worker supposed to go back to school and learn a new trade when he has a mortgage to pay and a family to feed? In 2019 Joseph Biden told coal miners that they should "learn to code,"[39] but that is not a realistic option for most people. The harsh reality is that creative destruction will result in a permanent loss of income for many workers and their families.

Creative destruction is hard, but it teaches a lesson—the *virtue of failure*. Even when technology isn't changing, markets are in a constant state of flux. Sometimes firms lose their mojo. They may get a new CEO who lacks vision, or they may adopt harmful management techniques like stack rank and ruin their workplace culture. But other hungry firms will fill the void, and the market as a whole stays competitive. It's just like survival of the fittest. Animals with bad genes don't survive, but this means that the species as a whole remains fit.

I wouldn't want to be an animal that is too slow to escape predators, but in virtually every other context, failure teaches powerful lessons. This will be a running theme throughout the rest of the book. Back in its glory days Nike created some of the most inspiring commercials ever made. Arguably the greatest of them all was *Failure* with Michael Jordan. In the commercial he narrates some of his low points:

> I've missed more than 9,000 shots in my career. I've lost almost 300 games. Twenty-six times I've been trusted to take the game-winning shot and missed. I've failed over and over and over again in my life. And that is why I succeed.

Jordan had to fight with Nike to get this commercial made. They teamed him up with the director Oliver Stone, who wanted to make a commercial highlighting Jordan's many successes. But Jordan pushed back: "The idea is to tell young kids, 'Don't be afraid to fail, because a lot of people have to fail to be successful—these are the many times that I've failed but yet I've been successful."[40]

Islands give us insight into the virtue of failure. A lot of weird things are going on with islands, like founder effects and reduced biodiversity, but one of the most important factors is that natural selection is weaker on islands. The two main reasons why birds fly are to escape predators and find food, but some island animals find that they have no natural predators and easy food sources. Island life is so easy that some species of birds, like dodos and kiwis, lose the ability to fly. That is what a lack of competition will do. What is it like to be a bird that used to be able to fly, but is now earthbound? My dog twitches his legs when he dreams of chasing squirrels. Do kiwi birds twitch their vestigial wings and dream of flight?

Perfect Competition

Here is what might be a fatal flaw in the parable of the pin makers. There must have been thousands of workers who made pins by hand. That's clearly enough competition to keep the pin makers from colluding to rip off consumers. But after assembly lines, there may have only been a handful of factories making pins. Suppose these factories colluded to keep prices high. That might allow the factories to rip off consumers.

Historically the case for free markets has been based on the assumption of *perfect competition*. That only happens when the following assumptions are met:

1. There are many buyers and sellers of a good.
2. The *barriers to entry* into the market are low or nonexistent.
3. The goods produced by different firms are essentially identical.
4. Consumers are acting with *perfect information* (about prices and quantity of goods being sold).

A better term for perfect competition is ruthless competition. It is impossible for firms in a perfectly competitive market to gouge consumers because some other firm will come along and undercut them. In fact, it is impossible for firms in perfectly competitive markets to even make a profit. If one firm makes a profit of just 2 percent, then some other firm will come along and cut prices so that it only makes a profit of 1 percent. And then another firm will come along and charge even lower prices. What about collusion? What if all the firms colluded to set high prices? Then that creates a powerful incentive for new firms to enter the market and undercut the cartel. And what if the new entrants are brought into the cartel? Then yet another firm enters the market. The final outcome of this ruthless competition is that prices are cut to the bone.

Most markets are not perfectly competitive. The closest we get is commodities like gold, pork bellies, and hard red winter wheat #2. In these markets there are hundreds or thousands of producers all making an identical product and competing ruthlessly on price. If a farmer sells his hard red winter wheat #2 for even a penny more than another farmer, he'll lose his entire market to his rival. But what happens in other markets where these assumptions are not true? That leads to *imperfect competition*, which gives firms *monopoly power* that they can use to raise prices.

The Real Story of Standard Oil

Popular mythology of monopolies evokes images of "robber barons" who exploited consumers, but in reality they were innovators who found ways to lower prices. Standard Oil is the textbook example, as the economist Thomas DiLorenzo explains in *How Capitalism Saved America*. Back in the late 1800s, the oil industry was going through a boom. The Industrial Revolution was ramping up and everyone knew that oil was going to be huge. Investors threw money at oil companies the same way they would later throw money at questionable tech firms. There were hundreds of oil companies, but not all of them were going to last. One of these startups was Standard Oil. In 1870 it only had 4 percent of the market, but John D. Rockefeller had a vision that separated him from his competitors.[41]

The first plank of Rockefeller's strategy was to improve both the safety and efficiency of the refining process. Oil refineries used to be extremely dangerous because they were prone to massive fires. Standard Oil instituted better quality control that made manufacturing safer and cheaper. That was good for workers and the firm's profits. Rockefeller also began to buy competitors. Critics argue that this is proof of the predatory ways of Standard Oil, but remember that this was a boom period with massive overinvestment. There were simply too many oil companies, and the result was a wasteful duplication of services. Standard Oil brought these refineries under unified management and introduced their superior safety and quality.

Another improvement Standard Oil made was to vertically integrate. They made the other products that were needed to sell and distribute oil, such as barrels to store the oil and wagons to carry it. Vertical integration is not always a good strategy, but it makes sense when one firm is unusually efficient. An example of their penny-pinching ways was that Standard Oil reduced the number of rivets in an oil barrel from sixty to fifty-nine. A small change, but it added up over millions of barrels. Standard Oil also hired chemists to make new products from the waste oil left over from refining. Examples include lubricating oil, paint, and another little-known product called gasoline.

The results were extraordinary. In 1869, the year before Standard Oil was formed, refined oil cost thirty cents per gallon.[42] By 1885 Standard Oil had improved its market share to 85 percent while dropping the price of refined oil to eight cents per gallon.[43] These massive price cuts are a useful rule-of-thumb to use when reading history. I've noticed many times that seemingly even-handed historians get to the Gilded Age and start to show their bias. They discuss the ruthless competitiveness, the lack of child labor and workplace safety laws, and low wages. But they don't mention the huge price cuts and how much ordinary consumers benefited. Instead, they frame the discussion around the Sherman Antitrust Act as protecting consumers from dangerous monopolies. If that happens, they've been cherry picking their facts to create a narrative.

Fears of Standard Oil's monopoly power were unfounded. It's tough to stay ahead of the competition forever. Standard Oil's market share peaked at about 88 percent in 1890 and then went into a decline. By the time the Supreme Court upheld the Sherman Antitrust decision against Standard Oil in 1911, its market share had already dropped to 64 percent.[44]

Did Standard Oil reap windfall profits along the way? Of course they did. The way to encourage firms to innovate is by rewarding them with windfall profits. Standard Oil won, but consumers won too. The only people who didn't win were Standard Oil's competitors. That's why the Sherman Antitrust Act is not generally used by consumers who are being unfairly "gouged," but by rival firms. Unsuccessful firms that cannot compete in the marketplace may win in the political arena. Thomas DiLorenzo studied all the cases in which firms were charged by the Sherman Antitrust act. He found that they were dropping prices faster than the industry average.[45]

Economies of Scale

One of the assumptions of perfect competition is that barriers to entry in the market are low. So how do you get barriers to entry? One of the most important ways is through *economies of scale*. Bigger is better. A cook can grill two hamburgers with about the same amount of effort as it takes to grill just one. A truck can haul two TV sets as easily as it can carry one. Assembly lines are a great way to create economies of scale.

The good thing about economies of scale is that they let firms build things quickly and cheaply. The bad thing about them is that they create barriers to entry. Suppose a worker wanted to make pins before there were assembly lines. Then all he needed was a bit of metal and a few hand tools. The barriers to entry into the pin market were very low. After assembly lines, he needed a large building, a team of twenty workers and some machines. The barriers to entry got a lot higher.

A *natural monopoly* is what happens when economies of scale continue until there is only a single firm left. A bridge is a good example of a natural monopoly. It doesn't matter how much traffic crosses the river each day; it is cheaper to build one bridge than two bridges. That puts consumers between a rock and a hard place. If there is only one bridge, then the bridge company can abuse its monopoly power by raising tolls. If there are two bridges, then the cost of two expensive construction projects has to be passed on to consumers. That's why the

IMPERFECT COMPETITION

conventional wisdom used to be that only the government could solve the problem of natural monopolies. One firm should be granted a legal monopoly, and then the government would regulate that firm to keep the prices low.

In reality the cost of a second bridge is trivial compared to the lack of innovation that results from granting a firm a government-granted monopoly. Jim Cox gives the following example to show that government regulation is designed to prevent competition:

> Airlines were regulated beginning in 1938, and in the 40-year period from then until 1978 [when the airlines were deregulated] no new trunk airlines were granted a charter. These four decades saw a huge change in the airline business as airplane technology advanced from propellers to jets, from 20 seaters to 400 seaters, from speeds of 120 mph to speeds of 600 mph. Yet, the Civil Aeronautics Board (CAB) found no need to allow new competitors into the growing industry. This fact alone makes it quite clear that the purpose of the regulation was not to protect the consumer but to protect the market of the established airlines.[46]

Manufacturers like Boeing and McDonnell Douglas were building much better airplanes. And yet the government did not think that this massive increase in technology warranted even a single new airline being granted a national charter. Only after the airline industry was deregulated were we able to benefit from innovative new airlines like Southwest Airlines and JetBlue.

Compare airlines to cell phone service. Verizon, AT&T, and T-Mobile each have their own network of cell phone towers, which means that the cost of three rival networks had to be passed on to consumers. Yet cell service has gotten much cheaper over time. I remember the dark ages of worrying about going over my minutes for voice calls. My wife and I did this a couple times when we were engaged, and the increase in our cell phone bills was shocking. But now all carriers have unlimited talk and text as table stakes. These days many carriers have unlimited data, so I often forget to connect to Wi-Fi networks with my phone. Ten years ago that would have been economic suicide. Compare cell phones to airlines, and it's clear that competition is better than government regulations.

Monopolistic Competition

There is another factor which works against monopolies. Perfect competition assumes that the goods made by different firms are essentially identical. That's fine if you want to buy a commodity like hard red winter wheat #2, but it is not true for most goods. The French fries at McDonald's are different from the fries made by Five Guys. A Honda Accord is different from a Toyota Camry, and both are different from a Corvette or a Tesla. Pizza places specialize in deep dish, brick oven, and New York style. In the real world, firms compete on price *and* features. Competition based on features is called *monopolistic competition*.

Economists used to criticize monopolistic competition. They felt that it led to an inefficient duplication of services. Think about all those fast food restaurants across the street from each other. Add in the advertising costs, and the result is higher prices. Modern economists have a different view. They realize that consumers are willing to pay a premium in order to have a variety of choices. No one wants to live in a world with just one type of pizza. That does mean that firms do have a small amount of monopoly power. A firm with a winning formula like McDonald's French fries can make a profit.

The overall impact of monopolistic competition is positive because it creates a check on monopolies. Think about the classic natural monopoly of a bridge. It is true that a single bridge can supply the entire market with the service of "crossing the river." However, no one wants to drive to the bridge in North Jamesport when they are in South Jamesport. Just as consumers are willing to pay a premium to have different kinds of fast food, they are also willing to pay a premium for the convenience of having multiple bridges. Let's suppose that the pin industry is a natural monopoly. That means that a single mega-huge pin factory could cheaply supply the entire market with pins. But some consumers might want larger pins, or smaller pins, or skinnier pins, or pins with a sharper point, or pins made out of a stronger metal, or less expensive pins made out of a weaker metal, or pins made out of plastic. Monopolistic competition benefits consumers by giving them choice and variety.

Another safeguard is that rival firms can copy the winning formula of successful firms. McDonald's and Popeye's each created crispy chicken sandwiches inspired by Chick-fil-A. Coca-Cola started distributing Dasani when bottled water became a popular alternative to soda. The success of the iPhone with its touchscreen interface has led to Google's Android phones implementing their own touchscreen interface. Firms are copycats.

This imitation process teaches an important lesson. Good ideas like touchscreen phones spread by imitation. Think of markets in evolutionary terms. The "touchscreen phone mutation" appeared for the first time with Apple's iPhone, proved successful, and spread to dominate the market when Android copied them. That's how the ecology of free market competition produces efficient outcomes. Firms are always trying to innovate and create the next big thing, but as soon as they do, a bunch of other firms are going to rip off their idea and drive down prices.

However, monopolistic competition does have an important downside. Libertarians often argue that free markets work against racism, and I made that point in the previous chapter in the discussion of rent control. With rent control there are more applicants than vacancies, so racist landlords can easily choose white tenants. With free markets, turning down a qualified black applicant costs the landlord thousands of dollars of lost rent money. Monopolistic competition changes this dynamic. A landlord could offer the product of "apartments with no black people" to cater to racist tenants. That's what the former NBA owner Donald Sterling did—he rented apartments that excluded blacks and Hispanics.[47] Economists call this *consumer-driven racism*. In the Jim Crow South, consumer-driven racism led to virtually all white-owned businesses in town enforcing racist business practices.

Oligopolies and Experimental Economics

Most markets are *oligopolies*. That means that there are just a few firms. Soda is dominated by Coke and Pepsi. Computers are dominated by Microsoft, Apple, and Google Chromebooks. Cellular services are dominated by Verizon, AT&T, and T-Mobile. Even so, most firms make surprisingly small profits. In 2023 Walmart had a profit margin of about 2.5 percent[48] and ExxonMobil had a profit margin of about 11.5 percent.[49] Average profits for firms in the United States are usually around 4 to 7 percent, depending on the strength of the economy in a given year.[50] Microsoft is one of the most successful firms in the country with a near-monopoly over personal computing, and yet their profits are a relatively modest 35 percent.[51] Firms do not have much power to "gouge" consumers.

Why are these firms' profit margins so low? For the answer, we turn to Vernon Smith. He had the seemingly crazy idea of actually putting economic principles to the test. He did this by creating simulated markets with real human beings in the laboratory. In the process he almost single-handedly created the field of *experimental economics*, for which he received the Nobel Prize in 2002.

In a classic experiment, he took college students and assigned them to the roles of buyers or sellers in a market that worked a bit like the New York Stock Exchange. The students were told that they were free to negotiate with whoever they wanted, and however they wanted, in order to maximize their profits. The students described these markets as "unorganized, unstable, chaotic, and confused."[52] If you've seen footage of the New York Stock Exchange, then you can understand why. But it worked. The students naturally converged on a selling price, and no one was able to collude to exploit other buyers or sellers. "Students were both surprised and amazed at the conclusion of the experiment when the entrusted student opened a sealed envelope containing the correctly predicted equilibrium price and quantity [of the good being sold]". In other words, the market was imperfect, but the outcome was about what you'd expect with perfect competition. Smith concluded:

> In many experimental markets, poorly informed, error-prone, and uncomprehending human agents interact through the trading rules to produce social algorithms which demonstrably approximate the wealth maximizing outcomes traditionally thought to require complete information and cognitively rational actors.[53]

Experimental economics tells us that perfect competition is overkill. Consumers don't need perfect information; barriers to entry don't have to be low; and there doesn't have to be many buyers or sellers. Don Coursey summarizes the research[54] and finds that most markets will reach a competitive outcome as long as there are about four firms in competition. Even a single competitor can make a big difference. Reuben Kessel found that in the bond markets, adding a second firm to the bidding cut profits in half.[55]

In theory oligopoly firms should collude and charge the same price as a monopoly firm. In practice this is very difficult because each firm has an incentive to backslide and undercut their rivals. That's because the Sherman Antitrust Act has a provision that makes colluding illegal. Otherwise oligopoly firms could create legally binding agreements to sell their goods at a high price. They could even designate an arbitrator when they disagreed about how to update the price in response to market changes. Instead, firms must collude implicitly and unofficially, and it is easy for these tacit agreements to break down.

Network Monopolies

Now let's take a look at the most stubborn monopoly of them all: a *network monopoly*. It is more fun to play basketball if you can find other people to play with. It is better to have a cellphone if you have other people to call or text. We call these goods *network goods*. Networks grow more and more useful as they get bigger. Having one big network is better than having two small networks.

These network effects explain a lot of seemingly unrelated things. Why are acting jobs clustered in Hollywood, programming jobs clustered in Silicon Valley, and financial jobs clustered in New York City? Because of network effects. If an entrepreneur wants to start a tech firm, he has to go where the programmers are. And if a programmer wants to get a tech job, he has to go where the tech firms are. Stanford University's engineering department was a crucial pioneer in computers, and that gave Silicon Valley its head start. Network effects took over from there as young programmers flocked to Silicon Valley the way young actors flock to Hollywood. Networks also explain the rise of popular platforms like the Xbox and PlayStation. The game players choose the console with the most games, and the game developers choose the console with the most players.

Network monopolies are good. We want to enjoy the benefits of participating in the largest network possible. The objection is that they might cause a new type of market failure called *lock-in*. Consumers might become locked in to an inferior product. The classic example of lock-in is the war between VHS and Betamax. For younger readers, think of it as the Xbox versus PlayStation of watching movies. According to popular mythology, the wrong format won. VHS beat out the allegedly superior Betamax because consumers were already locked in to the VHS standard. Who would want to switch to Betamax when the video stores only rent VHS movies? And who would want to open a video store with Betamax tapes when all consumers have VHS players?

These days it is difficult to trot out the old "VHS versus Betamax" argument as an example of lock-in. The market had no problem switching from VHS to DVD, then to Blu-Ray, and finally to streaming services such as Apple and Amazon. This alone should be enough to refute the network lock-in theory, but let's take a deeper look anyway. In reality, Betamax and VHS had comparable technology. The main difference is that Betamax tapes were smaller but could only record one hour of programming. VHS tapes were larger but could record two hours—enough for a full-length movie. The only real advantage of Betamax was that it had a special form of tape threading that made it more suited for editing and adding special effects. But most consumers didn't want to add special effects; they wanted to record and watch movies. The longer recording time of VHS made it the clearly superior product.

Sony quickly realized that Betamax was in trouble, so they doubled the recording time to two hours. VHS responded by doubling theirs to four hours—enough to record a football or baseball game. Betamax ultimately increased their recording time to five hours and VHS to eight hours. However, VHS was always able to offer a better tradeoff between image quality and recording time due to the larger tape size. Sony gambled that people would want small, portable tapes and that gamble came back to haunt them. If any tape was superior, it was the VHS standard. In fact, Betamax was actually released a year before VHS, but that did not stop VHS from taking over the market. The real story of VHS versus Betamax is the opposite of the myth: The superior VHS format took on an established but inferior rival and won. So much for lock-in.

Another classic example of lock-in is the arrangement of keys on a keyboard. Standard keyboards are called QWERTY after the arrangement of letters on the top row of the keyboard. QWERTY was designed back in the days of manual typewriters that were prone to jamming. It slowed down typists and prevented jams. However, typewriters became less likely to jam as the technology improved. That made faster typing possible. In 1936 August Dvorak patented the Dvorak Simplified Keyboard. It moved all the commonly used letters to the middle row of the keyboard. It also put the vowels under the left hand to encourage load balancing between the right and left hands. This reduces finger travel and increases typing speed. Yet despite its merits, the Dvorak keyboard never caught on because we are all locked in to the inferior QWERTY keyboards. The result was a market failure. Or was it?

Dvorak keyboards minimize finger travel, and they do a better job of load balancing between the two hands. But there is one area where QWERTY is stronger: it does a better job of alternating hands than Dvorak. That was the real secret behind QWERTY's ability to prevent jams. If you are old enough to have used a manual typewriter, then you know that the best way to get a jam is to hit two keys that are close to each other at the same time. QWERTY was designed with the primary goal of alternating between the left and right hands. That made users less likely to hit successive keys that are near each other. It also has the by-product of speeding up typing. Alternating hands is fast.

The modern research on QWERTY supports this view. The original studies that are widely cited in the debate are old and do not meet modern standards for research quality. (We'll see in a future chapter that modern studies are not a whole lot better). Stan Liebowitz and Stephen Margolis review the modern ergonomics literature and find that Dvorak is only about 2 percent to 6 percent faster.[56] Still, does the fact that Dvorak keyboards are faster mean that we are locked-in? No, because the cost of switching has to be counted. If the costs of switching exceed the benefits, it is not a market failure.

Firms make many decisions that they might like to change with the benefit of hindsight. Maybe Subaru wishes they made the Outback four inches longer. Maybe a toy company wishes they built a factory in Indonesia instead of Taiwan. Perhaps the owner of a local pizza restaurant wished he rented the space in that fast-growing warehouse district instead of the slowly declining downtown area. Hindsight is 20:20. It's only a market failure if the benefits of making a change exceed the costs, but for some reason the firm is stuck and can't make the change happen. That's the essence of the argument about lock-in.

The story of QWERTY versus Dvorak has a modern twist. These days computer hobbyists have a cottage industry of creating ever-better keyboard arrangements such as Colemak and Maltron. These days you can even do a software analysis and create your own keyboard arrangement based on the words you tend to use in your own writing. Are Dvorak typists locked in to an inferior standard? No. For hobbyists, it's worth investing the time in the pursuit of the perfect keyboard. For the rest of us, QWERTY is good enough.

The real story of network monopolies is not lock-in, but *serial monopolies*. Betamax was conquered by VHS, which was conquered by DVD, which was conquered by Blu-Ray, which was conquered by Apple and Amazon's streaming. One product is released and establishes a network monopoly, but then it is conquered by a superior product. We've seen that this can happen, but how? Insurgent technologies face a seemingly hopeless task. The benefits of building a better mousetrap are overwhelmed by the benefits of having a large, established network.

Firms have a few different weapons in their arsenal but the most important is monopolistic competition. Consumers like variety and can support multiple networks. Social media is a network monopoly, and yet we have Facebook, Twitter/X, Instagram, Snapchat, YouTube, TikTok, and more. Each social network offers different benefits to different types of users. Facebook is the current leader, but Snapchat will become the new king if young people stick with it as they get older. For video game platforms, we have the Xbox, PlayStation, Nintendo, and PCs. Nintendo has some great exclusive games like Mario and Zelda. It's also a good choice for young gamers and casual gamers. PCs are great for serious gamers who want the best performance possible no matter the price. The Xbox and PlayStation fall somewhere in between. Streaming services are similar. I don't even want to think about all the different streaming services that I'm paying for because someone in my family is currently watching a show on one of them.

George Stigler was right: "Competition is a tough weed, not a delicate flower."

Social Norms

> It is those we live with and love and should know who elude us.
>
> – Norman McLean, *A River Runs Through It*

At this point in the book the focus moves to shoestring and duct tape: the social norms and moral values that hold society together when free markets don't work. There will still be economic parables, but they will teach general truths about human nature, not about the magic of supply and demand. This chapter will be a good example.

With that disclaimer in mind, let's move on to the most unfortunately named theory in economics: *The First Fundamental Theorem of Welfare Economics*. It's a mathematical proof that free markets will reach the most efficient outcome possible provided that a few assumptions are met. Many assumptions go into the theory, so we'll focus on just three.

1. Perfect competition.
2. People are rational.
3. People's choices will not hurt others, even indirectly.

The lesson of the last chapter was that perfect competition only exists in a stagnant world without technological change, so that's one assumption we don't have to worry about. The other two assumptions are problems, but they are problems that teach deep lessons. The basic idea of the conservative worldview is that unwritten rules, social norms, and moral values are the only way to deal with these two problems effectively. Cultures that celebrate these norms and values survive and thrive; cultures that don't decline and fall.

The Marshmallow Test

The next parable in our tour of human nature is the marshmallow test by Walter Mischel. The test involves giving preschool-aged children a marshmallow and then making a deal. They could eat the marshmallow immediately, or they could wait fifteen minutes while the experimenter left the room, and if they hadn't eaten it when he returned, they could have two marshmallows. It tests children's ability to control their impulses and defer gratification. Bruce Wydick explains in *Games and Economic Development*:

> Some of the children immediately crammed the marshmallow into their mouth with Augustus Gloop-like voracity as soon as the researcher left the room. Others were able to wait a few moments, but then succumbed to the overpowering temptation of the marshmallow. Another group of children engaged in a variety of self-distraction exercises: covering their eyes so they could not see the marshmallow, walking over to sit in a corner, singing, and playing clapping games with themselves. When Mischel returned, he rewarded these children with their second marshmallow. Then he waited for the children to grow up.
>
> What he found fourteen years later was astonishing. The children who had waited for the second marshmallow scored an average of 210 points higher on the SAT than those who couldn't wait. The two-marshmallow children grew up to be better adjusted, more able to get along with peers, and, by most measures, more successful young adults. In contrast, the grown-up one-marshmallow children were more likely to be stressed, disorganized, and generally less successful, not only in school but in other activities and relationships.

A good part of economic development is about not eating the marshmallow.[57]

A study by William Galston, a Democrat who worked as an advisor to President Clinton, has found there are three rules that people need to follow in order to avoid being poor.

1. Graduate from high school.
2. Wait until age twenty to marry.
3. Wait until marriage to have children.

Do these three things, and your odds of being poor are only about 8 percent. Don't do them, and your odds of being poor are 79 percent.[58] The striking thing about Galston's three rules is that they are all factors that people should be able to control. This suggests that willpower and the inability to defer gratification is a major cause of poverty.

Liberal readers may be thinking, "I knew it! He had me going for a couple chapters, but I knew he was going to blame the poor sooner or later." But I'm not blaming the poor. I'm blaming our own unwillingness to change our culture. If someone who is conservative doesn't want the government to help people who are poor, then that's a black mark on them. And if someone who is liberal doesn't want to change the culture so that people don't become poor in the first place, then that's an even bigger black mark.

The main thesis of this book is the power of ordinary people when socialized by the right norms, values, and culture. And it is with poverty that we begin to see the importance of *social norms*—unwritten rules about how to live a good life. Each of Galston's three rules should be a social norm, but unfortunately, they are not. Or at least, they aren't anymore. There is an old joke that goes like this: If the world were to end tomorrow, the headline in The New York Times would say, "World ends tomorrow! Women, minorities hardest hit!" But in the case of the Sexual Revolution, the old joke is 100 percent true. The Sexual Revolution happened, and women and minorities were the hardest hit.

The irony is that the Civil Rights movement had just ended institutional segregation. Black people were looking forwards to moving into mainstream middle-class American life. Unfortunately, the fragility created by 350 years of oppression left black culture uniquely vulnerable to the downstream consequences of the Sexual Revolution. In 1917, the earliest year we have data, only 12 percent of black children were born to single mothers.[59] Today that number is up to 70 percent, according to the Centers for Disease Control. Teenage pregnancy has declined, but single motherhood has increased.[60]

The old joke was right. The consequences of the Sexual Revolution fell primarily on women and minorities. I'll bet that many younger readers didn't even know that just a few generations ago, most black children grew up with married parents and lived in neighborhoods where it was safe to walk the streets at night. That generation is growing old and will begin passing away soon, which means there will be no living black people who remember a time when most black children were raised by their mother and their father.

As a society we need to collectively bring back the old social norms about marriage and childrearing. This would create a virtuous cycle around Galston's three rules. Increased marriage would result in more children being raised in stable homes with involved fathers. That would result in higher rates of children graduating from high school, which would lead to more young men getting good jobs and marrying. But we can't change our social norms unless society as a whole collectively agrees to do so.

The marshmallow test is one of the most famous and insightful studies in all of the social sciences, but no idea is above criticism.

Some liberals object to the marshmallow test by raising an alternate explanation: "A bird in the hand is worth two in the bush." They believe conservatives got the arrow of causation backwards. Poverty creates insecurity about the future. A poor person might want to get his car fixed so he can find a better job that can't be reached by bus, but he has to spend his money on food instead. For the poor, life teaches them to take the sure thing now. This creates a poverty trap: Poverty creates uncertainty about the future, which in turn changes the incentives to become a one-marshmallow person, which in turn leads to more poverty.

Tyler Watts and colleagues revisited the marshmallow test. Their initial results were similar to Mischel's, but after doing a *multiple regression analysis* to control for family background, early cognitive ability, and the home environment, about two-thirds of the results disappeared.[61] The liberal theory that poor willpower was a downstream consequence of poverty seemed to be vindicated. However, words like "control" and "regress" should always make your spider sense tingle, and that applies here.

Multiple regression analysis is a robust statistical technique, but it can be abused. Sometimes multiple regression helps to separate correlation from causation, but it can also make real relationships disappear. In this case it made a real relationship disappear. As a general rule you don't need to be suspicious when people control for the "usual suspects" like age, sex, and education. But when you see unusual items on the list of controls, like early cognitive ability, then you should start to get concerned. It might be fine, but it might not be. One of the main tools that prevents multiple regression analysis from being abused is to *pre-register* studies. That means scientists publish the methods they will use before actually gathering data, including what controls they will use in a multiple regression analysis. No one plans to do a biased analysis—that's plan B when their first approach fails.

In the paper *Same Data Set, Different Conclusions,* Laura Michaelson and Yuko Munakata use the exact same data set that was used above, but they pre-registered their analysis. Their more rigorous approach supports Mischel's original findings. The two marshmallow children did better in school, had better social skills, and had fewer problem behaviors.[62] If we care about the poor, then as a society we need to create social norms around not eating the marshmallow.

Supernormal Stimuli

Developing willpower and learning to defer gratification is a problem that has been with us since the dawn of time, but the more technology advances, the harder it gets. The obesity researcher Stephen Guynet explains:

> During the 1940s and 50s, an Austrian psychologist named Konrad Lorenz studied the behavioral patterns of geese.
>
> One of the things he observed was the egg-retrieving behavior of the greylag goose. When an egg rolls out of a goose's nest, it gently uses its bill to roll it back in. However, when Lorenz took an egg from the nest and placed it next to a larger round white object, the goose preferentially rolled the larger object back into its nest while ignoring the real egg. He called this larger object a superstimulus. It was an abnormally strong stimulus that was able to hijack the bird's normal behavioral pattern in a maladaptive way.
>
> Our brains are wired to respond to the stimuli with which they evolved. For example, our natural taste preferences tell us that fruit is good. But what happens when we concentrate that sugar tenfold? We get a superstimulus. **Our brains are not designed to process that amount of stimulation constructively, and it often leads to a loss of control over the will, or addiction.**[63]

Graylag geese chase the *superstimuli* (large, bright white fake eggs) and ignore their real eggs. Humans are the same. We chase the superstimuli (donuts and ice cream) and ignore healthy foods like fruit. Drugs are another type of superstimuli. Take heroin for example. Our bodies produce many natural opioids that make us feel good when we do things like exercise, have a pleasant conversation, listen to music, or accomplish something at work or school. Drugs like heroin concentrate that good feeling dramatically, much the way that donuts and ice cream concentrate sugar. Drug users chase the superstimuli (drugs) and ignore their jobs and relationships.

Another way of thinking about this is that we live in an *evolutionarily novel environment*. We evolved for fruit but have donuts and ice cream. We evolved for satisfying work and pleasant conversations but have heroin. Our willpower is strong enough to handle fruit, but not Oreos. Technology was supposed to solve our problems, but instead it created new ones. Yes, these new problems are smaller than the old ones we used to face. People in the developed world do not have to worry about chronic starvation, high rates of infant mortality, and dangerous air quality from unventilated stoves. But technology is not an unmitigated blessing. Instead of creating utopia, technology has created new challenges.

My favorite example of a supernormal stimuli is the Australian jewel beetle. In a peculiar turn of events, a type of beer bottle known as a "stubby" looked like a female jewel beetle. The females have brown bodies with textured bumps on them, and the stubby gave a stronger "brown with textured bumps" signal than the female beetles. The result was that the male beetles attempted to mate with the stubbies and ignored the real females. It ultimately reached the point where the species was in danger of going extinct. Fortunately, the manufacturer changed to a green bottle, and the jewel beetle was saved. The scientists

Darryl Gwynne and David Rentz were awarded the 2011 Ig Nobel prize for their research.[64]

The Ig Nobel prize is given to research that might make people laugh, but the best Ig Nobels teach surprisingly deep lessons, and this study is one of them. There are millions of failing marriages because the husbands are chasing a superstimuli (pornography) while ignoring their wives. We aren't that different from the beetles. Pornography has been around forever, but there's a difference between unlimited videos on your phone and a stack of Playboy magazines in your best friend's dad's closet.

Pornography is like alcohol and other drugs. Most people can drink in moderation without becoming addicted, but others are not as lucky, and alcohol can ruin their lives. For men who are addicted to pornography, it can lead to erectile difficulty and unwanted fetishes. For women the consequences are more harmful. Most men who are addicted to pornography are too ashamed to tell their wives, but at least they know what's going on. The women who are trapped in sexless marriages are left wondering what they did wrong. Does her husband no longer find her attractive? Has he fallen out of love? Is there another woman?

A recent article in The New York Times, called *The Troubling Trend in Teenage Sex*, shares research that two-thirds of college women in the United States have been choked during sex. It documents the rise of choking through shows and movies like *Californication*, *50 Shades of Grey*, and more recently with HBO's *Euphoria*. On the song charts, Jack Harlow raps that "I'm vanilla, baby, I'll choke you, but I ain't no killer, baby."[65] Our society has become so tolerant that it's become morally wrong to kink-shame, but socially acceptable to vanilla-shame—a point the article makes about the social scorn teenage girls who don't want to be choked receive.[66] And while I'm yelling at clouds, I remember when rappers prided themselves on their lyrical complexity.

Yet the left defends pornography. It is filled with sexist, degrading, and violent behavior towards women, and the left continues to maintain that pornography is healthy and empowering. The liberal take on pornography is that "What happens in the bedroom stays in the bedroom." But if a boy starts watching violent pornography at ten or twelve—and as Jack Harlow points out, choking is vanilla these days—how is he supposed to have a healthy relationship with a woman when he's in his twenties and thirties? More importantly, how is a woman ever supposed to be safe with him? What happens when it's no longer the power of grabbing a woman's throat that excites him, but the fear in her eyes when the line between fantasy and reality begins to blur? This is not a theoretical concern; there has been a 90 percent increase in the use of the "rough sex defense" when a woman dies during sex.[67] Women cannot consent to their own murders.

Reason and Passion

If Alicia likes chocolate ice cream and Blake likes vanilla, then there is no rational argument to prove that one of them is right. Tastes are ultimately based on feelings, or as philosophers used to put it, passions. The Enlightenment skeptic David Hume takes this insight to its logical conclusion and says, "Reason is, and ought only to be the slave of the passions".[68] If someone likes chocolate ice cream, then the role of reason is to help them get it. This was a sharp break from most philosophers, both modern and ancient, who felt that reason and passion were in opposition to each other.

If it seems like Hume's statement sounds like something that a reasonably bright high school atheist would come up with, then you're right. When I was in high school, one of the boys in my circle of friends started joining the stoners who snuck off to the river to smoke pot. This was decades before pot was legalized so it had a much greater social stigma back then. I could not understand his choice, and neither could another one of our mutual friends. The best we could come up with was "Feels good, might as well do it." But we meant it sarcastically. The slogan was so obviously wrong that no one was supposed to take it literally. But by the time we went to college, we had also succumbed to temptation and began to say "Feels good, might as well do it" non-ironically. It took a long time for us to recover the wisdom of ancient philosophers.

Hume did not actually say that we should all start doing drugs, because people have many passions and some of them conflict with each other. Take the popular meme: "I want a hot body, but I also want a taco." How does someone trade off between these two goals? Hume's literary style does not let us do this. Luckily for us, but unluckily for Hume, his insight is now baked into modern economics. That allows us to make this trade-off in a mathematically rigorous way. In both cases the goal is to satisfy as many desires (*preferences*) as possible. The only role for reason is to help achieve that goal. That's what economists mean when they say people are *rational utility maximizers*. The more preferences someone satisfies, the higher their *utility*. The goal of reason and rationality is to create the highest utility possible.

Gary Becker and Kevin Murphy took Hume's idea to heart and created the model of the rational drug addict.[69] In this model, drug addicts freely choose the poor health, damaged relationships, and disappointing lives that come with the high of taking drugs. The idea is that poor health and damaged relationships are far in the future, but the benefits of getting high are immediate.

It is rational to discount the future because there is legitimate uncertainty about what the future will bring. Think about it this way, it's probably not a good idea to work overtime your entire life and save all your money so that you can have a spectacular retirement. You'll miss out on many important moments of life along the way, and besides, you might get hit by a bus on your last day of work. In other words, sometimes eating the marshmallow is the rational thing to do. Economists explain this using what is called *exponential discounting*. It's exactly the formula used to calculate interest rates. Using the rational actor model and exponential discounting, Becker and Murphy were able to show that choosing drugs over a fulfilling life is rational.

Their model has some power because in many ways, drug addicts do behave rationally. The first lesson of economics is that people respond to incentives, and drug addicts are no exception. Henry Saffer and Frank Chaloupka use data from the National Household Survey of Drug Abuse and find that drug legalization would result in a 100 percent increase in the use of heroin and a 50 percent increase in cocaine.[70] Behaviors that are punished are done less often, and that applies to drug users.

Nevertheless, the model of the rational drug addict does not withstand a closer look. Drug addicts resolve to quit taking drugs, but then break their resolution. I remember asking my stepmother, who ultimately did quit smoking, if she ever tried to quit. Her answer was "twenty times a day." Broken resolutions are the hallmark of irrational behavior. Economists have a name for this—a *preference reversal*. They also have a way to model this mathematically called *hyperbolic time discounting*. In a heavily cited review paper, Shane Frederick and colleagues show that hyperbolic time discounting is a better fit for the evidence, including of drug addicts.[71]

Broken resolutions are not just a problem for drug users. We all take the marshmallow test many times each day. We resolve to exercise but stay home to watch TV. We resolve to eat healthy but grab donuts or ice cream. We resolve to get our work done on time but end up procrastinating. We resolve to live more frugally but spend money on frivolous things.

When you eat a donut, you are being nice to your present self—the "you" who exists right now, in the present. Your present self gets to enjoy a tasty snack. On the other hand, eating donuts is bad for your future self, the "you" who will exist tomorrow, and the next day, and the day after that. Your future self has to suffer all of the unhealthy consequences but doesn't get any of the fun. Conversely, when you go to the gym to exercise, you are being mean to your present self, but nice to your future self.

The psychologist George Ainslie points out that this is a form of bargaining between our present self and our future selves. All things being equal, we'd like for our future selves to live happy and flourishing lives. But in order to give them that, we have to repress the needs of our present self. Ainslie uses techniques like hyperbolic time discounting to show that unhealthy behaviors are not the result of rational choices. They are a breakdown of will.[72]

David Hume got it exactly backward: Reason is, or ought to be, the master of our passions. Unfortunately, that's easier said than done. Our passions come from a part of the brain called the *limbic system*. It is a robust and well-developed part of the brain in both animals and humans. Our impulse control comes from the *prefrontal cortex*. We know this because people who have suffered damage to the prefrontal cortex have poor long-term decision making abilities, despite being completely normal in all other ways.[73] Animals have only small prefrontal cortexes because they can't actively plan for the future. The prefrontal cortex is significantly larger and more developed in humans, but it should probably be even larger still, because it's not always up to the job of reigning in the limbic system. That's particularly true now that we live in an evolutionarily novel environment filled with superstimuli from junk food, drugs, and pornography.

That raises a question: Is life just too hard? Why live a life of self-denial, repression, and guilt over our inevitable missteps? If we could just let it all go, we could be free and happy. That was David Hume's vision. Edmund Burke disagreed:

> Men are qualified for civil liberty in exact proportion to their disposition to put moral chains upon their own appetites, — in proportion as their love to justice is above their rapacity,—in proportion as their soundness and sobriety of understanding is above their vanity and presumption,—in proportion as they are more disposed to listen to the counsels of the wise and good, in preference to the flattery of knaves. Society cannot exist, unless a controlling power upon will and appetite be placed somewhere; and the less of it there is within, the more there must be without. It is ordained in the eternal constitution of things, that men of intemperate minds cannot be free. Their passions forge their fetters.[74]

So there you have it: Hume says reason should be slave to the passions, and Burke says the passions enslave us. This distinction is arguably the single biggest fault line in the divide between right and left. Hume was pretty conservative, and even Burkean, in many ways, but his high school atheist skepticism ultimately puts him on the left.

The conflict between these two visions of freedom shows up in many political issues. We've already seen this conflict with Galston's three rules to avoid being poor, and the debate over the marshmallow test. The harm caused by pornography is another example of this gap between the left and right's vision of freedom. It will continue to be a running theme throughout the rest of this book.

Woke Postmodernism

> The embrace of gender-identity ideology was part of mainstream feminism's shift away from seeking to improve the lives of ordinary women and towards a self-congratulatory, performative, postmodernist style with its origins on campus.
>
> – Helen Joyce, *Trans: When Ideology Meets Reality*

In 2002 John Fonte published an article called *Liberal Democracy vs. Transnational Progressivism*. He was concerned about the growing trend of Western intellectuals abandoning Enlightenment principles of reason and rational thought. He called this emerging movement *transnational progressivism*. In his article he identified nine key points of this new ideology,[75] but I'll only list five, and I'll paraphrase them.

1. The group someone belongs to is more important than the individual.
2. Groups can be categorized as either oppressor groups or victim groups, with immigrants automatically belonging to victim groups.
3. Group outcomes must be proportional to their representation. If 10 percent of the population is Latino, then 10 percent of insurance salesmen should also be Latino.
4. The values of major institutions, such as corporations, universities, and news outlets, should be changed to reflect the values of victim groups.
5. A redefinition of democracy away from majority rule and towards power-sharing among groups, including non-citizen groups.

This list should be instantly familiar to anyone who follows modern politics. Fonte anticipated the rise of "Woke" ideology by almost twenty years. These are the principles behind Critical Race Theory and the de-facto open borders policy of the Biden administration. The New York Times reports that illegal border crossings after the Covid pandemic have been over 2 million per year, which is more than four times the yearly rate of illegal crossing during the eight years before the pandemic, which included both the Obama and Trump administrations.[76]

There is nothing new about Woke ideology. It's just a somewhat debased form of *postmodernism*, and its close cousin, critical theory. Postmodernists rejected Enlightenment principles of reason and individual rights decades before Fonte sounded the alarm. Fonte is clearly familiar with postmodernism and nods at it with his occasional use of postmodern buzzwords, but never made the connection explicit. But whether you want to call it Wokism, transnational progressivism, or postmodernism, it's all the same thing: the rejection of both individual rights and Enlightenment reason in favor of group-based politics and power plays.

Postmodernism

Postmodernism is a philosophy that rejects the idea of objective truth and holds that people are motivated by a quest for power. Hence the slogan "all truth claims are power plays." This core insight should resonate with conservatives who are used to truth claims, such as those about Hunter Biden's laptop, being used to advance political goals. When the universities, news outlets, non-profits, and the professional managerial classes of large corporations are all drawing from the same ideology, then it's easy to create a false consensus about truth. But postmodernists take this to an extreme where objective truth either doesn't exist or is essentially unknowable.

The reason why it's called postmodernism is because the period known as *modernism* ran from the late nineteenth century through the middle of the twentieth century. Modernists upheld principles of reason and rationality that date back to the Enlightenment, if not much earlier. These principles are the way for liberals and conservatives to come together in the public square and discuss, debate, and seek the truth on neutral terms available to everyone who embraces rational thinking. By denying the possibility of ever knowing the truth, postmodernism became a post-rational, or post-modern, movement. The philosophers Bradley Dowden and Norman Swartz explain that:

> The most radical postmodernists do not distinguish acceptance as true from being true; they claim that the social negotiations among influential people "construct" the truth. The truth, they argue, is not something lying outside of human collective decisions; it is not, in particular, a "reflection" of an objective reality. Or, to put it another way, to the extent that there is an objective reality it is nothing more nor less than what we say it is. We human beings are, then, the ultimate arbiters of what is true. Consensus is truth.[77]

Since the truth is unknowable, reality is a *social construct.* Reality is constructed by people with power to serve their own ends. Once again, conservatives already know many examples of socially constructed "truths" such as the Hunter Biden laptop story that might have swung 12,000 votes in Georgia. However, the best example of a socially constructed truth is not about laptops, but racism. The left has so much social power that conservatives can't make an argument without being accused of racism. That kind of power play is textbook postmodernism.

My favorite example of weaponized accusations of racism is from the Munk debate on media bias. Matt Taibbi, best known for the Twitter files that revealed government censorship of the Hunter Biden laptop story, briefly mentioned that the public had a high degree of trust in the news anchor Walter Cronkite. One of the participants on the other side of the debate was Malcolm Gladwell, who immediately pounced on this. He spent a good chunk of each speaking segment in the debate accusing Taibbi of racism because of his obvious fondness for the way America used to be.[78] Gladwell did this despite the fact Cronkite had a track record of fighting for civil rights.

The real magic of using social power to construct reality does not come from shaming people, but from silencing them. There is no need to even have a debate if people are too afraid to speak up for fear of the consequences. Power silences dissent. Power protects authorities from even having to pretend to care about the truth. So before you dismiss postmodernism as fuzzy-headed nonsense, keep the social power of the modern left in mind. They probably won't have this much power forever, but for now they are an accessible example of an important principle of postmodernism.

Since postmodernists believe we can't ever know the truth, the best we can do is *deconstruct* truth claims to find out who is gaining power from them. By teasing out the ambiguities, contradictions, and hidden meanings in a text, postmodernists claim to be able to learn the nature of the power plays found within, and perhaps even the fears and insecurities of the author who made them. It may seem ridiculous, but the concept of deconstruction has merit. Now that Hollywood has gone "Woke," conservative pop culture influencers have become positively giddy deconstructing the not-so-hidden-messages in the latest *Star Wars* or superhero movies. They don't call it that, but that's exactly what they're doing. They aren't analyzing these movies for their admittedly flimsy literary value; they're exposing the biases coming out of Hollywood. Deconstruction is a real tool with real value, but I wouldn't consider it an upgrade over Enlightenment reason.

The debate over Enlightenment reason versus postmodern power plays misses a key point: The truth is not something that is wielded in the public square to score talking points, but the nature of reality itself. Postmodernists can use their social power to implement their ideas, but they can't change reality. They can make everyone act as though poverty is caused by structural inequalities, but unless that is actually true, it won't do anything to help. It might even make poverty worse. Reality is the ultimate judge of all ideas, and it cannot be swayed by social power.

In the final analysis, postmodernism is false because it is self-refuting. Consider the proposition "all truth claims are power plays." That proposition is a truth claim, so by its own standard it's a power play. If power plays are false, then postmodernism is false. If power plays can still be true, then postmodernism can still be true, but so can the truth claims made by everyone else. Either way, the main weapon of postmodernism is rendered completely useless. (We can play the exact same game with other skeptical philosophies, and we'll see a couple later in the book.) Of course, most postmodernists don't worry about pesky details like logical consistency, or even distilling their philosophy into simple principles. But some of them do, and they have come up with various ways to moderate their position. Their goal is to retain most of their original power while still avoiding the trap of self-refutation. If they moderated their position all the way to "social power is often more important than the truth," then I would agree with them, but alas, they do not.

I don't claim to be able to penetrate the writing of postmodernists like Jacques Derrida and Judith Butler. Postmodernists are notorious for writing in a style of gibberish called *obscurantism*. To get an idea of how bad their writing really is, here is a random sentence from page 114 of Judith Butler's seminal book *Gender Trouble*: "To what extent is that Cartesian dualism presupposed in phenomenology adapted to the structuralist frame in which mind/body is redescribed as culture/nature?"[79] These are all valid terms from *continental philosophy*, although postmodernists use them in more literary ways.

Obscurantism is a defense mechanism. It means that no critic will ever get credit for winning a debate against a postmodernist. Any criticism will be uniformly met with the objection that the critic badly misunderstood the source material, and clearly couldn't be bothered to take the time and effort to actually read it. The philosopher John Searle, who made the naïve mistake of thinking that he could honestly engage with postmodernists, complained about obscurantism in an article in The New York Review of Books called *The World Turned Upside Down*.[80]

Obscurantism defeated the honest sincerity of philosophers like Searle, but it also exposes postmodernism to ridicule. It has been a repeated victim of intellectual hoaxes such as the Sokal Affair[81] and the Grievance Studies Affair.[82] These were fake papers that used all the right buzzwords and were published in reputable postmodern journals. The Grievance Studies Affair was actually a series of fake papers on various topics. One of them was about what dogs humping at dog parks reveals about fragile masculinity, and another was a proposal for an alternative to bodybuilding competitions where the competitors get as fat as possible. As long as you hit the right buzzwords, even postmodernists can't tell the difference between a real paper and an obvious troll.

Here's the real problem with postmodernism, and it has nothing to do with philosophy. It's just a trick that some people fall for, most notably John Searle. Postmodernism is based on rejecting reason and rational thought. That includes science. In theory that's because science is the biggest truth claim/power play of them all, but in practice it's because deconstruction is what postmodernism is all about. They treat science like any other text and deconstruct the *phantasms* found within. A phantasm is a distorted picture of reality caused by fear, insecurity, and a will to power.

In *Higher Superstition: The Academic Left and Its Quarrels with Science* Paul Gross and Norman Levitt discuss what has become the textbook example of the abuse of deconstruction. A group of postmodernists wrote a famous paper about what feminism can contribute to cellular biology. Yes, they actually did that. One of their examples was of fertilization. They misleadingly claimed that male biologists portrayed fertilization of an egg by sperm as a type of "martial gang rape" in which armies of sperm take turns actively attempting to fertilize the passive egg, which is portrayed as a whore, a damsel in distress, and finally a redeemed lady of worth when fertilized. Then they dropped their trump card: these patriarchal metaphors were wrong because modern studies with electron microscopes showed that eggs have agency and actively participate in their own fertilization.

There are so many things wrong with this argument that it's hard to even begin. Everything in my nature as a modern internet denizen screams that I'm being trolled, and not in a particularly subtle or clever way. Admittedly this happened in the late 1980s and the world was a simpler place back then. USENET existed and they had trolls, but internet trolling was not yet the fine art that it would someday become. On modern internet forums like Tumblr, anyone who made the sperm and egg argument would be six layers deep in irony, and if you responded to any of the top five layers you would lose. Even as I write this, I'm terrified that there is a secret postmodern bulletin board from 1988 and I'm being added to the list of victims who took their sperm and egg trolling seriously. But I'll bite anyways.

First, thinking about eggs as "passive whores" says a lot more about postmodernists than it does about scientists. Second, the argument that it was feminism and not the invention of the electron microscope that led to the discovery of the active role of eggs also says a lot more about postmodernists than it does about scientists. Finally, Gross points out that scientists had long since known through other methods, such as artificial parthenogenesis and maternal RNA, that eggs are not passive.[83]

Because of this type of shoddy reasoning, many Enlightenment-inspired interlopers are tricked into thinking that they can drag these fuzzy-headed postmodernists back into reality. The Sokal hoax, John Searle's attempt to sincerely engage with postmodernists, and the sperm and egg saga were all a part of the *science wars* that took place in the early 1990s when scientists tried to engage postmodernists. They accomplished nothing. The postmodernists didn't learn, and they didn't change. If you want to understand postmodernism then your best bet is to think of them as the internet trolls of academia, but without the six layers of irony to make them interesting. The more you feed them, the more powerful they grow. That's the trick.

Gender Ideology

Postmodernists like Judith Butler give us the sharpest conflict between the conservative Burkean view of freedom and the liberal Humean view. That is *gender ideology*, which is the movement driving the rise of transgenderism. The liberal argument for it is simple: people who are transgender deserve the freedom to be their authentic selves. It's basically just a repeat of the fight for gay marriage, in which gay people wanted the freedom to live their own lives without conservatives getting in the way. But just as my simple understanding of taxes fell before real-world complexities, so does the simple liberal understanding of gender ideology. It will almost certainly go down in history as a bigger medical scandal than lobotomies.

Gender ideology has been around for a while so here is a brief history. In the case of gender roles, truth claims like "women are passive" and "women are more naturally oriented towards children and family" were created by men to oppress women. Men don't have to force women into being homemakers if they willingly choose that role. In the past, *radical feminists* fought to abolish these oppressive gender roles. Note that radical means going to the root of the problem, not extremist. Radical feminists see these gender roles as the root of female oppression. Instead of socializing girls in female ways and boys in male ways, we should socialize all children in gender-neutral ways. This would liberate women from oppression and men from narrow and confining gender roles.

Unfortunately, that creates a problem. Radical feminists want to replace rigid gender roles based on femininity and masculinity with the equally rigid roles of sexless monks. Throughout history we do find various groups experimenting in gender-neutral societies, such as the eighteenth-century Shakers and the twentieth-century Israeli Kibbutz movement. These groups are based around communal living with non-gendered clothing, jobs, and social roles. The Shakers were celibate and didn't have children, and members of the Kibbutz movement raised children collectively so that women were not stuck in a domestic role.

These are admirable experiments, and I usually root for novel subcultures when I read about them. I don't want to be Amish, but I'm glad the Amish are out there showing us what a simpler life built around faith, family, and community looks like. However, these gender-egalitarian communities never last more than a generation or so without major changes.

In the case of the Kibbutz movement, the anthropologist Melford

Spiro found that the return to a more traditional lifestyle was led by the first generation of women who had been born and raised in the movement.[84] They were grateful for the Kibbutz movement and what it gave them, but they nevertheless wanted something different for their own children. I'm not suggesting that all radical feminists want to create a communal society, although some of them do. Rather, the point is that the Kibbutz movement shows the difficulty of creating a sustainable world based on the abolition of gender roles.

In some ways the radical feminists were quite Burkean: freedom meant having to repress your sexuality to some degree. That was doomed to collide with the liberal vision of freedom. The backlash was inevitable, and a new generation of *liberal feminists* arose. One of the most important tenets of liberal feminism is *sex positivism*. This new generation protested against double standards where sexually active men were celebrated and sexually active women were shamed. They also championed the personal autonomy of women as sexual beings and argued that promiscuous sex could be empowering for women.

The school of gender ideology contributed the idea that since gender roles were not innate, they could be subverted. We see this most clearly with people who are gay or transgender. Both groups take power away from heterosexual men who want to dominate women. Gay people opt out of this heterosexual oppression, and transgender people subvert these roles by switching sides. Members of these marginalized groups can then form their own families that subvert the heterosexual nuclear family. For example, older gay men can play the mother role to younger gay men.

These oppressive gender roles can be further subverted by sexual kinks that reject stereotypical power dynamics between men and women, which is why the queer community is becoming increasingly kink-friendly. A female dominatrix who sexually dominates men is subverting traditional gender roles, as is a woman who forms a polyamorous relationship with multiple male and female partners. Andrea Long Chu is a Pulitzer Prize winning journalist and a biological male who identifies as female. He writes openly in his book *Females* about the role that sissy porn played in making him transgender. In fact, Chu identifies the essence of being female with sexual passivity: "an open mouth, an expectant asshole, blank, blank eyes."[85] How big would the backlash be if a conservative like Jordan Peterson had made that statement? But when it's a liberal like Chu, they give him a Pulitzer.[86]

The idea that women are passive sex objects is precisely the stereotype that radical feminists had fought against for decades. This is one of the most important criticisms that radical feminists make against gender ideology—they aren't subverting sexist stereotypes, they're amplifying them. The liberal definition of woman is anyone who feels like a woman. But what does it mean to "feel like a woman?" The answer invariably involves a collection of sexist stereotypes like being pretty, having long hair, wearing dresses, and enjoying makeup—all things the radical feminists had been fighting against associating with women.

The radical feminist-inspired 1970s gave us children's shows like *Free to Be ... You and Me*. It was about learning to be yourself and appreciating the body you were born with. It had frequent images of boys and girls challenging gender stereotypes such as boys dreaming of becoming cooks and girls dreaming of becoming construction workers. It also had a duet with a young Michael Jackson and Roberta Flack dreaming about what they would be like when they were adults, and the chorus goes, "You don't have to change at all."[87] The liberal feminist-inspired 2020s would pounce on a boy having slightly feminine interests and conclude that he's not a boy at all. Then they would send him down a lifelong process of attempting to change his sex. And that takes us to youth gender medicine.

Youth Gender Medicine

The TV show, *The Problem with Jon Stewart*, made the usual case for "gender-affirming" care. It featured parents of feminine boys whose gender nonconformity emerged in early childhood.[88] These are the boys who wanted to grow their hair long and wear Disney princess dresses as small children. If there is such a thing as someone who is born transgender, it would be these boys. However, the psychologist James Cantor reviewed the research and found that about 60 to 90 percent of these children stop identifying as transgender by adulthood.[89] Another study found that 83 percent of transgender children eventually stop identifying as transgender.[90] Most of these feminine boys grow up into gay men, so at some point during puberty they realize "Oh, I'm not a straight female, I'm a gay male." Puberty is not the enemy of gender dysphoria—it's the cure.

The children who stopped identifying as transgender were following a *watchful waiting* paradigm. That meant their gender dysphoria was acknowledged and they were given therapy, but they weren't transitioned, either socially or medically. These days the standard practice is to socially transition these children, which sends them inexorably down the path towards transitioning medically. The theory is that early transition helps children get the socialization of the opposite sex, and that transitioning before puberty increases their ability to pass as the opposite sex. Liberals also argue that social transition improves the mental health of these feminine boys, but the Cass Review that we'll meet shortly shows that it does not.[91]

Medical transition carries a heavy price. There is very little research on puberty blockers despite them having been used by tens or even hundreds of thousands of children. However, what little research we do have suggests that they cause lower IQs, brittle bones, and problems with sexual development.[92] In the past few years the highly progressive Nordic nations of Sweden, Finland, and Norway have all dramatically scaled back youth gender medicine.[93]

Meanwhile, the National Health Service of England launched an independent investigation into youth gender medicine spearheaded by the pediatric specialist Hillary Cass. The interim Cass Review led to England closing its only youth gender clinic, and the final Cass Review led to England banning puberty blockers except for clinical trials.[94] After the final review, Scotland said they would also ban puberty blockers,[95] and Belgium and the Netherlands are planning to review their use.[96]

The Cass Review is the most thorough and comprehensive literature review of transgender youth medicine in existence. In fact, four years ago the World Professional Association for Transgender Health (WPATH), the leading medical organization for transgender medicine, commissioned a literature review from scientists at Johns Hopkins. When the scientists concluded that there was no good evidence for youth gender medicine, WPATH blocked them from publishing and continued to advocate for "gender affirming" care for children.[97]

Liberals have bombarded anyone who exhibits even the smallest amount of skepticism with a chorus of "the science is settled." But the science is not settled, or at least, not in the way liberals think. The Cass Review examined 23 clinical guidelines such as the WPATH Standards of Care. They found two important patterns. The first pattern is that many guidelines review the research and find insufficient benefit to justify medical treatments, but then go on to recommend medical treatments anyways.[98] The second pattern is circular citations. The 23 different clinical guidelines and standards of care cite each other. Cass concludes that, "The circularity of this approach may explain why there has been an apparent consensus on key areas of practice despite the evidence being poor."[99]

Another problem with transitioning boys before puberty is that they will never be able to have a sexually fulfilling relationship. Boys have to go through male puberty for their genitals and sexual functioning to develop. In leaked documents from WPATH, the president Marci Bowers admits to not knowing of a single case of a child whose puberty was blocked at Tanner Stage 2 who was able to experience an orgasm.[100] Children cannot consent to losing something that they have never experienced.

A third problem is that these feminine boys are usually gay, so if they are going to transition, they generally want a surgically created neovagina. (Trans-identified men who are attracted to women typically do not get this surgery). It is a dangerous surgery with extremely high rates of complications. It amounts to essentially creating a permanent wound and requires a lifelong practice of dilation to keep the neovagina from closing. It is also prone to complications such as fistulas, which are abnormal connections between the colon and the neovagina, and necrosis, which is when the tissue that is grafted to the inside of the neovagina does not receive an adequate blood supply and begins to die.

Jazz Jennings, the star of the reality TV show *I Am Jazz*, has literally been the poster child for gender affirming care. Jazz has the best surgeons in the business, including Marci Bowers, the president of WPATH. And yet Jazz has had three revisions to this surgery and may need a fourth.[101] A long-term study of everyone in Sweden who has had gender reassignment surgery found that their suicide rate increases to twenty times as high after about ten to fifteen years.[102] I suspect that's when these patients give up hope that one more revision will solve their medical problems. I realize that transgender individuals want to look as much like the opposite sex as possible, but this surgery has such terrible complications that it is cruel and unethical. Jazz got this surgery as a minor.

In theory, the goal of these treatments is to reduce the suicidality of transgender children. That's the threat hanging over the heads of parents who have concerns about making irreversible medical decisions for their children: "Would you rather have a live daughter or a dead son?" How many parents have the courage to stand up to bullying gender clinicians? However, this is just a manipulative tactic that has no substance in fact.

The Cass Review found that the suicide rates for transgender children is the same as for children who have comparable mental health problems but who are not transgender. It concludes that the evidence does not support the claim that gender affirming care reduces the suicide rate.[103] Leor Sapir also reviewed the evidence and came to the same conclusion.[104] If you're skeptical of research studies, and you should be, then looking at the raw data is a good sanity check. If the gender clinicians were right, then we should have seen a large drop in teenage suicides in the 2010s when children began transitioning in significant numbers. Instead, the teenage suicide rate has continued to slowly increase.[105]

I'll admit that conservatives have not made it easy for young gay boys. And yet there is no getting around the fact that the rise of transgenderism happened after same-sex marriage became socially acceptable. There is also no getting around the fact that it is a phenomenon that is concentrated in liberal states, liberal communities, and liberal families. And most importantly, there is no getting around the fact that many liberal parents, upon noticing that their young son likes to wear dresses and play with dolls, immediately pepper him with leading questions about gender. Young children, always eager to please their parents, oblige.

The BBC journalist Hannah Barnes wrote *Time to Think* to provide an insider's account of why England closed the nation's only youth gender clinic. She opens the book with a question from a soul-searching clinician: "Are we hurting children?"[106] She then proceeds to answer the question affirmatively with a procession of exploited children and flimsy science. The question was not, "do you want a live daughter or a dead son?" The question was, "Do you want a straight daughter or a gay son?" Barnes notes that gender clinicians used to joke that when they were done, there would be no more gay kids left.[107] Somewhat ironically, liberals have created the most widespread and medically damaging form of gay conversion therapy ever invented.

The transgender movement started with feminine boys, but it spread to girls who were happy being girls until the struggles of adolescence. When England's youth gender clinic began, the patients were almost exclusively pre-adolescent boys, but over the past decade there was a 5,000 percent increase in the number of teenage girls.[108] Barnes writes:

> Whereas most of the literature on gender non-conforming children was about boys who had a lifelong sense of gender incongruence, GIDS's [England's youth gender clinic] waiting room was overpopulated with teenage girls whose distress around their gender had only started in adolescence. Many of them were same-sex attracted – the same was true for the boys attending GIDS – and many were autistic. Their lives were complicated too. So many seemed to have other difficulties – eating disorders, self-harm, depression – or had suffered abuse or trauma.[109]

You never see liberal TV shows and puff pieces that feature girls with mental health problems who became transgender after getting bullied during adolescence, but they are the ones filling up the waiting rooms.

Everyone feels uncomfortable with their body during puberty, but it is a more difficult transition for girls. They have to deal with painful breast growth, menstruation, and sexual attention from boys their own age as well as from men older than their fathers. That's compounded by the fact that female social dynamics are more fluid and complex than male social dynamics. The socially awkward girls, particularly the ones with mental health problems, struggle to follow the unwritten rules and end up lonely, isolated, and hurt.

Socially awkward teenagers can grow into confident adults, but not without pain, embarrassment, and many nights spent crying into their pillows. Instead, psychologists and doctors are telling these girls that their problems are the result of being transgender, so they put their energies into their transition instead of developing basic life skills.

The Free Rider Problem

> I have noticed
> that when
> chickens quit
> quarreling over their
> food they often
> find that there is
> enough for all of them
> i wonder if
> it might not
> be the same way
> with the human race
>
> – Don Marquis, *The Lives and Times of Archy and Mehitabel*

This chapter, and not the social norms chapter, is the one that lays the foundation for the rest of the book. It may take a while for that to become clear.

The Tragedy of the Commons

Garrett Hardin invented the *tragedy of the commons* to be a counterexample to the magic of supply and demand.[110] In the case of the tragedy of the commons, the pursuit of self-interest promotes the "greater bad." Here's a simple version of the parable.

> A group of ranchers graze their cattle on a *commons*—public land that everyone is allowed to use. In order to maintain the long-term health of the grass, the ranchers should follow a quota of perhaps fifty cattle each. The problem is that each rancher has an incentive to break the quota and graze extra cattle. But every rancher has the exact same incentive, so they all double the sizes of their herds. The

outcome is that there were more cows than the commons could feed, and the cows grew weak and sickly.

Let's think about the incentives for a moment. We're going to do this many times over the course of the book, so it's worth making sure you understand now. Each rancher can either cooperate or defect. If they cooperate, they'll do what's in the group's interest. That means follow their quota of 50 cows. If they defect, they'll do what's in their own self-interest. That means they'll break their quota and graze perhaps 100 cattle on the land.

Suppose that Alicia is one of these ranchers, and the other ranchers choose to defect (break their quota). She's only one of many ranchers, so if the others all defect the commons will be overgrazed no matter what she does. So her best option is also to defect (break her quota). It's better for her to have 100 sickly cows than 50 sickly cows. Now suppose the other ranchers choose to cooperate (follow their quota). Then there will be plenty of grass for everyone no matter what Alicia does. So her best option is to defect (break her quota). It's better for her to have 100 healthy cows than 50 healthy cows.

No matter what the other ranchers do, Alicia's best option is to defect. If everyone else cooperates, she should defect. If everyone else defects, she should still defect. In game theory terms, the tragedy of the commons has a single *Nash Equilibrium* of always defect. A Nash equilibrium is when a player can't single-handedly improve her outcome by making a different choice.

That's how the pursuit of self-interest leads to the "greater bad." Libertarians emphatically disagree. They claim that the real lesson of the parable is the need for private property. The commons aren't all that different from the Chinese communes. Even the names are similar: commons and commune. The solution is to divide the commons into privately-owned lots. No farmer is going to graze 100 cattle on a lot that is only large enough for 50. Lester Thurow explains.

> Capitalism requires profits, and profits require ownership. Property ownership generates responsibility. A decade ago I wrote an article about communism entitled, "Who Stays Up with the Sick Cow?" Without ownership the answer was too often "No one," and the cow and communism died.[111]

The problem is that not everything can be divided into privately-owned lots. Most environmental problems—like global warming, poor air quality, endocrine disruptors that lead to early puberty for girls, and overfishing—are cases of the tragedy of the commons. Private property would instantly solve all of our environmental problems. Imagine if we could somehow divide the atmosphere into privately-owned lots. Everyone would live inside a large bubble that contained their own personal air supply. People wouldn't need the government to make them drive a car with low emissions because no one wants to breathe in their own car's exhaust fumes.

Suppose Alicia built a factory on a river and Blake lives downstream. Alicia's factory pollutes the river, which damages Blake's property. Economists call this pollution an *external cost*. Normally all the costs to make a product are included in the price, but that's not the case with pollution. Instead, the costs of pollution are passed on to an unconsenting third party. Suppose a widget costs $100 of materials and labor to make, but it also does $10 worth of damage to Blake's property. Then Blake is forced to spend $10 cleaning up for each and every widget that Alicia sells. The standard solution to external costs is for the government to step in and tax or regulate Alicia's factory. Suppose that Alicia is required to install a filter that removes the pollution, and the cost works out to $5 per widget. Then she sells widgets for $105 but now all the costs are *internalized* in the price of the widget.

Let's see how that happens with a solved environmental problem: the hole in the ozone layer. Ozone is a molecule that filters the harshest effects of sunlight. A thinner ozone layer would result in high rates of skin cancer and cataracts that cause blindness. In the 1970s, scientists noticed that the ozone layer in the atmosphere was thinning and even had a large hole over the Antarctic. The problem was traced to the use of chlorofluorocarbons (CFCs) in spray cans. In 1987 twenty-four nations signed the Montreal Protocol to limit the use of CFCs, and today the hole is the smallest it has been in decades and still shrinking.

Public Goods

Public goods are a type of good that can only be built by the government. Rockets are not a public good, but for some reason, the government builds rockets anyways. We can take advantage of that to give us a head-to-head comparison of the efficiency of free markets versus the government. The SpaceX Falcon Heavy rocket costs about $1500 per kilogram to launch a payload into space.[112] By contrast, NASA's SLS rocket costs about $43,000 per kilogram to launch a payload into space.[113] That means SpaceX is about thirty times more affordable. Liberals can "yes, but" this in various ways, but all this "yes, butting" accomplishes is to highlight how rigid and inflexible governments are compared to firms. The lesson is that we should never have the government build something that can be built by free markets.

Public goods cannot be built by free markets. The military is the classic example. We can have private firms build tanks and planes on a cost-plus basis, but they can't actually provide the service of national defense. Suppose a private company called DefendTech sold the service of national defense. Alicia signs up for it, but her neighbor Blake

THE FREE RIDER PROBLEM

does not. Then Canada invades the United States, as Canada is prone to doing.[114] So DefendTech unleashes a bunch of tanks, fighter jets, and infantry to drive the warmongering Canadians away. The problem is that Blake is equally safe even though he didn't pay for national defense. Economists would say that national defense is *non-excludable*—there is no way to stop people who didn't buy it from benefiting from the service.

This leads to what economists call the *free rider problem*. If you think it through, it's the exact same dynamic as we've already seen with the tragedy of the commons. People can either pay for national defense (cooperate) or save their money (defect). If everyone else cooperates, then you can defect and free ride on the national defense everyone else paid for. But if everyone else defects, then you'd be a sucker to be the only one cooperating. Your piddly $5,000, which is what the average taxpayer spent on national defense in 2022, isn't going to buy many tanks and fighter jets. The free rider problem has a single Nash equilibrium, which is to defect. Once again, the standard solution to the free rider problem is the government. The government taxes everyone and uses the money to pay for national defense.

Roads and railroads are another example of public goods. Suppose Alicia planned to build a railroad from San Francisco to Los Angeles. So she starts buying up land along her proposed route. Unfortunately, Blake's house lies along this route, and he refuses to sell unless she pays him ten million dollars. Even in California, houses in the remote desert are not worth ten million dollars. I think. And there are a lot more holdouts like Blake along her route. The cost of meeting their exorbitant demands would sink her project.

In theory *options* could help. She could buy options on land, which means she pays a small fraction of the property's value for the right to buy the property later at a predetermined price. Options give her more flexibility to connect the dots and find a viable route. But options only reduce the holdout problem, they do not eliminate it.

The solution to building railroads is the government. It has the power of *eminent domain*. That means the government can force Blake to sell his home at a fair market-value price. In theory eminent domain should only be used for genuine public goods like railroads. But the notorious *Kelo v. New London* set a legal precedent that local governments can use eminent domain even for private developers. At the time of the Kelo decision, there was a liberal majority on the Supreme Court, and the vote was 5-4 along party lines. Perhaps Kelo can be overturned now that the Supreme Court has a conservative majority.

The Reality of Property Rights

Over a century ago, the United States built about 200,000 miles of railroads using hand tools. Today we can't even build a single 700-mile railroad segment with modern construction equipment like bulldozers and ballast tampers. In 2008, the state of California set out to build a light rail system to connect San Francisco to Los Angeles for what seemed like an astronomical $33 billion. Fifteen years later and the price tag has ballooned to $113 billion, yet construction has only recently begun on a short "starter" segment.[115] Even with the benefit of eminent domain, the project has been bogged down in problems over land use and environmental regulations. If the state of California, with the benefit of eminent domain, can't build anything, then a private developer has almost no hope at all.

So how did we get here and what is the solution? Ezra Klein, who founded the magazine Vox, writes about this problem in The New York Times. His core insight is that there are too many people with veto power over projects, and making them all happy is both slow and expensive.

THE FREE RIDER PROBLEM

When you construct a new building or subway tunnel or highway, you have to navigate neighbors and communities and existing roads and emergency access vehicles and politicians and beloved views of the park and the possibility of earthquakes and on and on. ...

I ran this argument by Zarenski [a construction industry insider]. As I finished, he told me that I couldn't see it over the phone, but he was nodding his head up and down enthusiastically. "There are so many people who want to have some say over a project," he said. "You have to meet so many parking spaces, per unit. It needs to be this far back from the sight lines. You have to use this much reclaimed water. You didn't have 30 people sitting in an hearing room for the approval of a permit 40 years ago."[116]

One of the main reasons why there are so many people with veto power over projects is because of our increased understanding of external costs. The original understanding was "it's my land and I can do what I want with it." But economists realized that you don't have the right to spew pollution onto your neighbor's property, or the right to open up a nightclub that plays loud music until 2:00 a.m. in a residential neighborhood. Over time property rights have been weakened to recognize that there are more and more people who may have external costs from pollution imposed on them.

The economist Thomas Sowell has a famous slogan in conservative circles: "There are no solutions, there are only trade-offs."[117] We shouldn't allow people to build nightclubs in residential neighborhoods, but at some point we have to swing the pendulum back towards stronger property rights and weaker environmental protections. That's true even if you are a staunch environmentalist.

The Cape Wind Project was a proposed offshore wind farm near the island of Nantucket. The island's wealthy residents thought it would ruin their beautiful views, although they were savvy enough to couch their opposition in environmental terms like saving the whales and protecting birds from the propellers. So they fought a sixteen-year battle against the project and ultimately won.[118] The US Government fast-tracked the SunZia wind farm, and it still took seventeen years to get a permit.[119] And of course the light rail in California was not intended primarily to speed travel, but to protect the environment. One of the main outcomes of the environmental movement has been to make global warming even worse. The law of unintended consequences strikes again.

Here's how to think about stronger property rights in environmental terms. Suppose a proposed renewable energy plant would impose $1 million of external costs on immediate neighbors. That's because of concerns like roads, sight lines, and water usage. However, the plant will prevent $1 billion of external costs by reducing global warming. We've got such weak property rights that the immediate neighbors have a veto, and the planet ends out worse off. If the goal is to protect the environment, property rights have to be stronger, not weaker.

Private Information

The market for lemons is the next parable in our tour of economics. George Akerlof won the 2001 Nobel Prize in economics by thinking about the market for used cars. It is a humble topic, but one with vast and far-reaching implications. We will see it throughout the rest of the book so you may want to give this section extra attention. For the sake of simplicity, let's divide used cars into two categories: peaches and lemons. Peaches are good cars that run well, and lemons are bad cars that have a lot of problems. Let's say peaches are worth $24,000 and lemons are worth $16,000. The problem is that only the car's owner knows whether or not the car is a peach or lemon. Very few people know how to change a car's oil, let alone perform a detailed inspection. In other words, the owner has *private information* that the buyer lacks.

The consequence is that used car buyers have to guess whether the car is a peach or a lemon. If half the cars are peaches, and the other half are lemons, then consumers would be willing to pay $20,000 for a used car. If it is a peach, they come out ahead, and if it is a lemon, they come out behind, but overall it's a fair bet. The problem is that someone who owns a peach would not want to sell a car that is worth $24,000 for a mere $20,000. So his best option is to hang onto his car. This would drive peaches out of the market. Free markets fail when it comes to selling peaches—high quality used cars.

Ranchers can also be divided into peaches and lemons. Peaches follow their quotas, and lemons break them. Employees at firms can also be divided into peaches and lemons. Peaches are team players who are honest and work hard. Lemons are free riders who shirk on the job and perhaps even steal from their employer. I'll bet you know a lemon or two at your own office.

Even the Mafia has the problem of sorting out peaches from lemons. In their case, the peaches are gang members who will go to jail rather than "snitch" against their fellow criminals. Part of the reason why organized crime is based on family ties is because people are less likely to "rat out" their own family. Even spouses can be divided into peaches and lemons. It is an unhappy fact of life that many people thought they were marrying a peach but found out they were stuck with a lemon. The problem of private information runs very deep and dominates most of this book.

False Market Failures

Ironically, one place where private information isn't much of a problem is, well, the market for used cars. Dealers have the technical ability to assess quality, and they can offer warranties on certified used cars. Consumers can buy cars from their friends and use third party services such as CarFax and Auto Critic. The market for used cars is actually pretty efficient.

This is a good lesson for liberals who tend to be skeptical of free markets. One of the signature examples of a market failure isn't actually a market failure. We saw the same thing earlier, where for decades, QWERTY keyboards and VHS tapes were wrongly held up as market failures. The Nobel laureate and famous liberal Paul Krugman has an entire chapter in his book *Peddling Prosperity* called "The Economics of QWERTY," where he wrongly championed network monopolies and lock-in as market failures.[120] I'm not blaming Krugman for getting economic principles wrong. Everyone who enters the public square gets things wrong sooner or later, and Krugman's been in the public square longer than just about anyone.

My point is that even Nobel prize winners can underestimate the flexibility of bottom-up processes. It's easy to think that free markets must follow the path of least resistance, like a ball rolling downhill, and must therefore get stuck in ditches and holes before it reaches the bottom. But just because an economist with no skin in the game couldn't think of a solution, that doesn't mean that no solution exists. Windfall profits are a powerful incentive for entrepreneurs with skin in the game to think about the problem with more determination and creativity. If you are an economic liberal, then it is good to learn about market failures, but keep in mind that George Stigler was right: "Markets are tough weeds, not delicate flowers."

Signals

The movie *The Sixth Sense* was about a boy who could see ghosts. The catchphrase of the movie was, "I see dead people. They're everywhere. They don't even know they're dead." Economists have their own version of this: "I see people signaling. They're everywhere. They don't even know they're signaling." *Signals* are how people share their private information with others.

Signals are also the first example of the parallels between evolutionary biology and economics. We'll see more of them in this book. In biology, signals are a way that animals share private information about their fitness. Peacocks signal by taking on a *handicap*—a large tail. Female peahens prefer males with large and beautiful tales because they are the fittest. Gazelles signal their fitness to cheetahs by stotting—jumping up in the air. That is a risky thing to do in the middle of a high-speed chase with death on the line, but cheetahs will often stop chasing gazelles who stott.[121] If you played tag as a child, then you've probably learned the same lesson: Don't chase the kid who takes a lot of dumb risks, because he's the neighborhood fast kid.

Good signals have two important traits: They are costly and easy to broadcast. A peacock's tail does both. It's harder to survive dragging around such an enormous tail, and yet when unfurled they are beautiful and impossible to miss. By contrast, most of what we call, "virtue signals" are quite cheap. Changing a Facebook background to a pride flag is not costly except for people who live in a conservative subculture. Most so-called virtue signals serve as loyalty oaths rather than as genuine signals.

Advertising is a great example of a signal that meets both requirements. A firm that makes widgets is in the exact same position as the person selling a used car. Consumers don't know whether a widget is a peach or a lemon until after they buy it. By contrast, the firm that makes the widget has a pretty good idea of its true quality. The engineers who designed the widgets should know it intimately, and the marketing department would do research and focus group testing to see how consumers feel. So how do firms that think their new product is a peach share this private information? With advertising.

Critics object to advertising because it is uninformative and manipulative. They claim that advertising is not a case of the invisible hand informing consumers, but a market failure in which firms manipulate consumers into buying stuff that they don't need. The critics are correct when they say that most advertising is uninformative, but signaling explains why. Even firms whose widgets are lemons can create a commercial that says, "Our widgets are the best! They clean the toughest spills and make the tastiest coffee!" Only a foolish consumer would actually believe the information in an advertisement. Talk is cheap.

What matters is not the content of the advertising, but how much money the firm spends. Talk is cheap, but money talks. It doesn't make sense to spend millions of dollars advertising a lemon. Consumers will buy the product once but never again. They will tell their friends not to buy the product and go on angry rants on social media about how terrible it is. Firms should only spend money advertising a product that they expect to be a success. In other words, the actual content of an advertisement is irrelevant. The only thing that really matters is to increase the broadcast efficiency of the signal—to get as many people to notice the signal as possible. Firms are better off making a commercial that is funny, creative, or sexy. That way more people will pay attention.

Signals also have a downside: They are so important that people sometimes care more about the signal itself than whatever real world thing they are signaling. In other words, perception is more important

THE FREE RIDER PROBLEM

than reality. A good example of this is Hitler's winter blunder. He invaded the Soviet Union in June and expected a quick and decisive victory just like he had in France. Instead, Germany made slow progress, and by autumn it became clear that they would not be able to conquer Moscow until winter at the earliest. And yet Hitler did not order winter clothing for his soldiers, so many of them either got frostbite or froze to death. It wasn't until late December that Germany sent winter gear to the front.

Why did Hitler make this mistake? Because ordering winter clothing acted as a signal that broadcasted private information, namely that the war with Russia was going badly and would take a long time. Hitler would rather let German soldiers die than reveal this private information. His propaganda couldn't say that victory would happen soon if he was settling in for a long campaign. The private information would hurt morale and weaken his political support. I hate to say anything nice about the second most abhorrent government that ever existed, but the Soviet Union took advantage of Hitler's mistake and would go on to do the lion's share of defeating the Nazis.

Firms play the same game. They find ways to provide signals that the firm is strong even though they have private information that it is weak. They do this with techniques that fall under the category of *earnings management* like income smoothing, deferring expenses, and cutting research and development to meet quarterly profit targets. If you've ever worked for a firm that has refused to pull the plug on what everyone knows is a failing project, it's not because management is incompetent, but because they don't want to write down bad assets. They can either say that their billion-dollar investment will start earning 10 percent returns next quarter, or they can write it down as a billion dollar loss. A CEO's stock options only have value if the firm's stock price goes up, so this is an easy call to make. Audits and accounting standards are supposed to prevent this, but there is a lot of money to be made in the gray areas of life. Sometimes signals do more harm than good.

Other times signals succeed in conveying private information—and then fail because of it. Think about how showy displays of wealth don't impress people from "old money" backgrounds. Yes, they signaled wealth, but they also signaled self-importance and bad taste. Or consider how an artistic woman with a unique style won't be impressed by a woman in the latest European fashions. Yes, she signaled the social acumen to navigate the ephemeral world of high fashion, but she also signaled a lack of genuine creativity. And although we haven't reached that part of the book yet, consider how my repeated use of Jane Austen won't impress someone with a deep knowledge of literature. Yes, it signals a certain middlebrow sophistication, but it also signals the lack of curiosity and fortitude to read more challenging books.

My favorite example of this phenomenon comes from Samuel Johnson's *Lives of the Poets*, which I learned about from the historian Robert Bucholz.[122] In the late seventeenth century, the poet and diplomat Matthew Prior was given a tour of the magnificent palace of Versailles in France. It was built by King Louis XIV, the "Sun King." Historically, most European kings could only raise taxes by negotiating with a body like the Estates-General or Parliament. But Louis XIV was an absolute monarch who had the power to tax. He used that power to bleed his peasants dry and then built Versailles as a way to show off his enormous wealth. If you read about Versailles today, it is often described as a monument to French decadence. That's true, but that was not the real reason why Louis built such a luxurious and opulent palace.

He built it to be a threat. Versailles was a signal of France's wealth. Versailles broadcasted the private information that Louis XIV could raise more money than his enemies. Even in the early modern period of history, wars were won by money, not by guns. Visiting dignitaries would be given a tour, and then they would report home that war with France would be suicide. But Prior was not impressed. After the tour he was asked, probably with a tone of smug superiority, what he thought about the palace. Prior said, "The monuments of my master's actions, are to be seen every where but in his own house."[123] In other words, the French spent their money on a palace; the British spent their money on a navy. Prior was right. Shortly after his visit, the French and the British fought the War of the Spanish Succession, and Louis XIV was forced to make major concessions to the British.

The reason why the signal failed is that Prior's tour happened at a turning point in history. Louis XIV had taken absolute monarchy as far as it could go. Kings can only raise so much money by sucking the blood out of impoverished peasant farmers. If they really want to raise a lot of money, they need a tax base that includes trade and commerce. Britain did not have an absolute monarchy, so they didn't have the same crushing tax burden as the French. But that didn't matter. Britain was beginning to reap the benefits of having a relatively free and educated population, and the dynamic economy that comes with it.

The question of how Britain, and the West in general, became free and industrialized will dominate the rest of this book. We won't be able to answer it until we get to the chapter on the greatest free rider problem of them all: the Hobbesian problem. But if you want a glimpse, pay attention to the next chapter on firms, because firms also suffer a type of Hobbesian problem.

Jack Welch and the Fall of Boeing

> The most valuable of all capital is that invested in human beings.
>
> – Alfred Marshall, *Principles of Economics*

There is a paradox at the heart of capitalism. Firms like Microsoft and SpaceX are just like the Chinese communes. Each individual firm is a Soviet-style command economy with a central planner (CEO) at the top and a hierarchy of bureaucrats beneath him, all the way down to ordinary front-line workers at the bottom. Employees in firms aren't responding to incentives—they're given orders and told what to do. That's exactly what the Chinese communes were like. Workers in the communes got an equal share of the harvest whether they worked hard or shirked on the job. And employees in capitalist firms make the same salary regardless of whether they work hard or shirk. People respond to incentives, so economic theory predicts that workers in both communes and firms will shirk.

If you think it through, this is yet another example of the free rider problem. The firm will succeed if everyone works hard, but no matter what everyone else does, each individual worker has an incentive to shirk. Work effort in firms has a single Nash equilibrium of always shirk.

That's the paradox. Why do Microsoft and SpaceX succeed while the Chinese communes failed? Perhaps that's what managers are for—to motivate workers and fire the ones who shirk. But the Chinese communes had managers too. If Microsoft caught a worker repeatedly shirking, they'd be fired. If the communists caught a worker repeatedly shirking, they'd be imprisoned or killed. That's a powerful incentive not to shirk. Why do managers work for Microsoft but not for communes? Why did capitalism solve the free rider problem but not communism? Once again, the answer is social norms, not incentives.

Change the Incentives

The obvious solution to the free rider problem is to give workers better incentives. Instead of giving workers the same salary regardless of whether they work hard or shirk, find a way to incentivize effort. Taxi drivers are the textbook example. Think about the nature of the taxi business. It is impossible for the boss to monitor his drivers when they are spread throughout the city. If taxi drivers were paid by the hour, they'd find a remote location and sleep on the job. So how does the boss make sure his drivers work hard? By changing the incentives.

Taxi companies do this by renting taxis to drivers. The driver pays $150 or so to rent a taxi for one day, but he gets to keep all the money he makes. That gives him an incentive to work hard. If he sleeps on the job, then he won't get any customers and won't even be able to cover his rental fee. If he works hard and gets a lot of customers, then he will be able to pay back the rental fee and make money for himself. The outcome is that taxi drivers work very hard.

Taxis are an elegant solution to the problem of motivating workers. Unfortunately, taxis are the exception. In most cases, changing the incentives will not help very much. Different incentives can even be harmful. Canice Prendergast reviewed the research in his article *The Provision of Incentives in Firms*.[124]

The first problem is the *ratchet effect*. Suppose that a firm does come up with a way to reward hard work. The problem is that employees fear that if they work hard, the firm will respond by cutting their pay. This happened to my mother-in-law. She used to sell X-Ray machines for a major medical supply company. She earned a commission of $1500 for each machine she sold (and this was twenty years ago). She is a charming and tech-savvy person, so she excelled at her job. She did the little things like visit the doctors periodically after the sale was complete. She wanted to make sure that they were still happy and hadn't run into problems. Doctors have informal social networks, and her reputation grew by word of mouth. Her informal quota was to sell twelve X-ray machines each year, but soon she was selling thirty, forty, and even sixty per year. In response, her commission was cut. Over time she saw her commission cut to $1100 per machine and then down to $800 per machine. Then her commission dropped to $800 *per hospital*. It didn't matter if the hospital bought one X-ray machine or ten, she would only get $800. That is the ratchet effect at work.

Employees are not dumb. They do not always trust management, and they anticipate the ratchet effect. That's why employees typically guard against it by establishing workplace norms of low effort. A good example of that is from the movie *Big*, starring Tom Hanks. In the movie, Tom Hanks' character is a boy named Josh who wished to be a grownup. When his wish was granted, he got an entry level job working in computers. After a few minutes on the job, a fellow worker named Scott leaned over to chastise him:

SCOTT: "Listen, what are you trying to do? Get us all fired?"
JOSH: "Huh?"
SCOTT: "You've gotta slow down. Pace yourself. Slowly! Slowly!"
JOSH: "Sorry. Today's my first day."
SCOTT: "I know!"[125]

The employees set a norm of a low work output, so it's important to initiate the new employees into the norm. Otherwise, the new employee will make the others look bad by doing a lot more work, and the gig will be over for everyone. Once these norms are in place, people who work too hard are informally punished by their peers with scorn and ostracism.

Solving the ratchet effect takes trust between workers and management. The Lincoln Electric Company was able to use a piece rate payment system for their workers for over a hundred years, because they developed a reputation for never lowering the piece rate, and never laying off workers.[126] The workers could safely work hard without fear that their efforts would be punished. The workers and the firm both made more money, but it only happened because of mutual trust. Let me say that again because it is a radical concept in this era of treating workers like commodities: It only happened because of mutual trust between workers and management.

The other problem with relying on incentives is called *multitasking*. And no, I don't mean browsing social media while watching TV. Prendergast explains multitasking with the story of Ken O'Brien, a football quarterback in the early 1980s. He had a problem with throwing too many interceptions, so his team gave him a new contract that penalized him for each interception he threw. It worked—he threw fewer interceptions. The problem was that he stopped throwing the ball as often. He would just hold onto the ball for fear of making an interception. The football great Joe Namath, who knows more about motivating people than most management consultants, said, "I see him hold onto the ball more than he should . . . I don't like incentive contracts that pertain to numbers."[127]

That's multitasking. If workers have contracts with incentives built in, then they will usually do better at whatever the incentives measure. But they will shift their effort away from other areas, which can easily make the overall performance worse. In New York, surgeons are penalized if their mortality rates are too high. Andrew Leventis finds that surgeons stop taking on high-risk patients if they get too close to the threshold.[128] Once again, surgeons do better at what is being measured (mortality rates) at the expense of the overall level of care. The sickest patients who need the best surgeons are the ones who suffer. Robert Drago and Gerald Garvey use Australian survey data to show that pay-for-performance incentive schemes result in employees helping their co-workers less often.[129] Workers do better in what is being measured (their own performance) at the expense of things that are not measured (the overall team performance).

The obvious answer is to create a multidimensional rubric to measure quality. And this idea takes us to the only part in this entire book where I draw from my own knowledge. My day job is as a computer programmer, but the software I write is quality assurance software. Our clients include many Fortune 500 companies, and I am a member of the services group that has a client-facing focus. I've been in countless design meetings working with clients to refine their rubrics, and then implemented their designs. Of course, even in this area I'm just the tech guy, not the quality assurance expert, but at this point in my career I've learned how to fake it well enough.

What our most sophisticated clients know, and this is reflected in our best practices, is that these rubrics are great for finding patterns of problems that need to be fixed. But they are terrible at rating the performance of individual employees. There are two reasons for this. The first is that you have to make subjective judgment calls whenever you want to turn two or more numbers into one number.

Think about a rubric for rating sports cars. You start with one rating for acceleration and another rating for handling, but how do you turn these two numbers into a single number? You could just average them together, but what if one car enthusiast wanted a classic American muscle car that accelerates really quickly, and another wanted a smooth, graceful European roadster? The average would be completely useless for both customers. In his article *The Order of Things*, Malcolm Gladwell showed that by changing how different factors that go into Car and Driver's ratings are weighted, he could make other cars, like the Lotus Elise or the Chevrolet Corvette, have the highest rating instead of the Porsche Cayman that they picked.[130]

Skeptical readers might be thinking that there should be a method to objectively compare the different factors that go into picking the best car. Sometimes there is. I'm sure that Formula 1 teams have a very good idea how to weight acceleration, handling, braking, and aerodynamics when designing cars. But they have several advantages. They have an objective standard for success: the fastest car around the track wins. They also have computer-enabled cars that generate enormous amounts of hard data about performance. And finally, they have huge budgets that allow them to hire armies of engineers to crunch these numbers. Most fields are not so lucky when it comes to creating metrics. Take Malcolm Gladwell for example. Which book is his best? How could you possibly create an objective metric to rate this?

Another problem is that rating people invariably requires creating a threshold: A score of 90 percent or higher results in a good rating, and below that the employee gets a bad rating. But that means that one or two ticky-tacky questions can put an employee beneath the threshold for a good rating. Sometimes the lower scoring result is actually better work. If you're an NFL fan, may have seen this. A running back may get a bonus if he runs for 1200 yards, but he happens to come up just a few yards short. However, he had a monster season with great receiving yards and improved blocking. Most NFL teams are smart enough to just give the player his bonus. Otherwise, they'll end up with a disgruntled player, and rightly so.

Employees know perfectly well that these rubrics do not capture the true complexity of their jobs. Could your job be captured with a rubric of twenty or thirty questions? They are justifiably resentful when they get low scores despite doing good work. These ratings undermine worker morale and create hostility between workers and management. Most firms that embark on using these high stakes rubrics are wise enough to back off after a few years. All this goes back to my initial point: Multidimensional rubrics are best used to identify broad patterns, and not rate employees. Employees do benefit from regular and high-quality feedback, but that feedback should be "no stakes" evaluations built around coaching and improvement.

Lean Manufacturing

The belief that worker quality could be accurately measured was almost enough to ruin the American auto industry. For a long time, the prevailing philosophy for how to run a factory was based on the ideas of Fredrick Winslow Taylor. He was an engineer who created the management philosophy of *Taylorism*. He felt that each worker on an assembly line should have a simple well-defined task that he did repeatedly. This would maximize efficiency and let worker performance be accurately measured.

Here's how it works in the auto industry. A job might be "rivet door panel A to door panel B." This is a simple well-defined job that makes it easy to measure worker performance. The problem with Taylorism is that firms need an extensive supply of spare parts to make it work. Suppose that door panel A was not shaped quite right, perhaps because of a mistake by an upstream worker on the assembly line. Then the riveter wouldn't be able to make it fit door panel B. The solution is to keep a supply of extra door panels so he could swap in one of those instead.

In other cases, the shape of door panel A might be a little off, but not too bad. So he'd rivet it to door panel B and send it down the line. These small errors would snowball as the car worked its way down the assembly line. The rest of the pieces of the door wouldn't fit very well, and the door wouldn't open and close properly. Assembly lines based on Taylorism have poor quality and need to do a lot of refitting work. That means paying mechanics to fix brand-new cars that have never been driven.

If you are old enough to remember the 1980s, then you're familiar with the constant anxiety about the success of Japanese firms. They were steadily chipping away at American successes in both heavy manufacturing and electronics. Firms like Toyota and Sony were the Apple and Microsoft of the 1980s. It took another engineer turned management consultant to explain the problem. James Womack spent five years studying Toyota, and he changed manufacturing forever when he released *The Machine That Changed the World: The Story of Lean Production* in 1990. In this book he explained the major principles of *lean manufacturing*, or *just in time manufacturing*, which was how Toyota was able to produce such high-quality cars.

The main idea of lean manufacturing is to create small batches on demand using flexible teams. Japan developed the technique during and after the World War II years, and they were too poor to have the luxury of extensive reserves of spare parts. With lean manufacturing, the employees work in teams with flexible job descriptions. If door panel A wasn't shaped quite right, one worker would fix it on the spot. Another worker would jump in and take over the riveting as the next part came down the assembly line. Workers had to be more skilled to fix defects and fill in multiple roles on assembly lines. It also turned out to be more efficient because they didn't need the extensive reserves of spare parts, and it prevented quality issues from snowballing. However, lean manufacturing also made it a lot more difficult to objectively evaluate employees. When workers fluidly switch between tasks, then it becomes impossible to objectively measure one worker's output.

Managers

If objective measures of worker quality aren't realistic, then what about relying on managers? Managers do develop subjective opinions about the quality of their workers, and those opinions are usually pretty accurate. Managers are a step in the right direction, which is why every organization in human history has had them, but managers are not a magic bullet.

The first problem is that managers have a conflict of interest. They may exchange good reviews for loyalty. A study of Navy supervisors showed that they distorted performance reviews in order to help their favorite subordinates move up the ladder.[131] This allows supervisors to develop a small army of loyal subordinates that he has groomed and developed.

An example of this from pop culture is in the movie *The Devil Wears Prada*. The character Miranda Priestly was Editor-in-Chief of a fashion magazine that was expensive to produce. Her boss wanted to bring in a new editor who was younger and cheaper in order to cut costs. However, Miranda could not be fired because she had "the list" of models, designers, editors, and photographers whose careers she had advanced and who were personally loyal to her, not the magazine. That led to her winning a crucial power struggle at the end of the movie.[132]

The second incentive problem is that managers want to look good to their own bosses. Unpopular managers risk having their employees stir up trouble in a variety of ways. Disgruntled employees may go to the next layer of management behind their boss's back, or make excuses to file complaints with HR, or stir up trouble with colleagues to undermine workplace morale. Managers don't want to get a reputation as an ineffective and unpopular manager, so they have an incentive to keep their own employees happy.

Managers do this in two ways. The first is to give everyone good reviews. This is called *leniency bias*. A related phenomenon is that managers tend to compress everyone's ratings. The good workers are evaluated as being only slightly better than average, and the bad workers are evaluated as being only slightly below average. This is called *centrality bias*. These biases happen because giving poor performance reviews puts managers into a delicate situation.

A study by David Card and colleagues confirms these difficulties. They found that employees are very unhappy when they get below average reviews and pay.[133] (Apparently, we had to do a study to prove this.) These disgruntled employees become much more likely to stir up trouble or look for another job. By contrast, employees with above average reviews aren't really any happier. If a firm bases pay and bonuses on performance reviews, high turnover, low morale, and rebellious employees will be a problem.

Small Businesses

Managers are a good solution for small businesses where the owner is the manager. The dual role of owner and manager eliminates the conflict of interests. The healthier the workplace culture, the more money the owner makes. So the owner has a strong incentive to keep workers happy without ignoring genuine problems. But even this approach has issues.

One of the TV shows that my wife got me into was *Tabatha's Salon Takeover*. It is about an expert salon owner with an outsized personality who helps turn around struggling small salons. I like it better than *Gordon Ramsey's Kitchen Nightmares* because restaurants live or die by their food. Good food can cover a lot of management sins, so reforming a failing restaurant largely means improving the food. I'm more interested in improving the workplace culture.

You see the same patterns of failure over and over again. One common pattern is the absentee owner. Many people start a small business, not because they want to be their own boss, but because they don't want to work at all. Their thought process is that they'll start a business, hire a manager, and then they'll spend all day watching TV and live on the profits. The problem is that the manager does not have an incentive to do a good job. It's not her money; she gets a paycheck whether she does a good job or a bad job. On the rare occasions that the owner is around, the manager and her team all put on a good show. Then they promptly slack off when the owner leaves.

Another common pattern is owners with poor social skills. There is a human side to building a successful business. Managers that are too tough alienate their employees and lower workplace morale, which results in high turnover and poor work effort. But managers who are too soft get walked all over. They can't enforce discipline and run a tight ship. Good managers have to strike a balance of professionalism while genuinely caring about the welfare of their workers. Workers can spot a phony. The upshot is that many firms have an unhealthy workplace culture. Trust is easy to lose and hard to regain.

Despite these pitfalls, having an owner as a manager usually works reasonably well for small businesses. The owner is the primary manager and has an incentive to be present and to set a good tone. The problem is that it does not scale to large firms. Sometimes family can help. Two or three siblings may go into business together, and they can each be managers. This method also explains why incompetent relatives are often put into positions of authority in low-trust societies. It makes more sense to have an incompetent relative you can trust in a position of power than a competent stranger you can't. But family is a stop-gap solution. Even the biggest families will run out of relatives as their firm grows. Moreover, the "incompetent but trustworthy nephew" theory of management is not going to build firms that can go toe-to-toe with Microsoft or SpaceX.

Who Will Monitor the Monitors?

Large firms need managers who are not owners, and that creates the same problem we saw in *Tabatha's Salon Takeover* with the absentee owner. What's to stop the manager from shirking on the job? The manager gets paid the same salary regardless of whether she works hard or shirks on the job. So the managers themselves need managers. Large corporations try to solve this problem by having a hierarchy of managers with CEOs at the top. The CEO and senior managers get stock options, which make them like owners. But this has problems.

Here is a good way to think about firms. There is a line in the sand between making money and losing money. Free market competition will weed out any firm that consistently loses money, so when a firm starts sinking into unprofitability, the alarm bells go off. New leadership is brought in. Divisions are reorganized. Money-losing departments are spun off. Senior management's pet projects are finally cancelled. That's another virtue of failure—the mere threat of failing keeps firms honest.

Unfortunately, there is no line in the sand between being a healthy firm that makes a 20 percent profit and a somewhat inefficient firm that makes a 4 percent profit. There is a lot of "slack" between a 20 percent profit and a 4 percent profit. And there are three special interest groups fighting for this slack: shareholders, senior management, and regular workers.

The special interest group of "CEOs and senior management" want the firm to make high profits—but then they want to use their power to capture some of these profits in the form of stock options and bonuses. The best way to do that is to skew the firm towards short-term performance. Economists call this *short-termism*. There are many sneaky ways to do this that fall under the category of *earnings management*. The textbook example is cutting spending on research and development. Cutting expenses boosts profits in the short term, but in the long run the firm's competitiveness will suffer as their pipeline of innovative new products dries up. However, stock options usually vest over four years and CEOs and senior managers don't usually stick around longer than five or ten. CEOs make decisions that help the firm in the short term but hurt it in the long run.

The shareholders are another special interest group. They obviously want high profits, but there is a debate about whether shareholders can drive short-termism. Are they pressuring management to produce quick results so they can "flip" their stock? If so, then we should insulate management from the shareholders. Or are they generally focused on the long run? In that case, we should do the opposite and make management more accountable. Research by Lucian Bebchuk shows that shareholders are aligned with the long-term health of the firm.[134] He has also shown that the way CEOs and senior managers are compensated, such as with stock options that vest in four years, creates incentives for short-termism.[135] When it comes to firms, shareholders are the good guys and CEOs are, potentially, the bad guys.

The special interest group of workers are the simplest. In some unionized industries they can use their power to demand some of the firm's profits for themselves. But most of the time workers take in "slack" by setting lower norms of effort. I wouldn't call it outright shirking, but workers want to set norms of lower work effort and take things a bit easier. I learned this first-hand in my own career when I went from working for a large bank to a small startup. The bank was a typical firm with moderate work effort but the people at the startup were passionate and hard-working. It was a culture shock at first, but I eventually came to appreciate what the CEO told me when I was hired: "If you're not at a small company, you're doing it wrong."

Now that the ulterior motives of senior management are clear, let's tackle the "who will monitor the monitors" problem. In theory the CEO must answer to the board of directors and the shareholders. But membership on the board of directors is like joining a cabal. Many board members are CEOs or senior managers who draw from the same management philosophy and culture, so they collectively use their power to set norms of high CEO pay and low standards of accountability. Did the firm do well? Stock options. Did the firm do poorly? Golden parachute. It's a win-win for CEOs. Non-CEO board members may use their membership to trade power and influence with the other board members in mutually beneficial ways. Even in the rare cases where there is a true outsider on the board, their outsider status means that they don't have deep industry knowledge. This means they can be bullied into agreement by better-informed board members, even if those board members are acting in their own self-interest rather than the interest of shareholders.

An even bigger problem is that most board members are lazy. Activist investor Nell Minow noted that "Some big names on the boards . . . barely show up due to other commitments, and when they show, they're not prepared."[136] Sometimes a single activist investor can pull off a hostile takeover. That means that the investor buys enough shares to grant himself voting control over the board. Economists call this the *market for corporate control*.

Unfortunately, the market is rigged against the activist investors. One method is with "poison pills" built into how stocks must be bought that make it expensive for investors to gain a majority stake in the firm. The second line of defense is anti-hostile takeover laws such as the Williams Act of 1968. It includes disclosure requirements that prevent activist investors from covertly buying up stock until they reach voting control.

You might wonder why we have laws designed to protect incompetent CEOs. Of all the creatures in the world that need help, how did incompetent CEOs shoot up to the top of the list above orphans and baby seals? The answer is because activist investors don't just fire senior management when they pull off a hostile takeover. They often have mass layoffs and spin off unprofitable divisions. The activist investor gets rich, and thousands of workers lose their jobs. This is part of the process of creative destruction that we saw back in the chapter on imperfect competition, but it also makes hostile takeovers an easy target for liberals. So who watches the watchers? Most of the time the answer is "no one."

The Legacy of Jack Welch

Firms are another case where we can learn from Akerlof's parable about the market for lemons. The main insight of the parable is that the owner of the car has private information about the car's quality: whether it is a peach or a lemon. Firms are just the same. A good way to think about firms is that they have two bank accounts. The first bank account is *short-term performance*, and the second bank account is *long-term excellence*. The short-term performance bank account is public information. Anyone can look up a firm's stock price, quarterly earnings or calculate metrics like the return on net assets.

Unfortunately, the long-term excellence bank account is private information. That's because it consists of things that are impossible to objectively measure. Some of them are worker quality, worker morale, institutional knowledge, workplace culture and norms of effort, efficiency of business processes, and technical debt. People who work in the core business have a reasonably accurate subjective feel for the status of the long-term excellence bank account, but it can't be measured. Peaches are firms with a healthy long-term excellence bank account.

This creates a problem. It's easy to take money out of the long-term excellence account and boost the short-term performance account. If I were somehow made CEO of a Fortune 500 company, I could do it on my first day on the job. I would cut research and development, eliminate bonuses, layoff staff, replace senior programmers with junior programmers, and outsource IT and other departments to high-turnover shops based overseas. In the short term my firm's costs will go way down and profits will go way up. In four years my stock options will vest and I'll be set for life. But these measures will also drain the firm's long-term excellence bank account and cripple it. It is much harder to go the other way. But if firms are going to be successful, they need managers who invest heavily in the second bank account.

The long-term excellence theory of management was the prevailing school of thought during the boom years after World War II. We think of the era of lifetime employment at a single firm as an uncompetitive relic where firms gave people lifetime jobs like an act of charity. But long-term employment creates long-term accountability. These days employees have an internal clock that tells them how long they have before any failures are blamed on them and not their predecessors. When that clock starts to run out, they move on to a new firm and start it over again. Here is an old joke that's been around for a long time.

> A firm hired a new CEO, and on his first day, he found three sealed and numbered envelopes in the drawer of his desk, along with a note that said: "When you get into trouble, open one of these envelopes."

He closed the drawer and forgot all about them until a particularly bad quarterly earnings report. Then he remembered the envelopes and opened the one labeled #1. In it was a short note that said: "Blame your predecessor." So the CEO held a press conference and blamed his predecessor. The press conference worked, and the firm's stock price recovered.

A year later he had another bad quarter, so he opened envelope #2. The note said, "Announce a reorganization." So he held another press conference and announced a major reorganization. Once again, the press conference worked, and the firm's stock price recovered. Another year passed, and he had yet another bad quarter, so he went to the final envelope. Inside the note read: "Prepare three envelopes."

Modern workers understand the lesson of the joke quite clearly: Find a new job after opening the second envelope.

Two major events ended the long-term excellence theory of management. The first was the rise of libertarian economics spearheaded by Milton Friedman. He wrote a famous article in The New York Times called *The Social Responsibility of Business Is to Increase Its Profits*.[137] Friedman was arguing against the idea that firms should voluntarily cut pollution to help the environment, or lower prices in order to fight inflation. He did not focus on internal stakeholders such as workers, but the takeaway was that firms exist solely to increase profits, and that workers were therefore not stakeholders in a firm's success. The era of workers as interchangeable commodities had begun.

The second change was when Jack Welch became the CEO of General Electric. He launched a management revolution that put Milton Friedman's ideas into practice. GE was founded by Thomas Edison in 1892, and it is single-handedly responsible for most of the major technological advances that took place over the twentieth century. The products that GE invented would require their own book-length treatment, but some of them include the electric lightbulb, the diesel locomotive, the jet engine, and the refrigerator.

Jack Welch changed everything after he was appointed CEO. He began a string of cost cutting, layoffs, and outsourcing. He invented a management practice known as *stack rank*, in which all employees were ranked, and the bottom 10 percent were fired, year after year. Steve Ballmer adopted stack rank for Microsoft, and it almost ruined the company. Today Ballmer is remembered as being one of the worst CEOs in tech history. Marissa Mayer adopted stack rank for Yahoo, and it almost ruined that company too, and she is also known for being one of the worst CEOs in tech history.

Welch seemed to have better luck. He was CEO for twenty years, and GE met its earnings forecasts for all eighty quarters of his tenure. But GE's success was a house of cards that could not last. On Welch's watch, GE did not create any new products like the lightbulb or the jet engine. Instead GE grew by acquisitions. Welch turned GE Capital, which was created to help consumers finance their first refrigerator, into what was essentially an unregulated bank. Then using financial shell games and creative earnings management, GE could meet its quarterly targets. The investors did not know the extent to which GE Capital was involved. Even Jeffrey Immelt, Welch's hand-picked successor, did not know how vulnerable GE Capital had become.[138]

The *efficient markets hypothesis* (EMH) comes in both a strong form and a weak form. The strong form is that the stock market price reflects *all* the information about a firm, both public and private. In other words, both the short-term performance and long-term excellence bank accounts are reflected in a firm's stock price. Economists haven't defended the strong form of the EMH in a long time, probably since Sanford Grossman and Joseph Stiglitz's 1980 paper *On the impossibility of informationally efficient markets*.[139]

The weak form of the EMH is that firms reflect only the publicly available information—the first short-term performance account. The second long-term excellent bank account is largely invisible to investors (in addition to CEOs and senior management). In a world of naïve economic models based on perfect information, any shady dealing is immediately punished with a drop in stock price. In the real world, shady dealing by one CEO wasn't even known by his hand-picked successor.

It turned out that Jack Welch benefitted from extremely good timing, retiring two days before 9/11. As Immelt put it, "My second day as chairman, a plane I lease, flying with engines I built, crashed into a building that I insure, and it was covered by a network I own."[140] The crash revealed the extent of GE Capital's exposure, but the real turning point happened a year later when Enron's accounting fraud came to light. In response the government passed Sarbanes-Oxley, which led to increased oversight of accounting and financial dealings. This would have made Welch's playbook difficult or even impossible to execute. The final blow came with the housing crash in 2008, because GE Capital had bet heavily on subprime mortgages. Eventually the company was split into three pieces. The greatest firm in United States history had essentially ceased to exist. The brand name lives on, but the firm does not.

Yet Welch was lionized in the press and was widely considered the CEO of the century. His management style became the standard way to run a business. The idea that American businesses only look to the next quarter? That came from Welch. The idea that people should not expect to have a long-term career at a company? Also Welch. That workers are disposable commodities? Welch. That certain metrics such as return on net assets have a magical ability to measure the value of a firm? Once again, Welch.

Welch didn't just influence GE; many of his proteges became CEOs of other firms and brought Welch's management practices with them. The outcome was a consistent track record of failure at a wide variety of firms like 3M, Fiat, and Home Depot. One of the few exceptions was Tom Tiller, who left GE to become CEO of a snowmobile company called Polaris. But Tiller explicitly rejected Welch's principles and ran Polaris as a high-trust family business.[141]

The most spectacular failure of a Welch disciple was Harry Stonecipher. He managed to ruin not one, but two, of America's greatest firms: McDonnell Douglas and Boeing. In his book, *Flying Blind*, Peter Robison explains that Boeing was once the world's leader in aviation with a corporate culture that was dominated by its engineers. Boeing's archrival, McDonnell Douglas, hoped that Welch's cost-cutting ways would allow them to overtake their more storied rival. So they brought in Stonecipher, who promptly ran the company to the ground. But Stonecipher was able to arrange a buyout by Boeing that got him a powerful voting block on Boeing's board. As some Boeing employees put it, "McDonnell Douglas bought Boeing with Boeing's money."[142]

Stonecipher's voting block allowed him to ruin Boeing the same way he ruined McDonnell Douglas. He began a number of cost-cutting strategies such as outsourcing design, manufacturing, and computer programming. Programming jobs that were once done in-house by high-quality Boeing engineers were done by contractors from India making as little as nine dollars an hour. They also cut back on test pilot time and pilot training. But the ultimate sign of Boeing's cost-cutting was that they chose to update their aging 737 plane into a new iteration called the 737-MAX. What they should have done was design a new plane to compete with the fuel-efficient Airbus A320. For airlines, the more fuel efficient the plane, the cheaper the tickets. Fuel efficient planes are essential in the cut-throat airline industry.

The 737-MAX was so technologically out of date that it didn't even have an electronic checklist, something that Boeing's engineers pioneered thirty years earlier with planes like the 757 and 767. But the main problem with updating the 737 was that it was designed back when engines were much smaller. Modern engines are much more fuel efficient, but they are also much larger. There was no good spot to put the larger engines on the 737 frame, so they had to mount them relatively high up on the wing. This was a major design compromise that made the plane more prone to stalling.

To fix this potentially fatal flaw, Boeing created special anti-stall software for the plane. Planes are not supposed to need special software in order to be safe to fly. Until recently, computers simply weren't powerful enough to do the necessary calculations in real time. But this was a necessary design compromise to allow the old 737 frame to accommodate the much larger modern engines. The software was designed to level the plane out if there was a danger of going into a stall. However, it was connected to a single sensor with no redundancy. Yes, you read that correctly: no redundancy. Airbus uses triple redundancy, and the space shuttle uses 5x redundancy. Boeing used no redundancy whatsoever. If that single sensor was faulty, it would cause the plane to literally dive straight down into the ground as if on a suicide mission. And sure enough, that's exactly what happened. Twice.

The only way to avoid a fatal crash was for the pilot to follow a complicated troubleshooting procedure. An hour or two in the simulator would have been enough to train the pilots what to do. This is the point in the story where I should mention Boeing's most tragic cost-cutting decision. They outsourced the design of the 737-MAX's simulator to a firm that didn't even have an engineering staff when it was awarded the contract. Not surprisingly, it was late making the delivery. Boeing used their lobbying clout to get the plane approved even though the simulator was not ready.

The result was two crashes of a brand-new plane within the span of five months, which killed 346 people. Because these crashes took place in the developing nations of Indonesia and Ethiopia, Boeing was initially able to blame pilot error before the truth finally came out. The crashes were the most tragic and visible sign of a long process in which Boeing's invisible long-term excellence bank account had been gradually sucked dry into stock dividends and bonuses for management. Internal emails and group chat transcripts of Boeing employees showed that the engineers were designing a plane that they would never let their own families fly on. One employee colorfully said, "This airplane is designed by clowns who in turn are supervised by monkeys."[143]

The final irony is that outsourcing does not even save money, even in the short-term performance bank account. In an internal document called *Outsourced Profits*, a Boeing employee named John Hart-Smith explained how outsourcing impoverished Boeing, while enriching its third-party vendors. The paper covers many ways this happens, so we'll only look at the most important.

When firms outsource a part, they have to give their vendor a specification that the part must meet. This gives suppliers enormous leverage if a part needs to be redesigned. They have a signed legal contract on their side. The vendor can say "Hey, you gave us a specification the part had to meet, and we met it. If you want to go to court on this, that's fine with us. We'll drag it out for years while Airbus keeps selling more and more A320s. And ultimately, we're going to win because we upheld our end of the deal to the letter."

Firms like Boeing are aware of this problem, but the only way to avoid it is to spend a lot of time over-engineering the design of every single part that they outsource, which is slow and expensive. And even that process isn't foolproof. It's inevitable that some parts are still going to need a redesign. The reality is that designing a part is an iterative trial-and-error process. Firms can't just create a specification and expect it all to work without any real-world feedback. Even if the part seems perfect in isolation, it may run into problems when they start assembling and testing actual airplanes, which is exactly what happened to Boeing.

In the end, Boeing was forced to buy up the suppliers that they had outsourced work to at the staggering cost of $50 billion—all so that they could finally tell them to make a tiny change without having to go to court.[144] Boeing originally decided against building a new cutting-edge plane that could have leapfrogged past the Airbus A320 because they didn't want to spend the $20 billion it would have cost. Instead, they spent $50 billion on a plane that was worse than the A320. Bad firms treat everything like a number and operate in the world of formal contracts. Good firms foster trust between senior management and rank-and-file employees and operate informally. What is the value of trust? In the case of Boeing, about $50 billion.

The Jack Welch school of management was based on the libertarian philosophy that everything that happens in a firm can be reduced to a number. Or as economists would put it, that employees are governed by complete and costlessly enforced contracts. But that view is simply wrong, and it took another libertarian economist, Ronald Coase, to figure out why. Coase wondered why firms even exist. Instead of having 20,000 employees, why don't firms have literally zero employees, with every single task outsourced to a subcontractor?

Coase's answer is that the costs of creating formal well-defined contracts to get work done are greater than the costs of simply hiring someone to do the work in the first place. If you have ever been tempted to interrupt a meeting and say, "For crying out loud, in the time we've been talking about this, I could have just done it myself," then you have an idea of how that dynamic works. That's exactly the problem Boeing ran into when they outsourced their parts.

Welch and his proteges thought of themselves as alpha males who made the tough decisions that weaker CEOs were unable to make. But their real legacy is that they were fearful and timid leaders. Leaders can't dare greatly when their only guiding principle is the fear of a short-term setback. I'll take creators like Steve Jobs, Elon Musk, and Satya Nadella over Jack Welch and his cronies every time.

Social Status

> If only there were evil people somewhere insidiously committing evil deeds, and it were necessary only to separate them from the rest of us and destroy them. But the line dividing good and evil cuts through the heart of every human being. And who is willing to destroy a piece of his own heart?
>
> – Aleksandr Solzhenitsyn, *The Gulag Archipelago*

Two hikers were walking through the woods when they came across a grizzly bear. They immediately began to run away, and the bear chased after them. The first hiker said, "Why are we running? We can't outrun a bear!" The second hiker said, "I don't have to outrun the bear. I only have to outrun you!" Economists would say that the two hikers were in an *arms race*. The funny thing about arms races is that it doesn't matter how many armaments someone has. All that matters is that he has more than the other guy.

Let's suppose that two hypothetical nations were mortal enemies. Let's call them Athens and Sparta. And to keep things simple, let's suppose that their economies only produced two goods: guns and butter. Butter was used to feed the population, and guns were used to defend it. At first, both nations devoted virtually all of their economies to butter and only 1 percent to guns. Since Athens was a bigger nation with more people, it had a bigger military and more guns. So the Spartans decided to spend 2 percent of their economy on guns, putting Sparta on top. Athens matched and Sparta escalated again by spending 5 percent on guns. The cycle continued until both nations were spending half their economy on guns. Now many people in both nations were starving due to a lack of butter, and yet the relative rank of Athens and Sparta was completely unchanged. Athens had the bigger military before the arms race, and they had a bigger military after. Arms races lead to economically inefficient outcomes.

Once again, our old friend the free rider problem shows up. Nations can dedicate most of their economy to butter (cooperate) or they can shift much of it to guns (defect). If they think their enemy is going to cooperate, then their best option is to defect and crush their enemy like a bug. But if they think their enemy is going to defect, then they have to defect also, or else they'll be the one crushed like a bug. No matter what their enemy does, their best option is to defect. The free rider problem has a single Nash equilibrium of always defect.

Wherever there is competition, there is an arms race. Bodybuilders are in an arms race to build the biggest muscles. Freestyle skiers are in an arms race to do the most flips off of the biggest cliffs. Models are in an arms race to be the most beautiful. Cheetahs and gazelles are in an arms race to run the fastest. Trees are in an arms race to be the tallest and get the sun's light.[145] Firms are in an arms race to make the best widgets at the lowest price. Lawyers are in an arms race to learn the most case law. Hackers and computer security experts are in an arms race to either break into or secure corporate servers.

Social Status

The most important arms race of them all is for *social status*, or what high school students call popularity. Social status is the informal hierarchy that people spontaneously create when they form groups. However, the need for social status does not go away when students graduate from high school. The desire for social status is wired deep into our genetic makeup. The lion that defeats his rival acquires a pride of females and will pass on his genes. The lion that loses will see his genes go extinct. Females have similar status competitions hard-wired into them. Hyenas are violent killers and bonobos are the peaceful hippies of the great apes, but they do have one thing in common: High ranking females can secure more of the group's food for their children than low-ranking females. The children of high-ranking females survive and thrive; the children of low-ranking females languish and starve.

Humans work the same way. The anthropologist Napoleon Chagnon found that among the Yanomamö hunter-gatherer tribe, the single best predictor of a man's reproductive success was whether or not he had killed another man. These men had more social status, more wives and three times as many children as men who had not killed.[146] The anthropologist Lawrence Keeley shows in his book *War Before Civilization* that hunter-gatherer societies fight for land, women, honor, and revenge.[147] Arms races are literally built into our DNA.

Once you start paying attention, you will notice status competitions everywhere. Why do liberals and conservatives always argue with each other? Why do runners immediately compare half-marathon times? Why do two sports fans often start quizzing each other on esoteric knowledge? Why is it that two pretty women are often rivals? Why do a man and a woman who feel a spark of attraction play games and tease each other? Why does that "frenemy" at work always try to one-up you? In all these cases, they are testing and sorting each other for relative social status.

Signals

Social status and signaling go hand in hand because many signals are aimed at social status. In the chapter on the free rider problem, we saw that advertising is a costly signal of a product's quality. But consumers can buy a product for its usefulness in the real world (a watch that gives them accurate time) or for its social status (a watch that makes them look wealthy and sophisticated). Social status is a lot more expensive. A quality mechanical watch like the Tudor Prince costs over $3,000 and it doesn't keep time nearly as well as a $30 Timex.

Social status is where we see the manipulative side of advertising. Beer is a great example. If advertising were about objective real-world performance, then heavily advertised beer would taste better than other beers. But in one study, regular beer drinkers were put to a blind taste test, and it turned out that they couldn't even recognize their own brand with consistency.[148] People buy beer to obtain an image of themselves as rugged and cool, not for taste. Wine drinkers don't fare any better. In one study researchers dyed white wine red and then asked experts to describe it, and the experts used terms for red wines.[149] They didn't catch on to the fact that they were actually drinking a white.

The easier it is to sort out relative social status and create a hierarchy, the less conflict there will be. Well-defined and stable hierarchies reduce conflict, but fuzzy hierarchies fuel conflict. If two runners meet, one of the first things they'll do is exchange 5K or half-marathon times, and instantly the hierarchy is settled. Skiing works differently. There isn't anything like a 5K time for skiing, so it is much harder for skiers to settle their relative rank. The only good way to do it is to actually ski together. So online ski forums frequently erupt into status competitions because skiers use their gear or advice as signals of relative rank as skiers.

Money is as easy to measure as 5K times, so you'd think people would be able to settle relative rank by checking their bank accounts, but that runs into a different problem. I remember a viral video of a man at a bar trying to pick up a woman by doing exactly that—showing her his bank account on his phone. It was every bit as difficult to watch as you might imagine. All he accomplished was proving that he was painfully lacking in social skills. Signals give us plausible deniability. If the man were wearing a Tudor Prince, then he wouldn't have to show the woman his bank account. He'd just pretend that he didn't notice her quick glance down at his wrist, and she'd pretend that she didn't notice his eyes follow hers. The real game is not showing her that he is rich but showing her that he is capable of having a wordless conversation.

Near and Far Beliefs

Smoking and touching hot stoves are both bad for you, but no one ever thought that touching a hot stove was cool. Why is that? The first time you touch a hot stove, you will get a nasty burn. The immediate feedback tells you not to do it. By contrast, cigarettes do not give immediate feedback. Cigarette smokers don't live as long as non-smokers, but the reality check comes decades after they start smoking. Besides, there is no guarantee that they'll even get lung cancer. Some smokers live long and healthy lives and some non-smokers die young. However, the social status and coolness factor of smoking is available immediately.

The economist Robin Hanson connected social status to the research of *psychological distance*. He showed that the importance of social status increases with greater psychological distance.[150] Touching hot stoves is *near*. There are immediate consequences. Even if society collectively decided that touching hot stoves was cool, no one would do it. Cigarette smoking is *far*. The harmful consequences are in the distant future. When things are near, we care about real world fundamentals (whether the watch keeps accurate time). When things are far, we care about social status (whether the watch signals wealth and sophistication).

Purity Spirals

I have a tongue-in-cheek theory that every forty-seven years (it should be a prime number) the spirit of Jean-Jacques Rousseau emerges from dormancy and captures the soul of modern liberalism. Then after about twenty or so years of forcing everyone to be free, a backlash occurs, and it goes dormant for the rest of the cycle.

Charles Darwin laid the foundation for the eugenics movement with *The Descent of Man*. I think Darwin was actually trying to reign in the growing scientific racism of his time, yet it is a shockingly racist book which takes for granted the idea that blacks are morally and intellectually inferior to whites. In his book, Darwin casually predicts a global genocide: "At some future period, not very distant as measured by centuries, the civilized races of man will almost certainly exterminate and replace throughout the world the savage races."[151]

It wasn't until the progressive movement of the early twentieth century that scientific ideas like social Darwinism and eugenics would cross over to mainstream politics. In 1916 Margaret Sanger founded Planned Parenthood. In the article *My Way to Peace*, she explained that her goal was to increase the national IQ by reducing the population of, in her words, "morons, mental defectives, epileptics."[152] In 1927 the Supreme Court decision *Buck v. Bell* set the precedent that state laws for sterilizing the "feebleminded" were constitutional. Canada was following the same trends, and in 1928 and 1933, two Canadian provinces passed laws about sterilizing Indigenous people. Then World War II and the horrors of the Holocaust repudiated the eugenics movement, so the spirit of Rousseau went dormant again. But it returned sometime in the liberal 1960s.

The 1960s and 1970s gave us the usual suspects like rampant inflation and even more rampant crime, but the environmental movement was the real villain. Except that in the 1960s, the concern was over population growth, not climate change. Think of the Earth as a giant petri dish filled with food. Initially the bacteria will grow exponentially, but once they finish all the food, they will die off in a mass starvation. That was the doomsday scenario environmentalists were worried about—exponential population growth and mass starvation. Intellectuals like Paul Ehrlich warned of this in books such as *Population Bomb*. These intellectuals championed mass sterilizations as the only way to keep the population beneath the amount the Earth could feed.

The Indian Health Services began a policy of sterilizing Native Americans in the United States in the 1960s and the 1970s. Denmark began sterilizing indigenous women in Greenland in 1967. They were worried that population growth among the Indigenous people would cause a drain on the nation's welfare state. Ultimately, about half of the women in Greenland were sterilized, and the policy continued informally as late as 2018.[153] However, the majority of victims were in the developing world. Millions of Chinese and Indian citizens were sterilized to alleviate the rapid population growth in those nations.

When liberal became a dirty word in the 1980s, the spirit of Rousseau went dormant once more. Bill Clinton was only able to win the presidency by promising the voters that he was a "new Democrat," and a change from the far-left liberals that had come before him. But even as early as the 1990s, the far left was attacking Clinton and the moderate Democratic Leadership Council for being "Republican-lite," so it was just a matter of time until they re-emerged and seized the moral high ground once more. It happened sometime in the 2010s, and now the left, which once believed in Enlightenment principles of reason, rationality, and individual rights, has gone fully postmodern and is imposing two unfalsifiable hypotheses on the American public.

The first is *antiracism*. Superficially it is just a collection of interrelated unfalsifiable hypotheses. One is the belief that structural racism is the reason why there are different outcomes between whites and blacks, and any argument otherwise is a power play to justify white oppression. Another is that all white people are complicit in racism, and any argument whites make otherwise is proof that they have a sense of fragility about their own racism. Whites can either confess their racism, or they can deny it and prove that they are even bigger racists. At an only slightly deeper level, which is as far as you can go, antiracism is white saviorism. Blacks are trapped in oppression, but their antiracist allies are nobly fighting to free them.

The second unfalsifiable hypothesis is gender ideology—the belief that anyone who identifies as a woman is a woman. That's the essence of the self-ID policies that are granting men access to women's spaces, such as prisons, locker rooms, and domestic violence shelters. The domain of science is objective facts, not subjective opinions. Self-identification is a subjective opinion.

This "Rousseau cycle" happens because of *purity spirals*. In his article, *How Knitters Got Knotted in a Purity Spiral*, Gavin Hayes explains that "A purity spiral occurs when a community becomes fixated on implementing a single value that has no upper limit, and no single agreed interpretation. The result is a moral feeding frenzy."[154] Purity spirals are a major problem for the left because they are the party of top-down processes driven by the ideas of scientists and intellectuals. Scientific ideas like "the gene pool is declining in quality", "overpopulation will lead to mass starvation", and "climate change will lead to runaway global warming" are all examples of these values. Of course, these propositions are false, but that doesn't matter. What matters is that scientists believed they were true, and plenty of other people were happy to follow the lead of scientists in the moral domain.

A purity spiral will get halted in its tracks if it hits a ceiling, so not having an upper limit is important. Take climate change for example. If Alicia says that climate change is real, but it's not as big of a problem as activists make it out to be, she'll be accused of climate denialism. If Blake says that we should cut carbon emissions by 10 percent in ten years, someone else will say we should cut them by 20 percent in five years. And then a third person will point out that China's emissions are much higher than the United States' emissions and rising rapidly—that if we really care about climate change, we need to do something about China. Once again, a liberal purity spiral collides with the developing world. Hayes points out that with purity spirals "a bidding war for morality turned into a proxy war for power."[155] That's why people who consider themselves to be the most moral are often the most dangerous.

The fascinating thing about purity spirals is that they can lead to astonishing outcomes that no one could have possibly predicted earlier in the cycle. This follows from the "not having an upper limit" property. Gender ideology is a textbook example. Many conservatives objected to gay marriage on the grounds that it would lead to a slippery slope, and they were routinely mocked. But after the Supreme Court legalized gay marriage, LGBT groups pivoted towards transgender issues as the next great civil rights struggle.

Here's a small sampling of things I did not have on my slippery slope bingo card: men in women's sports; liberal nations like Australia denying lesbians the right to gather without including men;[156] doctors surgically removing healthy body parts from autistic teenage girls;[157] states such as California passing laws like SB 132 that allow male rapists to transfer into women's prisons without even having to take hormones or get "bottom surgery";[158] parents taking their children to drag shows where they see the exposed breasts of transgender drag queens;[159] the police refusing to arrest sex offenders walking around naked with erect penises in women's locker rooms;[160] states passing laws allowing schools to transition children to the opposite gender without disclosing this to parents;[161] parents being charged with child abuse and losing custody of their children for not transitioning them;[162] and the Biden administration withholding federal free lunch from poor students if their school's administration didn't let boys change in the girl's locker room.[163]

If I had suggested these things would happen back in 2015 when the Supreme Court upheld the right of gay people to marry, I would have been accused of creating the most ridiculous straw man argument in all of human history. In 2024 the same argument makes me a bigot.

So how did we get here? Purity spirals show how at every step people can signal that they have greater empathy and kindness than the people one step behind, but as the purity spiral progresses, it leaves behind all but the true believers and the con men. Here's how the purity spiral unfolded for men who identify as women.

Step One: Transgendered individuals have an untreatable mental health problem. Their physical bodies are causing them enormous unease and distress. They need hormones to relieve their gender dysphoria, not gatekeeping psychologists who try to convert them into being cisgender.

Step Two: Being transgender is not a mental health problem. It's who they are. We used to say that being gay was a mental health problem too. Trans women may not have female bodies, but what matters is that they are women on the inside. (If you're keeping score at home, this is the point where the left abandoned its long-held position that there is no such thing as "pink brains" and "blue brains.")

Step Three: They aren't just women on the inside. Trans women are women. We wouldn't tell an intersex woman that she isn't really a woman just because she looks masculine. If a trans woman wants to take estrogen to look more stereotypically feminine, then that isn't any different from a cis woman getting breast implants to look more stereotypically feminine. But regardless of whether or not a trans woman chooses to alter her appearance, she was always a woman.

Step Four: Conservatives are weaponizing trans women in prison. They're making it a wedge issue to force liberal allies to admit that they don't really believe that trans women are women. But it's cruel and barbaric to lock women in men's prisons, regardless of whether they are cis or trans. Cis women also commit horrible crimes like rape, but we don't send them to men's prisons.

The purity spiral started with the desire to have empathy for people with a mental health problem. It ended with men in women's prisons, which is a violation of the Geneva Conventions. In 1823 England passed the Gaol Act which created separate prisons for women staffed by female guards. 200 years later the prisoners and the guards are often male. (While the topic of men in women's prisons is relevant, we need to get rid of the male guards. There are more women raped in prison by male guards than by male prisoners. All prisoner-facing jobs in women's prisons should be done by women.) Martin Luther King Jr. said that the arc of the moral universe is long, but it bends towards justice. Well, it also takes a lot of wrong turns along the way.

Many liberals are opposed to locking rapists in women's prisons. At least, I hope they are, but I can't be sure because they don't speak out. That's because purity spirals have three important methods to suppress dissent. The first is *loyalty tests*. In current times, it might be putting your pronouns in your email signature and displaying a pride flag on your social media profile in June. Loyalty tests help isolate dissenters for scorn and ostracism early in a movement and make it hard for them to mobilize resistance. Conservatives have loyalty tests too, but they involve American flags instead of pride flags.

The second method is *self-censorship*. Critics keep quiet for fear of getting fired from their job and being socially ostracized by their friends and neighbors. In *The Coming of the Terror in the French Revolution*, the historian Timothy Tackett gives a concrete example.

> Even before the Girondins [moderate revolutionaries] went to their death, contemporaries were becoming much more cautious as to what they set down in writing. Many ceased correspondence altogether. For those who continued, the transparency of their thoughts and opinions was frequently clouded by fear and self-censorship. Some burned everything they had previously written or received, or tore out and destroyed whole sections of their diaries.[164]

The main idea was that the people involved in the French Revolution were worried they might be put on trial and then executed at any time for not being sufficiently on board with the revolution's more radical goals. So they were careful to purge any evidence of even the faintest hint of criticism. The French Revolution is the greatest purity spiral in history, which is why both liberals and conservatives have been fascinated with it ever since. There are very few things that France does better than the United States, but creating interesting history is one of them.

The third method that purity spirals use to suppress dissent is *preference falsification*, which is when people pretend to believe things that they really don't. Preference falsification is usually more subtle than lying about what you believe. It's more along the lines of, "The world is changing, and I need to change with it." But it also means that people are weakly attached to these new ideas. That weak attachment is important when the purity spiral collapses.

Purity spirals are not a liberal problem but a human problem. Conservatives have purity spirals over abortion, taxes, the military, and much more. Conservatives care about purity, which is why *rino* (Republican in name only) is one of the worst insults that conservatives can use against another conservative. This is unfortunate because conservatism, like liberalism, is a diverse and multi-faceted movement. But I do understand the instinct because the left has more social power, and many conservatives cannot escape the left's gravitational pull.

Nevertheless, purity spirals are a smaller problem for conservatives because they aren't chasing new ideas but preserving old traditions. That's why Britain has gone over 300 years without a revolution and America has gone over 200. In the time since America's one and only revolution, France has had five different republics, two dictators, and two restorations of the monarchy. Maybe the French made a bad choice when they embraced Jean-Jacques Rousseau and turned their backs on the wisdom of the past.

In fact, many conservative purity spirals aren't technically purity spirals at all, at least according to Hayes' definition. That's because traditions do have an upper limit. For example, conservatives admire the high rates of stable marriages in both the black and white communities before the Sexual Revolution,[165] but conservatives can't outbid each other on this. What are they going to do—propose that everyone gets married twice to show that they like marriage twice as much? Upper limits stop purity spirals.

The final lesson of the French Revolution is that purity spirals can end as quickly as they begin. That's because self-censorship and preference falsification create an illusion of widespread support that doesn't actually exist. Sooner or later everyone but the con men and the true believers hop off the bandwagon. The problem is that critics are afraid to speak up. Speaking up is a recipe for a quick trip to the guillotine. All totalitarian regimes intuitively understand the importance of censoring dissent, and the French were no exception. What the people need is something that gives them a clue that they are not alone—that everyone else feels the same way they do. Once that happens, purity spirals can collapse with astonishing speed.

The Reign of Terror ended because the ringleader, Maximilien Robespierre, would make fiery speeches before the National Convention to rousing cheers. But on July 26th, 1794, Robespierre made a speech in which he suggested there were still more traitors in the National Convention. In this speech he made the fatal mistake of not naming names, so this time, no one cheered. Everyone thought that they would be the next person sent to the guillotine. Robespierre was arrested the next day and put on trial and executed the day after. The purity spiral, and the Reign of Terror, was over.

Government Failure

> It is very easy to accuse a government of imperfection, for all mortal things are full of it.
> – Michel de Montaigne, *Essays (1580-88)*

We've spent a lot of time looking at market failures and implicit in the debate is that the government can do a better job. That is an odd assumption considering that most of us are happier with our cars than we are with our government. In this chapter free markets get their revenge. The discipline of *public choice theory* applies an economic analysis to the government instead of free markets.

Public Choice Theory

Consumers who are buying a car have an incentive to do their homework because otherwise they may end up buying a lemon. That is not true of politics. It is unlikely that a single voter will change the outcome of an election. A voter can do all the research in the world, but if the other voters want a lemon, he's getting a lemon. The first lesson of economics is that people respond to incentives. Voters are not rewarded for doing their homework or punished for being ignorant. So the outcome is that most voters don't do their homework. Economists call this *rational ignorance*. Only about half of the general public knows that each state has two senators, and only about a quarter of them know the length of a senate term. Less than half of the public can name their congressional representative, and only about 60 percent can name one of their senators.[166] I'm not any different. I can name my state's senators, but I can't name any congressional representatives.

Regulatory capture is perhaps the most troubling example of government failure. It is what happens when regulatory agencies become captured by the corporations they are supposed to regulate. Regulatory capture has been documented by critics on both the right and the left. On the left there is the socialist historian, Gabriel Kolko. In his book, *The Triumph of Conservatism*, he makes the case that the sweeping reforms of the progressive era were not a win for liberals who wanted to "reign in" Big Business, but for conservatives who wanted to make Big Business more powerful.

Regulatory capture has also been documented by critics on the right, such as the Nobel Prize winning economist George Stigler.[167] Stigler's argument is a defense of free markets, and an argument against government interference in the economy. In both cases their arguments were directed against moderate liberals who believe that the government can act as a limit on corporations. The reality is that the government often amplifies corporate power.

Stigler's insights begin with the realization that firms in regulated markets have the most skin in the game. Regulated firms have the strongest incentive to influence regulations and manipulate them for their own advantage. They use expensive regulations to create barriers to entry that protect them from small nimble firms with innovative new products. They can also use their power to get government subsidies and to collude in order to fix prices. Every dirty trick that liberals accuse scheming firms of doing secretly is actually done right out in the open by government regulatory agencies.

Boeing is a good example of regulatory capture. As we saw in the chapter on Jack Welch, their 737-MAX airplane had two fatal crashes within the first five months of release. One of the many failure points that led to these crashes is that Boeing pressured the FAA to allow them to self-certify many aspects of the plane's design.[168] If the government worked in the public interest, then this never would have happened. But because the government works to amplify the power of large politically connected firms, the FAA said, "Sure, we trust you."

The biggest problem with regulatory capture is that it can stifle competition. The captured regulatory agencies increase the barriers to entry and prevent rival firms from entering the market. Kolko made this point many times in his book. The major meat packing firms, such as Swift and Amour, supported the Meat Inspection Act of 1906 to drive small competitors out of business because they could not afford to comply with the regulations.[169] Corporations also supported the Clayton Antitrust Act and the creation of the Federal Trade Commission for exactly the same reason.[170]

The classic example of regulatory capture is the Interstate Commerce Commission (ICC), which was embraced by the railroad industry. The Transportation Act of 1920 gave the ICC the power to set both minimum and maximum rates for shipping.[171] In other words, it was legal collusion and price-fixing. The airline industry worked the exact same way. Jim Cox explains in *The Concise Guide to Economics*.

> Airlines were regulated beginning in 1938, and in the 40-year period from then until 1978 [when the airlines were deregulated] no new trunk airlines were granted a charter. These four decades saw a huge change in the airline business as airplane technology advanced from propellers to jets, from 20 seaters to 400 seaters, from speeds of 120 mph to speeds of 600 mph. Yet, the Civil Aeronautics Board (CAB) found no need to allow new competitors into the growing industry. This fact alone makes it quite clear that the purpose of the regulation was not to protect the consumer but to protect the market of the established airlines.[172]

Innovative low-cost airlines like Southwest Airlines and JetBlue could not have happened before the deregulation of the airline industry.

So how does regulatory capture happen? The main method is the revolving door between industry and the government. The government likes to hire experienced workers from the regulated industry because they already have deep knowledge of how the industry works. Similarly, the regulated firms like to hire workers from the government agency. That's because they have insider connections and know how to manage the red tape. If a firm wants the government to stay off its back, they hire someone from the government with a lot of connections who can ease them through the process of regulatory compliance.

Workers at regulatory agencies are well-aware of the existence of the revolving door. A good example comes from a study of the US Patent and Trademark Office. Patent examiners grant significantly more patents to firms that eventually hire them, and that this leniency extends to other prospective employers as well.[173] Basically, patent examiners know the job is a stepping-stone to a higher-paying corporate job and they curry favor by granting patents to firms they'd one day like to work for.

Regulatory capture is a problem that voters can't easily solve. First, we have to deal with our old friend the free rider problem. Voters can research issues and petition the government (cooperate) or enjoy their free time (defect). If all the voters cooperate then the government *might* be able to control the regulated firms instead of the other way around. But it's in the interests of each individual voter to enjoy their free time instead of spending it reading 2,000-page bills about airline regulations. Even if someone was masochistic enough to do that, they don't have the deep industry knowledge needed to understand proposed regulations. They wouldn't realize that complying with clause 9a of subsection 12.8 on page 1,254 will be extremely expensive and drive small firms out of business. The government is supposed to solve the free rider problem, but the government itself suffers from the free rider problem.

Regulatory capture does not have to be as sinister as bribing politicians. It results from the fact that creating regulations is a cryptic process, and few people have the time, knowledge, and political connections to make a difference. Donald Kettl explains:

> To participate requires knowing that a particular issue is in play, following the *Federal Register* [where proposed regulations are published - it totals about 80,000 pages per year] closely to read the draft regulations, and the ability to write persuasive comments. ... Effective participation requires policy and technical knowledge and, especially, the ability (and often the contacts) to get the right information to the right people at the right time. That makes it hard for ordinary citizens to participate in most regulatory issues. ... it increases the influence of members of the issue, who have established relationships with each other ... Influencing the regulatory process thus is largely an insider's game. This is one reason why former government officials, from both the executive and legislative branches, are in such demand as lobbyists. They know who to call and, when they telephone, their calls are more likely to be answered.[174]

This is a game that only deep-pocketed firms that have taken advantage of the revolving door between industry and government can play.

Wittman's Criticism of Public Choice

The essence of public choice theory is that the government itself suffers from the free rider problem. Donald Wittman disagreed. He argued in *The Myth of Democratic Failure* that politics is more like a free market.[175] Economists even have a term for this market: the *political economy*. Instead of firms, there are rival political parties battling to increase their market share by getting more votes. If one political party gets arrogant, out of touch, or otherwise loses its mojo, the ecology of the marketplace will punish it as voters switch their allegiance.

Wittman's vision fits more neatly with how both liberals and conservatives feel about government. The 2024 presidential election is coming up, and both parties feel that the other has become radical and authoritarian, and both parties are hoping that the voters will reward them and punish their rival.

Let's take a look at how Wittman's theory works by highlighting a few of the more important points, starting with the rational ignorance of voters. Sure, voters are ignorant of specific facts about politics, but consumers are ignorant of the technology of their cars. I drive a Subaru Impreza but couldn't tell you a thing about its engine. I bought the car because my family likes to ski, and it has all-wheel drive. I can write a whole book about my politics but only one sentence about my car. Most voters don't know much about specific political issues, but they can tell you if they are a Republican or a Democrat and why. Voters rely on brand names, and brand names allow even the rationally ignorant to make informed choices.

Individual voters don't need much information to make good choices collectively. That takes us to the next parable in our tour of economics, the parable of the ox contest. The statistician (and eugenicist) Francis Galton analyzed the results of a contest in which people tried to guess the weight of an ox after it was slaughtered. These days we have contests about the number of jellybeans in a jar, but apparently back then they used animals. After the contest Galton collected the entry forms and calculated the average of all the guesses. James Surowiecki explains in *The Wisdom of Crowds*.

> Galton undoubtedly thought that the average guess of the group would be way off the mark. After all, mix a few very smart people with some mediocre people and a lot of dumb people, and it seems likely you'd end up with a dumb answer. But Galton was wrong. The crowd had guessed that the ox, after it had been slaughtered and

dressed, would weigh 1,197 pounds. After it had been slaughtered and dressed the ox weighed 1,198 pounds.[176]

Wittman points out that voting is like the ox contest. Suppose voters have to pick between two candidates. If they were completely ignorant, then the only way they could pick would be at random. They'd have to guess or flip a coin. But although voters are ignorant, they are not completely ignorant. They do know a little bit about politics. Let's suppose that they have enough information to pick the better candidate 51 percent of the time. That means the better candidate would get 51 percent of the votes and win the election.

Rational ignorance is not a problem, but what about special interest groups and regulatory capture? Wittman has an argument for that too. Suppose the Democrats are in power and create a lot of new regulations that voters don't like, such as government-granted monopolies that don't innovate. This would damage their brand name and give the Republicans a golden opportunity to run against them. The fact that the voters haven't chosen to systematically roll back the regulatory state is proof that these regulations serve the interests of voters.

Facing the wrath of voters prevents one party from going heavy into creating bad regulations. But what if the harm happens "under the table"? It's not so much that the Democrats want to create anti-competitive regulations, but that individual politicians from both parties are trying to help their own reelection prospects, even if it means making bad deals for the nation as a whole. Neither the Republicans nor the Democrats will officially endorse pork barrel spending, but if a senator can get a Bridge to Nowhere for his state, then he's helped his voters and his chance of getting reelected.

Wittman responds by pointing out that political parties have effective means to maintain party discipline. They can punish disobedient politicians by taking away their committee assignments. They can withhold campaign funding in the next election. They can even run a primary challenger against the disobedient politician and then fund the primary challenger. It is political suicide to go against the party. (This argument made more sense twenty years ago when I first read Wittman than it does in today's political environment where renegade politicians are more common.)

Wittman's takeaway is that the government is pretty efficient. Sure, it has its warts, but as we've seen, free markets have their warts too. Wittman's theory also explains a phenomenon called the *Tullock Paradox*, named after the discoverer, Gordon Tullock. He found that there isn't very much money being spent influencing politics. One study found that only three billion dollars was spent by candidates, political parties, and political organizations during the 2000 election cycle.[177] That may seem like a lot of money, but the federal budget was $1.8 trillion that year. The amount of money spent buying influence amounted to about one tenth of a percent of the federal budget.

Ultimately there are two ways to think about Wittman. The first is that Wittman refutes the arguments of public choice theory. On this view, whenever a libertarian or conservative wants to use public choice theory to criticize the government, liberals can play their Wittman trump card and win.

I don't think that's the correct interpretation, although I believed it for a while. According to the incentives described by public choice theory, the government would collapse in about five minutes. For example, rational ignorance means that turnout in elections would be much closer to zero than the 66 percent we got in 2020. Voters would be so uninformed that government corruption would be more rampant than in a banana republic. Special interest groups and political insiders would devour the entire gains of creating a government in the first place. The fact that the government didn't immediately collapse five minutes after George Washington was sworn in back in 1789 means that there must be countervailing powers to keep it working.

One of these countervailing powers is that voters aren't wholly self-interested. They care about the greater good and take their civic duties seriously. That's why turnout in elections isn't close to zero. Another countervailing power is Wittman's theory. Public choice theory and Donald Wittman give us the tools we need to evaluate what we already know about government. The government does some things reasonably well, such as creating public goods like national defense and roads. That's where you lean more on Wittman. But it also has regulatory capture and special interests tilting the playing field in favor of politically connected insiders. That's where you lean more on public choice theory. Liberals and conservatives still argue about the government, but we now have a more precise vocabulary for doing so.

Voters are Systematically Irrational

We still have one major problem. Wittman shows that the government responds to the demands of the people, but what if the people are systematically wrong about what they want? This is what the economist Bryan Caplan persuasively argues in *The Myth of the Rational Voter*.[178] Caplan builds on the theory of *expressive voting*, which holds that people vote to express their values and personal identities instead of achieving specific policy goals. Caplan uses this concept to argue that voters can easily end up supporting policies that actually work against their desired goals.

Critical readers might be thinking, "Wait a second, the wisdom of crowds shows that the group converges on the truth. Individual voters might be mistaken, but groups of voters are usually right." That is not always true. There is some fine print attached to the wisdom of crowds. First, it assumes that people make their choices independently. Second, it assumes that errors are random. The ox contest meets these two requirements. The trials are independent because each person who entered the contest made their own guess. Sure, some people may have talked it over with a friend or two, but for practical purposes, the guesses were independent. The second requirement is that their errors are random. One person might guess that the ox is 100 pounds too heavy, but someone else might guess that the ox is 100 pounds too light. Overall, those errors will cancel out.

Voting fails to meet both assumptions. First, voters do not make their political choices independently. People constantly discuss and debate politics and share sarcastic political memes. Voters use their social power to shame, scorn, and ostracize black sheep and bring others back into the herd. Secondly, errors are not random because voters must get their information from sources like newspapers, websites, and books with strange animals on the cover. Most media companies lean left and a few like *Fox News* lean right. No one tries to be objective. The upshot is that voters are systemically biased, which means that the wisdom of crowds cannot work its magic.

Caplan says that voters are *rationally irrational*. Suppose Alicia is a socialist who lives in the West. Objectively speaking, socialism is a terrible system that creates poverty and oppression. But her one vote isn't going to change the outcome of the election. Alicia is insulated from the real-world consequences of her political beliefs. On the other hand, her belief gives her social status. They gain her admittance into the high-status world of left-wing artists, activists, and intellectuals. It also lets her think of herself as someone who is kinder and more compassionate than others, not just conservatives, but also more moderate liberals.

Think back to the previous chapter on social status and the concept of psychological distance—near and far. As we've seen, democracy insulates us from the consequences of our beliefs. That means that political beliefs are in far mode. However, your political ideology can negatively impact your friends, family and even cost you your job. The smart thing to do is to choose your political beliefs based on social status. Social status is near.

A striking example of this is the recent war between Israel and Hamas. Jewish people in the United States tend to side with the Palestinians, but Jewish people in Israel reject "Free Palestine from the river to the sea." For Jewish people in America, the war is far. For Jewish people in Israel, it is near. This distinction is even more true for American university students with "Queers for Palestine" flags. They seem to be unaware of the fact that even high-ranking leaders in Hamas are executed for being gay.[179]

In theory, political debates force us to confront contradictory evidence. Liberals put their evidence on the table, and conservatives do likewise. The person with the most evidence wins. In practice, cognitive dissonance is a powerful thing, and there aren't always simple rubrics for judging the truth. That's why the economist Robin Hanson holds that social status is the "One Ring that rules them all" of biases and logical fallacies. The only purpose of other biases and errors in reasoning is to enable us to hold false but high-status beliefs.

A bigger problem is the fact that the best way to change someone's mind is not with evidence, but with scorn, ridicule, and insults. People don't respond to reason; they respond to social status. If one political party is higher in status than another, they'll almost effortlessly win votes and gain political power. We saw this dynamic in the discussion of postmodernism in the chapter on social norms, so there is no need to rehash it again here. But the power of social status to change beliefs is the reason why I don't dismiss postmodernism as fuzzy-headed nonsense. Social status is how the idea that truth is a social construct originated.

The biggest problem with the intermingling of social status and politics is that it leads to an implicit groupthink. Low status ideas are systemically purged from the public sphere, even if they're true. Obviously that's happened with conservatives, but we were only the first. Liberals who still believe in the Enlightenment project of using public reason have been pushed into an intellectual ghetto called *heterodoxy*. That means holding different and unorthodox ideas. Some examples of heterodox liberals include Jonathan Haidt, Bari Weiss, and Glen Loury. But when did believing in Enlightenment reason become heterodox to the left? The answer is at the exact same time the left got into postmodernism and became Woke.

No one intentionally chooses beliefs based on social status. We all have to believe we've chosen to aim our beliefs at the truth, even though we're all deeply influenced by status. I can't do much about self-deception, but I can give some advice on how to enter the public square in an honest and truth-seeking way. This is just my take, there are many others, including John Rawls' more comprehensive doctrine of *public reason*. This is a bit simpler than Rawls and hits the main problems that come up on social media and internet forums.

The Principle of Courtesy. Be polite. Don't use insults or scorn. Your goal is not to shame black sheep into complicity but to exchange information. Treat your opponents as intellectual and moral equals, even if they are not. Especially if they are not. Ultimately the use of scorn and insults reflects poorly on you, not your opponent.

The Principle of Charity. Consider arguments in their strongest and most persuasive form. Most people immediately pounce on the first chink in their opponent's armor to score points, but you should instead try to repair their faulty argument. A *straw man* is when you misinterpret or oversimplify an opponent's argument so as to knock it down more easily. Create steel men, not straw men. Moreover, keep in mind that effective communication is a two-way street. Language is messy, and we aren't philosophers with the luxury of spending a lot of time defining terms. Effective communication relies on the listener actively interpreting what is being said and charitably filling in the needed details.

The Principle of Humility. Appreciate that you might be the one who is wrong. Most people can admit it when they know for sure that this happened. "I'm conservative, but we were wrong about the Patriot Act," or "I'm liberal, but Donald Trump was right to warn Germany about their dependence on Russian oil." If you knew that your belief in something had a fatal objection, then you would drop your belief in it. But if you've done your research and still haven't found the fatal objection, then it's easy to become overconfident. Realize that there are unknown unknowns, and that you don't know what you don't know.

You have probably heard of the *Dunning-Kruger effect*.[180] It is often bastardized into an insult: "You're so stupid you don't even know how stupid you are." That is a possible interpretation, but that's not what's usually going on. What it really means is that when you learn about a subject, you also gain *meta knowledge* about it. That's basically the roadmap of everything else there is to learn about that subject. If your roadmap is incomplete, then you won't know about the potential landmines and fatal objections that await you. The real lesson of Dunning-Kruger is that people only step on landmines that they don't know are there.

A more practical piece of advice is to avoid arguing about politics at all, at least with people you know in real life. Instead suggest a book or a podcast episode. Even if you stay calm and make reasonable points, everyone knows that a battle of wills is going on. The person you're debating is going to become defensive. A book or podcast can be consumed at leisure when the heat of the moment has passed. Give people a chance to reflect on new ideas on their own terms.

Evolutionary Psychology

> Marriage is like a golden cage with the birds on the outside singing "let me in!" and the birds on the inside singing "let me out!"
>
> – botched version of a quote by Michel de Montaigne

Nature is often harmonious and beautiful. Suzanne Simard's *Finding the Mother Tree* is about how she came to learn that trees in the Pacific Northwest would share resources and information with each other, even across different species, through fungal networks that connect their roots.[181] But nature can also be ugly and even, to anthropomorphize a bit, evil. The biologist David Barash points out in *The Myth of Monogamy* that, contrary to the claims of feminists like Susan Brownmiller, there are many animal species that commit rape.[182] So fasten your seat belts because we're going to grapple with the highs and lows of human nature as we look at the greatest arms race of them all—the war between the sexes.

Female Choosiness and Male Promiscuity

The first principle of the war between the sexes is that when it comes to making babies (and everything else?) women do most of the work. Women must carry their unborn child for nine months and then nurse their babies for the first year or three of their lives. And even in modern egalitarian families, women typically do most of the childcare. An even bigger burden is that until modern medicine, women had a roughly 1 percent chance of dying in childbirth.[183] By contrast, the only work a man does to make a baby is a brief period of pleasurable effort.

Biologists have found that this is a general truth that applies to virtually all animal species. Most mammals come together for mating season, and then the males go their separate ways without ever seeing their own children. The females do all the work of carrying, nurturing, and protecting their offspring by themselves. Even the size of a female's egg is much larger than the male's sperm, which means that the female has to do more work to make an egg than a male does to make sperm. In a day and age when most people on the left have trouble defining what a woman is, biologists have long had a definition: Females make large *gametes* (eggs), and males make small gametes (sperm). Sex is a binary, not a spectrum. There are intersex people who have a genetic condition that alters their sexual development, but there are no medium-sized or intersex gametes.

This creates the central conflict in the war between the sexes: If women are going to take all the risks and do most of the work, then sex isn't something they will take lightly. It doesn't make sense for a woman to procreate with a man who has low quality genes. She would spend nine months pregnant, risk her life in childbirth, spend a couple years nursing her baby, and then close to two decades raising a child who inherits his low-quality genes.

Her best strategy is to turn the low-quality man down and wait for someone who is smarter and stronger. Then her offspring will inherit his high-quality genes. The opposite is true for men. From an evolutionary perspective, men should procreate with women who have low-quality genes. Sure, her children may have a somewhat lower chance of survival, but that more than justifies the small amount of effort a man invests in making a baby.

The downstream consequences are profound: women are choosy, men are not. Of course, no one actually thinks this way. People out at the bars and browsing Tinder don't make spreadsheets where they calculate the genetic quality of their potential hookups. Most people at bars and clubs don't even want children and are using birth control. But millions of years of evolution have given us a sex drive that makes us act that way. An engineer at the dating app Hinge found that the top 5 percent of men who use the app get 41 percent of the likes.[184] And Hinge, at least relative to Tinder, is considered an app for relationships rather than hookups.

Polygamy

The collision between male promiscuity and female choosiness leads to *polygamy*. The males fight, and the females choose the winners. In some species like elephant seals, it is common for a dominant male to acquire a harem of fifty females. The other forty-nine males don't reproduce at all. Humans aren't that different except that our societies are more complex, which can lead to even larger harems. Kublai Khan had four queens and 7,000 concubines. King Tamba of Benaras was said to have had over 16,000 women in his harem.

Polygamy has many downstream consequences. Figuring out what to do with the extra males is one of them. Elephant seals just go their own way and try again at mating season next year. But with humans, large numbers of unmarried men can stir up violence and unrest. The usual way to get rid of them is through war. If they die, they won't be a problem anymore, and if they survive, they may earn the honor and status needed to take a wife. Among the Yanomamö tribe in Brazil, men who have killed in battle have three times as many children as men who haven't killed.[185]

Another consequence of polygamy is infanticide. When a rival male defeats the reigning alpha, the first thing he does is kill the infants. When this phenomenon was first discovered, scientists were shocked and appalled because they naively believed that evolution worked for the good of the species. The biologist Sarah Blaffer Hrdy figured out the reason. Killing the infants brought the females into heat sooner. That meant that the newly crowned alpha male could reproduce sooner and have more lifetime offspring. The alpha male maximizes his own reproductive fitness, but at the expense of the females and their children. This pattern of infanticide is found in many species such as lions, bears, langur monkeys, and prairie dogs.

Infanticide doesn't happen because langur monkeys pull out an Excel spreadsheet and start calculating their expected number of lifetime offspring if they kill infants versus letting them live. It happens because they form an emotional attachment to infants that were born while they were the reigning alpha, and a sense of antipathy towards all other infants.

This pattern of infanticide holds for humans too. In their book *Homicide*, Martin Daly and Margo Wilson have found that children are at seventy times the risk of being killed by a stepparent compared to their married biological parents.[186] Preschool children living with their mother and stepfather were forty times more likely to be abused than preschool children living with married biological parents.[187] Children are the main source of collateral damage in the war between the sexes.

Biologists call this the *Cinderella Effect*. In modern times we're used to stories of children being abused by stepfathers and live-in boyfriends, but throughout most of history, it was the stepmothers who were the potential threats. Before modern medicine, women often died in childbirth, which meant that her husband often remarried. It was common for children, particularly girls, to grow up with an abusive stepmother.

Cinderella is a nearly universal story found in many cultures throughout the world. China has the story of Yeh-Shen, a beautiful and kind-hearted young woman who lived with her wicked stepmother and stepsister. Instead of a fairy godmother, she had a magical fish who was her reincarnated mother. Her stepmother discovered this and cooked and ate the fish, and the heartbroken Yeh-Shen buried the bones in the garden. Soon after this came the spring festival, and the stepmother and stepsister dressed in their finest gowns and went, leaving Yeh-Shen behind. She fled to the garden in tears where she discovered that the fish bones were magical. She made a wish, and her rags were transformed into a beautiful green gown and golden slippers so she could attend the spring festival. Her fine clothes, beauty, and gentle manners attracted many admirers, including the king. But Yeh-Shen was forced to flee when she was recognized by her stepsister, and she lost one of her golden slippers while making her escape. The king vowed to marry the owner of the slipper and used it to track her down. In the story, Yeh-Shen married the king and lived happily ever after, but in the real world, Cinderella is just a fairy tale.

Another consequence of polygamy is an arms race between males. I've been using the term arms race metaphorically throughout this book, but in this case, it is literally true. Since males fight for the chance to reproduce, the largest, strongest, and most aggressive males pass on their genes. There are three classic signs of a polygamous species. The first is that males are larger than females. The second is that males delay adolescence compared to females. This gives young males extra time to mature before becoming a threat to older males. The third sign is that males are more aggressive than females. Passive males who don't like fighting don't pass on their genes. Humans show all three of these signs.

Anthropology provides another line of evidence for the polygamous side of human nature. C.S. Ford and Frank Beach surveyed 185 human cultures and found that only twenty-nine were monogamous—about

16 percent. G.P. Murdoch found similar results. His survey of 238 human cultures found that only about 20 percent of human societies are monogamous prior to contact with Western Civilization.[188] In fairness, polygamy is not as lopsided in humans as it is among elephant seals. Only high-ranking men had multiple wives, and about half the men were in monogamous relationships with a single wife. At the bottom of society there were large numbers of unmarried men with no wives and no prospects.

The Blank Slate Theory

It's hard to argue against the fact that men are bigger than women, but many liberals do dispute the point that men are more aggressive. That's because they subscribe to the *blank slate theory* of human nature. The idea is that humans are born as "blank slates" without any instincts or innate traits, and thus can be arbitrarily shaped by their culture and environment. A good way to understand it when it comes to differences between the sexes is with the slogan taught to children, "the difference between boys and girls is what's between their legs, not what's inside their head." Our bodies may be different, but there is no such thing as pink brains and blue brains. Instead, the patriarchy socializes girls to want to be pretty and passive and boys to be aggressive go-getters. That's where the idea that gender is a *social construct* comes from—our culture creates oppressive gender roles to keep women in their place.

The blank slate theory was popular on the left before gender ideology took over. Now statements like "the difference between boys and girls is what's between their legs, not what's in their head" violate more important creeds like "trans women are women" and "some men can get pregnant."[189] Still, I believe that many liberals continue to believe in the blank slate theory, so that's what I'll address.

EVOLUTIONARY PSYCHOLOGY

This book is about the power of culture, so I am sympathetic to the blank slate theory. Culture is a weaker version of the blank slate, a version that is more constrained by the weaknesses of human nature. But even so, human culture is enormously flexible. Think about the many different types of societies throughout the world and human history. People who live in England today are different from people during the pre-Victorian Era when Jane Austen was writing her novels, and both cultures are radically different from the Yanomamö or the Roman Empire. Culture can socialize women to have a sense of purpose and agency, or it can squash it. I appreciate the way Jane Austen subtly pushed back against the social norms of her times. In *Persuasion*, Mrs. Croft says, "I hate to hear you talking so, like a fine gentleman, and as if women were all fine ladies, instead of rational creatures. We none of us expect to be in smooth water all our days."[190]

Nevertheless, there are good reasons why conservatives part ways with blank slate liberals, and the idea that differences between men and women are 100 percent the result of socialization is one of them. Steven Pinker reviews the evidence and makes an overwhelming case against it in his appropriately named book, *The Blank Slate*. We'll only consider two of his arguments. First, Donald Brown has compiled a list of *human universals*. These are traits that anthropologists have found in every known human society whether primitive or advanced, Western or Eastern. Two of these human universals are that men are more aggressive and violent than women, and that women spend more time on childcare than men. That was even true in the Israeli Kibbutzim, which were gender neutral communities determined to stamp out sex-specific roles.[191]

Another line of evidence for differences between men and women is that the brains of boys and girls diverge during development. That's because the male fetus' testicles produce testosterone and other male hormones while still in the womb. These hormones trigger permanent changes to the male brain.[192] In fact, females with a condition called congenital adrenal hyperplasia produce larger than normal amounts of androstenedione, the prohormone made famous by the muscular baseball player Mark McGuire. Stephen Pinker explains in *The Blank Slate* that these girls "grow into tomboys, with more rough-and-tumble play, a greater interest in trucks than dolls, better spatial abilities, and when they get older, more sexual fantasies and attractions involving other girls."[193]

Even in societies where girls are socialized to become rational creatures instead of fine ladies, men and women will be different. And in fact, that's how Western culture works. Pinker points out that research literature shows that parents give boys and girls similar amounts of warmth, nurturing, restrictiveness, and discipline.[194] The only real difference is that fathers discourage their sons from playing with dolls, out of the fear that it will make them gay. Pinker points out that boys who play with dolls are more likely to be gay, but the doll is not the mechanism that makes that happen. My mother is a lifelong liberal, and she good-naturedly tells the story of when her gender-neutral parenting collided with human nature. She bought me a doll as a child, and I promptly grabbed its arms like a steering wheel and tried to drive it like a truck. My mom does not like shopping or gossip, so I suppose she dodged a bullet.

Equality between the sexes requires treating people like individuals and respecting the choices they make. And yes, that means women will be more likely to choose the role of homemaker than men. The logical fallacy of *begging the question* is when someone assumes the truth of a point that is under debate. There is a lot of diversity within the feminist community, but the purist adherents of the blank slate theory commit this fallacy. They argue that the point I just made—that we should respect the choices of individual women to work or stay home—is just a subtle way of using the truth-claim "women are natural homemakers" to socialize women into a domestic role. But that objection assumes that the blank slate theory is true. Instead, blank slate feminists want to socialize women as a class to achieve goals that are not always shared by individual women, including women who want to make the choice to be stay-at-home moms.

The blank slate vision is even more harmful when it comes to encouraging women to have sex like men. First, there is the fact that female choosiness means that most women prefer to have a sense of intimacy and connection with a man before they sleep with him. Secondly, promiscuous sex puts women at a much greater risk of sexual assault and rape. The standard of evidence in a criminal trial is reasonable doubt, and the difference between rape and consensual sex is whether or not the woman said "no" when she was alone with her rapist. That makes it hard to convict men of acquaintance rape, and many men realize that hookup culture gives them a free pass to prey on women.

Female Status Competitions

So far we've been guilty of a largely male-centered view of evolutionary psychology, but it turns out that females have their own brutal power struggles. This shouldn't come as a surprise to any woman who has survived adolescence. The zoologist Katherine Rolls points out that in many species—such as moon rats, jackrabbits, marmosets, and bats—females are larger than males. Sarah Blaffer Hrdy explains one such case in her book *Mother Nature*.

> Both fishermen and male fish seek out these "big mothers" – the former for their cachet, the latter for their greater fecundity. Depending on the species, big mothers produce bigger babies, deliver larger

quantities of rich milk quickly (as whales do), outcompete smaller females so as to monopolize resources available in their group, or, as spotted hyena females must do, not only defend their place in the chow line but also defend their infants from carnivorous and extremely cannibalistic group mates.[195]

It is with the social species that the quest for alpha female status really takes off. One of the dilemmas that every woman faces is how to choose between the career path and the motherhood path. Many women think that this is a modern dilemma created by rising technology and progressive social values. However, Hrdy's research shows us that it is ancient. The choice is really between two different strategies for raising children. The motherhood path is hands-on, but the career path goes for wealth and social status. This wealth and status can then be cashed in for food and "day care" for her children.

Females even have a rational reason to commit infanticide. In some cases, it means that females will kill the children of a rival. With less competition, their own children will get a larger share of the group's food. This explains why female chimpanzees are typically reluctant to hand their babies over to other adult females—they might not get their baby back alive. It also explains why human babies get stranger anxiety. It is a defense mechanism that gives the mother a face-saving justification to avoid handing her baby over to a stranger.

Even more radically, mothers have a rational reason to kill their own children. As economists put it, "sunk costs are sunk." Females should stop putting time and energy into a bad investment. Instead, they should kill their own baby so they can move on. Hrdy explains.

> At first, it seems counterintuitive that any female would ever produce fewer offspring than she is capable of, much less terminate investment in a fetus or an infant in whom she has already invested so much. But the art of iteroparity (or, breeding more than once over a lifetime)

involves knowing when to cut your losses and weather poor conditions, the sooner to breed again under better ones.

… For such creatures, survival of at least some young requires reproductive discretion. This is why being pro-life means being pro-choice.[196]

I understand Hrdy's evolutionary logic, but the most common reason humans commit infanticide is to get rid of unwanted girls. The historian JC Russell has documented that the sex ratio in ancient Italy was 140 males to 100 females.[197] Jack Lindsay studied inscriptions at Delphi and out of 600 families, only 6 raised more than one girl.[198] Female infanticide was staggeringly widespread until the rise of Christianity, at which point it became illegal. Even in modern times, selective abortion to kill unwanted girls has been common in China and elsewhere in the developing world.

The secular historian Tom Holland points out in *Dominion* that during the Roman Empire, two groups of people were rescuing infant girls left to die of exposure at refuse heaps. The first group was brothel owners who would turn them into prostitutes when they got older. The second group was Christians. The historian Will Durant writes that "in many instances Christians rescued exposed infants, baptized them, and brought them up with the aid of community funds."[199]

One of the most important of these early Christians was Macrina the Younger, who was later sainted by the Catholic Church. She was a remarkable woman in many ways, only one of which was that she took the babies that were left to die at the refuse heaps and raised them as her own.[200] It's worth noting for both feminist and conservative readers that Macrina was once engaged, but her fiancé died before the wedding. Even though she was from a wealthy family, Macrina chose to become a nun and lived the rest of her life as a single mother to her adopted children, with Jesus as her bridegroom.

Monogamy and the Mixed Strategy

Baby deer can walk within minutes of birth, but baby birds are not so lucky. They cannot fly and are stuck in the nest dependent on others for food and protection. This helplessness explains why birds are the champions of monogamy. If a baby is a little helpless then it may need its mother. But if a baby is truly helpless, then it will need both parents. The mated pair can take turns looking for food while the other protects the nest. With just the mother herself, she'd have to choose between leaving her babies unguarded and not being able to feed them. That's why David Lack has found that birds are the champions of monogamy, with 92 percent of bird species being monogamous.[201] Humans also have unusually helpless children, which is why there is a monogamous side to human nature.

Monogamy is a contract in which the male promises to help raise the children, and the female promises to be faithful. And that brings up our old friend, the free rider problem. How can the male and female birds trust each other? The evolutionary biologist Robert Trivers found that the most successful tactic is to use a *mixed strategy* between monogamy and polygamy. Males should form a monogamous commitment to a female, procreate with her, and spend at least some time and energy into raising their offspring. However, when he is away from his family, he should try to procreate with other females. Sure, the time he is looking for other females is time he is not spending feeding his children, but this will maximize his reproductive success. What he loses by having less well-fed children, he gains by having more offspring. Many human females have come to the sad realization that the male in her life is doing essentially the same thing.

The mixed strategy for females is to choose the best mate that she can, but to keep her eyes open for a roaming alpha male with better genes. If she gets the chance she should procreate with him. Her mate will then invest his time raising another male's children. As a general rule, males cheat to increase the *quantity* of their offspring, and females cheat to increase the *quality* of their offspring.

So how do females choose a male with good genes? Once again, we run into an economic problem. Males have private information about their genetic quality that females lack. So how do males with good genes communicate their status to females? With signals. There are a few different types of signals. The first is that females prefer males who have the most highly developed secondary sexual characteristics—traits that males develop at puberty. In humans that would be large size, big muscles, a square jaw, and a deep voice. Among barn swallows that means long, deeply forked tales. Barn swallows are like peacocks in that males develop large tales as a signal of their genetic quality.

Symmetry is another signal. The left and right sides of animals should in theory be perfectly symmetrical. However, in practice there are slight differences between them. Disease, malnutrition, and toxins can interfere with growth and development, and that will usually result in one side developing differently than the other. The healthiest animals will be the most symmetric. Female barn swallows don't just prefer males with long, deeply forked tails. They also prefer males whose left and right tail forks are of equal length.[202] Humans are similar. A study of 200 college students found that men who were rated as being more symmetrical were more likely to cheat on their romantic partners, even after controlling for other factors such as socioeconomic status.[203]

In most animals it's the males who are the beautiful ones, and the females have drab colorings designed for camouflage. Humans are a striking exception to this pattern. One of the more controversial insights of evolutionary psychology is that beauty is a signal of a woman's health and fertility. It is how women share their private information with potential suitors. In a famous study, Devendra Singh found that women with a waist-to-hip ratio of about 0.7 were considered more attractive, and that this was also a reliable indicator of a woman's youth, health, and fertility.[204] What's interesting is that we see the same ratio of 0.7 going back to the 1950s when curvier women like Marilyn Monroe were more popular. This is not a grand unified theory of female signaling, but it is striking how consistent the 0.7 ratio is across a wide variety of body types.

Female beauty is also based on differentiating feminine traits from masculine traits. Women have longer legs relative to their height than men, so women often wear high-waisted pants and skirts to create the illusion of legs that are even longer. The use of makeup to accentuate high cheekbones and full lips is similar, because women have higher cheekbones and fuller lips than men. Men use the same strategies, such as wearing baggy clothing to make their upper bodies look bigger and growing beards to accentuate a distinctly masculine feature.

Cads and Dads

The alpha male is the animal with the best genes, but all is not lost for the beta males in a monogamous species. David Barash explains in *The Myth of Monogamy*.

> Female barn swallows, for instance, have an opportunity to assess the quality of a male's future parenting: by the type of nest he has built. In this species, nest-building occurs after mating. It appears that effort expended in nest-building serves as a "post-mating male sexual display," whereby males indicate to females that they are ready and willing to invest in reproduction. It turns out that female barn swallows actually invest more in reproduction when their mates have constructed a large nest.[205]

In human terms, there are cads and dads. The cads are the alpha male barn swallows. In biological terms, cads follow an *r-selected* strategy. That means they invest their time and energy into procreating with as many females as possible. The cads choose quantity over quality. They have a lot of children but don't do much for them. The dads are the beta male barn swallows. Biologists would say that dads follow a *k-selected* strategy. That means they invest heavily into the relatively small number of children they have with their partner. The dads choose quality over quantity.

Female barn swallows hope to partner with an alpha male who has a long, deeply forked tail, but they will remain faithful to a beta male who builds a big nest. What they lose in genetic quality they make up with healthy, well-fed children. What they don't want is a beta male who thinks he's an alpha but isn't a good provider. That's when they cheat with a real alpha. If she can't get a good provider, then she will at least get good genes.

Building a healthy civilization requires socializing men to be dads instead of cads, even if the man is high in status and could take the cad path if he wanted to. There are many harmful downstream consequences of a society of cads neglecting their children while chasing every woman in sight. To paraphrase Edmund Burke: "It is ordained in the eternal constitution of things that an r-selected people cannot be free. Their passions forge their fetters."

Humans are a social species, so succeeding in the cad path takes more than being six feet tall and having a jawline that can cut glass. Several generations of young men have come to learn the hard way that kindness and empathy do not get them very far in the bars and clubs. They had to develop an edge to succeed in the modern sexual marketplace. Psychologists have a name for this edge: the *dark triad*. It consists of three negative personality traits called narcissism,

Machiavellianism, and psychopathy (sometimes they add sadism to create the dart tetrad). There is a large body of research showing that dark triad traits are negatively correlated to both *cognitive empathy* (the ability to understand another's perspective) and *affective empathy* (the ability to share in another's emotions).[206]

It shouldn't come as a surprise that research by Peter Jonason and colleagues shows that dark triad men do better when it comes to short term hookups and dating.[207] That's because it hurts to be rejected by a woman, particularly for empathetic men. Empathy allows men to see and feel their own lack of desirability from the woman's perspective. Dark triad traits like narcissism give men a sense of grandiose self-importance, and make them feel that other people, particularly women, are inferior and are only valued for instrumental purposes. In other words, dark triad men see women as objects. That prevents them from getting hurt and gives them the right attitude to be playful and aggressive in the bars and clubs. But that only prepares them for the game. Playing it takes something else.

If you've made that initial connection with someone from the opposite sex, then you've felt the excitement and energy flowing back and forth between the two of you. Most people can't fake that energy, but dark triad men can. They can make a woman feel special even if they are inwardly bored. They do this by mustering energy and affect to invest in the conversation, feigned displays of empathy and mirroring, pretending to have shared values and opinions, a push-pull of banter and flattery, and strategically overselling themselves, but framing it as self-deprecation.

Ordinary people can't fake these behaviors, but many of them happen spontaneously when they feel a genuine connection. Dark triads are mimics, and they use this ability to worm their way into the affections of others. However, ordinary people catch on to the phoniness of dark triads sooner or later. In *Persuasion,* Anne Eliott, the most perceptive of Jane Austen's heroines, decided not to accept her cousin's attentions because she never saw anything spontaneous or genuine beneath his perfectly polished manners.[208] It made her suspicious.

Most people take a lot longer to penetrate the surface of dark triad individuals than Anne, but once they do, it's like a switch flipped. It's not just that the charm no longer works, but that it seems fake and triggers a sense of disgust and revulsion. You want to get away from the same person who once charmed you. The mimicry of dark triad individuals is an advantage in the short term, but the honesty of ordinary people is an advantage in the long term.

Ordinary people struggle to fake what they don't feel, which makes them easier to trust. The movie *Kissing Jessica Stein* was largely forgettable, but it had one scene that stuck with me. The protagonist was in a lesbian relationship, but she was not out of the closet to her family. She kept making excuses to her girlfriend about why she wasn't invited to her brother's wedding. Eventually her girlfriend got fed up with the transparent excuses and said, "Stop saying that. You're a terrible liar. It's one of your best qualities."[209]

The strategies of dark triad men inspire the vision that *red pilled* conservatives have internalized. The term red pill comes from the movie *The Matrix*. In the movie, the hero had the choice of taking a red pill or a blue pill. The red pill represents ugly truths, and the blue pill represents comforting myths. In the context of sexual politics, the ugly truth of the red pill is that women don't want kind and empathetic men. They are the men that she puts into her "friendzone." What women really want is a high-status alpha male who is muscular and domineering, even if he is an aggressive jerk.

The red pill vision is more or less correct when it comes to the bars and clubs. However, dark triad behavior is counterproductive in the long run. Jonason's research also shows that dark triad men do *worse* in long-term relationships.[210] That should not be a surprise at this point in the book. Real cooperation requires empathy and self-sacrifice, not narcissism, fake charm, and control. The only way to build a healthy and lasting relationship is by deescalating the unspoken power struggle between men and women. I realize research studies may not convince red-pilled readers, so I'll try two more times, once with pop culture and again with the Bible.

I'm not a big *Star Wars* fan but there is one scene that has become a favorite. It happened when Luke was training under Yoda, and he came across a cave that radiated evil from the Dark Side of the Force. Yoda told him he must go into the cave. When Luke asked what was in it, Yoda said, "Only what you take with you." As Luke walked towards the cave, he strapped on his trusty lightsaber and blaster. Yoda told him, "Your weapons—you will not need them."[211] But Luke ignored Yoda's advice and took his weapons anyway. It seemed like the right decision because in the cave he came across a vision of Darth Vader. Luke won the battle and beheaded his enemy, but then Vader's mask disappeared to reveal Luke's own face inside the helmet.

The scene is rich in symbolism and draws on a long literary tradition from Orpheus's journey to the underworld to Boromir's corruption by the One Ring in *The Fellowship of the Ring*. Our fears and insecurities become the source of our own downfall. Luke was afraid of Darth Vader and that led to his symbolic death. I sometimes wonder what would have happened if Luke didn't feel the need to bring his lightsaber. My guess is that Luke would have met a redeemed vision of his father, which would have shown him his future destiny (oops, spoiler warning). The key to healthy relationships is taking Yoda's advice and leaving your weapons behind.

Jesus told his followers, "Enter through the narrow gate. For wide is the gate and broad is the road that leads to destruction, and many enter through it. But small is the gate and narrow the road that leads to life, and only a few find it." (Matthew 7:13-14). The wide gate is when you bring your weapons into your relationships. In that case the red pill can teach you the strategies to gain power and claw your way up the hierarchy—but it will ultimately destroy your relationships, and your own heart along with it. The narrow gate is when you leave your weapons behind and choose love, empathy, and kindness. It can be scary to walk into an unknown cave without any weapons, but that's the secret to healthy relationships.

A textbook prediction from evolutionary psychology is that the dark triad personality traits will increase as society becomes more tolerant of premarital sex. More men will take the cad path, and women will have to match them as the arms race escalates and the game playing becomes both more subtle and more vicious. That is exactly what we have seen. Jean Twenge and colleagues reviewed eighty-five different surveys of college students who took the Narcissistic Personality Inventory, and they have documented a consistent trend of increasing narcissism since 1979.[212]

There is a conflict at the heart of the liberal worldview. One liberal goal is to increase human freedom by allowing people to have promiscuous sex without shame or financial hardship. Another liberal goal is to minimize or even eliminate personality differences between men and women. These two goals work against each other. No one on Tinder cares how many flowers grow in your heart. They only care if you're smoking hot and know how to play the game. This drives men to become as masculine as possible and women to become as feminine as possible.

The *egalitarian gender paradox* is the well-documented phenomenon in which there are bigger personality differences between men and women in egalitarian nations like Sweden than in developing nations like Rwanda.[213] I suspect the modern sexual marketplace influences this. Men and women are both playing the same game, but in highly gendered ways.

Multilevel Selection

In popular imagination we think of nature as "red in tooth and claw." The strong survive and the weak die. Historically, biologists have rejected this brutal vision. They mistakenly believed that evolution worked for the good of the group. Good groups help each other out and consequently prosper. Bad groups that cannot cooperate wither and die. The downfall of this benign view of evolution came in 1962 when V.C. Wynn-Edwards attempted to show the precise mechanisms by which self-sacrificing behavior benefited the group.[214] However, by trying to explain these mechanisms, he only succeeded in making it clear that evolution for the good of the group was unworkable.

George Williams realized the fatal flaw, which is our old friend the free rider problem. This is yet another of the many parallels between economics and evolution. Suppose a group of deer are facing a tough winter, and there isn't much foliage left to eat. Then they are, literally, in a tragedy of the commons. They can cooperate (eat a bit less) or defect (eat as much as they can). It is in their collective self-interest to reduce their food intake to ration the scarce supply of food, but it is in the self-interest of each individual deer to eat as much as possible. After the winter ends the altruistic deer would be weak and scrawny, but the free riding deer would be strong and fit. If they are male, they would win the battles for females and have more offspring. If they are female, they would have healthier children. This process would continue until there are no altruistic deer left. Altruistic genes would be relentlessly weeded out of the population.

Williams's response was so devastating that it was almost laughable to argue for group selection. Raghavendra Gagagkar tells a revealing story about this. John Maynard Smith, who was another leading critic of group selection, was giving a lecture at a conference when he was interrupted by the loud buzzing of cicadas. "Nonplussed, Maynard Smith said, 'If Wynne-Edwards were here he would surely have argued that the cicadas are singing in unison so as to assess their population density and adjust the rate of reproduction so that they do not overexploit the habitat and eventually drive their species to extinction.'"[215] The audience laughed. Evolution for the good of the group had become a joke.

The evolutionary biologist D.S. Wilson championed a new theory of *multilevel selection* against both ridicule and settled science. Wilson explains how it works with a colorful parable. Imagine a bunch of castaways stuck on an island. Some of the castaways are evil, and some of them are good. What do you think would happen? The good castaways would be shark food. The evil castaways would kill or exploit them for personal gain. Competition at the level of individuals favors selfish free riders. Now suppose that there are two islands. The people on the first island are all good, and the people on the second island are all evil. Now what do you think would happen? The good island would cooperate and prosper, and the evil island would collapse. Competition at the level of groups favors moral behavior.

Now, let's extend our thinking just a little bit more. Suppose that we have an archipelago with many islands. Some islands are mostly good, and other islands are mostly bad. Now what happens? The islands with mostly good members will grow and thrive, even to the point of colonizing other islands. Islands with many evil members will wither and die. However, within each island we expect the number of evil members to increase as they kill and exploit the good members. At the group level, evolution is eliminating evil genes from the population. But at the individual level, evolution is eliminating the good genes. Since both levels of selection are at work, there will always be a mix of good and evil.

I've framed evolution at the level of the group as being the good side of evolution, but that isn't quite true. Steven Pinker explains.

> Group selection, in any case, does not deserve its feel good reputation. Whether or not it endowed us with generosity towards the members of our group, it would certainly have endowed us with a hatred of the members of other groups, because it favors whatever traits lead one group to prevail over its rivals. (Recall that group selection was the version of Darwinism that got twisted into Nazism.) ... As Williams put it, "To claim that [group selection] is morally superior to natural selection at the level of competing individuals would imply, in its human application, that systemic genocide is morally superior to random murder."[216]

Evolution at the level of the group explains why humans are naturally tribal. It explains why we divide people into those who are "Like Us" and "The Other." It explains our instincts towards bigotry and racism. It even explains why politics can get so ugly, and why we dehumanize people with different beliefs.

A running debate in anthropology and philosophy was about the essential nature of mankind. Jean-Jacques Rousseau championed the theory of the *noble savage*—the idea that primitive people are naturally peaceful and live in harmony with the land and each other. Lawrence Keeley shattered the myth of the noble savage with his book *War Before Civilization*. He found that primitive societies are extremely warlike, much more so than civilized governments. They lose about 0.5 percent of their population to combat each year, or 5 percent per decade, or 25 percent of the population every fifty years.[217]

Primitive tribes also commit acts of genocide. One tactic of the Maring of New Guinea was to surround an enemy village at night and set fire to the huts. The warriors then kill the men who try to escape.[218] Keeley highlights the brutality of primitive warfare with the story of a Māori chief who taunted the preserved head of a defeated enemy.

> You wanted to run away, did you? But my war club overtook you: and after you were cooked, you made food for my mouth. And where is your father? He is cooked:- and where is your brother? He is eaten:- and where is your wife? There she sits, a wife for me - and where are your children? There they are, with loads on their backs, carrying food, as my slaves.[219]

When anthropologists ask people in primitive societies why they fight, their answers are blunt and honest. They fight for women, revenge, cattle, honor, and land. Keeley points out that these societies frequently abduct women from neighboring tribes.[220] We also find evidence for fighting over women in pre-historic hunter-gatherers. Archeologists uncovered the bones of about 500 people killed in the Crow Creek massacre, but there were no female skeletons in the age range of 12 to 19. The young women had been taken captive by the raiders. The massacre was dated to 1325 AD, so it happened 175 years before Columbus discovered America. Rousseau felt that the original sin of humanity was private property, but evolution teaches that it's primarily sexual competition.

To get an idea of the omnipresent threat of violence, the anthropologist Napoleon Chagnon explains in his book *Noble Savages* that he was almost killed by the Yanomamö the first time he encountered them. Not because they randomly killed strangers, but because seven women had been abducted by a neighboring group the night before. The men had chased after them and fought a nighttime battle with heavy clubs. They were able to get five of the women back, but their enemies promised to return with bows and kill them all the next day.[221] The tribesmen thought he was a member of the neighboring group making good on this threat.

Primitive tribes can be cruel even when there is no rational reason. Robert Edgerton describes some of these cases in *Sick Societies*. Yanomamö women who become pregnant are prohibited from having sex with their husbands until their child is weaned, which means that many Yanomamö men simply kill their own children in order to resume having sex. Some Innuits teach their children to torture small animals and birds to death and mock mortally wounded animals. That's a stark contrast from the movies where we see primitive hunters solemnly thanking animals for their meat. The Mbuti, who rely on dogs for hunting, "kicked them mercilessly from the day they are born to the day they die."[222]

I've been underselling the violence of primitive life. Chagnon explains that Yanomamö women have bodies covered with scars from their frequent beatings by their husbands. They are beaten with clubs, shot with arrows, wounded with axes and machetes, and have burning firewood held against their bodies, all by their husbands.[223] About 20 percent of women are abducted, and when that happens, they are repeatedly gang raped by the men in the abducting tribe for days until conflicts between the men starts to flare up. At that point the headman gives her to one of his younger relatives as a wife.[224]

The Yanomamö sex ratio is about 135 males to 100 females despite the fact that many men die from warfare.[225] So why is the sex ratio so heavily skewed towards males? Because of infanticide. There are many reasons why the Yanomamö practice infanticide, such as a baby being born with a deformity, or too soon after another baby that is still nursing—the mother doesn't have enough milk for them both. But factors like this don't explain the sex ratio. The most important clue is that among the Yanomamö, infanticide is practiced by women. Chagnon is a scientist who's not going to speculate ahead of the evidence, but as a reader I felt like he was leading me to this conclusion: The women were killing their own daughters out of mercy. They felt that the life of a Yanomamö woman was a fate worse than death.

I don't understand how this is allowed to happen. The Yanomamö women are full citizens of Argentina and Brazil. They have rights. Their governments know how they are treated. I can't understand why their governments don't send a special police detachment to protect these women from rape, abduction, and torture. Are we so far lost in moral relativism that we don't understand that Yanomamö women are human beings who have rights?

Superorganisms

In humans there is a constant struggle between the group level of selection and the individual level. But some animals have solved that problem completely. Biologists call them a *eusocial* species, but I prefer Bert Hölldobler and Edward O. Wilson's more colorful name: a *superorganism*. That's because the entire group acts like a single organism with a unified purpose. There are not many superorganisms in nature, and with the exceptions a few species like the snapping shrimp, the naked mole-rat, and its close cousin the Damaraland mole-rat, they are all insects.

What makes a superorganism tick? How do they get individuals to sacrifice for the good of the group? There are two main principles. The first is the existence of a *reproductive caste*. Only the queens and a limited number of males can reproduce. The workers are sterile. This is like the nuclear option for eliminating sexual competition. If only the queen can reproduce then the sterile workers really have no choice but to sacrifice for the greater good of the colony.

The second principle is *haplodiploidy*. That means females develop from fertilized eggs, but males develop from unfertilized eggs. So females have a pair of each type of chromosome, but males only have one of each. The workers in these colonies are female. They get all of their father's genes but only half of their mother's genes. This means that workers share 75 percent of their genes with their sisters, but only 50 percent of their genes with their mother.

There is a method to this madness: Workers have a stronger incentive to help the queen have more offspring than to try and have offspring themselves. If a worker somehow has a child through fertilization, she passes on 50 percent of her genes. If she helps her queen have a child, she passes on 75 percent of her genes. Even insects respond to incentives, and this channels the energies of workers to the good of the group.

The evolutionary theory of *kin selection* holds that animals will behave more and more altruistically towards relatives as they share more and more genes. Kin selection means that worker ants have stronger altruistic ties to each other than they do to their queen. If ants could write epic poetry, you would be able to read about the powerful bonds of love and sisterhood that tie the colony together. It is this sisterhood that makes ant colonies function like one cohesive whole, not the love that the queen has for her daughters. This literature would be filled with epic tales of ants who nobly died in battle so that their sisters could survive.

There is an interesting debate in evolutionary circles about which principle is the most important—haplodiploidy or a reproductive caste. My outsider's take is that the reproductive caste is more important for two reasons. The first is that naked mole-rats, Damaraland mole-rats, termites, and snapping shrimp are superorganisms that are not haplodiploid. But they do have a reproductive caste in that only the queen and a limited number of males can reproduce.[226] The second reason comes from research by Jacobus Boomsma. He shows that in order for an insect species to become a superorganism, it must go through a *monogamy window* in which the queen practices lifetime monogamy with a single male partner.[227] This suggests that eliminating sexual competition is the most important driver for becoming a superorganism.

Once an insect species goes through the monogamy window, the assumption of strict monogamy can be relaxed. In some superorganisms the queen may mate with multiple male drones, or there may be a colony with multiple queens working together. But the purest superorganisms do continue to practice lifetime monogamy. That's true for termites. For ants and bees, the male drones are generally breeders who donate sperm and die, but a male termite spends a lifetime with his queen, and they form a monogamous partnership.

Unfortunately, there is a moral problem with superorganisms—they are tyrannical and oppressive. They are the ultimate in top-down control. There will never be an ant who writes, "We hold these truths to be self-evident, that all women are created equal, that they are endowed by their Creator with certain inalienable Rights, that among these are Life, Liberty and the pursuit of Happiness." Ants will never have a "masculinist" movement designed to bring equality to male ants. Sometimes secular people base morality on the evolution of cooperation or on our moral intuitions, but if we were ants, we would unquestionably accept living in a caste system, inequality between the sexes, and being ruled by a queen. Ants would see both freedom and equality as threats to their cooperative hierarchy. Even Rousseau, with his "forced to be free" philosophy, would think ants are a bit too intense. At least, I hope he would.

Humans will never be a superorganism. We would need the strong, top-down control of a queen and a caste system for that. But a social norm of lifelong monogamy provides many of the same benefits in a freer and more equal way. Human cooperation happens through bottom-up processes like the nuclear family rather than the top-down control of a caste system. Without the nuclear family, men fight to claim more women, and the women scheme and plot to claim more of the group's food and resources for their own children. The nuclear family tames both of these effects.

The incentives created by promiscuous social norms mean that both men and women are socialized to become game playing and narcissistic. But female choosiness means that women demand monogamy if they have the power. There are two good lines of evidence for this. The first comes from comparing the gay and lesbian communities. The gay male community is extremely promiscuous. Even when two gay men fall in love, they often prefer being "monogamish," as the columnist and gay man Dan Savage put it. By contrast the lesbian community is inclined to monogamy. It seems hard to believe that a butch lesbian with a man's haircut and clothing is choosing monogamy because she's been brainwashed by the idea that good girls don't sleep around.

The second line of evidence comes from sex ratios on college campuses. Most colleges have more women than men. When that's the case, the men have the negotiating power because many women are seeking relationships from a small number of men. On these campuses, the men demand "situationships" where they get sex from their female partners but without commitment. The dynamic plays out differently on college campuses where there are more men than women. On those campuses, the women have the negotiating power, and they demand monogamy from their male partners.[228]

There is an important lesson here, which is that the root cause of single motherhood is found in the choices men make, not in the choices women make. If men can have sexual relationships with multiple women, most of them will take it. This arrangement is not what women want, but it's what men demand when they have the option. Single motherhood is a downstream consequence of male sexuality.

The idea that women prefer monogamy is common sense to everyone except liberal feminists and red-pilled conservatives. Most women do not go through a "ho phase." Instead, our promiscuous social norms hurt women in subtle ways. It has become table stakes for women to sleep with a man if they want a second or third date. Most women would prefer to wait until the relationship gets serious, but they can't because they don't want to lose him to a woman who won't wait. For men, particularly high-status men, this means they can juggle multiple women in casual but sexually active relationships. Meanwhile each woman he's with hopes that he'll take the relationship to the next level with her. For women, this means having a lot of transactional sex that falls somewhere in the gray area between "good" and "date rape". In *The Case Against the Sexual Revolution* Louise Perry writes:

> The liberal feminist narrative of sexual empowerment is popular for a reason: it is much more palatable to understand oneself as a sassy Carrie Bradshaw, making all the decisions and challenging the patriarchal status quo. Adopting such a self-image can be protective, making it easier to endure what is often, in fact, a rather miserable experience. If you're a young women launched into a sexual culture that is fundamentally not geared towards protecting your safety or wellbeing, in which you are considered valuable in only a narrow, physical sense, and if your only options seem to be either hooking up or strict celibacy, then a comforting myth of 'agency' can be attractive.[229]

The comedian Sinbad once joked that marriage is rare because it takes two people realizing at the same time that neither of them can do any better. That's exactly right, but it doesn't have to be so hard. In the old days, it was relatively easy. A woman was courted by many men, and she picked the man she felt the strongest connection with. The courtship process gave her real feedback on her true marriage market value. If a man felt like he was out of a woman's league, then he didn't court her. In *Pride and Prejudice* Miss Bingley may have wanted Mr. Darcy's attentions, but no matter how much she fawned over him, she never got them. Perhaps the single biggest benefit of lifelong monogamy is that it stops men from pursuing women who are lower than them in terms of social status.

A downstream consequence of sex before marriage is that modern women rarely get feedback on their real marriage market value. Because women are choosy and men are promiscuous, the outcome is that women who are a "6" or "7" will often find themselves in a casual relationship with a man who is a "9" or a "10." Of course, we don't walk around with numbers floating over our heads. If we did, it would make things a lot easier. A woman could just look up and see that she is a "6" and that the man who is hitting on her is a "9." At that point it would be obvious that he just wants sex.

Instead, women have to reason along these lines: "I think I'm above average? But it's not like I'm a model or anything." That covers a lot of ground and can easily lead women into overestimating their status. How is a woman supposed to know that she's really a "6" when men who are "9s" and "10s" make her feel special and beautiful? She may intellectually understand the nature of hookup culture, but it's very easy for her to be misled into thinking she is really a "7" or an "8".

Even when women do form committed relationships with men, they sometimes run into an even bigger problem. Suppose a woman started a relationship with a man she loved at age twenty-six. He said all the right things about wanting marriage and children someday, but the day never seemed to come. Finally, after five years or so of gradually escalating demands, the woman gave her boyfriend an ultimatum: marriage and children, or we're done. And the man shrugged and said that he's not ready for children yet. So the woman went back into the dating market, but at age thirty-one instead of twenty-six. Giving her youth to her boyfriend caused her more harm than simply sleeping with him.

Somewhere between long-term committed relationships and casual "situationships" lies yet another minefield: serial monogamy. Think back to Sinbad's observation that marriage requires two people both realizing at the same time that neither of them can do any better. Serial monogamy happens when one person realizes "yeah, but they're cute and make me laugh." Once the initial honeymoon period is over, the person who is lower in status is in for a miserable time. They are going to watch as their partner slowly slips away until they are finally dumped. Then they move onto the "hurt people hurt people" stage of their dating life, as they realize that their last relationship failed because they lost power relative to their partner, and they resolve not to let that happen again.

The Bonobo Defense

If monogamy is too difficult, then perhaps bonobos have the answer. They are the peaceful hippies of the great apes. Bonobos make love, not war. In fact, they literally use sex to resolve conflicts. So far we've been seeing sexual competition as the root cause of conflict, but in the case of bonobos, it's the solution. Frans de Waal gives an example of how this works in *Our Inner Ape*:

> One day, two adult males were introduced after a long separation. They both screamed and turned around each other for six minutes

without any physical contact. We feared a bloody confrontation (most animals fight when introduced to relative strangers of the same sex), but Kevin, the younger male, kept stretching out his hand, and flexing his fingers, as if beckoning Vernon to come closer. Occasionally, Kevin shook his hands impatiently. Both males had erections, which they presented to each other with legs apart, in the same way that a male invites a female for sex. It was as if each male wanted contact but did not know whether the other could be trusted. When they finally did rush towards each other, instead of fighting, they embraced frontally with broad grins on their faces, Vernon thrusting his genitals against Kevin's. They calmed down right away and happily began collecting the raisins[230]

This example is of males, but it is the female-female sex that really makes bonobo society tick. Female bonobos form very strong alliances with each other, reinforced with frequent genital rubbing. The result is that bonobos are a female-dominated society, one of the few such societies in the animal kingdom. That is even more surprising because male bonobos are about 15 percent larger than females and have sharp canine-like teeth. Individually, the male bonobos can dominate the females, but the females form stronger and more cohesive groups, which give them the power. Females use that power to control the food supply and male bonobos eat by begging from the females.

There aren't many female-dominated species, so it's worth taking a brief look at what makes bonobos tick. The starting point to understanding the bonobos is their solution to the problem of infanticide. It's in the interest of each individual male to kill the offspring of his rivals. That way the mothers of the dead infants will be ready to reproduce again sooner. In theory, that should lead to an arms race for alpha male status, but bonobo females have an excellent counter strategy: disguised fertility. The labia and clitoris of female bonobos regularly swell to the size of a small soccer ball. Female chimpanzees only have these swellings when they are fertile, but bonobo females have frequent fake swellings even when they are not fertile. These fake swellings, combined with the bonobo's promiscuous sexuality, disguise the paternity of bonobo infants. Male bonobos won't kill an infant that might be their own child.

Males don't fight because there are too many seemingly fertile females to control, but that does not mean that bonobos live as equals. Once again, we see the big mothers effect that Sarah Blaffer Hrdy described earlier in the chapter. The females form a hierarchy with an alpha at the top. Alpha females have two important but ugly strategies which benefit themselves at the expense of the group. The first is securing a larger share of the group's food supply for her offspring. The second tactic is to use their social status to enhance the reproductive success of their sons. Bonobo females form lifelong attachment to their sons, and these males derive much of their social rank through their mothers. The sons of high-ranking females get more food and more sexual access to females than the sons of low-ranking females. Bonobos still have a hierarchy, but it's different from chimpanzees and most other animals.

Chimpanzees have a more typical hierarchy. Chimpanzee males fight and the strongest becomes the alpha. However, chimps are a socially adept species, so reaching alpha status usually requires forming an alliance with another powerful male, who becomes the lieutenant. In *Our Inner Ape*, de Waal tells the poignant story of Luit, who was an effective and even empathetic leader, who was ultimately killed by two rivals who formed an alliance against him. Male dominated hierarchies are aggressive and based on fighting. The female-dominated hierarchies of bonobos are softer but just as real.

The animal that we should look to is not bonobos, but wolves. The term "alpha" was coined by studying the dominance hierarchies of wolf packs. But in a seminal paper called *Alpha status, dominance, and division of labor in wolf packs,* the biologist David Mech, whose earlier research gave rise to the alpha myth, showed that wolves only form hierarchies in captivity. In the wild, wolves do not have alphas. How is that possible? What is the secret to their equality? The answer is the nuclear family.

Wolves in the wild form lifelong monogamous bonds and live with their children like a suburban nuclear family. There are no rival males in the pack, only family members. The parents tend to be the leaders, and they will use acts of dominance against their older children, but only to make sure that younger children get their share of the food. (Every human parent of two or more children can relate.) Eventually the older children leave the family to form their own monogamous union, and the younger children step up. Wolves teach us the importance of the nuclear family. Hrdy explains.

> Sociobiology is not a field known for the encouraging news it offers either sex. Yet its most promising revelation to date has to be that over evolutionary time, lifelong monogamy turns out to be the cure for all sorts of detrimental devices that one sex uses to exploit the other.[231]

Bonobos have more sexual liberty, but wolves have more freedom to make their own lives on their own terms. Bonobos are not nearly as socially aggressive as chimpanzees, so overt fighting is rare. But they do have a hierarchy and it works exactly the same way as hierarchies in other animals: females compete for food and males compete for females. In *Bonobos: The Forgotten Ape*, Franz de Waal points out that high ranking females will claim prized foods like fruit and meat from lower ranking members,[232] and the top two ranking males usually team up to suppress the reproductive opportunity of lower ranking males.[233] The low-ranking males do manage to sneak off with females sometimes, but the top two males claim the lion's share of reproductive opportunity.

The nuclear families formed by wolves have three advantages over the hippie communes formed by bonobos. First, it eliminates female conflict to monopolize the group's supply of high-value foods. Second, it eliminates male conflict to monopolize females. Third, it promotes male investment into children.

Bonobos solved the problem of males committing infanticide with disguised paternity. Male bonobos don't kill infants because they don't know whether or not they are the father. But they also don't invest into providing food for children for the exact same reason. In order for males to be involved fathers, they have to be certain about paternity. Monogamy channels male energy away from sexual competition and into their children.[234] The dad path versus the cad path. Bonobos take the cad path; wolves take the dad path.

Liberals pride themselves on being opposed to hierarchy, but in fact the opposite is true. There are two main engines of hierarchy: communal living and promiscuity. Communal living results in the big mothers effect where females scheme for status and rank to funnel more of the group's resources to their own children. And promiscuity results in males fighting for status and rank to gain access to females. Wolves solved both of these problems with the nuclear family.

Wolves have one final advantage over bonobos: love. Birds are the champions of monogamy, but most birds practice serial monogamy. They partner up, raise a nest of hatchlings, and then go their separate ways and repeat the cycle with a different partner the following year. Only a few animal species actually mate for life. They include wolves and beavers along with several bird species such as swans and turtle doves. Humans are lucky to be one of these rare species.

The Philosophy (and Abuse) of Science

> Extinguished theologians lie about the cradle of every science as the strangled snakes beside that of Hercules.
>
> – Thomas Huxley, *Lay Sermons, Addresses, And Reviews*

I didn't want to get too philosophical in this book, but we have to do something about the phrase, "The science is settled."

The Philosophy of Science

Rationalism. Let's start with the ancient Greeks. They were an impressive civilization whose advances in mathematics, philosophy, and the arts remain relevant today. Greek science was also wildly successful, but it has not passed the test of time. That's because the ancient Greeks were hobbled by a philosophy called *rationalism*. That meant that they used the same technique for science that they used for mathematics: Start with self-evident principles and then make deductions from those principles.

A good example is Aristotle's theory that everything has a natural place, and that the Earth's natural place is the center of the universe. It's self-evidently true that earth is heavier than water. If you throw a stone or a clump of dirt into a lake, it will sink to the bottom. From this principle, Aristotle was able to deduce that the Earth would continue to "sink" until it reached a point where it couldn't sink any further—the center of the universe. That was the Earth's natural place. Clearly the rationalist approach is not very good when it comes to science.

Inductivism. The single most important event in the philosophy of science was realizing that the ancient Greeks got it backwards. We need to make observations first and create theories second. This led to the philosophy of *inductivism*. The idea is that scientists gather more and more facts about the world. For example, they may encounter a group of swans and notice that they are all white. Then they would make some generalizations about them, like "all swans are white." But inductivism has two major problems. The first is that it doesn't do a good job when a theory is *underdetermined*. That means that multiple theories can agree with the facts. Take the Sun-centered and Earth-centered models of the solar system. They both made accurate predictions about the position of the planets in the night sky. So how do we know which theory is right?

The second problem with inductivism is that it's based on the assumption of *uniformity*—that the world worked the same way yesterday as it does today, and that it will work the same way tomorrow. Uniformity has a few issues but arguably the biggest is the *black swan problem*. That means that sometimes rare events do happen. Bertrand Russell had a great example: the chicken happily awaits the farmer who feeds it until that one fateful day when he wrings its neck and cooks it for dinner.

Falsification. The philosopher Karl Popper solved both of these issues with his philosophy of *falsification*. His main insight is that all ideas are subject to criticism, regardless of how well established they are, and how much scientific consensus they have. It doesn't matter how many white swans scientists find—they can never prove that all swans are white. However, finding a single black swan would be enough to falsify the theory.

Falsification also helps when there are two underdetermined theories. Suppose one theory says that white feathers help swans stay cool in the summer, and another theory says that they are for camouflage—the white feathers blend in on large lakes where the sun reflects off the water. Scientists might falsify the first theory by looking for swans that live further north where it's colder. And they might falsify the second theory by looking for swans that evolved to live in marshes and bogs with dense foliage. In these cases, swans would want to blend in with the foliage, not the open water.

Popper realized that this meant taking a step back towards how the ancient Greeks did science. Scientists should go back to their theory and make deductions that could then be tested with new observations. Popper's key insight was not falsification *per se*, but the importance of making risky predictions that could be easily falsified. These risky predictions tell scientists where to look for more evidence. If they just kept hanging out at the same lake where they saw their first white swan, they'd never falsify either theory.

One of Popper's main goals was to separate science from pseudo-science: Science can be falsified but pseudo-science cannot. Some examples of pseudo-science are astrology, the Marxist theory of history, and the idea that anyone who identifies as a woman is a woman. Falsification seems like an ideal way to do this, but it runs into two problems. The first is that it is too strong. Falsification rules out other types of knowledge like most of philosophy, culture, acquired skills, and even simple things like using your senses to navigate and understand the world. The second problem is that falsification is self-refuting. How do we falsify the principle of falsification? We can't. Falsification collapses, and astrology seems to be back on the same level as real science.

The term pseudo-science seems to mean "worthless junk." If so, we can rescue falsification by upgrading pseudo-science to "maybe worthless, maybe not." Some pseudo-science like falsification, philosophy, and cultural traditions can be used to seek the truth, but others like astrology cannot. But now we've just kicked the can down the road. How do we separate good pseudo-science from bad pseudo-science? There is no easy answer, so we'll let go of Popper's project and shift the focus back to science again.

Engineers are lucky because the difference between success and failure is clear. Either the airplane flies or it doesn't. A longstanding quest in the philosophy of science is to create a test like "does the airplane fly?" for scientific theories. Then we wouldn't need to make judgment calls between two rival theories. It would also mean that no one could claim that the science was settled unless the science really was settled. Falsification seemed to do that.

Lee Smolin provides a great example in *The Trouble with Physics*. Physicists are always on the hunt for a grand unified theory that can unify several different forces. The theory of symmetry, which is called SU(5), managed to unify the strong and weak nuclear forces with electromagnetism. It was a simple and beautiful theory that also had the virtue of making a novel prediction that protons would decay. So scientists filled an underground tank with ultrapure water and waited to see if a proton would spontaneously decay. But it never happened. Eventually scientists had to accept that the theory was wrong. Smolin's friend said "SU(5) was such a beautiful theory, everything fit into it perfectly—then it turned out not to be true."[235]

Social status. Stories like this are often used to valorize scientists as noble and disinterested searchers for the truth, willing to abandon a lifetime of work if that's where the evidence leads. In reality scientists are just as biased and status-seeking as the rest of us. Maybe more so. The golfer Jack Nicklaus once said that every great athlete has a mean streak. I think that's true of everyone who has fought their way to the top in a highly competitive profession. Whenever two scientists discover things at roughly the same time there is almost inevitably a battle for recognition. Isaac Newton was an all-time great scientist, so you might think that he wouldn't need to worry about his legacy. And yet he fought battles with Robert Hooke over the inverse square law of gravity, and with Gottfried Leibnitz over calculus.

The book and movie *And the Band Played On* were about the early years of the AIDS virus. Much of the plot was driven by the American scientist Robert Gallo trying to steal credit for discovering the HIV virus away from the French team led by Luc Montagnier. Gallo denied the accuracy of his portrayal, but in 2008 Montagnier and his colleague Françoise Barré-Sinoussi were awarded the Nobel Prize in Medicine for discovering the HIV virus. Gallo was conspicuously left out.

If scientists fight battles over recognition for discoveries, then they fight scorched earth warfare over whose theory is right. No scientist wants to see their legacy crumble because their life's work proved to be wrong. In fact, Smolin's book is an argument that string theory is a failed theory zealously protected by a powerful group of physicists. There's a quote that is usually attributed to Max Planck that goes, "A new scientific truth does not triumph by convincing its opponents and making them see the light, but rather because its opponents eventually die, and a new generation grows up that is familiar with it." This is sometimes shortened to "science advances one funeral at a time." Take the origins of the coronavirus. There are a lot of people who are going to spend the rest of their lives defending a belief they chose for political purposes in March of 2020. (I've flip-flopped on it twice.[236])

Models are useful. The pursuit of social status infects everything it touches, but even if we lived in a humbler world, falsification does not work. George Box said it best: "All models are wrong, but some are useful." Until scientists are ready to close the book and proclaim that they have the final and ultimate theory of everything, all theories are going to be at least a little bit wrong, which means that all theories can be falsified. The best we can do is to find theories that are useful, such as by making predictions of the position of the planets in the night sky.

This may or may not send you down the *anti-realism* rabbit hole. Anti-realism basically follows from Box's insight—that our theories are useful, but they aren't true, and they don't tell us about the nature of reality. If you can't wrap your head around how theories can make accurate predictions without describing reality, then realize that every theory that has been relegated to the dustbin of history once made accurate predictions. Sure, those old theories were eventually falsified, but the theories we have now will probably be falsified someday too.

Anti-realists have a deeper motivation for their skepticism. Some philosophers, going all the way back to Plato, have sat down in their armchairs and thought deep thoughts which they felt revealed a hidden world that transcended the real world that we can see and touch. Anti-realists are hard-headed skeptics who wanted to destroy these hidden worlds. The main weapon they used was evidence—that all beliefs have to meet strict standards of evidence to be rational.

Plato had no evidence for his signature ideas like the theory of forms, so Plato's ideas fell beneath their skepticism. Anti-realists felt the power of their new weapon and began to wield it more ferociously. The idea that science can reveal hidden truths about the universe became one of their new victims. The anti-realists were staunch supporters of science, but they followed along with Box's slogan that "all models are wrong, but some are useful." In their view, science cannot cross the bridge from useful to true.

This was an ironic turn of events. The postmodernists are fuzzy-headed English majors, and the anti-realists are hard-headed skeptics, and yet they both ended up at the exact same place: that science is useful, but it can't tell us about the truth. That means anti-realism is false for the same reason postmodernism is false: It is self-refuting. Both philosophies hold that the truth is unknowable, but that is itself a statement of truth. By its own standard, the truth of anti-realism is unknowable. Anyone who believed in anti-realism would be irrational for doing so. So the anti-realists went back to the drawing board and tried to soften their philosophy while preserving its core values, and the debate continued.

Fallibilism. I'm not an anti-realist, but I am struck by two mildly skeptical principles. The first is that scientists will probably create many new theories in the future, which means that many of the theories we believe today are going to be overturned. SU(5) was a bust, but I suspect physicists will get their grand unified theory someday, and when they do, the standard model of quantum mechanics will be replaced. This leads to the philosophy of *fallibilism*—that even the most secure beliefs might be wrong. I think fallibilism is obviously true, and it is the consensus belief of scientists, but it could be proven wrong someday.

The second skeptical observation is that science doesn't work by gradually homing in on the truth, but by paradigm shifts—scientific revolutions that radically change our understanding of the universe. Einstein's theory of relativity is a textbook example. I'm going to lump both special and general relativity together, but here is a quick hit list of a few things that were changed: that space and time are woven together into the fabric of spacetime; that gravity is not a traditional force like magnetism but rather curvature in the fabric of spacetime; that matter can be converted into energy which is the source of nuclear power; that the speed of light is the speed limit of the universe; and that time slows down as you approach the speed of light.

The biggest item on the hit list of things Einstein changed is also the most novel prediction in all of scientific history: that the universe began with a Big Bang about 14 billion years ago. From the time of the ancient Greeks up through physicists like Isaac Newton, scientists had always believed the universe was eternal. Einstein himself did not realize the implications of his own theory, and he added a cosmological constant to his equation that made the universe static. The constant was to offset the force of gravity—otherwise his theory predicted that the universe would collapse back in on itself and be destroyed. Adding the cosmological constant prevented this collapse. It took the work of the physicist and Catholic priest Georges Lemaître to figure out the correct way to solve this potential problem.

I suspect his faith played a role in the discovery, even though Lemaître was careful to keep his two careers separate. As both a working physicist and a working Catholic priest, there was no human being in history more acutely aware of the fact that every scientist on the planet for the past 2,500 years agreed that the universe was eternal, and yet the Bible clearly taught that God created the universe out of nothing a finite time ago. Lemaître's key insight was to realize that the cosmological constant was unnecessary if the universe was expanding. And if the universe was expanding, then in the past it must have been smaller. The further back into the past, the smaller the universe would have been. At some point billions of years ago, the universe would have been just a tiny "primeval atom." And before that, nothing at all. What emotions must Lemaître have felt after that flash of insight?

Lemaître went on to lay the theoretical groundwork for the Big Bang and an expanding universe. Sometime later, the astronomer Edwin Hubble independently made the discovery, and then he confirmed the expansion of the universe experimentally by measuring the red shift of stars. Einstein would later call adding a cosmological constant to the theory of relativity his "greatest blunder." But in yet another twist of the fallibilistic knife, it was later realized that the expansion of the universe was actually accelerating. The cosmological constant was brought back with a higher value to explain this acceleration.

Paradigms. Moving on from fallibilism, we come to the most famous person in the philosophy of science: Thomas Kuhn. He's the one who came up with the concept of paradigm shifts. He said that science had two different modes: *normal science* and *scientific revolutions*. Let's start with normal science. That's when scientists work within an accepted *paradigm* like Newtonian physics or the Earth-centered model of the solar system. Normal science involves refining existing theories, exploring their implications, and solving remaining puzzles. Kuhn refers to this as "mopping up." During these periods, scientists tend to ignore or explain away anomalies.

Ignoring anomalies is not a bad thing. Kuhn appreciated that scientific theories need some degree of protection from falsification, otherwise they'll never get off the ground. If the idea that theories need to be protected doesn't make sense, then here are two different times when Newtonian physics could have been falsified. The first was by the planet Uranus and the second by the planet Mercury. Both planets failed to follow the orbit predicted by Newtonian physics. Both anomalies were known for decades before the solutions were found. Should physicists have said, "another beautiful theory slain by an ugly fact"? Of course not. Scientists ignored the anomalies and stuck with Newtonian physics.

Urbain Le Verrier and John Couch Adams solved the mystery of Uranus's strange orbit. They thought it could be explained by the gravity of a mystery planet that no one knew about. They did the calculations and made a prediction about where this mystery planet should be, and sure enough, astronomers found Neptune. This was a remarkable discovery because all the other planets had been found by direct observation. Neptune was the first planet found by mathematical calculations. The anomaly that could have falsified Newtonian physics instead led to a novel prediction that was arguably the theory's greatest triumph.

The mystery planet trick did not work for Mercury (fun fact: They named the mystery planet Vulcan). So they tried other tricks, like including gravity from other known planets, including the existence of clouds of dust acting like a mystery planet, and adjusting for the fact that the sun is not a perfect sphere. Nothing worked, so scientists just lived with the anomaly until Einstein came along and discovered the theory of general relativity. Einstein was certain that it would explain the orbit of Mercury, and when they ran the numbers, it did so perfectly. An anomaly for Newtonian physics had become a novel prediction for general relativity.

When the anomalies build up and reach a critical mass they can precipitate a crisis. That's when science enters into the second mode that Kuhn called scientific revolution. When this happens, scientists abandon their old paradigm for a new and better paradigm. That is the meaning of the phrase *paradigm shift*. The switch from Newtonian physics to general relativity was a textbook paradigm shift, as was the switch from the Earth-centered model of the solar system to the Sun-centered model.

Kuhn's theory is controversial because he thought that different paradigms couldn't be compared based on scientific merit, and that paradigm shifts were the result of a power struggle. This is where the idea that paradigms of *theory-laden* comes from. That basically means that when all you have is a hammer, everything starts to look like a nail. If the idea that paradigms are theory-laden seems wrong, then think about politics. Are people really changing their beliefs based on facts? Probably not. A single fact can't outweigh the mass of an entire worldview.

A good example of my own thinking being theory laden is the debate over taxes. As we saw in the chapter on free markets, the first lesson of economics is that people respond to incentives. Behaviors that are punished are done less often, and behaviors that are rewarded are done more often. That leads to the economic slogan "you get less of what you tax and more of what you subsidize." Because of this, I ignored or explained away the fact that the economy improved after President Clinton raised taxes and the fact that the economy declined after President Bush cut taxes.

Economies are complex systems, so I assumed there had to be something else at work. That assumption was true because Clinton was president during the dot.com boom and Bush was president after it went bust. But I used external factors like the business cycle to explain away a myriad of cases where taxes didn't affect the economy like I expected. It was only after learning about the income and substitution effects that I finally had another economic principle to counterbalance the principle that you get less of what you tax. Once that principle was in place, I could finally "see" the evidence that had been staring at me in the face the whole time.

Research Programs. The philosopher Imre Lakatos did not consult my evolving thoughts on taxes, so he rejected Kuhn's idea that science was driven by "mob psychology." He came up with a new philosophy that has nevertheless become my favorite. You can quibble with various minor details, but at a high level I think it's just about right. One of Lakatos' main insights is that rival theories are often competing at the same time, and that this competition can drive scientific progress. That insight led to his philosophy of *research programs*. (Lakatos was a great philosopher, but he wasn't nearly as good at thinking of compelling names as Kuhn.)

Research programs are like paradigms, but there can be multiple research programs competing at the same time. In this book we've been juggling three different research programs: a liberal one based on government; a libertarian one based on free markets; and a conservative one based on culture. Because research programs are competing with each other, supporters are constantly trying to find flaws in their rivals while covering up their own program's weaknesses. (I hope I haven't been too egregious in that department, but I probably have.)

Lakatos says that research programs have core beliefs that must be protected,[237] such as, "gravity follows an inverse square law." The way they do that is by surrounding these core beliefs with a *protective belt*. They are other theories that are designed to protect the core beliefs from falsification, such as "There must be a mystery planet." Lakatos distinguishes between *progressing* research programs, where anomalies lead to novel discoveries like finding new planets, and *degenerating* research programs, where anomalies lead to more theories being added to the protective belt for defensive purposes.

Note that the orbit of Mercury did not mean Newtonian physics was a degenerating research program, even though there were many failed attempts to explain it. Newtonian physics was a wildly successful theory and was not in danger of being considered degenerating by a single anomaly. Instead, it was replaced by a new theory that was even more wildly successful: general relativity.

The classic example of a degenerating research program is the Earth-centered model of the solar system. It couldn't explain why the planets sometimes appeared to reverse direction and move backwards. This is called *retrograde motion*. This anomaly was fixed by adding an *epicycle*, a circle within a circle, to the protective belt. Popular mythology holds that as our observations of the planets became more and more precise, more anomalies emerged, and more epicycles were added to fix them. Eventually, scientists realized that this was ridiculous and switched to a Sun-centered model of the solar system.

To this day "adding epicycles" is a slur that scientists use to dismiss rival theories that they believe are degenerating. However, this story is a myth, and there is no evidence that astronomers ever used more than two epicycles.[238] Instead the Sun-centered model was mathematically simpler and more accurate than making calculations based on even two epicycles.

Ideology. The switch to the Sun-centered model is the textbook example that paradigm shifts happen because of power struggles, not scientific merit. The power struggle between Galileo and the Catholic Church happened at a time of conflict between Catholicism and Protestantism. Aristotle's philosophy was tightly woven into Catholic theology, so if Aristotle was wrong about the Earth-centered model, then it might seem like Catholics were wrong elsewhere. The debate over the Earth versus Sun-centered models turned into a proxy debate over the truth of Catholicism versus Protestantism. The scientists themselves did not want this to happen, and Copernicus and Galileo were both devout Catholics. Yet Galileo would be declared an honorary Protestant.[239]

Nevertheless, Galileo escalated the conflict by having the not-very-clever Aristotelian in his dialogues voice one of the Pope's own arguments in a clearly mocking way.[240] Galileo and the Pope had been friends, so this must have come across as a personal betrayal. The Roman Inquisition put Galileo on trial for heresy, and he was convicted and imprisoned, although his sentence was immediately changed to house arrest due to his age and poor health.

Galileo's trial is usually turned into a parable about religious superstition versus scientific truth, but we get the same power struggles today, and they don't have anything to do with religion—they're about ideology. Take Napoleon Chagnon, the anthropologist who studied the Yanomamö and used his research on them to debunk the myth of the noble savage. The main idea of the noble savage is that primitive societies lead communal lives of peace and harmony. According to Jean-Jacques Rousseau, the root cause of all our crime, wars, horrors, and misfortunes happened when someone fenced off some land and said, "this is mine."[241] In other words, shifting from communal living to capitalism is the root cause of all our problems.

Chagnon's research showing that primitive societies fight for women made him many powerful enemies. Anthropologists at the time were generally Marxists, who were willing to concede some amount of primitive violence, but only in the Rousseau sense of fighting over scarce resources. The idea that the Yanomamö fought over women was as big of a heresy to Marxists in cultural anthropology as Galileo's arguments were to the Pope. Chagnon explains:

> The second discovery I made that first day was that most Yanomamö arguments and fights started over women. This straightforward ethnographic observation would cause me a great deal of academic grief because in the 1960s "fighting over women" was considered a controversial explanation in "scientific" anthropology. ... For an anthropologist to suggest that fighting had something to do with women, that is, with sex and reproductive competition, was tantamount to blasphemy, or at best ludicrous.[242]

When an outbreak of measles occurred among the Yanomamö, his enemies had a chance to get revenge. Chagnon cared deeply about the Yanomamö people. They had a wildness and nobility about them that other primitive societies with more direct contact with the developed world lacked. He arguably violated professional ethics to treat them with Western vaccines. But the journalist Patrick Tierney accused him of actually spreading measles among them in his book *Darkness at El Dorado*.[243] That led to a flurry of headlines like *Scientists killed*

Amazon Indians to Test Race Theory in respectable newspapers like *The Guardian*.[244] Chagnon was attacked by many of his peers and subjected to a professional ethics investigation, although the findings were later rescinded, in large part because Tierney's book was full of holes and misleading footnotes.[245] Chagnon went on to write about the experience in his appropriately titled book, *Noble Savages: My Life Among Two Dangerous Tribes—the Yanomamö and the Anthropologists*.

Edward O. Wilson was also persecuted for his scientific research. What could a guy who studied ants have done to earn the wrath of his professional colleagues? Recall that ants, and our friend the naked mole-rat, are superorganisms. They are so effective at cooperation that individuals put the good of the group over their own welfare. It's tempting to think that liberals would celebrate superorganisms because they are about as close as living things come to communism. However, there's a catch: The only reason they cooperate so effectively is because they eliminated sexual competition.

Anthropology and evolutionary biology were both converging on the same truth: That sexual competition, and not private property, are the root cause of human conflict. That was a dangerous thing to say back in the 1970s. The Sexual Revolution was still in its infancy, and the blank slate theory of human nature reigned supreme.

Evolutionary psychology is now widely accepted among biologists, and it has roots that go all the way back to Darwin himself, but it was a novel idea in 1975 when Wilson published a textbook on the subject called *Sociobiology*. If Wilson had confined his discussion to ants, he might have stayed safe, but in the controversial final chapter of his book, he suggested the same principles about sexual competition applied to humans. His Harvard colleagues Stephen Jay Gould and Richard Lewontin tried to get him fired and blackballed professionally. Other scientists came to Wilson's aid, most notably Richard Dawkins, and the conflict escalated into what became known as the *sociobiology wars*.[246] Human nature hasn't changed since Galileo.

Sun-centered solar system. The debate over the Sun-centered model of the solar system was almost as big within the scientific community as it was with the Catholic Church. So once again Kuhn's thoughts on paradigm shifts as power struggles make sense. There were a few reasons for this. First, it required making a break from the ancient Greeks and abandoning the rationalist approach to science in favor of observation-based science. Second, the Earth-centered model was tightly bound to both Aristotle's theory of natural places, and his theory of motion. This was such a difficult problem that Copernicus, who was the first scientist to create a mathematical model of a Sun-centered solar system, foreshadowed the anti-realists and said that his model should only be used to make predictions, and not as a description of reality. It took the work of Issac Newton, about fifty years after Galileo was put on trial, before a replacement for Aristotle's theory of motion was found.

The final problem was that the Sun-centered model had some troubling anomalies of its own. Perhaps the most important was that the stars didn't move in the night sky the way scientists would have predicted if the Earth were orbiting around the sun. This movement is called *stellar parallax*. When you drive down an open road, the distant foothills seem unchanging and far away, but if you keep watching, you will notice that your angle to them does shift a bit over time. According to the Sun-centered model, the Earth is also moving as it orbits the sun, and yet the stars didn't appear to move even a little bit. (You do see a different portion of the night sky over the course of the year, but that's a different phenomenon.) The lack of stellar parallax seemed to falsify the Sun-centered model. Of course, we now know that's because stars are extremely far away, but they didn't know that back then.

Imagine being in a debate with another scientist back in the seventeenth century, and he challenged you on this point. What could you possibly say? "Stellar parallax is real, it's just that stars are so far away that we can't see it with our current level of technology. But if we had more powerful telescopes—which conveniently don't exist—we would see the stellar parallax." That's the exact same reasoning that string theorists use to protect their degenerating theory. When challenged about why none of string theory's predictions have been proven true, they say "String theory is true, it's just that the energy levels are so high that we can't test it with our current level of technology. But if we had more powerful particle accelerators—which conveniently don't exist—we would find evidence for strings."

Both defenses come across as equally absurd rationalizations. So how did the Sun-centered model of the solar system manage to win, whereas string theory is degenerating? The key difference is that the Sun-centered model of the universe was successful in other ways. It was both easier to use and more accurate than using the Earth-centered model, and it had other advantages like explaining the phases of Venus. But the lack of observable stellar parallax was an anomaly that lasted for about 300 years. It wasn't until 1838 that much better telescopes let Friedrich Bessel measure the parallax of the star 61 Cygni.

String theory is in a much deeper hole because it doesn't have any successful predictions. The physicists Lisa Randall and Raman Sundrum tried to fix this. In 1999 they created an elegant model of strings that could be tested by the Large Hadron Collider. It was a new particle accelerator that would be the most powerful in the world. The catch was that it was under construction and wouldn't be ready for another ten years. But in some ways the delay was a good thing. Having to wait a long time forced scientists to commit to a side. When the collider was finally built, it falsified Randall and Sundrum's predictions.

In response, string theorists tweaked their models a bit so that ever more powerful particle accelerators would be needed to test their theories. But that seemed to be one epicycle too many. My outsider's take is that most physicists now consider string theory to be a degenerating research program.

The final lesson from the philosophy of science is that the goal of an objective test for science is doomed. All research programs have anomalies. There is no bright, clear line like falsification to separate degenerating research programs from productive research programs. Instead, we have to make subjective judgment calls between them.

Bayesian Reasoning

Bayesian reasoning is almost good enough to believe that it's the "One Ring that rules them all" of the philosophy of science. It's worked its way into high-brow politics, which is why you may sometimes hear pundits talking about "priors" and "updating." Here is an overview that will teach you enough to fake it. That's what everyone else is doing.

Suppose you see a swan and notice its striking white color, so you wonder if all swans are white. You have no idea, so you guess 50 percent. This is called your *prior*. It is your degree of certainty that "all swans are white" is true. It's called a prior because you choose it prior to gathering evidence. With Bayesian reasoning, you are allowed to subjectively choose your priors. If you have no idea, then 50 percent is a good starting point. But your gut may tell you something else, and that's also fine. Maybe you're an experienced bird watcher, and your gut tells you all swans are white, so you start at 80 percent. You may also have some objective real-world knowledge. Maybe you are wondering whether swans are monogamous, and you remember David Lack's research that 92 percent of bird species are monogamous,[247] so you make that your prior. Priors can be based on subjective opinion or objective fact.

This honesty is refreshing. While I would love to have an objective test like "Does the airplane fly?" for scientific theories, we don't have one. Instead, philosophers sometimes go on benders where they pretend to have one and wield this test like an imaginary sword to vanquish their enemies. Anti-realism was one of these benders. These projects invariably end up in embarrassment and failure, but they are vexing while they last. The honesty of Bayesian thinking avoids these unproductive detours.

After you choose your prior you need to gather evidence. You find another swan and sure enough, it is also white. So you *update* your belief that 'all swans are white' to 66 percent. Be aware of the fact that you don't get to decide how much to change your belief. That is governed by a formula called *Bayes' Theorem*, but I'm not going to do the math. You continue to see swans and continue to update your belief to 80 percent, then 89 percent and so on. The more swans you see, the higher your certainty, but you'll never quite get to 100 percent.

What if you did see a black swan? Then you would be forced to update your belief that all swans are white to zero. This captures what we saw with both inductivism and falsification. Finding white swans helped a lot at first, but it never got our theory to 100 percent certainty, even after finding many white swans. But finding a single black swan falsified it. Both inductivism and falsification are subsumed into Bayesian reasoning. This should give you an idea why it is so powerful.

What about the orbit of Uranus? Shouldn't it have falsified Newtonian physics according to Bayesian reasoning? Not necessarily. Think about it this way. Suppose you looked out your window and saw a dinosaur. You could conclude that your belief that dinosaurs went extinct was just falsified. But you'd be more likely to believe that your buddy was playing a trick on you, or that there is a new *Jurassic Park* movie being filmed. Even if you couldn't think of any reasonable explanation, you could still conclude that the dinosaur isn't real and that there must be some unknown explanation for it. Choosing your priors isn't the only subjective choice in Bayesian reasoning. Sometimes you also have to make judgment calls about the likelihood of your evidence.

This same logic applies to the mystery planet defense. Scientists were so sure of the truth of Newtonian physics that they applied extremely high probabilities to a mystery planet. That way Newtonian physics wasn't falsified or even significantly weakened. In the case of Uranus, they were right. In the case of Mercury, they were wrong. But in both cases, they applied Bayesian reasoning correctly.

Given all these strengths, why isn't Bayesian reasoning the "one ring to rule them all"? First, there may be too much freedom. Think about the subjective priors. Yes, it's honest, but it's also unsatisfying. Priors that are really low or really high can dominate the evidence. Someone who believes in the Earth-centered model of the universe can choose a really high prior that makes his belief rational even in the face of mountains of evidence. Also think back to the mystery planets—we were also able to subjectively choose the likelihood of the evidence we observe. Bayesian reasoning may be too flexible.

Another problem with Bayesian reasoning is that it is not intuitive. Most people are notoriously bad at understanding how Bayesian statistics work even under normal conditions. It's much harder under unusual conditions or with complex models. It can result in beliefs rapidly converging to true or false on what seems like a very small amount of evidence. Sometimes this is because the evidence is strong, but sometimes it's the result of a poorly designed scientific model. Since even scientists struggle to intuitively follow Bayesian updating, this means that their intuition cannot sanity check what their model is doing. They may be lulled into a false sense of security that their belief is true.

Another problem is the concept of *overfitting*, which is when a complex model seems to be perfectly confirmed, but all it's really doing is adapting to random noise and has no predictive power. The great John von Neumann wittily captured the problem of overfitting with his famous quote, "with four parameters I can fit an elephant, and with five I can make him wiggle his trunk." By "wriggle his trunk," von Neumann meant: "make the model predict anything I want it to predict."

At the end of the day, I think Bayesian reasoning is best for well-defined problems, like the probability that a positive test means that a patient has the disease. When it comes to bigger questions with many unknown unknowns, then Lakatos's research programs are better. Research programs help us intuitively compare the strengths and weaknesses of two different theories. Bayesian thinking can lead us astray if a formal model needs to be tweaked a little. The blogger Scott Alexander explains.

> Nobody - not the statisticians, not Nate Silver, certainly not me - tries to do full Bayesian reasoning on fuzzy real-world problems. They'd be too hard to model. You'd make some philosophical mistake converting the situation into numbers, then end up much worse off than if you'd tried normal human intuition.[248]

Problems in social science tend to be big and messy, which means the smart thing to do is stick with research programs. Maybe one day high-brow politics will replace talk of priors and updating with talk about protective belts and degenerating.

The Replication Crisis

Physics is the science that studies matter and energy. Biology is the science that studies life. *Meta science* is the science that studies science. The results are disappointing. Meta science has been around in some form or another for a long time, but it really took off in 2006 with an article called *Why Most Published Research Findings Are False* by John Ioannidis. The article precipitated the *replication crisis* in both medicine and the social sciences.[249] It turns out that a lot of shady science has been going on.

The Open Science Collaboration tried to replicate one hundred of the most important studies in psychology and only about 40 percent replicated successfully.[250] Other attempted replications of large numbers of studies in both economics and psychology have also found that only about half can be reproduced.[251] It's also worth pointing out that Ioannidis focused on medical research, not social science, and medical research has even lower replication rates than social science.[252] I would not have predicted that.

Let's take a look at the shady science toolkit. The first technique is *p-hacking*. A good way to think about it is cherry picking. Suppose Alicia wants to prove that reading to children is good for them. What would she measure to prove this? The obvious endpoint is their reading level. But she could also pick how much time they spend reading, their vocabulary, their grades in English, overall GPA, self-esteem (children whose parents read to them feel loved), behavioral problems in school, depression, IQ, working memory, impulse control and much more. The standard cutoff for statistical significance in science is 5 percent. If she can think of twenty endpoints, then she'll probably get one statistically significant result just by chance.

If that doesn't work, she can start slicing and dicing her test subjects. Don't just measure these endpoints for all children; try it for just the boys and then for just the girls. Try it for preschoolers and then for kindergartners. Try it for different socioeconomic classes and different ethnicities. Try it for good readers and for bad readers. Each time she slices and dices her data in a new way, she gets another 5 percent chance for every single one of her different endpoints. Maybe the best she can do is find that reading raises the overall GPA of elementary age children. So she creates a plausible spin and says something like, "Although being read to does not translate to increased reading scores, it does foster a general love of learning that directly translates to higher grades." Then she picks up the advance for her new book and waits for the major newspapers to write stories about her discovery.

P-hacking is only the tip of the iceberg. Researchers have many *degrees of freedom* or "slack" in the design of an experiment. This freedom makes it easy for researchers to insert their own bias, either consciously or subconsciously. There are many low-level judgment calls to make about how to design an experiment. Each of these judgment calls allows scientists to subtly manipulate the results. Do they need to recruit more subjects to get more data? How should they handle outliers—data points that seem to be unusual? What about people who dropped out of the experiment partway through? Which dependent variables should they use, and which covariates should they regress for?

Another tool in the shady science toolkit is *publication bias*—don't publish null or negative results. The classic example of this is a 2008 study in the *New England Journal of Medicine* by Erich Turner and colleagues, which shows that the benefits of antidepressants were significantly overstated by publication bias.[253] Sometimes publication bias can be malicious. My favorite example is Laura Favaro, who was studying whether social scientists felt like they were being censored when it came to transgender issues. But she never got to complete her study because she was fired and locked out of her research.[254] On one hand, that's a great example of publication bias. On the other hand, I don't think there is a more powerful way to prove the truth of her thesis.

Another example of publication bias on transgender issues comes from puberty blockers. It's scandalous how little research on these drugs have been done given how many children are taking them, but Sallie Baxendale wrote a paper summarizing what little research we do have. What she found was a pattern of the drugs causing lower IQs. In animal studies on a variety of species they resulted in animals performing lower on tasks like solving a maze. And in humans they create a deficit of about ten IQ points. However, she couldn't find a journal that would publish her results.[255] Parents and children have the right to be informed about the harmful effects of these drugs.

One last example from the train wreck of youth gender medicine is that the World Professional Association for Transgender Health (WPATH) commissioned researchers at Johns Hopkin's to do a literature review on the benefits of youth gender medicine in 2020. When the researchers, much like the Cass Review that would come along four years later, found no benefits, WPATH blocked them from publishing it.[256] Then they updated their standards of care guidelines, which are the industry standard, stating that expert consensus supported youth gender medicine.[257]

Meta scientists have found some cheeky ways to make the point that they can prove virtually anything. In a famous paper called *False Positive Psychology*, Joseph Simmons and colleagues use standard research techniques to prove that listening to *When I'm Sixty-Four* by the Beatles makes you younger.[258] The psychologist Scott Alexander illustrates the same point using parapsychology (the study of the paranormal). Parapsychologists have used generally accepted scientific techniques to prove the existence of ESP.[259] That leaves you with two choices. The first is that the science is settled, and ESP exists. The second is that generally accepted scientific techniques are hopelessly flawed.

Some steps have been taken to fix these problems. The most important is *pre-registering* studies. This means that the methodology for processing the data is specified before the data is collected. No one sets out to p-hack; they only do it when they don't get the original result they were hoping for. No one is going to pre-register a study with twenty different endpoints that will be measured against data that is sliced and diced in a dozen different ways.

Another major change would be to get away from the 5 percent level for statistical significance in favor of 1 percent or even lower. Unfortunately, this has not become common. A third change is that we need to pay attention to effect sizes. In most debates in social science, the debate is over whether or not academic preschool or smaller class sizes work. Even if it does work, but the effect size is small, it shouldn't be a major policy option. We have only limited tax dollars available, so we need to prioritize programs that make a big difference.

These changes move slowly, and they only address a small part of the overall problem. Not all studies are pre-registered. Journals don't like to publish null results. Replications are costly to do, and it is not the kind of innovative research that will launch a scientist's career. Moreover, replicating someone else's study is an aggressive act that can make enemies and can hurt a scientist's career. And there isn't much we can do about all the low-level slack in a study in terms of minor design decisions. And we can't do anything about *citation bias*—scientists ignoring good studies that have results they don't like while making use of studies that have results they do like. The upshot is that research quality is better today than it was twenty years ago, back when Ionnidis first published *Why Most Published Research Findings Are False,* but not by a whole lot.

Cultural Rationality

> For the scientist who has lived by his faith in the power of reason, the story ends like a bad dream. He has scaled the mountains of ignorance; he is about to conquer the highest peak; as he pulls himself over the final rock, he is greeted by a band of theologians who have been sitting there for centuries.
>
> — Robert Jastrow, *God and the Astronomers*

When I talk about culture, I don't mean going to the opera (high culture) or a Taylor Swift concert (pop culture). In *Not by Genes Alone*, Peter Richerson and Greg Boyd define *culture* as "information capable of affecting individuals' behavior that they acquire from other members of their species through teaching, imitation, and other forms of social transmission."[260] Culture takes the form of social norms, moral values, beliefs, and personal identities. I would define culture as aggregated and processed information about how to live a good life. How does culture aggregate and process information? There are three main ingredients: *innovation*, *transmission*, and *selection*.

Innovation

Let's start with innovation. Cultural innovation can be slow, but it adds up over time. In his book, *The WEIRDest People in the World*, Joseph Henrich uses the example of a poison recipe.

> What's amazing about the products of cumulative cultural evolution is that they are often smarter than we are—much smarter. ... To see this, let's begin with a case in which there's a well-understood goal: making a deadly arrow poison used by Congo Basin hunter-gatherers.

This is perhaps the deadliest hunting poison known, dropping prey in their tracks before they can vanish into the bush. The recipe combines 10 different plant varieties, including three powerful poisons — nightshade, poison rope, and sassy bark. Poison rope alone can bring down a hippo in 20 minutes. These ingredients are first thickened with fig latex and yam juice. Saliva is then stirred in until the mixture turns brownish red. Then, a marsh toad is added, presumably for its toxic skin. The concoction is brought to a boil before crushed beetle grubs and stinging ants are blended in. The resulting dark paste is set into a bark envelope, which is often placed inside the body of a dead monkey and buried for several days. Once it is unearthed, sap from the euphorbia tree is added to this deadly adhesive paste, which can then be applied to arrows. Do NOT try this at home.[261]

Innovation is everywhere. The first bodybuilder to keep the pump going by finishing the bench press and doing some push-ups was an innovator who invented drop sets. The soccer coach Vic Buckingham invented Total Football when he realized that his unusually skilled team could play a new style by fluidly shifting positions. The snowboard was invented when Sherman Poppen built a surfboard for snow. It was so dangerously unrideable that the prep school where my parents taught had to ban them because too many students broke their bones riding them. But the development continued by adding metal edges, a way to attach your feet, and high-back bindings. In the ski world, Shane McConkey invented the concepts of both wide skis and "rocker" when he decided to try skiing in fresh powder by mounting ski bindings onto water skis. The unusually wide and gently curved skis let him float close to the surface of the fresh powder. Rocker was such a useful innovation that it spread to snowboards as well.

Cultural innovation means that even though culture is a bottom-up process, it does have some top-down elements. Skiing has innovators like Shane McConkey. Free markets have innovators like Steve Jobs.

Every firm is led by a CEO who makes top-down decisions every day. Some cultural innovators are religious leaders like Jonathan Edwards, abolitionists like Frederick Douglas, and feminists like Betty Friedan. But cultural innovations do have to pass the test of being useful to other people, which takes us to the next property.

Transmission

Innovations spread through imitation. People can imitate in a few different ways. One method is called *content bias*—copy the most successful strategy. Suppose Alicia and Blake are fishing buddies. Alicia decided to fish the rapids and Blake decided to fish the still waters. If Alicia catches more fish than Blake, he will eventually give up and join Alicia in the rapids. This strategy may not work. I used to play *Street Fighter 2* with my next-door neighbor when I was a kid, and he always beat me with Chun-Li. I became frustrated and kept trying different strategies and still couldn't beat him. Finally, I demanded to play Chun-Li, and he still beat me. I could copy his choice of character, but not his skill at the game.

Another technique is the *conformist heuristic*—copy the most popular strategy. This is probably the smartest choice. The Toyota Camry is the best-selling midsize sedan on the market. There might be better cars in the class, but you can't go wrong picking the Camry. The same idea is captured in the slogan, "No one ever got fired for choosing IBM." It originated back in the 1970s when IBM was the 800-pound gorilla of the tech world. In the movie *Top Gun*, Maverick was an instinctive pilot who flew by the seat of his pants and threw out "the book." But if you aren't capable of going into a 4g inverted dive with a MiG-28, then you should probably stick to the book.

The most dangerous strategy is the *status heuristic*—copy the high-status people. Biggie Smalls once rapped, "Either you're slinging crack-rock or you've got a wicked jump shot."[262] There are 20 million black males in the United States, and only 450 people in the NBA. That's a math problem that can't be solved. On the other hand, imagine what the NBA would be like if Stephen Curry had said to himself, "Who am I kidding? I'm lightly recruited and undersized. Maybe I should become a dentist."

Despite this flaw, the status heuristic is very useful. There are many types of high-status cultural models including teachers, working professionals, and clergy. William Julius Wilson identifies the problems in the inner-city not to an unchecked "ghetto culture" but rather to the loss of middle-class blacks to the suburbs. This loss deprived inner city youths of positive cultural role models. It also resulted in the loss of other inner city cultural institutions such as churches and parent-teacher organizations. Without these valuable role models, the inner cities suffered a cultural collapse. We saw the loss of these institutions clearly during the Covid-19 lockdowns. Teachers' unions used their power to enforce remote learning longer in black neighborhoods than in white neighborhoods, because white parents had the institutional power to pressure the school boards to get their children back into the schools.[263]

Conservatives are often critical of Wilson, but I think he's onto something important. His insight applies to both the white and black communities. Historically very few people went to college, so most working-class white and black communities had large numbers of highly-skilled people who acted as leaders and role models. But with more people going to college, these high achievers were picked off and moved into upper middle-class communities.

Selection

Let's think about evolution by natural selection for a second. The prospect of getting killed by predators means that all animals have to meet a basic minimum standard for running speed. Even the slowest deer must be pretty fast, or else it would have been dinner for wolves a long time ago. The same principle applies to free market competition. All existing firms have to be relatively free of inefficiency, nepotism, and waste. Otherwise they would go bankrupt. One of the running themes in this book is that the only thing worse than failure is not being allowed to fail. The importance of selection teaches us why.

The same process of selection applies to culture. Unfit cultures are weeded out of the ecology. A textbook example is the Shakers. They were an unorthodox offshoot of the Quakers in the eighteenth century, and they had such a strong belief in the equality of the sexes that they organized their lives around simple communal living rather than along gendered roles in family environments. But they also believed in celibacy, and eventually they reached the point where they couldn't recruit new members fast enough. The Shakers, and their egalitarian ideals, literally died out.

The modern left may suffer the same fate as the Shakers due to the low birth rates in urban communities. Throughout human history, many young power couples have chosen to pursue wealth and social status rather than domestic tranquility. But without modern birth control, the babies were going to come whether they wanted them or not. So the couples cashed in their wealth and provided their children with the best education and childcare money could buy. They may not have wanted children, but their status-seeking genes spread to the next generation regardless. Now, it's easy for these young power couples to avoid having children, so status seeking individuals are voluntarily removing themselves from the gene pool.

Genes for the pursuit of social status are a textbook example of genes that increase fitness in one environment (before the birth control pill) and hurt fitness in another environment (after the birth control pill). That's a common dynamic in evolution. The classic example comes from research by Peter and Rosemary Grant, who studied the finches in the Galapagos Islands.[264] Finches with large, strong beaks do well during dry seasons when the only available food is hard seeds. The short but strong beaks are perfect for cracking them open. Finches with long, slender beaks do well during rainy years because their long beaks act like spears to grab scurrying insects. During rainy years the proportion of long-beaked finches rises and during dry years the proportion of them drops.

The birth control pill seemed to be a major win for the left, but it may be a pyrrhic victory. What will happen to our culture as status-seeking genes become less common? I suspect we will see a rise in humbler but more meaningful values as younger generations exchange social status for social connection.

That does not mean that every power couple is driven by status-seeking genes. Instead, genes and culture have a complex interplay called *gene-culture co-evolution*. Children inherit genes from their parents and a cultural blueprint from their society. The real innovation of culture is that can change much faster than our genetic makeup, allowing humans to rapidly adapt to new environments. And compared to genes, that's true. Compared to a single human's life, cultural evolution can still be stubbornly slow.

If you think back to the chapter on social status, culture is more like smoking cigarettes than touching a hot stove. If I choose a new type of ice cream, I can evaluate it because I've tried many flavors of ice cream. But most people only get to choose a life strategy once. A young couple can move to a major city and try to achieve successful careers, or they can stay in a small town and raise a family. What if the couple made the wrong choice? How would they even know? That means cultural feedback happens over a long period of time as the younger generations make choices based on the lives of previous generations. In terms of psychological distance, culture is far. We know that when things are far, people will choose social status over real-world fundamentals like fulfilling relationships and satisfying careers. The pursuit of social status can easily hijack entire cultures.

Selection is the check against cultural decline. Cultures are in competition with each other. The good cultures win, and the bad cultures lose. Jared Diamond's *Guns, Germs, and Steel* has an example of competition at the level of individual cultures. Most cultures go into decline sooner or later; it doesn't matter whether it is a modern democracy or a primitive tribe. Diamond theorized that aboriginal tribes in Australia periodically went into decline where they lost vital technologies such as the boomerang and barbed spears. However, their neighbors still had these technologies, so they would ultimately be reintroduced. Ideally a declining tribe would relearn their lost technology through peaceful means like trade, but if worst came to worst, it would be reintroduced through conquest.

Tasmania is an island off the coast of Australia that is about the size of West Virginia. It's a lot smaller than Australia, so the forces of competition were much weaker. That's also why we often find flightless birds like the kiwi and the dodo on islands. The selection pressures were so weak that the entire species lost the ability to fly. The aborigines who settled Tasmania were like the kiwi. They arrived with the full toolkit of Australian aborigines but ultimately lost many important technologies. Diamond lists some of these lost technologies including "barbed spears, bone tools of any type, boomerangs, ground or polished stone tools, hafted stone tools, hooks, nets, pronged spears, traps and the practices of catching and eating fish, sewing, and starting a fire."[265]

Island living got a reality check when the mainland species eventually arrived. The dodo is now extinct, and the kiwi is endangered because of invasive species such as dogs. And of course, Australian aborigines lacked the guns and steel to defeat the most invasive species of them all—other humans. The lower the threshold between success and failure, the further people and animals will sink. The only thing worse than failure is not being allowed to fail.

Ecological Rationality

The word rationality usually suggests things like gathering evidence, deductive reasoning, and making lists of pros and cons. The Nobel laureate Vernon Smith calls this *constructive rationality*. But another type of rationality has been developed by economists. Gerd Gigerenzer calls this *ecological rationality*. Gigerenzer's research has focused on using simple rules of thumb to make rational choices on limited information. This book will lean more on Richerson and Boyd. If an ecology has all three factors we've looked at so far—innovation, transmission, and selection—then it will produce rational outcomes. Culture has all three ingredients, so culture is rational.

Evolution by natural selection provides the basic blueprint for ecological rationality. The three key ingredients of evolution are *variation*, *natural selection*, and *differential reproduction*. They are different names for the three properties we've been considering. Variation happens because there are many different genes for different traits. Some of these genes are good innovations and others are bad innovations.

Natural selection is how the bad genes get weeded out. Animals with bad genes die, and animals with good genes survive. Differential reproduction refers to the fact that animals with good genes have more offspring. That's transmission—the good genes spread as they get passed on to the next generation. In short, evolution produces rational outcomes because the fittest animals survive and pass on their genes.

Free markets are ecologically rational. Innovation is creating new or better products. Selection happens when consumers reject bad ideas, and transmission happens when successful products gain market share and competitors rip off winning ideas. Think about the innovation for touchscreen phones. The iPhone came out of nowhere and took on the old guard like Motorola and Blackberry. Then Android was able to copy the touchscreen innovation and now virtually all phones have touch screens.

Mathematics is another example. The innovation step is when a mathematician creates a new proof for something like "the real numbers are uncountably infinite." The selection step is when other mathematicians double-check the proof to see if it is valid. If it isn't valid, then it gets rejected. If the proof is valid, then it gets published and added to the store of knowledge, which is the transmission step.

In math, it's relatively easy to tell if a proof succeeds or fails. I could never in a million years think up Georg Cantor's proof that the real numbers are uncountably infinite, but it's something that every high school calculus teacher shows his students, and they all get it. There are some exceptions, like the four-color problem. It is the theory that a map can be colored with just four colors such that no two countries that touch each other have the same color. In 1879 Alfred Kempe thought he had a proof for the four-color problem, but it turned out to be flawed. It took eleven years for mathematicians to realize that it had a flaw. But the four-color problem is a rare exception to this rule.

In math, most innovations can be quickly accepted or rejected. In terms of psychological distance, success or failure in math is near. In science, failed theories are not always obvious. Scientists knew that the orbits of both Uranus and Mercury were anomalous for decades before they figured out why. One solution confirmed Newtonian physics and the other led to a paradigm shift that replaced it. Failure in science is far—it's more like smoking cigarettes than touching a hot stove. And when things are far, social status takes over. The pursuit of social status is even more troubling when it has political implications, like research on how taxes impact the economy or the origins of Covid-19.

Despite these problems, science passes the ecological rationality test. It has all three ingredients: innovation by creating new theories, transmission of knowledge by publishing studies, and selection by falsifying failed theories. In fact, the only way our store of scientific knowledge can grow over time is because science is ecologically rational. Isaac Newton put it best: "If I have seen further than others, it is by standing on the shoulders of giants." This means that constructive rationality—such as doing research and gathering evidence—is subsumed into the realm of ecological rationality.

Despite being ecologically rational, science is a purely top-down process. But otherwise, it has a lot in common with culture. They are both ecologically rational, they both have weak selection forces, and they both get hijacked by social status as a result. The real battle is not between liberals and conservatives, or between science and culture, but between humility and pride.

The Parable of Chesterton's Fence

This conflict between humility and pride takes us to the next parable in our tour of human nature. This one comes from the famous Catholic writer G.K. Chesterton and is called The Parable of Chesterton's Fence.

> There exists in such a case a certain institution or law; let us say, for the sake of simplicity, a fence or gate erected across a road. The more modern type of reformer goes gaily up to it and says, "I don't see the use of this; let us clear it away." To which the more intelligent type of reformer will do well to answer: "If you don't see the use of it, I certainly won't let you clear it away. Go away and think. Then, when you can come back and tell me that you do see the use of it, I may allow you to destroy it."[266]

We learned about the law of unintended consequences back in the chapter on free markets. The parable of Chesterton's fence gives us insight into why it happens. Human society is complicated. There are many interacting social norms, moral values, and institutions all in a delicate balance with each other. If we mess with that balance, things fall apart.

Foreign aid is unfortunately one of the most common ways we see Chesterton's fence in action. The West is so rich that aid money can overwhelm the much poorer communities of the developing world. That's a recipe for harmful downstream consequences. It would take a book-length treatment to get into all the ways it can happen, which, conveniently, has already been done. In *Foreign Aid and Its Unintended Consequences*, Dirk-Jan Koch creates a taxonomy of all the different ways foreign aid can go wrong. We'll look at only a few branches of his taxonomy.

The first way foreign aid can go wrong is through *conflict effects*. This happens when aid in the form of food, supplies, or money is captured by powerful leaders at gunpoint and then sold at high prices to fund wars and genocide, such as in the case of Rwanda.[267] The second is through *price effects*. One way this happens is when food aid is sent to a region that is suffering a famine, which puts local farmers out of business. It's hard for farmers to compete with free. So the farmers give up and move to the city or find some other job. The outcome of food aid is that nations produce less food in the future, which makes it even more vulnerable to famine.

Another price effect is when the influx of peacekeepers and aid workers flood the local economy with money, which leads to rampant inflation, making life more expensive for locals. Koch tells the story of posh lakeside villas in Goma, a city in the Congo. As you drive around the lake, you see villa after villa inhabited by aid workers with the *de rigueur* white four-by-four Toyota Land Cruisers parked outside. Meanwhile, skyrocketing rents forced the locals far away onto bad roads with limited electricity.[268] We see the same phenomenon in the United States—the Airbnb effect where locals can no longer afford to live in the vacation communities where tourists expect them to work. Someone should tell foreign aid workers that they're not on vacation.

Another category is *marginalizing effects*, where foreign aid creates rising inequality. A good example is fair trade policies that make small farmers wealthier, but which also makes day laborers and seasonal workers poorer. Another type of marginalizing effect is when local elites capture the foreign aid and then direct it to their constituents.[269] The politically connected get richer and the rest of the country gets poorer. Moving on, we come to the category of *behavioral effects*. In the case of Nepal, aid workers tried to reduce deforestation by giving local Nepalese more fuel-efficient stoves that were less smoky. However, the improved stove technology led to locals using them more, which increased the deforestation. In one of the saddest stories, one of Koch's students mentioned a mother who starved one of her own children so that the entire family would be given food aid.[270]

I've only hit about half the categories in Koch's taxonomy, but I'll stop here. Koch is not opposed to foreign aid, and his main goal in writing the book is to improve foreign aid so that it can help people in the developing world. One way is by highlighting successful programs like deworming. Another way is to discuss how to reform aid programs to eliminate these unintended consequences. One example is to stop sending food to the developing world. Use the aid money to buy from local farmers instead. But you can only hope to avoid unintended consequences if you approach local communities with a sense of humility and respect. Aid workers and nongovernmental organizations need to realize that there is wisdom in local customs, norms, and values. That's the lesson of Chesterton's fence.

Chesterton's fence shows up in the developed world too. Nutrition science has had such a dismal track record that it belongs in the replication crisis Hall of Fame. In the 1980s, leading nutritionists and the Center for Science in the Public Interest (CSPI) campaigned to eliminate saturated fats from the food supply. That's because saturated fat was thought to be a major cause of heart disease. Restaurants and food companies replaced lard, beef tallow, and coconut oil with partially hydrogenated vegetable oils, and movie theater popcorn has never been the same. Well-meaning wives took away their husbands' butter and replaced it with margarine. But in a 2012 review article, Walter Willett points out that partially hydrogenated oils are much worse than saturated fat. He also points out that cutting saturated fat intake isn't helpful unless it's replaced with polyunsaturated fat, not carbs and sugar like we did in the 1980s.[271] The CSPI has since tried to memory-hole their role in encouraging the switch.[272]

This same story has been repeated many times in exercise science. The first chapter introduced the topic of bodybuilders and protein, but that's only one example. The same dynamic has played out with squatting with knees beyond toes, the value of partial reps, rounded back lifting, and more. Even the much-maligned "bro split" is making a comeback. To this day the term "bro science" is an insult for bad training advice based on folk wisdom like "chasing the pump"—another maligned bit of training advice making a comeback. The real story is that the bros, through trial and error, have figured out what works. When they find out what works, they tell their friends, and the knowledge spreads.

It's been a much slower and more difficult job for exercise scientists to prove what works using the scientific method, and in their hubris, they often dismissed the hard-won knowledge of the bros as being incorrect. The epigraph to this chapter is about scientists climbing the mountain of knowledge only to be met by a bunch of theologians. When exercise scientists climb to the top of their mountain, they'll be greeted by a bunch of bros in backwards baseball caps.

Intellectual hubris has led scientists to commit the fallacy of Chesterton's fence over and over again. Scientists didn't tell bumblebees to stop flying because our old models of fluid mechanics held that bumblebee flight was impossible. But exercise scientists felt free to tell bodybuilders to eat less protein. Nutritionists felt free to tell the American public to eat more margarine. Doctors felt free to perform ice pick lobotomies on people, mostly women, as a cure for schizophrenia and depression. Scientists in the 1920s felt free to sterilize women with low IQs and then send their children to institutions with almost no human contact. They then felt free to diagnose the children's constant rocking motions as symptoms of feeblemindedness, rather than self-soothing techniques of children taken from their mothers.

By the 1960s, scientists had finally learned the importance of nurturing, so they then felt free to blame autism on mothers for being cold and emotionally distant. How many women who deeply loved their children were unfairly shamed for being an unloving mother? Psychologists in the 1980s felt free to diagnose patients, mostly women, with false memories of sexual abuse. This resulted in innocent people going to prison and families being torn apart when parents denied sexually abusing their own children. And today psychologists feel equally free to diagnose adolescents, mostly girls (are you seeing the pattern yet?), with gender dysphoria and prescribing them puberty blockers, opposite-sex hormones, and double mastectomies.

It's comforting to believe that horrific medical scandals are caused by ignorance and superstition. That would mean that we've progressed beyond them, and they won't happen anymore. But imagine how ignorant and superstitious we'll seem to people fifty years from now: "I can't believe that people in the 2020s really believed that some men could get pregnant.[273] I guess that's what education was like back before everyone had a personalized AI tutor." In reality, medical scandals are caused by the power and hubris of a new discovery, such as how to use hormones to alter secondary sexual characteristics. This means that we will have more scandals in our future unless scientists learn to give ordinary people the same respect they give to bumblebees.

The Limit of Ecological Rationality

Ecological rationality is not a magic bullet. Sometimes the world changes without people even realizing it, so the old techniques and strategies no longer work. This has happened so often in military history that there is even a saying: Generals are always trying to win the last war. Military history buffs could provide hundreds of examples, but I'll only give one particularly famous case. The French were impressed by the lessons of World War I, which had settled into long static trench warfare. So the French dug trenches and built fortifications along the Maginot Line near the border with Germany. It would have been suicide for Germany to directly attack these defenses. But the

Germans realized that they could make effective use of the improving technology of tanks to get around these fortifications. They built their military on speed—the blitzkrieg tactics. They used their mobility to go around the Maginot Line. They drove their tanks through the dense and hilly Ardennes Forest and then smashed through the relatively light defenses found there.

Another problem is that ordinary people don't have organic bottom-up knowledge of technical subjects. Bodybuilders have a lot of organic knowledge of lifting. Soccer coaches have a lot of organic knowledge of soccer. Farmers have a lot of organic knowledge of farming. But regular people don't have bottom-up knowledge of engineering. Would you want to fly on an airplane collectively designed by ordinary people? Probably not. Ecological processes can work magic with organic knowledge, but they can't work magic with no knowledge at all.

What happens if people try anyway? Then we get a *cargo cult*. The closest thing that any humans have come to experiencing an alien landing must have been when the South Pacific islanders saw the United States' World War II Navy ships arrive. Imagine what life was like for an islander with hunter-gatherer technology, and his entire world was a few smallish, interconnected islands sparsely populated by other dark-skinned people. Then one day, out of nowhere, he saw a massive steel boat the size of a small island. From the ship emerged strange, white-skinned people with godlike technology. They built airstrips and air traffic control towers and soon magical flying machines descended from the skies.

These strange foreigners were generally nice, and they gave away valuable metal tools like knives, pans, and axes, along with warmer clothing and new types of food that could be stored for a long time. Then one day, as suddenly as they arrived, they disappeared. The natives wanted more of the steel tools that the Americans brought with them. So they built their own airplanes and air traffic control towers out of straw. If you do an image search for "cargo cult" you can see the pictures, and they are impressive models built to a realistic scale. But of course, they didn't work. Perhaps the gods didn't favor them the way they favored the white man.

It is easy to feel superior to cargo cults, but they happen the instant you step out of an area where you have domain expertise. I'm a computer programmer, but once you leave the realm of code and focus on what actually happens on a computer, I'm useless. I sometimes invoke cargo cults when I work with our devops team: "Hey JC, the server gods are angry again; I need you to take the fire out of their anger." I could have said something about heap space, but it would have been the exact same statement dressed up like *Star Trek* tech speak. At least the first way makes it clear that I have no idea what's going on.

Cargo cults happen in politics all the time, such as when a high-status expert in one field weighs in on education or gender ideology and shows very quickly that he doesn't know very much. I'm sure I've wandered into minefields that I don't know exist many times in this book. I know they're out there somewhere, but I don't know where.

The philosopher David Makinson called this the *preface paradox*.[274] An author writes a book filled with assertions, but in the preface, he apologizes for whatever he gets wrong. If he knew something was wrong, then why didn't he just remove it? The reason is that he has no idea which parts of the book he got wrong, so all he can do is apologize ahead of time. The real lesson of Dunning-Kruger isn't that stupid people don't know how stupid they are, but that people who are making a reasonable attempt to be truth-seeking only step on landmines that they don't know exist.

The fact that we don't want ordinary people building airplanes is not controversial. But it might be controversial to say that we should leave the Federal Reserve's monetary policy to the experts. Ordinary people don't have any organic bottom-up knowledge of monetary policy. They might know about it from reading books and articles, but that's different. We can't use the wisdom of crowds to aggregate the knowledge that ordinary people gain from reading articles and expect it to collectively outweigh the knowledge of the experts who wrote them.

That takes us back to the parable of the ox contest in the chapter on government failure. We saw that there is some fine print attached to the wisdom of crowds. We can only aggregate the knowledge of individuals if the errors are random. If there is systemic bias, then aggregating the knowledge of ordinary people will lead to systemic errors. That was exactly the nature of Bryan Caplan's critique of government—people are systemically misinformed and have beliefs aimed at social status rather than truth.

Unfortunately, systemic bias is just as big of a problem for the experts as it is for ordinary people. One of the many ways economists divide goods is into *experience goods* and *credence goods*. Consumers can judge the quality of experience goods on their own. If you like chocolate ice cream better than vanilla ice cream, then there's nothing an expert can do or say to change your mind. That's not true of credence goods. How do I know that my orthopedist was right when he recommended shoulder surgery over rehab? Even if the surgery went well, it could have been the wrong call. I can't bring my own knowledge into that decision; I just have to trust my doctor. But at least I don't have to worry about his politics influencing his judgment.

What happens with credence goods when the experts are too politicized to have any credence? Then you get a big problem. We've seen many examples already, such as how WPATH commissioned a comprehensive review of the research on youth transgender medicine and then blocked the scientists from publishing when they found that there wasn't any credible evidence to justify children transitioning.[275] And we saw it with the battles over the theory of the noble savage.

Here is one more example. Research by Elizabeth Kempf shows that credit rating analysts who are Democrats grant lower corporate credit ratings than Republicans when there is a Republican president and vice-versa when there is a Democratic president.[276] The idea is that they can use their small but still significant power to hurt the economy when someone from the other party is president. That will increase the chance of their own political party winning the next election. That's bad for the nation, but good for partisan ideologues. Getting experts you can trust is a hard problem to solve.

Peer Socialization

> A child's goal is not to become a successful adult, any more than a prisoner's goal is to become a successful guard. A child's goal is to be a successful child.
>
> – Judith Rich Harris, *The Nurture Assumption*

Much of our social science research is fatally flawed, but not because of shady techniques like p-hacking. It's because many studies don't have the power to separate nature from nurture. Suppose we do a study on how much time parents spend reading to their children. Then we track their children through school, and sure enough, we find that the children who were read to the most are the best readers. Case closed, right?

Not so fast. We don't know if the children were good readers because of nature or nurture. Perhaps intelligent parents spend more time reading to their children, and intelligent parents also have intelligent children who are good at reading. Were the children good readers because of nature (parents giving them genes for intelligence), or nurture (parents instilling a love of reading)? If we want to answer that question we need better tools. That's what *behavioral genetics* provides us.

Intuitive Behavioral Genetics

I'm going to talk a lot about genes and the environment, and I'm going to be sloppy about it. What I should say is "the variance found in genes explains 90 percent of the variance found in height." Instead, what I'll say is that height is 90 percent genes. Another way of putting it is that the *heritability* of height is 90 percent. That's a lot shorter and easier to say. But genes cannot be expressed except by interacting with the environment. If a man is seventy inches tall, that doesn't mean that he got sixty-three inches from genes and seven inches from the environment. The effect of genes and environment can't be partitioned like that. What it means is that men generally range from around sixty-four inches to seventy-six inches tall, and 90 percent of this clustering of different heights can be explained by genes. Keep this disclaimer in mind.

The main workhorse of behavioral genetics is *twin studies* where scientists compare fraternal twins to identical twins. But we won't get into them because they're complicated. Instead, we'll use other types of studies that give us essentially the same results in a more intuitive way. The first is comparing identical twins who are separated at birth. Luckily this is extremely rare, but it does happen, and when it does, it's a golden opportunity for scientists. Researchers track down a bunch of these twins and see how strongly they are correlated to each other for traits like height and IQ. Since they have the same genes but different environments, any correlations between them must be due to genes.

The second technique is adoption. Couples that adopt one child often adopt a second child. When that happens, there are two children who share the same home and family despite not sharing any genes. Any correlations between these two children must be due to their environment. We call this the *shared environment* because it is shared by siblings.

A third technique is to compare identical twins who were *not* separated at birth. Why would we want to do that? Because there is more to the environment than your home and family life. Once children walk outside the front door, they have to navigate the world of peers and teachers. Two identical twins may lead different lives outside the home. They may be in different classes, participate in different activities, and make different friends. That can lead to them being socialized in different ways despite being genetically identical. Suppose we find that identical twins who were raised together are 60 percent correlated for a trait like IQ. They have the same shared environment, and they have the same genes. So the remaining 40 percent must be due to environmental factors outside the home. We call this the *nonshared environment* because it is different for each twin.

To recap, here are the three main categories.

Shared environment. This is generally the home and family life—things that siblings would share with each other. It will also include the local culture of their neighborhood and schools since siblings would share those as well. These effects may not always be strong, but if they do exist, this is where we'll see them.

Genes. Here is a subtle point. Suppose we have two children. One is an extroverted jock, and the other is a shy nerd. This will result in their school environments being very different from each other, but our behavioral genetics studies would pick this up in their genes. It was their genes that led to them carving out separate niches in school. This teaches an important point: What we see as the effect of genes may be amplified by the environmental niches that children find. Awkward and shy students may be routed into a niche that amplifies their poor social skills.

Nonshared environment. Think of the nonshared environment as the random hand of fate. Sometimes that can be birth order effects if parents favor the oldest or youngest child in the family. Yes, this is home and family life, but two children from the same family can't both be the favorite. Or it could be a death, such as if a parent dies after one child reaches adulthood but before another child is fully grown.

It can also be due to peer effects. Genes play a large role in determining what kind of social niche a child will carve out, but luck is still important. Perhaps Alicia sits next to a girl on the cross-country team her freshmen year of high school. They start talking and the girl encourages her to join the team. Alicia isn't good at soccer and wants to make friends, so she agrees. She finds a new sport and a wholesome group of friends. But in an alternate timeline she gets placed in a different homeroom. She quits soccer because she'll only be a benchwarmer, so she falls in with the rebellious druggie crowd at her school.

The nonshared environment doesn't have to involve peers. Suppose Anthony gets hooked on a video game and it inspires him to start making his own games. He becomes obsessed and spends hours programming on his computer every day, but his twin Blake never found his passion. Then Anthony will end up with a higher IQ than his twin, simply because he happened to discover an intellectually stimulating hobby.

However, twin and adoption studies have a weakness. I'm going to call this the *between-group problem* because there isn't a standard term. Twins are members of the same family, so we can't use twin studies to compare rich people to poor people, or black people to white people. We do have adoption studies, but adoptive parents are carefully screened to be good parents and are almost always members of the middle class. So even if a woman puts two children up for adoption and they go to different homes, those homes are going to be very similar to each other. Stephen Pinker explains in his book *The Blank Slate*.

> Behavioral genetic methods address variation within the group of the people being examined, not variation between groups of people. If the twins or adoptees in a sample are all middle-class American whites, a heritability estimate can tell us about why middle-class American whites differ from other middle-class American whites,

but not why the middle class differs from the lower or upper class, why Americans differ from non-Americans, or why whites differ from Asians or blacks.[277]

A good example of the between-group problem is height. People in the developing world are much shorter than people in the West, but that isn't because of genes. It's because they have diets low in fat and protein. When people immigrate to the developed world, the children are five or six inches taller than their parents. Twin and adoption studies are great when scientists want to compare one middle class American to another, but they only capture a small sliver of all the possible environments.

The Results For IQ

Robert Plomin reviewed the literature on intelligence and found that it is about 60 percent genes.[278] However, there is some fine print because the role of genes increases throughout life. Intelligence is about 20 percent genes in infancy and increases to 80 percent later in adulthood. I usually just go with the 60 percent estimate from early adulthood.

Critics may wish to avoid this discussion by denying that IQ is a meaningful concept—that all IQ tests measure is the ability to take IQ tests. There is a kernel of truth to this in that all tests are imperfect proxies for real world knowledge or skills. But the research on IQ is robust and IQ tests are highly predictive of important real-world outcomes. Tarmo Strenze did a meta-analysis of eighty-five data sets and concluded that IQ explained the amount of education by 56 percent, the prestige of a job that someone has by 43 percent, and income by 20 percent.[279] The result for income is surprising, but some high-status careers don't pay particularly well. Another meta-analysis shows that

IQ has a 51 percent correlation to job performance.[280] Being intelligent gives people more education, a better selection of jobs, and higher performance in their chosen career. IQ matters, and it matters a lot.

The Shared Environment

The most surprising finding of behavioral genetics is that the shared environment is not nearly as important as we thought. Remember that the shared environment is basically family and home life—things that siblings share with each other. At young ages the shared family environment has a significant impact on children's IQs. But as children grow into adulthood the importance of the shared environment declines to zero.[281]

Another way of putting it is that parents have no impact on the adult IQs of their children, except for the genes they give them. If you're struggling to wrap your head around this concept, think of it this way. When children are young, their entire world is their parents, but as they grow older their world becomes bigger and the importance of their parents becomes smaller. Becoming an adult means, in some ways, breaking free of your parents' influence. I will always remember the bittersweet moment at a family birthday when my son, who was four or five at the time, decided that he'd rather sit with his cousins than with his parents. That was the beginning of the end for me and my wife.

The same pattern is true of reading. Parents have a large impact on their children's reading when they are young, but as they get older the influence declines to zero. Callie Little and colleagues did a meta-analysis of thirty-seven different twin studies on reading comprehension. In the abstract for the study, they report that the shared environment is 16 percent. However, most of the studies on reading are done on young children. If you check the body of the study, you will see that the shared environment declines to zero by the fourth or fifth grade.[282] Once again that fits the pattern of the shared environment declining as a child gets older.

The shared environment also has no impact on the Big Five personality traits of openness, conscientiousness, extroversion, agreeableness, and neuroticism.[283] If you find this list of things parents can't control distressing, then here is an olive branch: the shared environment does have lasting impacts on the amount of education[284] and religiousness.[285]

I realize this may be a depressing lesson for parents, but it has a silver lining. You can relax when it comes to "The Mission." I remember in the late 1980s when the movie *Parenthood* came out. It was a forgettable movie, but what stuck with me was a young couple raising their daughter to be a genius with flash cards and classical music. At the time it seemed strange, unhealthy, and obsessive. But it became part of the "generally accepted accounting principles" for middle-class parents. I don't think it's healthy for children.

Children need the freedom to play. They need to ride bikes and climb trees. They need to build forts in the woods and create jumps for their bikes, including the famous suicide jump over a ravine of concrete. They need to light small fires, play in the dirt and mud, and slide around on the ice of a frozen river in the winter. They need to sneak in through a window to the equipment room of the local high school gym and pretend to be professional wrestlers on the pole-vaulting mats. (Sorry coach.)

Children also need to negotiate their disagreements free of adult supervision. My neighbor was a much better athlete than I was, but he was a crier. Whenever a call went against him, such as when we were playing stickball or soccer, he would cry and go home. Then an hour later, he'd come back and join the game again. Kids need to learn the skills of advocating for themselves in a prosocial way, accepting when the group disagrees, and of making judgment calls free of bias or favoritism. We learned that when the older kids deigned to play with us. In hindsight I think they deliberately made calls against themselves when they saw how biased we were. We need resilient, psychologically healthy children. Free play away from the watchful eyes of grownups is a vital ingredient.

I'm perpetually astonished that educated liberals didn't pounce on the importance of unstructured play a long time ago. I remember reading an article in The New York Times about this when my children were little. I tried to find it but couldn't, however I did find a more recent article that was essentially the same called *Making Playgrounds a Little More Dangerous*. It was about children turned loose into a reclaimed junk yard where they could smash things, climb things, build things, and play tag or hide-n-seek amidst the junk. In other words, they could be normal kids. The article notes that:

> A 2017 randomized controlled trial conducted in New Zealand found that children (ages 6 through 9) who participated in what the researchers called "free range play" were happier at school, more engaged with other children and less likely to report being bullied during recess than those whose play time was more structured.[286]

That's almost certainly because unstructured play promotes social skills. It rubs down the rough edges and teaches children how to make friends. Because the children had good social skills, they were less likely to be bullied. One of my dad jokes used to be about liberal moms trying to find time to get together: "I'm sorry, I can't do Thursday, Cordelia has unstructured play from 3:15 to 4:45." Unfortunately, free play has never caught on. It turns out that this was just wishful thinking on my part. Helicopter parenting is more deeply entrenched than ever.

Peer Socialization

The fact that family and home life aren't as important as we thought was merely an interesting puzzle until Judith Rich Harris published her groundbreaking book, *The Nurture Assumption*. She showed the power of peer socialization and exposed the beating heart of what makes it tick. That takes us to our next parable in our tour of human nature. Judith Rich Harris explains.

> When I was a graduate student I lived in a rooming house in Cambridge, Massachusetts. It was owned by a Russian couple who, along with their three children, occupied the ground floor of the house. The parents spoke Russian to each other and to their children; their English was poor and they spoke it with a thick Russian accent. But the children, who ranged in age from five to nine, spoke perfectly acceptable English with no accent at all - that is, they had the same Boston-Cambridge accent as the other kids in the neighborhood. ... Even the five year old was a more competent speaker of English than her mother.[287]

Sometimes this dynamic is so strong that immigrant children struggle to hold a conversation with their own parents. Language and accents are the first clue to a powerful lesson in human nature: Children are more influenced by their peers than by their parents. Children will be teased if they have a funny way of speaking, so immigrant children quickly learn to speak without an accent. Meanwhile, their parents speak with thick, heavy accents their entire lives.

In *The Nurture Assumption*, Judith Rich Harris describes how children split up into groups. If there are only a small number of children, then they will all play together, even across large age ranges. But as soon as there are enough children, the older kids will break off and form their own group. When even more children are added, the groups will split again by sex. The end result is four groups: young boys, young girls, older boys, and older girls. In my opinion, this is the largest number of groups you can have and still get healthy socialization.

As you add more and more children to the mix, the children will split into groups based on interests and personality traits. The movie *The Breakfast Club* identified the most common cliques: the brain, the athlete, the basket case, the princess, and the criminal. The movie was about five students, one from each of these cliques, who were forced to spend an entire Saturday in detention with each other. At first their differences led to conflict, but over the course of the day they gradually learned to see past their differences and become friends.

The group that a child is routed into can amplify the features that put him there in the first place. If a child is shy and introverted, then he will probably end up in the brain group, and his shyness and introversion will intensify. But if he went to a small school, then every day would be like *The Breakfast Club*. That's because students in small schools have no choice—there is no one else their own age to hang out with. The children socialize each other to become well-rounded individuals. In the case of the introverted geek, the good social skills of the other children would rub off on him, and his intelligence and love of learning would rub off on them. Healthy socialization rubs off the sharp edges and makes people well-rounded. Unhealthy socialization routes geeky children into geeky social niches and amplifies their sharp edges and poor social skills as they become immersed in geek culture and geek norms of behavior.

The second problem with large schools is that they increase status competitions and bullying. Let's start by thinking about our small village with just enough children to form the four main groups: young boys, young girls, older boys, and older girls. There might be only eight or ten kids in each group, so the status distinctions between the children would be fairly large. The status hierarchies would be stable, and conflicts would be rare. Sure, sometimes two children happen to be closely matched in status, or a late bloomer threatens to overtake a rival and move up the status hierarchy. We're never going to get rid of bullying. Status competitions exist because they are deeply embedded in human nature. But we can minimize them.

Large high schools are like the *Lord of the Flies* on a grander scale. Take a thousand children from a narrow age range so they are all rivals. Then drop them onto a proverbial island and let them organize a status hierarchy. Since social status cannot be measured ("I'm a 6.14 and you're a 6.13, so you must defer to me") the outcome is more conflict and potential threats to social status. That means more bullying as children send messages to rivals and deter potential threats.

Most middle schools have a team-based structure where students are put on a team of perhaps 150 students. This creates a "school within a school" environment. There are many reasons for doing this, but I think the main reason is that the ecology of the marketplace has spoken: It's better for socializing children. But the "school within the school" approach is a stopgap. Children need smaller schools. Up through middle school, there should only be one class per grade, which is what usually happens with private schools. High schools should be bigger because sports and activities are an important social glue, and because at some point, the training wheels have to come off. But even high schools should be relatively small.

Age and Social Status

Children don't know what their lot in life is yet, so they start out by aiming high. That's why most young boys want to be professional athletes. That's also why high school students are so obsessed with popularity and coolness—they are still aiming pretty high, which makes status competitions particularly fierce. As children mature into adults, they moderate their expectations to their skills and talents, and the social niches they've carved out for themselves.

Children become socialized by imitation, and they follow the same heuristics that we saw in the chapter on culture. However, since children are particularly influenced by social status, they are much more likely to follow the status heuristic. Within the world of children, older children are higher in status than younger children. This means that there is a trickle-down effect. The older teenagers imitate young adults. The younger teenagers imitate older teenagers. The older pre-teens imitate the younger teenagers, and so on down the line.

The outcome of this trickle-down process is that children are socialized to meet the demands of the adult world they will someday enter. If children were as influenced by their parents as we once thought, then idiosyncratic or manipulative parents could cripple their children's life prospects by raising them in an unusual way. Children protect themselves against this by learning from their successful peers instead of their parents. Once again, this is why the shared family environment has less influence than we thought.

The unimportance of the shared environment explains a puzzle. There are no randomized controlled trials which show that single motherhood causes poverty. In theory we could get a representative sample of women and randomly assign half of them to marry and the other half to be single mothers, but that would be both unethical and impossible. The next best thing is to look for a natural experiment. And that's exactly what Kenneth Lang and Jay Zagorsky figured out how to do. The methodology is grim, but they looked for cases where married fathers died unexpectedly.

If single motherhood causes poverty, then it shouldn't matter if the father left because he found another woman, or because he passed away. Most single mothers are in relationships with their child's father initially,[288] so the situation isn't that different. In both cases we have fathers who are initially part of the family but then go away. Lang and Zagorsky found that children whose fathers died suffered loss and trauma, which is not surprising. The puzzling part is that as adults they made about the same income as their peers whose fathers who didn't die.[289]

At this point in the book the puzzle isn't actually a puzzle. It's completely predictable. First, the reason why the father is absent *does* matter. A neighborhood of children whose fathers passed away would be heartbreakingly sad, but it would otherwise be a normal middle-class neighborhood where children are socialized by norms such as William Galston's three rules to avoid poverty: graduate from high school, wait until age twenty to marry, and wait until marriage to have kids.[290] A neighborhood of children whose fathers left to be with other women has very different values and socializes children into a very different life script. In terms of evolutionary psychology, the first neighborhood socializes boys to take the dad path. The second neighborhood socializes boys to take the cad path.

I find this to be particularly heartbreaking because even if parents from low-income backgrounds marry and do everything right, their children will almost certainly end up poor. Their daughters will be single mothers and their sons will be absent fathers. It takes an extraordinary effort and force of will to overcome harmful peer effects.

The book *The Ditchdigger's Daughters* tells the story of a determined working-class couple. They built a house by hand in a middle-class neighborhood to get their daughters into a better school, and carefully screened their daughters' friends. Their father could be demanding and difficult, and he expected straight A's from his daughters. But it worked. Two of his daughters became doctors, and all five got a college education and became accomplished women with successful lives.[291] But that's not a realistic path for most hardworking married couples who are poor. As a society we can either change the culture, or we have to accept that even couples who do everything right won't be able to escape entrenched generational poverty.

The Lesson of Andrew Tate

For those who are not on social media, Andrew Tate is a young, physically fit man who has made a following of teenage boys by teaching them red pill techniques. If you recall from the chapter on evolutionary psychology, red pill is the dark triad techniques of manipulation and control. Tate himself is relatively unimportant. There are a million other social media influencers pushing red pill content who could just as easily have broken through. The key point is that our promiscuous norms have created a world where every teenage boy wants what he has: women, money, and six-pack abs. The left may frame it as, "We need to stop the alt-right from celebrating men like Tate," but Tate is not an alt-right phenomenon. He's a promiscuity phenomenon.

Rigid and inflexible gender roles are not the creation of conservative fathers or regressive religious leaders. They are the creation of social liberalism. The egalitarian gender paradox is the phenomenon where Western nations, which are supposedly feminist and egalitarian, have larger differences between the sexes for personality traits than patriarchal nations like Rwanda.[292] Once you understand peer socialization and evolutionary psychology, it stops being a paradox.

As soon as teenage boys leave their egalitarian homes and go to school, they have a high-stakes problem to solve: How to claw their way one step higher up in popularity. They might try looking to social media influencers like Tate, they might hit the gym and start lifting weights, or they might turn to hip hop artists and other cultural icons. One thing they are not going to do is listen to their parents regurgitate a *Vox* article like *How to Talk to Boys so They Grow into Better Men*.[293] That advice will help them have a healthier marriage as an adult, but it won't make them more popular in high school. Judith Rich Harris captured this dilemma perfectly in the epigraph at the start of the chapter: "A child's goal is not to become a successful adult, any more than a prisoner's goal is to become a successful guard. A child's goal is to be a successful child."[294]

Kim Kardashian is the female Andrew Tate. Tate is a talented athlete, but he wasn't quite good enough to make it as a professional kickboxer. And Kardashian is an attractive woman, but she never made it as an actress or a model. Instead, they both occupy niches where they are social media influencers for teenagers who want what they have. The girls want to be beautiful, sexy, and confident, and the boys want to be the kind of men who can get those women.

Monogamy does not produce famous social media influencers, so I will once again turn to the fictional world of Jane Austen to choose archetypes: Elizabeth Bennett and Mr. Darcy from *Pride and Prejudice*. They are both attractive people, as high-status individuals tend to be. But Elizabeth's appeal was not her looks, but her personality.[295] Her sister was the real beauty in the family, and Mr. Darcy originally took no notice of Elizabeth. It was only after he got to know her that Mr. Darcy revised his opinion of her beauty. Men don't care about the personalities of the women they meet at bars, but they do care about the personalities of the women they want to marry.

As a society, we have the collective power to choose either monogamy or promiscuity. Depending on which of these we choose, we set the goal that teenagers fight and claw their way up the social hierarchy to reach. That goal can be Elizabeth and Darcy, or it can be Kardashian and Tate. Maybe I'm overgeneralizing from my own experience, but most liberals are not like the muscular and domineering PC Principal from the TV show *South Park*. And research does suggest that compared to conservatives, liberals are more neurotic,[296] more introverted,[297] and have less upper-body strength.[298]

So I'm left struggling with this question: Why do the socially awkward outcasts fight so hard to create a system that prizes the Andrew Tates and Kim Kardashians of the world? Once again, I have to revisit my love-hate relationship with postmodernism, because only the postmodernists understand how people become willing participants in their own marginalization.

Strategic Behavior

> Humans have a *social epistemology*, meaning that we have reasoning processes that afford us forms of knowledge and understanding, especially the understanding and the sharing of the content of other minds, that are unavailable to merely "rational" creatures. This social epistemology characterizes our species. The bounds of reason are thus not the irrational, but the social.
>
> – Herbert Gintis, *The Bounds of Reason*

One of the assumptions that underpins modern economics is that people are rational. Libertarian economists have used this assumption to aggressively colonize other social sciences. Applying an economic analysis to politics colonized the field of political science and led to the discipline of public choice theory. Applying an economic analysis to the law has created the field of *law and economics*. This aggressive expansion into other fields is one reason why economics is, usually derisively, called the Queen of the Social Sciences.

The left needed a weapon to fight back against the assumption of rationality, and they found it with *behavioral economics*. Psychologists and economists began studying how people make decisions in the real world. And what they found is that people are not always rational. Liberals used behavioral economics to reclaim some of their lost territory back from libertarians. A good example is the model of the rational drug addict, where we saw that drug addicts experience regret and preference reversals, which means they aren't that rational after all.

The liberal counterattack came at a heavy price. In the process they missed the deepest and most exciting lessons of behavioral economics.

They invested enormous amounts of time and energy cataloging all the different ways that real people differ from purely rational members of *Homo economicus*, but they never thought about why.

Hawks and Doves

In what is probably the most famous experiment in behavioral economics, students were randomly selected to be given a coffee mug. The students who did not have a mug were asked how much they would be willing to pay to get one. The students who had mugs were asked how much they would be willing to sell their mugs for. The students with mugs demanded about twice as much as the mug-less students were willing to pay.[299] In other words, simply owning a coffee mug for a couple of minutes made the students so attached to them that they valued them a lot more. A rational being like Mr. Spock from the TV show *Star Trek* would not do this.

Behavioral economists call this by two related terms—the endowment effect and loss aversion. The *endowment effect* means that simply being given a mug causes people to value it a lot more. *Loss aversion* means that people would hate to lose a mug more than they would like to gain a mug. In other words, people hate losing more than they like winning. Richard Thaler and Cass Sunstein write in their book, *Nudge*, that "loss aversion operates as a kind of cognitive nudge, pressing us not to make changes, even when changes are very much in our interest."[300] The alleged lesson is that people are too irrational to promote their own self-interest, so we need the government to "nudge" us towards making rational choices. And if you read a book like *Nudge* or *Thinking Fast and Slow*, that is the end of the story. But in fact, it is just the beginning.

The real lesson is found in the next parable of our tour of human nature, the parable of hawks and doves. We are not literally talking about birds, but the strategies that people and animals use when they are in a conflict over a prize. For butterflies the prize may be a sunlit leaf because male butterflies who occupy sunlit leaves have more mating success. For feral horses, it can be a pool of fresh water. For baboons it can be food. Prizes are anything that has value. *Hawks* are fighters. When two hawks see a prize, they will fight over it. *Doves* are sharers. When two doves see a prize, they will share it. When a hawk and a dove both see a prize, the dove will defer, and the hawk will take it without having to fight.

Imagine a world of all doves. It is basically a communist utopia in which everyone shares everything without conflict. The fatal flaw of the dove strategy is that it is ripe for invasion by hawks. A hawk would have a field day in Dovetopia. Imagine how successful the first butterfly with the hawk mutation would be. Over time more and more doves would switch to the hawk strategy, and the newly minted hawks would have a field day of their own plundering the remaining doves. This means that dove is not what biologists call an *evolutionarily stable strategy*. Any strategy that can be invaded is not evolutionarily stable. But the hawk strategy has its own problem, which is that fighting is costly. The cost of fighting should be subtracted from the value of the prize. A world of doves is efficient but can be invaded. A world with hawks is inefficient. What can we do?

The evolutionary biologists John Maynard Smith and Geoffrey Parker found a third way: the *bourgeois strategy*.[301] If you're keeping track, this is yet another parallel between evolutionary biology and economics. The bourgeois strategy is 'play hawk when you own the prize, dove when someone else does.' The bourgeois strategy is as economically efficient as the dove strategy, but under reasonable assumptions, it cannot be invaded by hawks. I won't do the math, but the value of playing hawk comes from finding doves to plunder. When there are no easy victims there is no longer any benefit to being a hawk.

The bourgeois strategy is widely used in the animal kingdom. Herbert Gintis reviews the literature in *The Bounds of Reason* and finds that the bourgeois strategy is used by butterflies, spiders, wild horses, finches, wasps, lizards, primates, and many other species.[302] I've noticed that my dog follows the bourgeois strategy. It's always cute watching him make a beeline to another room when he's given a high value treat. By taking it to a new location, he's asserting his ownership, even though he's only had it for a few seconds. (Jake, I'm not going to take your pig's ear away from you.)

Humans also follow the bourgeois strategy. The fact that people who own coffee mugs place a higher value on them also means that they are willing to fight harder to keep them. Conversely, people who don't own mugs are less willing to fight to acquire them. Sure, that reduces the chance that two students can mutually agree on a price for a mug, but having the concept of ownership and property rights hardwired into our genes is more than worth it. Capitalism and free markets probably wouldn't even be possible if we didn't have this instinctive sense of property rights.

Loss aversion shows up in unlikely places. Gamblers are more likely to double down after losing a bet than after winning. Good students are more likely to cheat to avoid getting a bad grade than bad students are in order to get a good grade. Golfers are more likely to attempt foolish shots to save par than to get a birdie. NASCAR has even found that most accidents occur because a driver is trying to avoid being passed, and not because they are aggressively trying to make a risky pass themselves.[303]

The Ultimatum Game

The *ultimatum game* is played by two people who are anonymous to each other, usually because they are sitting at different computers in a crowded economics lab. So it's important to realize that the players really are anonymous. The purpose of the game is to divide ten dollars. One of the players is randomly chosen to be the first mover. He gets to decide how to divide the money. He could choose a 50:50 split, or 80:20, or something else. The second mover decides whether to accept or reject the offer. If he accepts, then they each get whatever the first mover proposed. If he rejects it, then no one gets anything.

If people behaved like rational members of *Homo economicus* then here is what would happen: The first mover would make an offer of 99:1 and the second mover would accept. That's because the second mover would realize that 1 percent of the pot is still better than nothing. In the jargon of economics, that would maximize his utility. Of course, no one in the real world would ever do this, but that's how economic models work.

In Western cultures the most common offer is a 50:50 split, and the average offer is about 44 percent.[304] In the rare cases when the first mover proposes 25 percent or less, the second mover usually rejects the offer, even though it means leaving money on the table. The ultimatum game taps into the *unwritten rules* of society. No one has to tell Western players that a 50:50 split is fair, and that an offer that departs too far from 50:50 will be rejected. It's just something that everyone learns by being a part of the culture. That's what Herb Gintis meant in the epigraph about humans having a *social epistemology*—a social way of knowing things.

There are two main differences between purely rational members of the mythical species *Homo economicus* and real human beings. The first is reputation. Members of *Homo economicus* would accept lopsided offers and gain a reputation as suckers. Once that happens, they'd be shark food. No one would ever deal with them as an equal again. There is nothing rational about making choices that will permanently mark you as a sucker. Our economic models are simply wrong, at least in the realm of informal cooperation outside of markets.

However, reputation still cannot explain the difference between real people and *Homo economicus*. That's because ultimatum is typically a one-shot game that is played anonymously, and interviews with players show that they clearly understand this. Instead what matters is your sense of *personal identity*. People want to be able to think of themselves as tough but fair. They want to think of themselves as a good partner that other people would want to cooperate with. And no one wants to think of himself as a sucker that other people would see as an easy victim.

We've talked about signals as a way to share private information, but the most important person you will ever signal to is yourself. We don't fully know our own character, so we go through life looking for clues for what type of person we really are, and we make choices with a sense of self-awareness about this. Even if it's a one-off game that is played anonymously, you'll know that you let the first mover walk all over you if you accepted an unfair offer.

Given the strong current of fairness and the desire to cooperate that emerges from the ultimatum game, liberals may see this as evidence that people are natural communists. This leads to the obvious conclusion that people would like to have a big government that "spreads the wealth." But a deeper look at experimental games clearly refutes that idea. In the ultimatum game, the first mover is typically chosen randomly. But in some versions, the first mover is the winner of a competition. This is typically done by choosing the person with the highest score on a quiz based on current events or a standardized test. In those games, the first mover only offers about 28 percent of the pot. Moreover, these offers are almost never rejected.[305] The first mover won the game fair and square and is claiming his just reward. The second mover knows this and accepts. If he punished the first mover by rejecting the offer, then he'd have to face the consequences of having to think of himself as a sore loser.

An even stronger line of evidence for fairness over altruism comes from the *dictator game*. It is just like ultimatum except that the first mover's offer is final. The second mover does not have the option of rejecting it. When the dictator game is played anonymously, and when the first mover is chosen by winning a competition, the average offer is only about 3 percent of the pot. There is no fear of having the offer rejected, so the winners feel like they can give themselves the entire pot. If that's not enough, then let's consider one more variation. In this version, the dictator is the person who *lost* the quiz. In these cases, the average offer is as high as 75 percent.[306] That is almost impossible to explain by altruism. We are not natural communists sharing the wealth. Instead, we follow unwritten rules of fairness and personal responsibility. In the case where the dictator is the person who lost the quiz, the first mover gets to think of himself as someone who plays the game fair and square, and who is gracious in defeat. That's worth more than money.

These fairness norms are relative to the local culture. Things that are fair in one culture may not be in another. A good line of evidence for this comes from a study by Joseph Henrich and colleagues. He has been at the forefront of trying to isolate what is unique about what he calls *WEIRD* cultures—Western, Educated, Industrialized, Rich and Democratic. In order to do this, they had people from fifteen different primitive cultures play the ultimatum game.[307] In all cases, they chose norms that suited their local environment and how their society was organized.

The Gnau were unusual in that first movers actually averaged offers of over 50 percent. Even more astonishing, these large gifts were routinely rejected. Why? Because people in that culture gain social status by offering large gifts (think of Oprah giving free cars to her audience). Accepting the gift means accepting a lower social status than the giver. The Lamalera and the Aché were different. They commonly made offers that were 50 percent or even a bit higher, but in these cases, the offers were almost always accepted. Why? Because the Lamelera and Aché have cultures based on sharing meat from large kills. They understand that sometimes you make the kill and share with others; other times your buddy makes the kill and shares with you.

The Machiguenga and Tsimané made low offers in the ultimatum game, but these low offers were almost always accepted. Why is that? Aren't they worried about being a sucker? The answer is *no*. These cultures have very little cooperation to begin with. People in these cultures do not trust strangers, and thus they don't have cultural norms built around punishing free riders and enforcing cooperation. People from selfish and uncooperative cultures are the closest thing we have to the purely rational members of *Homo Economicus*. Let that lesson sink in.

Strong Reciprocators and Sneaky Norm Benders

Let's draw a final lesson from the ultimatum game. People are not altruistic, but they are not wholly selfish either. Instead, they roughly fall into one of two categories: strong reciprocators and sneaky social norm benders. We'll look at *sneaky norm benders* first. They take advantage of the fact that social norms and unwritten rules are general principles. The lines are blurry, so some people like to push the bounds of acceptable behavior. The most common offer in the ultimatum game is 50:50, but many people make 60:40 offers. They know that if it is close enough to a fair offer that it will get accepted. They are able to "bend" the social norm of fairness.

Arguing over fairness norms is human nature. A first mover could defend the 60:40 division as equally fair: "The fact that I am the first mover means that I have a stronger claim to the money than you. It's only fair that I get a slightly larger share. You aren't a sucker for accepting this unequal distribution. Instead, you are showing empathy and moral imagination by recognizing when another has a stronger claim." That could be true, or it could be nonsense. But even if it's nonsense, it gives the second mover a face-saving way to get some money without feeling like a bully took advantage of them. These conversations don't actually take place, but they happen internally and become a part of the unwritten rules.

Luckily, not everyone is a sneaky norm bender. There is another group of people called *strong reciprocators*. Strong reciprocators are willing to punish free riders, even when it is costly to themselves. This is called *altruistic punishment*. The NASCAR driver Mark Martin is a strong reciprocator. We see that in his ethic of, "I treat another driver like he treats me. If he races me hard and clean, I do the same to him. If he doesn't, then payback is okay."[308] NASCAR is a perfect example of the themes in this book because cooperation on the racetrack happens informally, outside the realm of formal contracts. When is it ok to join a drafting line with another Chevy, and when do team loyalties take priority? There is no formal contract, just unwritten rules that can sometimes be bent.

Tit-for-Tat and the Folk Theorem

Let's simplify the free rider problem until there are only two players. This gives us a classic problem in game theory called the *prisoner's dilemma*. You may already know it, but here it is again:

Two bank robbers have been detained by the police. They separate the two robbers and make each of them the same offer: "Confess to committing the bank robbery, and you'll get immunity while your accomplice gets ten years. But keep in mind that we're giving your partner the same deal. So if you don't confess and your partner does, then he'll get immunity, and you'll go to prison for ten years." If neither partner confesses, then the police can send each robber to prison for two years for a lesser crime. If both partners confess, then they each go to prison for five years.

Suppose Alicia and Blake are the bank robbers. No matter what Blake does, it's in Alicia's self-interest to confess. Suppose Blake refuses to confess (cooperates). Then Alicia will get off scot-free if she confesses (defects). Now suppose that Blake confesses (defects). Then Alicia will go to jail for ten years if she cooperates, but only five if she also defects. Once again, she should defect. Economists would say that the prisoner's dilemma is a game with a single Nash equilibrium of always defect. A Nash equilibrium is virtually identical to the evolutionarily stable strategies we saw above. In both cases they mean that you can't single-handedly improve your outcome by changing your strategy.

Robert Axelrod attempted to solve the prisoner's dilemma when he hosted a famous tournament for social scientists. They were invited to create different strategies to play an iterated version of the prisoner's dilemma. That means the game was played repeatedly over many rounds. The reason why Axelrod chose an iterated game is because in the real world, people usually have ongoing relationships with each other, rather than one-time encounters. This makes it possible to learn from experience whether the other person can be trusted. The hope was that the strategies in the tournament could also learn from experience and reach cooperative outcomes. And sure enough, one strategy did.

STRATEGIC BEHAVIOR

Everyone expected the winner to be extremely sophisticated, but instead the surprise winner was a simple and humble strategy called *Tit-for-Tat*.[309] All the strategy does is cooperate on the first round, and then copy whatever its opponent did the previous round. If the opponent defected, then it will defect. If the opponent cooperated, then it will cooperate. Hence the name, "Tit-for-Tat."

Although it is a simple strategy, Tit-for-Tat does have three important virtues. Its first virtue is that it is nice. Tit-for-Tat always starts out cooperating. It may get drawn into a war, but only for self-defense. Its second virtue is that it is street-smart. Tit-for-Tat will punish defections by defecting in the next round. That means that it cannot be easily exploited. Tit-for-Tat's final virtue is its most important. Tit-for-Tat is a forgiving strategy because it does not have a memory of more than one round. It doesn't matter how much conflict the two players have had in the past. If the other player cooperates, then Tit-for-Tat will forgive all the past abuses and cooperate in the next round.

Tit-for-tat was so effective that many social scientists drew the wrong conclusion—that cooperative behavior is in our rational self-interest. They pointed to a famous theory in social science called the *Folk Theorem*, which says that it may be rational for self-interested people to cooperate with each other in repeated games. However, the Folk Theorem only says that rational, self-interested people *might* cooperate. It does not say that they *will* cooperate. The Nobel laureate Elinor Ostrom and her colleagues point out the following.

> Consistent policy prescriptions cannot be based solely on the Folk Theorem. It is a gigantic leap of faith to deduce that, simply because a mathematical solution exists to an infinitely repeated [prisoner's] dilemma, appropriators will automatically find such a solution and follow it.[310]

THE NAKED MOLE-RAT

In hindsight it's clear that Axelrod's tournament was rigged to get cooperative outcomes. There were only two players, and they each had perfect information about the other's actions. If one player defected, the other player would know who did it and who to punish. But what if there were ten players and three defected? What if there were 2,000 players and 600 defected? What if you have no idea who the 600 defectors were? You can't punish free riders if you can't identify them. Cooperation between two players with perfect information is easy. Cooperation between thousands of players with imperfect information is hard. And that is the lesson to take from the Folk Theorem. Cooperation is rational in small, intimate groups, but not in large, anonymous groups. Herb Gintis reviewed the research literature on the Folk Theorem in *The Bounds of Reason* and that is exactly what he found.[311]

Culture can help people cooperate. The *public goods game* makes this clear. It is a game designed to be a generic stand-in for all the cases where the group gains from cooperation, such as the decision to work hard for your firm. It is played anonymously with three players who are each given twenty dollars. They can put any amount of this into the pot. The amount put into the pot is increased by 50 percent and distributed equally among all the three players. I won't walk you through the analysis, but it's a lot like the prisoner's dilemma in that the game has only a single Nash equilibrium of always defect (not putting any money in the pot).

The anthropologist Joseph Henrich reviews the literature on the game in *The WEIRDest People in the World*. It turns out that WEIRD people have norms and values that are highly distinct from the rest of the world, and these norms and values are the foundation of cooperation between strangers. The branding of WEIRD is clever because our culture seems normal to us, but we really are the weird ones. It's the rest of the world that's normal. The rest of the world is enmeshed in deep kinship ties that help people cooperate with family, but also make it hard to trust strangers. Henrich finds that WEIRD people contribute much more to the pot than non-WEIRD people.[312]

The story gets more interesting with a variation of the game that takes place over multiple rounds, and which allows players to punish free riders. After each round of the game, the players get anonymous data on how much the other players contributed. Then each player has the chance to spend one dollar to remove three dollars from one of the other players. In WEIRD cultures, strong reciprocators punish the sneaky norm benders who didn't contribute. This results in even higher contributions to the pot in future rounds of the game. You can even visualize the sneaky norm bender sitting at his computer and realizing that he was punished. "Busted! Oh well, I guess I should contribute next round."

That's not what happens in non-WEIRD cultures. Instead, the free riders retaliate against the players who they think punished them. The punishments are completely anonymous, players don't even know that "player A" punished them. This meant that the free riders blindly lash out at high cooperators who they assumed were the ones punishing them. The outcome in non-WEIRD societies is that cooperation stayed low, even with the ability to punish free riders.[313] The takeaway is that we haven't quite solved the free rider problem, but we've sharpened the discussion to this: How do you make people WEIRD? That is the topic of the next chapter.

The Hobbesian Problem

> Palanpur farmers sow their winter crops several weeks after the date at which yields would be maximized. The farmers do not doubt that earlier planting would give them larger harvests, but no one, the farmer explained, is willing to be the first to plant, as the seeds on any lone plot would be quickly eaten by birds. I asked if a large group of farmers, perhaps relatives, had ever agreed to sow earlier, all planting on the same day to minimize the losses. "If we knew how to do that," he said, looking up from his hoe at me, "we would not be poor."
>
> – Samuel Bowles, *Microeconomics*

Society rests on a foundation of unwritten rules and moral values. If the foundation isn't strong, the legal system can't function. This is sometimes called the *Hobbesian problem*, after the philosopher Thomas Hobbes. The legal scholar Andrzej Rapaczynski explains.

> This is the old Hobbesian problem: when most people obey the law, the government can enforce it effectively and (relatively) cheaply against the few individuals who break it. But when obedience breaks down on a large enough scale, no authority is strong enough to police everyone. In such a setting, with enforcement becoming less and less effective, individuals have an incentive to follow their own interests, regardless of any paper constraints.[314]

Simply having a law that says "Don't steal" is not enough. The police have to be able to enforce it. If everyone follows the law, then it is easy for the police to arrest a few lawbreakers. But if too many people break the law, then the police will be overwhelmed and can't keep up. This problem is compounded by the fact that the police and legal system are part of society, so as society becomes more and more lawless, the police and legal system become more and more corrupt.

The Hobbesian problem explains why conservatives were so upset by the riots and looting that took place during the George Floyd protests. All societies have problems, and angry protests can happen anywhere. But if society is healthy, an angry protest won't cause the equilibrium to flip from "the police can arrest the rare few lawbreakers" to "there are too many people breaking the law for the police to do anything." The riots gave us a glimpse into a society whose unwritten rules are fraying. Conservatives were able to see the Hobbesian problem happening in our nation, in real time, right on our TV screens.

Amoral Familism

The best way to think about how difficult it is to solve the Hobbesian problem is to imagine life in its most basic and brutal form. The philosopher Thomas Hobbes called it a *state of nature*, but these days most people call it a zombie apocalypse. I think the appeal of the genre is that we have to imagine what life is like without the benefits of modern civilization. We would lose everything that we take for granted—not just cars and smartphones, but even the ability to walk down the street without risking life and limb. People would have to huddle together in small bands and slink around out of sight just to survive. That's life in a state of nature. Hobbes described it as "a war of all against all."

The most important lesson of the genre is that the real threat isn't the zombies, but the other humans. What happens when your band encounters another group of survivors? They might be nice, but there is always the chance that they have more guns and will kill the men in your group and capture the women. The smart thing to do is to avoid all other humans. If you try to stay away but still can't avoid them, then this is all the proof you need that they have bad intentions. At that point your best option is to preemptively attack them before they preemptively attack you.

On the other hand, if they stick to themselves then maybe they don't want trouble. Over the years you could build trust with the neighboring group. You could leave little gifts at the border between your territories, and they might reciprocate. Eventually this could grow into formal trade and perhaps even festivals and gatherings where you freely interact with the neighboring tribe. But simply walking up to strangers and saying "hello, we come in peace," is a recipe for a quick death.

The second way to wrap your head around primitive life is to think of prison. You may be familiar with movies like *The Shawshank Redemption* where a middle-class man is suddenly thrust into a hostile environment where he can't trust anyone. There is no one to protect him, and everyone else is a potential threat. He could be raped or beaten at any time, and no one would lift a finger to stop it, perhaps not even the guards. In prison people turn to gangs for protection. In a state of nature, they turn to their extended family.

A powerful goon can rob a single man, but it's too dangerous to rob someone who belongs to a large family. His brothers, cousins, and uncles will come looking for revenge. In a state of nature, your family is your police force, your legal system, and your national defense. The Pomo Indian William Saroyan wrote this in the 1940s.

> What is a man? A man is nothing. Without his family he is of less importance than that bug crossing the trail, or less importance than the sputum or exuviae. At least they can be used to help poison a man. A man must be with his family to amount to anything with us. If he had nobody else to help him, the first trouble he got into he would be killed by his enemies, because there would be no relatives

to help him fight the poison of the other group. No woman would marry him ... He would be poorer than a new-born child, he would be poorer than a worm .... The family is important. If a man has a large family ... and upbringing by a family that is known to produce good children, then he is somebody and every family is willing to have him marry a woman of their group. In the White way of doing things the family is not so important. The police and soldiers take care of protecting you, the courts give you justice, the post office carries messages for you, the school teaches you. Everything is taken care of, even your children, if you die; but with us the family must do all of that.[315]

Edward Banfield first noticed this dynamic when he was studying villagers in Southern Italy. He called it *amoral familism*. Francis Fukuyama summarizes the main lesson of amoral familism as, "take advantage of people outside your immediate family at every occasion because otherwise they will take advantage of yours first."[316]

Families are a safe refuge. People grow up with their brothers and sisters, aunts and uncles, and all of their cousins. That close contact fosters trust. The patriarch of the family also has the power to assign jobs in the various family businesses, along with land, money, and favoritism. He is a benevolent dictator who can reward cooperation and punish free riders. This creates *social capital*, which Robert Putnam defines as "features of social organization, such as trust, norms, and networks that can improve the efficiency of society by facilitating coordinated actions."[317] Throughout this book I've been talking about social norms, unwritten rules, and moral values. The reason why these things are important is because they create social capital. They create the ability to cooperate. Social capital is the solution to the Hobbesian problem.

The problem with amoral familism is that people cannot cooperate beyond the extended family. Members of the same village cannot even trust each other. Suppose Blake is the patriarch of an extended family that owns several small businesses. How does Blake make sure the employees don't shirk on the job? He could hire a manager, but if the manager is someone from another family, he'd rob the store and embezzle the profits. Instead, Blake puts relatives into management positions. And if there aren't enough competent relatives, then the incompetent ones will have to do. They are tolerated because they won't steal from the business, or at least, they won't steal more than what is considered socially acceptable. The incompetent nephew theory of management will never create a firm that can go toe-to-toe with Microsoft or SpaceX, but it is a good solution for low-trust societies. The research agrees. Rafael La Porta and colleagues found that cultures with strong families and a lack of trust have difficulty creating large firms and economies of scale.[318] Instead they are usually limited to small family businesses.

Amoral familism has difficulty scaling beyond the extended family, but cousin marriage can help. If you're relatively old like me, you've probably seen the generational turnover take place in your family. When my wife and I were newlyweds, family holidays were about my mother-in-law's siblings. My wife would see her aunts, uncles, and cousins. But as the younger generation married and started their own families, it became too big. So each family started going their own way. Now family gatherings are about my wife's siblings, and she rarely sees her cousins.

Cousin marriage prevents this. It helps keep the extended family in the fold. The problem is that cousin marriage also creates clannish communities that distrust outsiders. It increases social capital within the extended family but hurts social capital outside it. In the long run cousin marriage is a trap. If you want a quick rule-of-thumb for how effectively a society can cooperate, then simply look up the rate of cousin marriage. The higher the rate, the more corrupt and impoverished the nation.

Amoral familism explains why some cultures hold moral values that are hostile to economic development. Italian immigrants to the United States assimilated relatively slowly compared to other groups. They worked hard, had stable marriages, and generally behaved responsibly. But they were hostile to education. They wanted their children working, not in school. An educated person has options. An educated person can leave the orbit of the extended family. An Italian proverb says "Stupid is he who makes his children better than himself." Why spend decades investing time and money into the education of your children, only to have them go off on their own as soon as they are grown? If you look at children strictly as an investment, it is a foolish thing to do. Under amoral familism, families need sons to work and defend the family honor, and daughters to make babies. The Palestinian leader Yasser Arafat used to say that "the womb of the Arab woman is our greatest weapon." People from societies locked into amoral familism can relate.

Amoral familism explains why Southern Italy and Sicily have a history of organized crime. Their culture is literally made for it. Amoral familism gives them an increased willingness to break the law and exploit others, and it gives them extremely high trust within the family. Amoral familism literally solves the prisoner's dilemma. Going to jail without testifying against the family is a mark of honor in crime families, and prisoners are richly rewarded upon release. We've been grappling with the prisoner's dilemma for most of the book, and now that we've finally found a way to solve it, it's in order to further the interests of organized crime.

Reputation and Reciprocity

The main puzzle of amoral familism is why any culture would choose it when it is so clearly counter-productive. If someone lives in a village, then they must know some of the other villagers. Why can't they learn to build an ongoing relationship that leads to trust and cooperation? We can answer that question using game theory. This time we'll consider a game called *stag hunt*.

> Two people are out hunting. They can individually hunt rabbits and make $100 each, or they can team up and hunt stags and make $500 each. But it takes both people to catch the stag. If only one person hunts stags, then he'll come home empty handed. If only one person hunts rabbits, he'll still make his $100.

If you recall, the prisoner's dilemma has a single Nash equilibrium of always defect. The stag hunt is different. Suppose Alicia and Blake are hunting. If Alicia thinks Blake is hunting rabbits (defects) then she should also defect and hunt rabbits. It takes two to catch a stag, so she'd come home empty-handed. On the other hand, suppose she thought Blake was hunting stags (cooperating) Then she should cooperate too. It's better to make $500 from stags than $100 from rabbits. The stag hunt has two different Nash equilibriums. The bad equilibrium is hunting rabbits for $100. The good equilibrium is hunting stags for $500. The stag hunt is a type of *coordination game*. The challenge is to coordinate a switch from the bad Nash equilibrium to the good one.

Now let's apply the stag hunt to amoral familism. Blake can choose from two life strategies. The first is "exploit people from other families"; the second is "cooperate with other families that have a good reputation." This is also a stag hunt. If Blake thinks that other people are going to exploit him (defect), then he should also defect. Otherwise, they'll stab him in the back when he least expected it. But if he really did think that other people are going to cooperate, then his best strategy is also to cooperate. A lot of economic development is getting cultures to move from the "exploit others" Nash equilibrium to the "cooperate with others" Nash equilibrium.

If you're a college student playing these games in a computer lab because it's part of your economics homework, you can easily switch between strategies. If exploiting others doesn't work out, then try cooperation. But in the real world these strategies are part of how people are raised. They are deeply embedded into the culture. Diego Gambetta tells the following story.

> A retired [Mafia] boss recounted that when he was a young boy, his Mafioso father made him climb a wall and then invited him to jump, promising to catch him. He at first refused, but his father insisted until finally he jumped – and promptly landed flat on his face. The wisdom his father sought to convey was summed up by these words: "You must learn to distrust even your parents."[319]

Coordinating people's actions to change from one Nash equilibrium to the other is a hard problem to solve. It usually takes a major shock, like contact with a more vigorous culture or adopting a new religion. But if a society does manage to move to the good Nash equilibrium, it can do some impressive things, including solving the tragedy of the commons.

Historically, the debate over the tragedy of the commons was between liberals who favor government regulations and libertarians who favor private property. The political scientist Elinor Ostrom spent her career looking at more than 5,000 cases of actual commons. These included inland fisheries, forest management, and irrigation systems for farmers. She found that most commons were not managed using either method. Instead they were managed with spontaneously generated social norms and unwritten rules that bubbled up from the local users. Ostrom won the Nobel Prize in 2009 for her research.

The problem that libertarians and progressives both make is that they worry too much about the incentives and not enough about low-level information gathering. The real problem is telling the peaches (honest workers) from the lemons (free riders). Most people want to cooperate, but no one wants to be the only sucker. Communities of fishermen and farmers understand this better than most economists. Once people lose their ability to be anonymous free riders, the tragedy of the commons usually takes care of itself. In *Understanding Institutional Diversity,* Ostrom listed eight key requirements that had to be met for societies to manage their commons.[320] We will consider the first five.

Clear boundaries of group membership. If it is easy to tell the people who are allowed to use the commons from the people who can't, then it is tough to be an anonymous free rider. The most common method is basing membership on where people live. Locals can use the commons; others cannot. That makes it easy to find free riders: "Hmmm, I don't recognize that person—he shouldn't be fishing here."

Sometimes these boundaries are based on technology. For example, fishermen who use nets are allowed to use one particular fishing spot, but not others. This makes it easy for distant observers to monitor the commons. "What is that guy doing with a net? He can't use that here." Libertarians and progressives tend to favor usage fees, taxes, and quotas, but a game warden can't see from a distance who has paid the fee and who hasn't.

Proportional benefits. The benefits of using the resource have to be proportional to the costs that each person bears. Otherwise, the rules create resentment among people who feel like they are doing all of the work but not getting any of the benefits. Successfully managing the tragedy of the commons is based on everyone "buying in."

This is a lesson that applies more broadly, and it is why multiculturalism makes cooperation more difficult. If one subculture "buys in," but another subculture does not, then cooperation will collapse. Robert Putnam has spent his career studying social capital, and his paper *E Pluribus Unum* shows that trust and social capital is lower in diverse, multicultural communities.[321] Putnam explains that people in diverse neighborhoods tend to "hunker down" rather than integrate with other ethnic groups who have a different culture, and therefore different norms and values.

Two people can't dance together if they're listening to different music. And that's what culture is—it's music. Think about some of the tribal cultures from the chapter on strategic behavior. What would happen if a member of the Aché tribe, where kill sharing is normal, joined the Tsimané tribe, where sharing and cooperation is low? The first time the Aché member shared his kill he'd be marked as a sucker. He'd face exploitation from the rest of the tribe by this display of weakness. It would be like the prison movies where the middle-class prisoner gives the tough prisoner his commissary, only to realize that this made him a victim.

Alternately, suppose someone from the Gnau tribe joined the Aché. He'd be willing to share his kills, but in his culture gift-giving is a sign of status and rank. He would be offended that people who accepted his meat didn't pay him back with the increased respect he felt he deserved. The other members of the tribe would be equally offended that an ordinary act like sharing a kill made him think he was superior. The unwritten rules that allow people to cooperate in one culture lead to conflict in another.

There are relatively high-trust nations in Latin America, such as Uruguay and Costa Rica. But most immigrants come from low-trust nations like Mexico and Guatemala. They are willing for their children and grandchildren to assimilate into the American culture, but this process takes generations. If we get too many immigrants too quickly, they'll balkanize into low-trust subcultures and the Hobbesian problem will begin to rear its ugly head.

Circling back to the current lesson on how to manage commons,

THE HOBBESIAN PROBLEM

there is also a liberal lesson to learn. It's hard to coordinate actions when there is a large gap in wealth. Sometimes wealthy elites will use their power to draw more benefits from the commons than regular users. Ordinary people do not have the power to punish elites, but this does cause them to lose respect for the rules. Once that happens, they become free riders, and the tragedy of the commons soon follows.

This principle has a lesson for managing firms. Suppose the CEO and senior management are getting bonuses and stock options while regular workers see their pay hold steady or even cut. Then this will undermine the second long-term excellence bank account that was discussed in the chapter on Jack Welch. Workers will no longer see themselves as insiders on a team that shares the same goals, but as outsiders being exploited by management. They will cut back on their work effort and employee morale will go down. Ultimately the firm will suffer, although the CEOs and senior managers will probably have moved on by the time that happens.

Harry Stonecipher retired as CEO of Boeing in 2005, but the company remains tragically inept twenty years later.[322] As of the time I'm writing this, the firm is looking for a new CEO to get it back on track. My completely unsolicited advice: hire an engineer with a long tenure within the company.

Collective Choice. The people who actually use the common pool resource need to have a say about the rules that govern it. Locals are the first to know if a strategy is working, and they have skin in the game. Far-away bureaucrats do not. Once again, bottom-up methods work better than top-down methods. This is doubly true because creating rules to manage a common has to be done as a trial-and-error process. Elinor Ostrom explains:

No one can undertake a complete analysis of all the potential rules that they might use and analytically determine which set of rules will be optimal for the outcomes they value in a particular ecological, economic, social, and political setting. One must realize that policies involving rule changes must be viewed as experiments. ... For some readers, this is a depressing lesson.[323]

We saw earlier in the book how the Japanese invented lean manufacturing. A key aspect of this is *Gemba* or worker feedback systems. The workers who use machines for eight hours a day had a lot more insight into small innovations that might improve the efficiency of their workflow. This was a main driver of the continuous improvement of Japanese factories. The workers on the ground are the ones with the information.

Managing a commons is like managing a business. Even the smartest government planners can't know ahead of time whether or not a given rule will be a success. The rule may not work out, or it may create unintended consequences. The local users need the power to change bad rules: "Ok, we tried allowing people to use nets to fish by the red clay cliffs, but that didn't work. No more nets over there." Slowly, step-by-step, the usage of the commons will become efficient. But that can only happen if the people who use the commons have control over the rules.

Community input on monitors. Some common pool resources are small enough that people can police each other. But larger common pool resources need monitors. These monitors have to be accountable to the people. An easy way to make that happen is when the people choose a monitor from among their own ranks. The monitor is tied to the community and cannot do a bad job without risking social scorn and ostracism. By contrast, government appointed monitors can get away with shirking on the job or playing favorites for personal gain. They don't have to face the wrath of the community.

If you're interested in mining Ostrom's research for new management ideas, the clear takeaway from this is that upper managers should be from the core business. Think back to the chapter on firms and the failure of the Jack Welch school of management. Firms have a short-term performance bank account and a long-term excellence bank account. It's easy to measure the short-term performance by looking at quarterly earnings, stock price, or the return on net assets. But it's impossible to measure the long-term excellence account because it is composed of things like workplace morale, norms of effort, technical debt, efficiency of business practices, and institutional knowledge. Because we can't objectively measure it, it will be systemically undervalued. However, people who come from the core business will have a good subjective feel for the status of the second bank account and will fight to make it healthier.

Gradual punishments. The punishments for free riders need to be gradual, beginning with a purely symbolic slap on the wrist. This notifies the community that free riders have been dealt with but does not do anything to alienate the person who is punished. Anyone can make a mistake or suffer a momentary lapse in judgment. Treating rule breakers like scoundrels will lower their social status, breed resentment, and cause them to lose respect for the rules. A purely symbolic acknowledgement of wrongdoing is enough to teach a lesson. It then allows the violator to reenter the community as a member in good standing. Severe punishments should be reserved for repeat offenders.

Anonymous Strangers

When libertarians consider poverty in the developing world, they think the solution is easy: Get rid of socialism and instill strong property rights and capitalism. In reality they have—repeatedly. Hernando de Soto points out in *The Mystery of Capital* that Peru officially recognized the property rights of the people in the 1824 constitution. In fact, various Latin American governments have attempted these types of capitalistic reforms at least twenty-two times since the end of the Spanish conquests 400 years ago.[324] But capitalism has never taken root in Latin America the way it did in Europe and North America. This is De Soto's mystery of capital: Why does capitalism work in the West but nowhere else?

The answer is corruption. Let's start by looking at how difficult it is to create a legal business in Peru. De Soto writes:

> Our goal was to create a new and perfectly legal business. The team then began filling out the forms, standing in the lines, and making the bus trips into central Lima to get all the certifications required to operate, according to the letter of the law, a small business in Peru. They spent six hours a day at it and finally registered the business – 289 days later. Although the garment workshop was geared to operating with only one worker, the cost of legal registration was $1,231 – thirty-one times the monthly minimum wage. To obtain legal authorization to build a house on state-owned land took six years and eleven months, required 207 administrative steps in fifty-two government offices. To obtain a legal title for that piece of land took 728 steps. We also found that a private bus, jitney, or taxi driver who wanted to obtain official recognition of his route faced twenty-six months of red tape.[325]

Most people do not have the time and money to do this. Furthermore, maintaining the legal title to one's home and business is almost as difficult as getting it in the first place. That's why most people in the developing world own their homes and businesses under the table. That means paying bribes to the police, health inspectors, and other bureaucrats. De Soto points out that these business owners typically spend about 10 percent to 15 percent of their sales on these bribes.[326]

That's why capitalist reforms fail. Why would insiders in a corrupt government want to kill the goose that lays the golden egg? They will not relinquish their privileged status. The empirical evidence agrees. Transparency International maintains a Corruption Perceptions Index, which is an international measure of corruption. It shows a strong correlation between corruption and per-capita GDP.[327] Corrupt countries are poor.

Critics of the corruption-causes-poverty theory claim that the arrow of causation points the other way: Rich nations are low in corruption because bureaucrats don't need to take bribes in order to put food on the table. This raises the problem of separating correlation from causation. Does A cause B or does B cause A? The best way to separate correlation from causation is to use a randomized controlled trial. When scientists can't do that, then a natural experiment is the next best thing.

The economist Paulo Mauro used a natural experiment with the degree of "ethno-linguistic fragmentation" as a stand-in for corruption. People from different ethnic groups who speak different languages are going to have stronger in-group versus out-group distinctions, which will result in more corruption. However, poverty itself did not cause this fragmentation. This let him isolate the effect of corruption. Mauro's research confirmed the fact that corruption slows economic growth.[328]

De Soto is ultimately unable to answer the mystery of capital and can only urge for stronger property rights, but without solving the Hobbesian problem that is a recipe for a twenty-third failure. I agree with libertarians that capitalism is the greatest anti-poverty program ever created. But a nation can't have capitalism unless it has solved the corruption problem. That requires the greatest cultural shock of them all: getting anonymous strangers to trust each other.

The Marriage and Family Plan

The anthropologist Joseph Henrich documents this culture shock in *The WEIRDest People in the World*. Recall that the title comes from the acronym Western, Educated, Industrialized, Rich, and Democratic. His book is an investigation into the fact that people in the West are psychologically very different from people in the rest of the world. There are many differences, so we'll only focus on the fact that WEIRD people have a much higher level of trust for strangers. Henrich identifies the cultural shock that caused this as the Marriage and Family Plan (MFP) of the Catholic Church.[329] It was a group of policies that the Catholic Church implemented in Europe after the fall of Rome. It has several planks, so we will only look at a few of them.

Cousin marriage bans. Cousin marriage is what makes strong extended families tick, but it also makes it harder to trust strangers. The Bible bans sexual relations with close relatives (Leviticus 18:6), but how do you define close? In what may be the world's only purity spiral that worked for good, the Catholic Church went through increasingly strict standards until ultimately Pope Alexander II banned marriage even to sixth cousins. In practice these bans weren't always enforced, and sometimes they were only invoked after the fact, as a way for the Catholic Church to justify granting an annulment. "Oh yes, it turns out that the man and woman were fifth cousins, so the marriage never counted."

Nevertheless, the cousin marriage ban had profound downstream consequences as it was rolled out. These bans frequently meant that people were unable to find someone to marry in their own village, or even the next village over, so marrying people from distant villages became common. The boundary lines for marriage typically mark the boundary lines for trust and cultural interchange, and the MFP shattered those boundaries.

Nuclear family. The second plank of the Catholic Church's MFP was to promote the nuclear family. Genesis 2:24 says "Therefore shall a man leave his father and his mother, and shall cleave unto his wife: and they shall be one flesh." This has enormous implications for extended families. In most of the world, the newly married couple lives in the same household as the extended family. The Bible makes it clear that the married couple is the primary unit and should break away from their parents. The MFP promoted the typically WEIRD arrangement where the newlyweds live in their own house and form their own independent household. This is called *neolocal residence.* This gets them out from under the thumb of meddling fathers and mothers-in-law.

What's striking is that the Bible says a *man* shall leave his mother and father, not a woman. In most kinship-driven societies, women move into her husband's extended family. This is called *patrilocal residence.* This isolates the young bride from her biological family and kin. She no longer has her parents, brothers, and a small army of cousins and uncles to look out for her welfare. It puts her at the mercy of an abusive husband, and it also puts her under the power of her mother-in-law, which is a recipe for further abuse.

The Bible is taking a direct shot at this family dynamic. If you've lived in a Christian subculture, then you know that Genesis 2:4 (or Matthew 19:4-6, or Ephesians 5:31) is trotted out every time there is conflict between newlyweds and one of their parents. You can barely go to a church picnic without hearing someone complaining about a meddling mother-in-law, and someone else sagely concluding "and therefore a man shall leave his father and mother and cleave to his wife and they shall become one flesh." The lesson is always the same: The primary unit is the marriage between a husband and wife, and the meddling mother-in-law needs to respect that.

Consensual marriage. The Catholic Church's Marriage and Family

Plan also explains the wedding tradition where the bride and groom exchange statements of "I do." I had always assumed that it was a relic from more traditional times when the young couple must get the approval of their parents, church, and broader community to marry. Having a big ceremony and a public exchange of vows was to include the various stakeholders in the marriage and provide the community's blessing on the young couple. But I got it completely wrong.

Weddings were small affairs in the Middle Ages, but they did get a little bigger as the Catholic Church began to regulate marriage. They began requiring witnesses and a priest for the couple's public consent ("I dos"). The goal was to prevent women from being forced into arranged marriages. It gave both the woman and the man the chance to publicly state that they did not consent to the marriage. Extended families use marriage for dynastic purposes just like kings and other members of the nobility. Marrying a daughter to a violent older man from a powerful family is smart politics, but terrible for the daughter who is married against her will.

One of the most important downstream consequences of these reforms was to delay marriage. When a culture gives women the freedom to marry, but also expects lifelong monogamy, they'll shop around to pick the best partner possible. That means waiting so that they can get more information about the men who are courting them. Women don't know how a man is going to turn out at age sixteen, but as he gets older they can get a better idea. Consensual marriage also increased the soft power of women. They would not choose a brutish or domineering man, but a man who they believed they could form a cooperative partnership with. This changed the incentives of the medieval marriage market. Men under the Catholic Church's MFP were socialized in very different ways from, for example, the patrilocal Visigoths who had sacked Rome not that long ago.

The outcome was that couples married late, generally in their mid-twenties,[330] and had smaller families. This pattern holds throughout the Western world. For example, the historian David Hackett Fischer points out in *Albion's Seed: Four British Folkways in America* that the Puritans who settled the United States also married in the early to mid-twenties.[331]

The Catholic Church's MFP is what made us WEIRD. It is what created trust and solved the Hobbesian problem. Henrich uses data on the Catholic Church's expansion through Europe from about 500 AD to 1500 AD as a natural experiment to study the different "dosages" of the MFP that different parts of Europe received. Henrich found that more exposure to the MFP makes people WEIRDer in every measurable way, most notably for our purposes, in trust of strangers.[332]

Henrich's natural experiment also explains the puzzle of why Southern Italians are so low in trust that they are locked into an equilibrium of amoral familism. It seems strange because Southern Italy is so close to Rome, which is the epicenter of Catholicism. History buffs already know the answer—Southern Italy was controlled by the Byzantine empire and Sicily was controlled by a Muslim power called the Emirate of Sicily. They were not Catholic, so they were not exposed to the Catholic Church's Marriage and Family Plan. It was only with the Norman conquests in the eleventh and twelfth centuries that Southern Italy and Sicily became Catholic, which meant that they had much less exposure to the MFP than Northern Italy. These cultural differences between Northern and Southern Italy still exist 800 years after the Norman conquests.

The Protestant Ethic

Henrich's research with the MFP is impressive, but it leaves us with a puzzle. The Protestant world of Northern Europe had much less exposure to the MFP, and yet by all measurable standards, historically Protestant nations are much WEIRDer than Catholic nations. Henrich even refers to Protestantism as a "booster shot" of WEIRD psychology.[333] This booster shot led to profound differences.

One difference was in rejecting a king in favor of a republic. I have a soft spot for the Dutch Republic, which began in 1581. The official religion was Calvinism, and citizens had to be a Calvinist to hold office, but otherwise they had religious tolerance. This made the Dutch Republic a center of commerce, science, and the arts. It became a vital intellectual hub because the books that kings in other nations had banned were freely allowed in the Dutch Republic. Trips to Holland often inspired the most productive periods of the careers of visiting intellectuals. Some of them include John Locke, Baruch Spinoza, and René Descartes. Dutch freedom also made the people so wealthy that they developed a fondness for expensive tulips, which we discussed back in the chapter on free markets. Alas, the Dutch Republic was one of the many casualties of the French Revolution.

So with the Dutch people's forgiveness, the United States became the world's first republic of the modern era in 1789. England followed with the Reform Act of 1832. The Catholic nations took longer. In fact, it could reasonably be argued that they didn't achieve stable representative governments until after World War II, but if you want to be charitable, we could push it earlier. If so, France reached this milestone with the Third Republic in 1870. Italy took until 1912, and Spain didn't manage this until the Second Republic in 1931. Even so, all three of these nations were ruled by a dictator during World War II, so their democratic traditions were far more fragile than the ones in the United States and Northern Europe.

The historically Protestant nations are also wealthier and higher in trust. The World Values Survey is an international survey of the values of people from eighty-one countries which collectively make up 85 percent of the world's population. One of the questions asks, "Generally speaking, would you say that most people can be trusted, or that you can't be too careful when dealing with people?" Ronald Inglehart, who administers the World Values Survey, drives home the power of culture when he graphed the level of trust against per-capita-GNP in *Culture Matters*. See figure 15 below.

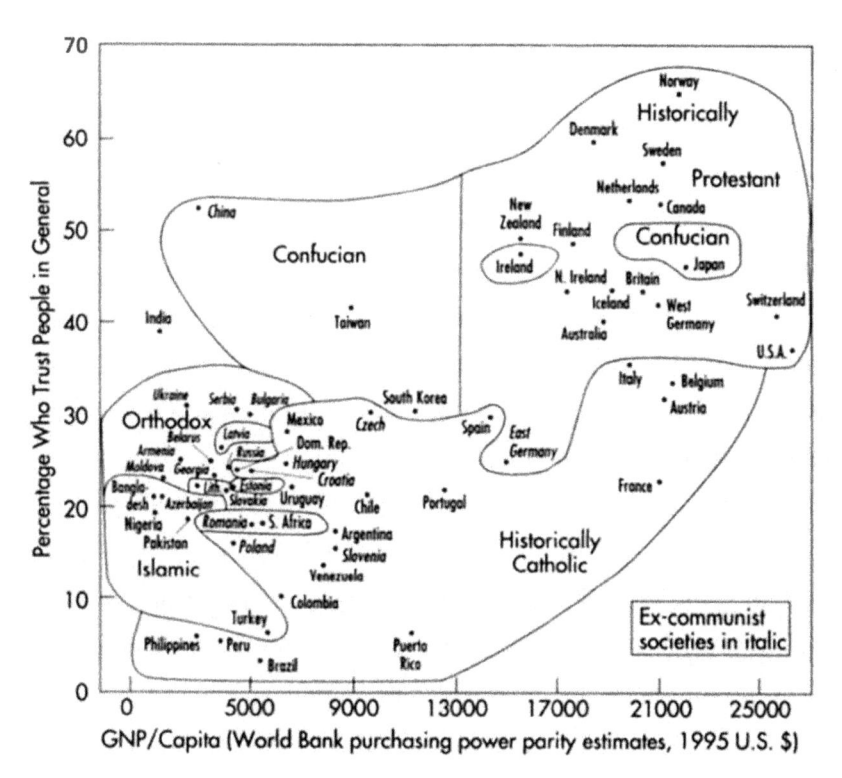

Figure 15: Interpersonal Trust vs Per-capita GNP. From *Culture Matters*.[334]

The cluster of affluent and high-trust Protestant nations is striking. However, the data is just a correlation. What we need is a natural experiment, and Henrich provides us with one: the Peace of Augsburg in 1555. After the Protestant Reformation, wars broke out between Catholics and Protestants. The Peace of Augsburg ended a war between Charles V and an alliance of Lutheran princes. The terms of the peace allowed each ruler to choose the religion for his land, which basically meant that different parts of Germany were assigned to be either Catholic or Protestant. This works as a natural experiment because most of the Lutheran princes were motivated by greed. One of the things that Protestant kings, French revolutionaries, and the Lutheran princes all realized was that they could make a lot of money by rejecting Catholicism and auctioning off church lands.

We don't have much data for this natural experiment, but what we do have shows that people from Protestant regions worked three to four more hours per week than people in Catholic regions, even after controlling for a variety of factors like age, education, marital status, and more.[335]

I said at the start of the chapter on free markets that we'd climb back to 30,000 feet. Now we're there. We have the exact same argument that was made in the opening chapter on three revolutions, but with a more rigorous foundation.

This tells us that Protestantism plays a causal role in making people extra WEIRD, but so far no one has isolated the "secret sauce" that makes it happen. It could be as simple as the fact that Protestantism is a bottom-up process, whereas Catholicism is top-down. If something works, more churches start doing it, and it spreads. Both churches and entire denominations can grow, then decline, and become extinct over time. But they are replaced by new churches and new denominations. Protestantism is an ecologically rational process.

The sociologist Roger Finke and Rodney Stark have argued in *The Churching of America* that religious competition leads to greater faith.[336] Without the benefit of state support, different denominations must compete with each other to win converts. By contrast, state religions become monopolies that refuse to innovate. Once again, the only thing worse than failure is not being allowed to fail. That's why the United States, with no established religion, is more devout than Europe, which does have established state religions. (Perhaps atheists should start advocating for the US to have an official state religion.)

Another possible reason for the Protestant ethic could be the emphasis on reading the Bible. Henrich starts his book by documenting how the Protestant Reformation led to universal literacy, including for women, for the first time in history. That's because Protestants felt that individual believers needed to read the Bible for themselves. The Catholics responded by also promoting literacy and Bible study, but outside of the Jesuits, their hearts were never really in it. Henrich observes that, "in the absence of competition from the literacy-obsessed Protestants, it's not entirely clear that Catholic missionaries had much effect on literacy at all."[337]

The O-Ring Economy

WEIRDness is essential for modern economics because modern jobs are more precise and demanding. In pre-industrial times workers could get away with doing a sloppy job. Gregory Clark explains in *A Farewell to Alms*.

> Consider the production of wheat in preindustrial agriculture. The ground was plowed, the seed sown, the grain reaped, and finally it was threshed and winnowed. If too much seed was sown then some of it was lost; if too little, then some land input was not fully utilized.

If the threshing was done poorly then some grain remained with the straw, which in any case was fed to the farm animals, so only part of the value was lost. But errors or poor performance at each step of the process tended to have only modest costs.[338]

In the past, economists assumed that low quality labor was a good substitute for high quality labor—that three low quality workers were as good as two high quality workers. That is true for preindustrial work like growing wheat, but not for modern economies. Michael Kremer calls this the *O-ring theory of economic development*. The name comes from the O-ring that caused the destruction of the space shuttle *Challenger*. The O-ring is just a tiny rubber seal that is barely worth a few pennies. Yet the failure of this one little part caused the loss of seven lives when the space shuttle exploded. The Industrial Revolution completely changed the dynamics of the labor force by putting a premium on high quality labor.

Worker quality is a combination of two different factors. The first is the worker's objective skill, and the second is their trust. We'll focus on trust. Clark points out that one of the most striking testimonies to the O-ring economy comes from the success of hand looms in India. They continued to exist alongside powered looms throughout the nineteenth century. In fact, as late as 1996 the hand loom market was about a third the size of the powered loom market.[339] By contrast, hand looms had disappeared from England by the 1830s.

Why did hand looms disappear in England but not India? The answer lies with the familiar problem of trying to incentivize workers. Workers with hand looms could be paid a fixed piece rate for the cloth they made. Perhaps ten cents per yard of defect-free cloth. That gave workers an incentive to be careful and work hard. Another way of putting it is that this incentive turned lemons into peaches. A worker who is a lemon knows that he won't get paid if he slacks off, or if he makes cloth with defects. So he pays careful attention and works hard.

Workers on powered looms make cloth collectively, so they have to be paid an hourly wage. This means that our old friend the free rider problem rears its ugly head. If the workers are lemons, then they will be careless and shirk on the job, so the firm will go out of business. If the workers are peaches, then they will be careful and work hard, so the firm will succeed.

Assembly lines mean that there is no incentive structure to turn lemons into peaches. England had a lot of trust and social capital, so they produced high quality workers and used powered looms. India did not have as much trust, so they stuck with hand looms. Assembly lines are great, but only for nations that have high-quality workers with high levels of trust. That's the O-ring theory of economic development.

Now we finally have the answer to our paradox: Why did the Chinese communes fail while firms like Microsoft and SpaceX succeeded? There are two reasons. The first is the ecology of the marketplace. Firms that are poorly managed and have poor workplace cultures fail. Firms that are well-run with healthy cultures succeed. You can't fail under communism, so you sink forever. But the second reason is the most important: We finally learned to cooperate with strangers.

The Rise of the West

> "Why is it that you white people developed so much cargo, but we black people had little cargo of our own?"
>
> – Yali, *Guns, Germs, and Steel*

The story of the last chapter is that Europe became free and prosperous because its culture was able to foster trust and cooperation. Liberals who champion cultural relativism needed a rebuttal to the cultural theory of Europe's rise, and they found it in a *structure matters* argument. The structure versus culture debate is one of the most important in all of politics.

The debate is this: Are unequal outcomes the result of systemic inequalities such as bad schools and racial oppression? If so, the unequal outcomes are the result of factors that are beyond anyone's reasonable control. Instead of blaming the poor, we need to eliminate the structural factors holding the poor back. Or are unequal outcomes the result of making bad choices? If so, then we need to change the culture to promote making good choices. In modern times, liberals generally take the structure matters side of the debate, and conservatives generally take the *culture matter*s side of the debate. In this chapter, we'll look at a structure matters argument that gives an alternative explanation for the rise of Western civilization.

Guns, Germs, and Geography

Our entry point to the debate is Jared Diamond's *Guns, Germs, and Steel*. The core of Diamond's argument is that the rise of the West can be explained by geography.[340] The key to understanding his argument is that the agricultural revolution was a game changer. The first society to develop agriculture had a huge head start over everyone else in the world. Agriculture lets societies extract far more calories out of the land than they could with hunting and gathering. That in turn leads to larger populations and bigger armies. Moreover, once a society has transitioned from being hunter-gatherers to farming, they are set down the path of gradual technological improvement. The debate over which society first developed guns and steel reduces to a debate over which society first developed agriculture.

Grains and Wheat. Complex civilizations need grains because only grains can be easily stored and used as a currency. Large, complex civilizations can't be built on bananas or sweet potatoes because they are too low in protein and rot too quickly. The dirty little secret of transitioning from hunting and gathering to farming is that farmers don't eat a varied diet and they don't eat much meat. That's why farmers tended to be smaller and scrawnier than hunter-gatherers until recent times. If people are getting the bulk of their calories from a single staple crop, then it needs to be a crop that is high in protein, and that can be easily stored year-round.

The Fertile Crescent of the Middle East had a tremendous advantage in that department, because it has many large, high-protein grains. Most importantly, it had wheat, the crown jewel of them all. Wheat is a large, high-protein grain, but the really nice thing about wheat is that it can be domesticated with only a single genetic mutation that happens naturally in the wild. This mutation makes it so that wheat would not naturally sprout and germinate. It made wheat easy to domesticate.

Geographic orientation. The Americas have a north-south orientation. If you look at them on a map, you will see that they are tall and skinny. That slowed down the spread of agriculture, because crops like corn had to adapt to colder and colder climates in order to spread north. This took a long time. In fact, corn had not yet fully spread through North America by the time European colonists discovered it. By contrast, Eurasia is shaped like a rectangle lying on its long side, so wheat only had to spread east-west. Wheat did not have to adapt to progressively colder climates as it spread. That let wheat spread rapidly through Eurasia and thus let the entire continent adopt agriculture sooner. The upshot is that Europeans had wheat-based agriculture for literally thousands of years before corn reached the northern parts of North America.

Size. Eurasia is big. One of the most fascinating lessons from *Guns, Germs, and Steel* is the need for constant competition between societies. It's a surprisingly conservative insight in a book that takes the structure matters side of the debate, but Diamond is a nuanced thinker. Competition is important because cultures frequently go into decline. This competition will inexorably lead to one of two outcomes: Either the declining society will reject the values that made them go into decline, or they will be conquered by other, more vigorous societies. Either way, healthy cultures will succeed, and unhealthy cultures will be weeded out. The forces of cultural selection are much stronger on large land masses than on small land masses like islands. The key point is that Eurasia is by far the largest continent in the world, so it had the strongest competition and produced the most vigorous civilizations. Big ponds produce big fish.

Diamond paints with a broad brush, and many points can be challenged individually, but there is some good empirical support for Diamond's theory.[341] Overall, I think Diamond sustains his case that the first advanced nation had to emerge from Eurasia.

The Rise of Europe

The million-dollar question is this: Why Europe? Why did Europe become the most technologically advanced civilization in Eurasia? Why not China, India, or the Middle East? Throughout most of recorded history, Europe was a backwater compared to advanced civilizations like the Persians and the Chinese. Suppose aliens visited the Earth back in 500 AD, or even 1000 AD. If they tried to guess which region would be first to industrialize, then Europe would be their last choice. How did primitive and inconsequential Europe manage to leapfrog past China?

Diamond spends relatively little time on this important question. It occupies just a few pages at the end of the book. The gist of his theory is that Europe had a more fragmented geography, which led to Europe having many nations in competition with each other. By contrast, China's geography was flatter and easier to traverse, which allowed a single culture to dominate the entire region and become a monopoly. Like all monopolies, China got lazy, whereas Europe became increasingly advanced. This is a geographic argument, but it still means that Europe had a better, more vigorous culture than China. Progressives needed a different theory to explain Europe's success.

Kenneth Pomerantz picks up the gauntlet for the structure matters side in *The Great Divergence*. His argument parallels Diamond's argument. In many ways humanity has been through two important revolutions. The first was the agricultural revolution. The second was the Industrial Revolution. The first nation to develop industrial technology had a huge head start over the rest of the world. Pomerantz argues that China was just as primed to create the Industrial Revolution as Europe, but that Europe had important geographic advantages.[342] Alan MacFarlane summarizes Pomerantz's argument:

THE RISE OF THE WEST

Apart from the matter of shipping and international trade, there was no appreciable superiority of the west over China by 1800. The Chinese were as well fed, clothed, housed, lived as long, produced as much through their agriculture, as Western Europe. It was only after 1800 that a divergence in standards of living and technical efficiency occurred.

There was no significant structural difference in the economies of China and Western Europe before 1800. They were both 'agrarian' and subject to the same structural constraints. There was no 'divergence' until the nineteenth century.[343]

If China and Europe were so equal, then why did the Industrial Revolution happen in Europe but not China? Pomerantz claims the answer is found in geography. England was lucky enough to have a lot of coal. The Industrial Revolution was built on steam engines, and steam engines needed coal. England's coal launched it ahead of the rest of the world. Critics of Pomerantz may wish to pounce on the fact that China developed steam technology long before Europe, but Pomerantz has an answer. Coal in China was confined to a remote part of the northwest, which meant that the coal was expensive and hard to acquire. That is the gist of Pomerantz's argument. There are many lines of evidence against it.

Europe's early convergence. Pomerantz argues that China was well ahead of Europe until about 1800, which is the time steam power emerged. If Europe caught up to China by 1400, then Pomerantz can't use the steam power defense. Three important datasets support the early convergence with China.

Angus Maddison was one of the first economists to make a quantitative study of history. He spent two decades painstakingly calculating data on the per-capita GDP for much of the world from the year 1000 AD and onwards. This kind of research is inherently vague and messy, but it is the best we've got, certainly better than Pomerantz's more subjective analysis. One of the key findings is that per-capita GDP grew slowly but steadily in Western Europe from 1000 AD onwards, but not elsewhere. Maddison's data shows Western Europe passed China by 1400.[344]

Stephen Broadberry and Bishnupriya Gupta use a different dataset on the world economy and reach the same conclusion.[345] They found that Europeans were about as rich as the Chinese when it came to the ability to buy grains. But when it came to the ability to buy silver, people in Northwestern Europe were far ahead of their counterparts in the Yangtze Delta of China. That's important. In terms of calories and nutrition, Europe and China were equal. They were also equal when it came to other factors that depend on nutrition, such as life expectancy. But Europeans had a big advantage in the ability to buy textiles and household goods. These were the early signs of Europe's industrial revolution and superior technology.

A third line of evidence comes from the Global Prices and Income History Group.[346] They are created by a team of economists who compare prices and wages across the world throughout history. Their research shows that Europe and China were comparable at around 1500 in terms of ability to buy grains and other necessities for survival, but Europe had a greater ability to buy capital goods like nails, and luxury goods including paper, soap, and candles. This also suggests that while China was about as good in agriculture as Europe, that Europe had superior manufacturing.

Rate of change. Another objection to Pomerantz's argument is that Europe was clearly developing faster than China. No one disputes that Europe was historically backwards compared to China. No one disputes that Europe caught up. If you see two people in a race and they are tied, you'd conclude that they are equally fast. But if someone pointed out that one of the runners had a huge head start, then you'd conclude that the other runner was a lot faster. And you'd be right.

Process versus outcomes. Macfarlane also makes the point that there is a difference between process and outcomes. Rome reached its magnificent heights on the backs of its slaves. However, after the Roman Empire became Christian, the people began to champion the spiritual equality of all individuals, and many slave owners voluntarily freed their slaves. Emperors began to pass laws regulating the treatment of slaves and making it easier to legally free them. The historian W.E.H. Lecky explains.

> St. Melania was said to have emancipated 8,000 slaves; St. Ovidius, a rich martyr of Gaul, 5,000; Chromatius, a Roman prefect under Ciocletian, 1,400; Hermes, a prefect under Trajan, 1,200. [And] many of the Christian clergy at Hippo under the rule of St. Augustine, as well as great numbers of private individuals, freed their slaves as an act of piety.[347]

More than a millennia later, the exact same book that inspired these early Christians would prove its timelessness and inspire the Quakers. They would go on to become the beating heart of the abolition movement. One fun fact about Quakers is that John Lilburne, the most important leader of the Levellers, would become a Quaker late in his life. Lilburne seemed to have his finger on the pulse of Protestant Christianity.

The Roman Empire would evolve away from slavery and towards a system called *Coloni*, which in turn evolved into medieval serfdom. Slavery did survive in pockets here and there, but surveys such as the Domesday book, which William the Conqueror commissioned after the Battle of Hastings, show that it was not widespread. It would continue to decline throughout the remainder of the Middle Ages.

Sometimes people argue that medieval serfs had it just as bad as slaves, but that is not true. Serfs had fewer rights, and they were clearly oppressed. They were prohibited from traveling in search of a better economic arrangement, which greatly reduced their negotiating power with their lord to improve their lot in life. They also owed labor to work their lord's land for a certain number of days each year. But they owned their own land and property, and they could marry whom they chose, so being a serf was still a big step up from being a slave.

Throwing more slave labor at farms was not an option, so Europe went down the technology path instead. In many cases, Europeans used technologies that were invented in China, even though they were never used on a widespread basis by the Chinese. These inventions included windmills, stirrups, the horse collar, and waterwheels. In other cases, Europeans invented new technologies, such as the heavy wheeled plow. Europe established a tradition of taking the technology path by substituting machinery and animals for human labor. It was just a hop, skip, and a jump to replace water and wind-powered machinery with steam-powered machinery.

A recent database from scholars at the University of Cambridge shows that Britain had industrialized at least a century earlier than history books traditionally date the start of the Industrial Revolution.

> Built from more than 160 million records and spanning over three centuries, the University of Cambridge's *Economies Past* website uses census data, parish registers, probate records and more to track changes to the British labour force from the Elizabethan era to the eve of World War One.
>
> The research shows that 17th century Britain saw a steep decline in agricultural peasantry, and a surge in people who manufactured goods: from local artisans like blacksmiths, shoemakers and wheelwrights, to an explosion in networks of home-based weavers producing cloth for wholesale.

Historians say the data suggests that Britain was emerging as the world's first industrial powerhouse several generations before the mills and steam engines of the late 18th century – long credited as the birth of global industry and economic growth.[348]

The Cambridge database teaches a general lesson that occurs over and over again in the study of history. The first wave of historians, with relatively few sources, may date the start of a trend, such as the Industrial Revolution, to a certain point in time. Later generations of historians, with many more sources, find that the trend stretches back much earlier.

Unlike Europe, China had been taking the *rice path*. China created an elaborate division of labor, which resulted in large rice harvests, but relied almost exclusively on human labor. This is also why the Chinese have such a disciplined and hard-working population, a cultural value that lasts to this day. China had largely maxed out what they could accomplish on the rice path. They couldn't increase their harvests any further with human labor. China was going to have to rebuild its economy by taking the technology path, if it wanted to improve.

Science. Pomerantz is correct that many of Europe's technologies were first developed in China. But China never developed the concept of science the way the West did. The absolute latest a historian could possibly date the start of Western science is 1687, when Isaac Newton published his theory of physics. But most historians would date the beginning of science much earlier, perhaps to Galileo or Frances Bacon in the middle of the sixteenth century.

However, the principle that recent historians with more sources find that gradual processes have much earlier roots is relevant to science. The historian James Hannam persuasively argued in *The Genesis of Science* that observation-driven science emerged from the work of Catholic scholars in the Middle Ages, and that seems to be the consensus of modern medievalists. That would mean Europe had science about five centuries before coal became important.

Integrated markets. In *A Farewell to Alms,* Gregory Clark points out that Chinese coal should not have been as scarce as Pomerantz claimed. As Pomerantz himself took great pains to point out, China had an advanced economy with many market institutions. Clark uses grains as an example to show that Chinese markets were about as well-integrated as English markets—and therefore the price of grain did not increase very much as it was transported over long distances.[349] If grain could be transported cheaply across China, then coal could too. The fact that China did not develop sophisticated steam engines and the Industrial Revolution cannot be blamed on the lack of coal, but on the lack of interest.

The Soft Bigotry of Low Expectations

> Which boys are you talking about? ... Which ones are you talking about? I come down on Bertier, I don't see you coddle him. I come down on Sunshine, I don't see you grab his hand, take him off to the side. Which boys are you talking about? ... Now I may be a mean cuss, but I'm the same mean cuss with everybody out there on that football field. The world don't give a damn about how sensitive these kids are, *especially* the young black kids. ... You aren't doing these kids a favor by patronizing them—You're crippling them. You're crippling them for life.
>
> – Denzel Washington, *Remember the Titans*

The civil rights movement began seventy years ago, and most people assume that blacks have been slowly catching up to whites since then. Unfortunately, that is not true. The National Assessment of Educational Progress (NAEP) is considered the Nation's Report Card. It is a test of a nationally representative sample of students in grades four, eight and twelve. It's the twelfth grade NAEP scores that we care about because that's when students are done with their education. If black students are graduating from high school having acquired fewer skills than white students, then they will be routed into less skilled and lower paying careers. A lifelong gap in earnings between blacks and whites is set at the time of high school graduation.

The NAEP data show that in the early 1970s black students were behind white students by about fifty points in reading and forty points in math. This was right after the civil rights movement, and black students were steadily catching up. By 1990 the gap had shrunk to about twenty points. Then in the late 1980s and early 1990s something happened.

The gap widened to about twenty-six points, and it's stayed there ever since.[350] Black students were closer to the level of white students in 1990 than they are today.

As a technical aside, you might be wondering if this gap is meaningful—it might be very small. In the case of the NAEP, a standard deviation is typically about thirty-four points.[351] This means black students are about three quarters of a standard deviation behind white students (a gap of twenty-six points divided by thirty-four). Z-tables let us convert standard deviations into percentiles. Checking these tables shows us that the average black student ranks with the bottom 22nd percentile of white students.

Why did black students take a step backwards in the 1990s? In *Towards Excellence with Equity*, Ronald Ferguson theorized that it was because of the rise of hip hop culture.[352] He points out that prior to 1988, there had only been three gold hip hop records, but in 1988 alone, there were seventeen. It was the year hip hop broke through and began to dominate urban radio stations. If so, the timing is ironic because the 1990s were when liberals in New York City and elsewhere began electing Republican mayors to enact tough-on-crime policies. Gangster culture went mainstream as the gang wars were deescalating.

If you're skeptical of the claim that a gap in high school test scores explains a lifetime earnings gap between blacks and whites, then we can turn to a different dataset that tracks workers and their salaries. The National Longitudinal Survey of Youth (NLSY) is a nationally representative sample of young men and women who were then followed to track their salaries and work experience in the labor market. The nice thing about the NLSY is that it gave the participants the Armed Forces Qualifying Test (AFQT) so we can relate test score performance to income.

Ronald Ferguson analyzed this data in *Towards Excellence with*

Equity. The unadjusted wage gap between blacks and whites is about 25 percent. But blacks are more likely to live in the South where both wages and the cost of living are lower. When Ferguson controlled for factors like years of schooling and region of the country, then you see a wage gap between blacks and whites of around 13 percent to 20 percent depending on the region of the country. But once he controlled for AFQT scores, the black-white wage gap closed to about 3 to 6 percent.[353]

What about the last 3 to 6 percent gap? Some of it is racism. A good argument for racism is that I left out the South, where the income gap between blacks and whites is 10 percent, even after controlling for AFQT scores. That seems like a smoking gun to me. But some of it is also *statistical discrimination*. A statistically discriminating employer is not racist. He wants to hire the most qualified applicant for the job regardless of skin color. He is not willing to pay a premium of even a single penny in order to hire a white applicant. However, since employers can't give job applicants the AFQT test, they hire the white applicant.

It's the same dynamic we saw with "Ban the Box" laws in the chapter on free markets—laws that prohibited firms from asking job applicants if they had a felony. It was designed to reduce the employment gap between blacks and whites, but it actually increased the gap—firms simply stopped hiring black applicants for low-skilled jobs. Still, even if we assume the remaining gap is 100 percent racism and 0 percent statistical discrimination, the black-white income gap is primarily caused by the gap in skills, not racism.

Funding For Minority Schools

A common liberal argument is that minority schools are underfunded, which explains the gap between blacks and whites. That argument is simply wrong and we've known this for a long time. The sociologist and Senator Daniel Patrick Moynihan was one of the all-time great Democrats, and he explained the problem in an interview with PBS.

> In the 1964 Civil Rights Act, as it was going through a long process, a little clause was put in saying there should be a survey of equality of educational opportunity. We had to demonstrate how separate schools were inherently unequal. And that was before things progressed such that the law outlawed dual school systems. But the little provision was still in there.
>
> And a friend of mine, James S. Coleman – a great sociologist – was asked to do this survey. And when he undertakes it, they said, "why are you doing this? Everybody knows these schools are unequal in their facilities and that's why they're unequal in their outcomes." He said, "Well, everybody knows it, but now we'll know it for once and all."
>
> And I'll tell you, early one evening, there's a reception at the Harvard Faculty Club, and Seymour Martin Lipset – the incomparable Marty Lipset – walks in, sees me, comes over and says, "You know what Coleman's finding, don't you?" And I said, "No." He said, "It's all family."[354]

James Coleman released his report in the middle of the sexual revolution of the 1960s. If you check Figure 17 below, you can see that the percentage of black children born to single mothers had already more than doubled from 12 percent to 25 percent. And the Sexual Revolution was just getting started.

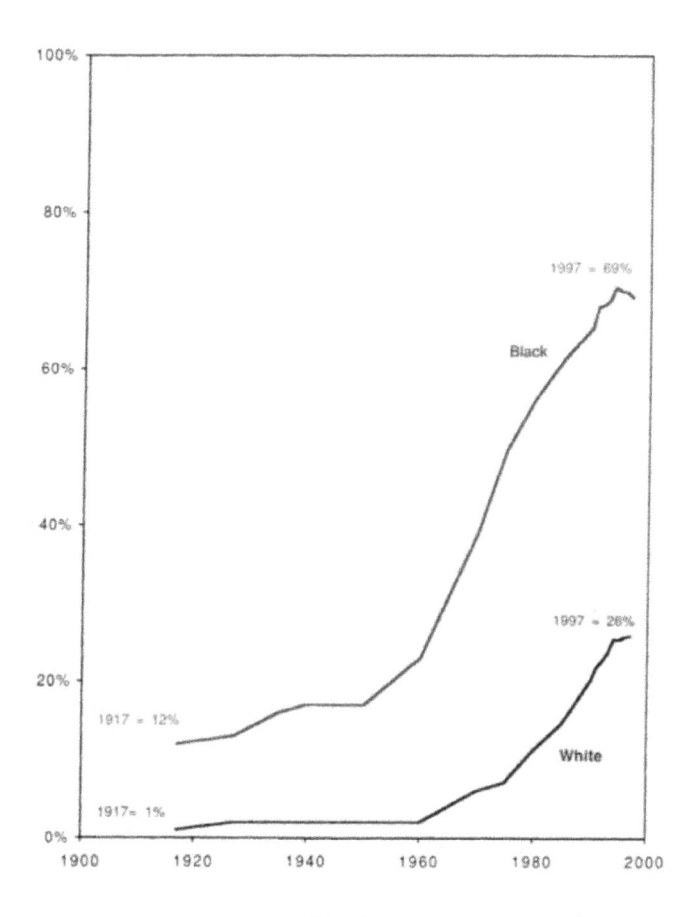

Figure 17: Nonmarital births as a percentage of all births. From *The First Measured Century*.[355]

Ferguson's theory about the rise of hip hop is interesting, but the 1990s were when the first generation of black children primarily raised by single mothers was in school. If hip hop played a role, I suspect it only catalyzed a change from the dad path to the cad path. According to the latest 2021 data from the Centers for Disease Control, the percentage of black children born to single mothers was 70 percent in 2021.[356]

The study Coleman ran was a massive survey of 600,000 students and 60,000 teachers. Coleman measured the *inputs* into school quality such as the amount of funding, class size, teacher experience, number of teachers with advanced degrees, the quality of the facilities, and more. He also measured the *outputs*—how much the students learned. Coleman went into the study with a very simple theory: The quality of the inputs determines the quality of the outputs—that bad schools provide a bad education. Coleman's theory was wrong.

Coleman found that black children attended schools that were about as good as the schools that white children attended, once regional differences were taken into account. Coleman's research has been replicated in the 1980s by Stephen Grogger[357] and in the 2000s by Derek Neal.[358] Black students go to schools with roughly the same funding and teacher-student ratios as white schools. Poor school districts don't bring in as much money from property taxes, but that is offset by more state and federal funding. Coleman also found that there was only a weak connection between school inputs and school outputs, with teacher quality being a notable exception. The research on school inputs has been replicated more recently by Erik Hanushek[359] as well as by Raj Chetty.[360]

If you're skeptical of these results, then keep in mind that it took a century to close the gap between black and white schools. Thomas Sowell points out in *Ethnic America: A History* that after the Civil War, Northern whites, generally from the American Missionary Association, moved to the South and established more than a thousand schools for the newly freed blacks. In the fifty years after the Civil War, Northern whites donated more than $57 million towards educating Southern blacks. The much smaller population of freed blacks donated another $24 million.[361]

Dereck Neal reviews several histories of black education in *Generational Change: Closing the Test Score Gap*. In the South in 1910, class sizes in black schools were 50 percent larger than in white schools, and the length of the school year was much shorter.

Black education began slowly but steadily improving after that, but the pace of improvements picked up in the 1930s. At that point black schools began to improve rapidly. Interestingly enough, there was no sudden increase in school quality after *Brown v. Board of Education*. For example, the teacher-to-student ratios improved at the same speed in the decade before 1954 as they did in the decade after.[362] It was ten years after Brown that Coleman did his famous study.

Overall Funding

Increasing school funding has been one of the most important items on the liberal agenda for the past sixty years, and they have achieved their goal and then some. The National Center for Education Statistics shows that inflation-adjusted spending in education has nearly quadrupled since 1960.[363] But has this increased spending made a difference? Once again, let's look at the NAEP results, but this time for white students. If the scores of black students goes up, then we don't know if its because of the end of segregation, or because of more funding. White students let us isolate the effects of increased funding. What the NAEP shows is that the scores of white twelfth graders have not budged.[364] We've quadrupled our spending on education, but the results have not changed.

It's worth dwelling on the stagnant scores for a bit. Since the 1950s, conservatives and liberals have taken turns dominating the educational agenda. The conservatives had the period after the Soviets launched the Sputnik satellite, which made Americans worried that we were losing the space race. Conservatives also had the 1980s when Ronald Reagan ramped up the Cold War, which once again made us worried that we were losing to the Soviets. Each time control flip-flops, the new group in power is convinced that they'll finally fix things. And yet the scores for twelfth graders never change. This fits with the lesson of the Coleman Report—inputs to school quality don't make much of a difference.

I would say that this is one of the most depressing lessons in the book, except that we are finally about to see a change in twelfth grade NAEP scores. Unfortunately, that change will be in the wrong direction. We don't have twelfth grade NAEP scores for the post-Covid era yet, but the only real question is how big the drop will be. We will probably see the gap between blacks and whites increase after decades of stagnation. All students suffered from the Covid lockdowns, as well as from recent educational fads like "Algebra for None."[365] However, Teachers' Unions have had greater power to impose remote learning on the black community[366] and black parents have less ability to hire private tutors to offset the harm of fads like "Algebra for None." This means the decline in education will be concentrated among poor and minority students.

The fact that we've quadrupled spending with no real change in test scores is the main conservative argument against increased spending. However, there is some fine print. In *Why Are the Prices So Damn High?* the economists Eric Helland and Alex Tabarrok give the next parable in our tour of economics.

> In 1826, when Beethoven's String Quartet No. 14 was first played, it took four people 40 minutes to produce a performance. In 2010, it still took four people 40 minutes to produce a performance. Stated differently, in the nearly 200 years between 1826 and 2010, there was no growth in string quartet labor productivity.[367]

The parable of the classical musicians is a counterexample to Adam Smith's parable of the pin makers. Recall that assembly lines increased the productivity of a pin maker from 20 pins per day to 5,000 pins per day. By contrast, the market for live classical music has made no gains at all. This is known as *Baumol's cost disease*, after its discoverer William Baumol. As a general rule, service sector industries have seen much less productivity growth than manufactured goods like cars, computers, and smartphones. Another way of putting it is that in relative terms, we have to increase spending on education simply to maintain the same level of quality. That may change as AI gets better, but it's not ready to be a private tutor yet.

Another reason for increased spending is because of special education. That's important, and I wish special educators all the resources they need, but it's narrowly targeted and won't do much to improve performance on tests like the NAEP. But the biggest problem is that much of this money goes to non-teaching administrators. There has been a 700 percent increase in the number of non-teachers hired by schools since 1950.[368] Some of those early staffing increases went to special education, but the surge in hiring non-teachers has expanded into inessential areas like Diversity, Equity, and Inclusion (DEI).

In fact, despite increases in school funding, teacher salaries have been stagnant. Non-teaching positions aren't just siphoning school funds as a whole, but they're taking money away from teachers, and therefore reducing the talent pool of teachers. What we really need is accountability in how schools are funded. More funding is not the solution unless the problem is a lack of DEI jobs.

Shaker Heights

Another way to refute the funding arguments is to look at how black and white students do when they go to the same school. Ronald Ferguson did a detailed study of Shaker Heights, which is an affluent middle-class school district, in *Towards Excellence with Equity*. About a third of the residents are black and the school district is strongly committed to racial integration. It draws each school attendance zone so that the school reflects the racial balance of the community. The district spent $10,000 per student at the time of his study, which was 50 percent more than the national average.

Ferguson found that black students were a full letter grade below whites. Black students averaged a C+ and white students averaged a B+.[369] Shaker Heights is not unique. It belongs to the Minority Student Achievement Network (MSAN). It gives us a sample of ninety-five schools across fifteen school districts in nine states. The results of Shaker Heights are typical of the MSAN network.[370] Thus we have a clear pattern. Black students do much worse than white students, even when they live in the same neighborhoods and go to the same schools.

Can socioeconomic status explain the gap? Shaker Heights is an affluent school district, and virtually all the parents are in the middle class. The white parents are a bit wealthier, but this difference is small. Ferguson found that controlling for the difference in education only narrowed the gap slightly. He also found evidence for cultural differences between blacks and whites. Black students were more likely to be raised by a single mother. Controlling for this narrows the gap slightly as well. Finally, controlling for differences in attitudes and behaviors closes the gap even more.[371] But these factors only explain a bit less than half the black-white achievement gap. What's going on?

This is where we get to the debate over *oppositional culture*, also known as "acting white." It dates to the work of the anthropologist John Ogbu. Black parents in Shaker Heights brought him in to figure out why black children weren't doing as well in school. They expected Ogbu to find hidden biases among whites, but instead he found an oppositional culture among blacks. Black students who did well in school were socially ostracized for "acting white."

There is an active debate about the strength of oppositional culture, and I'm not going to try and settle it here. But even critics of the oppositional culture theory, such as Ferguson, agree that black students who do well in school were under pressure to prove that they were not selling out. This forces them into a delicate balancing act. Good students sometimes had to hold back academically or dismiss praise in their achievements with a phony mock seriousness. Black girls in particular felt that they were socially isolated by other girls for doing well in school. The main way that good female students who are black can stay connected to other black students is through their male friends who bring them into the group, often to the consternation of less studious black girls.[372]

I suspect it is simply a matter of social norms. When I went from working for large corporations to working for a small startup, I had to raise my game even though I thought I was a pretty good worker before. Students are just like workers and want to set norms of low effort. Oppositional culture and acting white are just tools that students use to set norms.

Smaller Classes

Reducing class size is a liberal favorite but it won't help. The classic study on this is the Tennessee STAR study. About 6,500 elementary school students in eighty different schools were randomly assigned to small classes or large classes. Sure enough, students in the small classes did better. However, Eric Hanushek points out that the study ran for four years but most of the benefits were only found in the first year.[373] Hanushek also points out that the bulk of the literature disagrees with the Tennessee STAR study. There have been hundreds of studies on class size reductions, and about three quarters of them find no statistically significant results. Of the quarter that do reach statistical significance, about half find a benefit and the other half find that class size reductions don't help.[374] This suggests that small classes either don't work, or that they provide small benefits that are hard to measure.

There is a deeper problem with reducing class size that these studies do not address. Reducing class size means having to hire more teachers. But the talent pool for teachers is only so big. The more teachers a state hires, the deeper into the talent pool they must go to fill the extra vacancies, and the lower the average quality of the teachers becomes. In fact, improving teacher quality is one of the few things that does work in education,[375] so smaller classes with bad teachers could be worse than larger classes with good teachers. Studies on smaller classes do not have to make this tradeoff because they are small-scale studies. But if we roll out small classes state-wide, then we have to make the tradeoff and accept lower quality teachers.

Academic Preschool

We used to think that education was the solution to closing the gap between blacks and whites. But much of the gap is already in place by the time children get to kindergarten. Ron Haskins reviews the major studies in the book *Generational Change: Closing the Test Score Gap*. Data from the Early Childhood Education Longitudinal Study, Kindergarten Cohort shows that black children entering kindergarten are a bit over half a standard deviation behind white children.[376] Recall from above that the gap in the NAEP scores between twelfth graders is about three-quarters of a standard deviation. That means that most of the gap is in place before children even set foot in school.

Other studies paint an even darker picture. Both the Family and Child Experiences Survey and the National Longitudinal Survey

THE SOFT BIGOTRY OF LOW EXPECTATIONS

of Youth Child Data find that black preschoolers are a full standard deviation behind white preschoolers.[377] Another way of putting it is that black kindergarteners begin school with a large deficit relative to their white peers, but thirteen years of education can narrow this deficit, so they graduate having reduced it slightly. This view makes sense on the theory that black students are handicapped by extremely high rates of single motherhood, but that schools can partially offset this cultural disadvantage.

What do we do if black children have already lost the race before they even set foot inside a school building? The answer takes us to the very contentious world of preschool research. Suppose a patient was diagnosed with heart disease, and his doctor recommended a certain drug.

> PATIENT: Why should I believe this drug is any good?
>
> DOCTOR: Oh, that's easy, there was a study back in 1962 of 123 patients, and it showed a big benefit.
>
> PATIENT: That's a very small study from a long time ago. Have there been any studies since then?
>
> DOCTOR: Oh sure, lots of studies. They don't usually help, but they also only gave about one-third as much of the drug as the 1962 study.
>
> PATIENT: And which dose am I taking? Do I get the whole dose?
>
> DOCTOR: Oh, no, you're taking the one-third dose as well. It's a very expensive drug.

That is the research on preschool in a nutshell. The 1962 study is the Perry Preschool Project. It is expensive because it has a student-teacher ratio of about 6 to 1. It is joined by two other early preschool studies that also find benefits: the Abecedarian study and the Chicago Child-Parent study. They all find lasting benefits of preschool.[378]

The most famous preschool is Head Start. It was created as part of

Lyndon Johnson's War on Poverty with the goal of helping children from poor families prepare for kindergarten. There are many studies on Head Start, but the best is probably the Head Start Impact Study. It began in 2002 and had 4,500 students. It found early benefits, but they faded out by the end of kindergarten.[379] These initial results were criticized because some students in the control group went to other academic preschools. However, Peter Bernardy re-evaluated the data in light of this and found essentially the same results.[380]

Here's the rule of thumb to use when evaluating preschool research: Was the study small and done a long time ago? Then it probably found large and lasting benefits. Was the study large and recent? Then it probably found small benefits that fade out after a few years. In a meta-analysis of eighty-four different preschool programs, Greg Duncan and Katherine Magnussen find that preschool programs provide early benefits that fade out over time.[381]

The most recent academic preschool data comes from the Tennessee Voluntary Pre-K program. It shows that preschool actually *hurts* poor children.[382] In a commentary on the study, Jason Bedrick and Colleen Hroncich explain.

> In January 2022, universal preschool supporters received surprising news. Researchers from Vanderbilt University released a randomized study of Tennessee's Voluntary Pre-K initiative that found that children who participated in the program experienced "significantly negative effects" compared with the children who did not. The results were so shocking that the researchers had to "go back and do robustness checks every which way from Sunday," according to Dale Farran, one of the lead researchers. "At least for poor children," she concluded, "it turns out that something is not better than nothing."[383]

Don't tell anyone, but I do agree with progressive educators sometimes. One of the main concepts in progressive education is about how to make school more fun and engaging. The fact is that most students don't like school. They like seeing their friends, they like being in clubs and activities, and they like participating in sports. But most students don't actually like the school part of school. One of the main ideas of progressive education is about making school more fun. Unfortunately, progressive reforms have a dismal track record,[384] but I appreciate the motivation.

I don't know what it's like to be poor, but my son has ADHD. And the poor kids and the ADHD kids do have something in common: They are problems. And in both cases, the solution involves making school a bigger part of their young lives. The more a student dislikes school, the worse they are going to do. As eager, first-time parents, my wife and I sent our son to an academic preschool, but we sent our daughter to a regular daycare, which was far more affordable and had some wonderful young women working there. Our opinions as parents is that academic preschool is either not worth the extra money or is mildly harmful. Instead of starting academic work at age three, let's be more like Denmark and wait until age six, or Finland and wait until age seven. Let children finger-paint and play with blocks and have long recesses filled with unstructured play. Let them start out thinking school is fun. They'll figure out the truth soon enough.

Charter Schools

Charter schools are a favorite option of conservatives, but the results are mixed. The best way to figure out if A (going to a charter school) causes B (better grades or test scores) is by doing a randomized, controlled trial where half of the students are randomly assigned to go to the charter school and the other half go to a traditional public school. The next best thing is to use a natural experiment, in this case the charter school lottery. Some charter schools are so popular that more students want to go than they have spots available, so they have a lottery. Researchers can compare outcomes of students who won the lottery to the students who lost it.

In a review of the literature by Ron Zimmer and colleagues, lottery studies consistently find that charter schools do a better job than traditional public schools.[385] This is particularly true for the No Excuses charter schools that target urban areas using techniques like a longer school day, strict discipline, and an emphasis on reading and math. A separate meta-analysis by Albert Cheng found that No Excuses charter schools improve the performance of black students by a quarter of a standard deviation.[386] Education and liberal politics are filled with interventions predicated on making excuses for black people. And what is the one thing that actually works? Having uncompromisingly high standards for black children and holding them to it.

Nevertheless, there is a big problem with the lottery approach, which is that it only works for charter schools that have more applicants than spots available. That means, by definition, that we're only looking at the best charter schools. Most charter schools are not that popular and have to take every student that applies. If we really want to find out if charter schools are better, then we need an apples-to-apples comparison. For that we need methods that evaluate the quality of charter schools that do not use lotteries. Zimmer and colleagues use a variety of statistical methods to do this, and they don't find a pattern of charter schools outperforming traditional public schools.[387]

Despite these problems, charter schools have two important strengths. The first is the success of the No Excuses charter schools for poor and minority students. Minority parents have the right to send their child to a good school that won't patronize their children. The second is that some charter schools do outperform traditional public schools, so let's add them to the mix and force public schools to raise their game. Diane Ravitch is an opponent of charter schools, but she is an equal opportunity critic. In *Left Back*, she points out that there has been a constant gravitational pull within liberal education which results in dumbing down schools with programs like whole word language learning.[388] We need an automated system to fight against this gravitational pull, and market competition should do that. As soon as the regular public schools start dumbing things down, charter school attendance will go up.

School Choice

There are many reasons to like school choice. It will de-escalate the endless wars between the left and the right because liberals and conservatives can each send their children to a school of their choosing. We won't have to have elections so that 51 percent of the population can tell parents in the other 49 percent how to educate their children.

School choice may also result in cheaper housing. Elizabeth Warren, in her first career as an academic, published *The Two Income Trap* about the vulnerabilities of two income families. One of these traps is that the extra income that having a working wife brought to a household was captured by higher housing costs. Young couples want to raise their children in a "nice neighborhood" with "good schools." There aren't enough of these houses to go around. Since no one wants more cars and more traffic lights in their community, most towns are anti-growth. The result is a bidding war for a limited supply of housing. Entrepreneurs can't build more housing if the town won't zone for it, and it won't give them variances. If we break the link between housing and education, then young couples could buy houses in nice neighborhoods that fall on the wrong side of the school district boundaries.

THE NAKED MOLE-RAT

Having said that, the evidence that school choice will improve education is weak. According to libertarian sources, like the Friedman Foundation's review of the literature, they are a magic bullet.[389] A more careful meta-analysis by Danish Shakeel and colleagues found moderate evidence for benefits.[390] Both studies have methodological flaws,[391] but I'm more inclined to side with Shakeel. Overall, I suspect school choice will be like charter schools. It will result in some schools that outperform public schools, and thereby improve the ecology of the educational market. It will also keep public schools honest and force them to stay away from fads like whole-word language learning. But other than that, I doubt the average private school will outperform the average public school.

Ultimately the case for school choice is a moral one. When both Bill Clinton and Barack Obama were president, they put their children in expensive private schools instead of the Washington DC public schools. I don't fault any parent for doing what's right for their children, but I will fault even a President for hypocrisy. In poll[392] after poll[393] after poll,[394] blacks consistently support school choice. Although most blacks are not poor, as a group they have less ability to win the bidding war for houses in neighborhoods with good schools. Blacks who live in poor neighborhoods with failing schools would love to have the same freedom as powerful liberals.

Lessons from the Front Lines

The movie *Lean on Me* is about a charismatic but rebellious teacher who was brilliantly played by Morgan Freeman. He was tapped to become principal at a notoriously dangerous urban high school because no one else wanted the job. In the scene where he first meets the teachers, he gave a take-charge speech where he immediately made it clear that the teachers were the problem, and he was the solution. I looked over at my wife, who teaches in an urban middle school, and said, "I'll bet you've heard that speech before." She said, "Every single year." Except that she didn't use the word "single."

In twenty years as an urban teacher, she's had twenty-three principals. They all talk a big game at the start of the school year. One of them even passed out envelopes to all the teachers, and inside the envelope was a note with how many sick and personal days that teacher had used the year before. But when the school year starts, teachers quickly find out which type of principal they have: the ones that start out hiding in their office, or the ones that retreat more and more to their office as they realize they don't have the energy or force of personality required to deal with all the behavior problems. Sometimes teachers get lucky, and the new principal never retreats to his office. That was the case with the principal who passed out the letters. Once he learned what life in an urban school was really like, he apologized to the teachers and became a real ally. But good or bad, they will probably be gone after the end of the school year. The next year the same teachers get the same speech but from a new principal.

What most people do not realize about urban schools is that most of the students are great. They are not cynical and jaded like suburban students. They are sweet and want to learn. Urban schools do have bullying, but it is not a major problem like it is in suburban schools. The weird kids can be weird and no one's going to make them feel terrible about it. They may have violence and gang problems, but not the punching down on socially awkward kids.

The problem is that even the good students don't know how to learn. They struggle to sit still and be quiet, and even the best teachers have to tolerate some amount of low-level disorder. It's hard work to maintain classroom discipline, and most public-school teachers simply aren't up to it. Most new teachers switch to middle-class school districts after their first year in an urban school.

For the teachers who do stick it out, the results are worth it. My wife is a middle-school teacher, which means that they have a team-based system. In my wife's first year, she had a class from a team called Platinum, and their poor behavior and disrespectful attitudes made her cry in her car after school every day. She wasn't sure she would make it as a teacher. But by the end of the term, she had won them over, and they became her favorite class. It reminded me of the short book, *The Best Christmas Pageant Ever*, where the worst kids in town put on the most touching and meaningful Christmas pageant the town had ever seen.[395] Here is the plot, as summarized by Chat-GPT:

> The story is narrated by a young girl who, along with her brother, regularly attends Sunday School. The Christmas pageant is an annual event, and its traditional smooth sailing is upended when the Herdman children show up. They are rough, unkempt, and known for causing trouble. When they hear about the free snacks at Sunday School, they decide to attend and, much to everyone's surprise, end up taking over the main roles in the Christmas pageant.
>
> Despite concerns from the community and mishaps along the way, the Herdman kids bring a raw, honest, and uniquely sincere approach to the story of Christmas. Their interpretation of the Christmas story is unconventional but ends up touching the hearts of the congregation and bringing a new understanding and spirit to the usual holiday narrative.

That's why my wife loves teaching in an urban school. Like most teachers at urban schools, she feels a calling towards social justice. But she's also getting something back. If she taught in a middle-class suburb, she'd have less stress but also less joy. To this day, whenever she complains about a particularly rough class, I always respond with

"Best Christmas Pageant Ever," and she invariably wins them over. 90 percent of the kids in urban schools are great. The other 10 percent are . . . something else.

Most people don't understand just how challenging the bad apples are. In theory failing students are socially promoted to the next grade, but in practice it doesn't always happen. This means that even in middle school there are boys who are six feet tall and have a man's strength. Most of the female teachers can be easily overpowered by their students. I would be in jail if I did some of the things her students do. Teachers are physically assaulted by students; teachers are sexually harassed by students—"suck my dick you ugly bitch"—can come from either the boys or the girls; teachers are groped by their students; and teachers are routinely insulted by students.

In *Lean on Me,* the principal got the names of the 300 worst behaved students and expelled them all the next day. In 1989, principals could do that. My wife's jaw literally hit the floor when that happened. When she first became a teacher twenty years ago, the concept of *disparate impact*, where black students are punished at higher rates than white students, was already a major concern. For the past ten years or so, it's been the only concern. Forget expelling students—her school doesn't even have detention. Even in the case of sexual harassment or physical assault, students are typically back in class before the end of the day.

Even if principals want to have meaningful standards of discipline, they don't have much choice. They are under enormous pressure from superintendents, who are in turn under pressure from politicians all the way up to the President of the United States. Barack Obama made ending racial disparities in school punishments a key policy goal.[396] How is a principal supposed to fight the President?

If schools won't discipline children, then what about parents? Unfortunately, that won't work either. Most parents blame the teachers for their children's behavior. Or the parent feels defeated because they've already lost the power struggle with their adolescent child. If the teacher tries to involve these parents, the response is usually something like, "What do you want me to do? He's out of control at home too." My wife told me about one case where a girl got a text from her mother who told her to simply walk out of a class. The students are required to put their phones in special locked pouches before school begins, but with no standards of discipline, it can't be enforced. The only parents who support the teachers are the married parents, and their children don't get into trouble very often. My wife can tell which of her students have married parents based on their behavior before she even asks.

This lack of punishment leads to the greatest case of the law of unintended consequences in all of education: high rates of teacher turnover. College student-teachers are generally sent to nice suburban schools to get their initial taste of classroom experience, but when they apply for jobs after graduating, they find that most of the openings are in the urban schools. After a year of feeling unsafe and overmatched, most of them leverage their year of experience to get jobs in suburban districts. It's a great arrangement for suburban districts because they don't have to do the hard work of breaking in first-year teachers. Then, next year's crop of raw and inexperienced graduates moves into the vacated positions to get their initial seasoning.

The problem of teacher turnover runs deeper than having to constantly break in first-year teachers. Many teachers quit in the middle of the school year. That means students will have substitute teachers. I'm sure you remember being a child and the thrill of discovering that you had a substitute, which meant not having to learn that day. In urban schools, substitutes are common. In my wife's school, as of early May, there are currently more vacancies and substitutes than full-time teachers. Some kids haven't had a math teacher since October. Others have four substitutes out of six classes. When the next round of standardized testing is done and the children's scores drop, the public will blame the teachers. But those teachers were hounded out of the school a long time ago because of policies that made them feel unsafe.

Is this a good time for a reminder that teacher quality is the single most important input to school quality?[397]

Reforming urban schools is actually pretty easy. It doesn't cost money, only political will. We need to repeal the policies against disparate impact in punishment at both the federal and state levels. Then we need principals who are willing to fight for the teachers. In keeping with the Elinor Ostrom style of management, all principals should be former teachers with at least five years of full-time classroom experience. That should be a non-negotiable requirement. It's got to be long enough to face burnout.

Principals don't need PhDs. In fact, PhDs are worse than a waste of time—they're actively harmful. My love-hate relationship with postmodernism strikes again. That's because postmodernists understand hypocrisy better than anyone. The justification for requiring a PhD is, "We just want the best principals possible. Don't you want the best principals? You do care about the kids, don't you? Don't you think the kids deserve the best?" The reality is that it gets principals whose philosophy comes from the Teacher's College at Columbia University instead of from hard-won classroom experience. It allows top-down technocrats to impose their will on the schools. We need a bottom-up process where the wisdom of teachers governs the schools.

Principals are there to support teachers. They are there to be walking the halls and sitting in on classes. They need to feel the pulse of the building. They should know all the particularly tough classes off the top of their head. "Oh, Mrs. Bond has a class of thirty-two, and it has both Davon and Malcolm? We need to pull a teacher's assistant from another classroom and put them in hers, or we need to find another class for at least one of those two." Principals don't need a PhD for that, but they do need to know what it's like to be a teacher on the front lines. Principals can learn on the job how to handle all the red tape coming from the Department of Education. Or better yet, they can route it straight to the circular file where it belongs.

The next thing schools need is a transparent rubric for punishment that is followed consistently. This would start with the largely symbolic getting "buzzed out" of class and sent to the principal's office. Then comes detention, in-school suspension, out-of-school suspension, and finally being expelled. Every step should involve communication with the child's parents, including their explicit signoff acknowledging a problem. When my wife first started teaching, she was opposed to expelling students, but after twenty years, she has changed her mind. That one student who couldn't be expelled is making it so that twenty-five other students can't pay attention in class. Most of the students in urban schools want to learn, but we don't even give them a chance.

Teaching in an urban school is tough, but do not make the mistake of thinking that toughness will get teachers very far, because it won't. The only teachers who can get away with being tough are a few of the larger male teachers, typically the gym teachers. Suppose a new teacher planned to set a tough, no-nonsense tone, and the entire class was talking as they filed into the room. They also didn't go to their desks after the bell rang. What is he going to do? He can tell them to be quiet, but they won't listen. Maybe try yelling loudly to be quiet? Now, they know he is easily rattled. Maybe he can try walking right up to one of the loudest students and glaring at him? The student will glare right back. Acting soft doesn't work either. The students walk all over soft teachers.

So how does a teacher get students to behave? Effective teachers genuinely care about their students, who will pick up on this quickly. My wife will ask her students about their hobbies and the music they like, and often build that information into assignments. She also keeps fresh fruit, granola bars, and candy available. One of the small consolations of urban schools is that they don't have no-candy policies like middle-class schools. Candy wins the students over.

Her school offers free breakfast and lunch, but even so, not all her students have eaten, so she keeps food available. If a child seems to be behaving uncharacteristically, she will often give the class an assignment, and quietly ask if they are hungry and if things are ok at home. If they are hungry, she'll encourage them to choose something from the breakfast basket. The children pick fruit quite often because they eat a lot of junk food, and their mothers don't regularly buy fresh fruit. If there is stress at home, she'll ask if they want to eat lunch with her instead of at the cafeteria, and they usually take her up on that. My wife explains this with the phrase, "They don't care what you know until they know that you care."

Teachers have to hold the students accountable to standards that can be enforced within their own classrooms. That's because teachers have essentially no backup from the principal or from the parents. Sometimes that accountability is simply her own disappointment. Since she's already built trust and established rapport, that is often enough.

Another system that has evolved over the years is my wife's ticket-based rewards. She gives students tickets whenever they do something good. This allows her to reward more frequently. It could be working quietly for a while, picking up a piece of trash from the floor without being asked, or doing a good job on a task. When her jar is filled with tickets, she draws one at random, and that student gets a piece of candy. The second time she fills the jar, they all get a piece of candy. The third time she fills the jar, they get to watch a movie. The fourth time they fill the jar she bakes them cupcakes—and plays up how much she hates baking and hopes that they don't fill the jar that fourth time. Her complaints unify the class and creates a shared goal of filling the jar once more.

She also has class-based rewards. The world is divided into Mozart people and Beethoven people, and my wife is a Beethoven person. Every Friday is Beethoven Friday, and she will play a piece of his music for the class—but only if they are good. If they weren't good, she would say that they didn't deserve Beethoven that week. That tactic would never work in a middle-class suburban school where the students are jaded and cynical. But it works in her schools. "Shut up guys, or we're not going to get Beethoven Friday!"

My wife also has a charismatic ball-busting way about her. If she gives one student a ticket for working quietly and another complains that he too was working quietly but didn't get a ticket, she'll say something like, "That's because he's my favorite, and you're a pain in my butt." Teachers need to have the right personality to pull this off, but if they can, it creates a bond, particularly with the seemingly insulted student. It's similar to how good friends will trash talk each other, but casual friends do not. Teachers also need to be careful with this tactic because they can't be friends with the students, or the students will lose respect. My wife is sometimes a mom to her students, but never a friend.

Winning over students is crucial, and the bad students are the most important to win over. Don't treat them as enemies; instead make them allies. My wife does this early, often by making the bad kid one of her accomplices. When she is explaining her reward system, she might say, "Hey, Davon, remember when I had you back in sixth grade, and the first time your class filled the jar, I picked a ticket, but there was no name on it?" And then Davon will nod and explain that you can't get candy if you don't put your name on a ticket, and soon he's practically running the reward system for her.

The goal of this section is to give you insight into the challenges of teaching when the administration cuts teachers off at the knees and the married two-parent family has collapsed. I don't want to leave you with the idea that teachers are a part of the solution. I hope new teachers can benefit from my wife's experience, but any urban teacher who comes back for a second year is already one of the best teachers in the state. Urban teachers need to be supported, not held to even more impossible standards.

How Does a Dream Die?

> The law, in its majestic equality, forbids the rich as well as the poor to sleep under bridges, to beg in the streets, and to steal bread.
>
> – Anatole France, *The Red Lilly*

Congratulations—you made it to the final chapter. Although I've tried to avoid technical language, I have not dumbed anything down. This is a hard book and finishing it is an accomplishment. This chapter isn't too bad, so you should have smooth sailing to the end.

Moral Hazard

Moral hazard refers to the fact that if people are protected from the harmful consequences of a behavior, that behavior increases. A simple example is unemployment insurance, a government program that gives money to people who lost their job. The goal is to cushion the blow of a lost job, but in economics terms, it rewards people for being unemployed, and sure enough, the outcome was more unemployment.[398] I've been laid-off twice. Once when my firm's stock went from $40 to under $1 during the collapse of the housing bubble, and again when my firm outsourced the entire IT department. I was glad to have unemployment insurance, but all programs have trade-offs. That's particularly true with moral hazard.

You may remember the housing bubble and the too-big-to-fail logic. It resulted in the government bailing out the financial institutions that made reckless decisions. They were allowed to keep all the profits they made before the speculative bubble burst, but when the good times ended, they pushed their losses onto the taxpayers. Privatized profits and subsidized losses create a textbook moral hazard problem.

The standard solution to the problem of moral hazard is *insurance riders*. The basic idea is to try to fix the incentives that were just broken by providing insurance. Take unemployment insurance as an example. As soon as the government gives money to people who lost their job, it takes a lot of the sting away from being unemployed, so people can slack off on their job search. We address that problem with insurance riders. Unemployment insurance has several methods like making benefits smaller than the worker's previous pay, time limits on benefits, and activation plans where the unemployed have to check in with a case worker and document their job search efforts.

With health insurance that commonly means deductibles and co-payments. That way consumers still have some skin in the game. Exclusions are another common type of rider. Professional athletes are usually not allowed to participate in dangerous sports like skiing. I remember when Tom Brady, who either did not have this clause or was too untouchable to have to worry about it, gave New England a collective heart attack by posting a video of himself going over a ski jump. An example from the housing bubble is that large financial institutions that are deemed too big to fail have to undergo periodic stress tests. I doubt anyone will be surprised if it turns out that some institutions that were deemed too small for stress tests end up being declared too big to fail the next time the music stops playing.

In the case of welfare for single mothers, insurance riders take the form of *in-kind benefits*. That means the money is directed to a particular type of good. Section 8 housing is for housing. Food stamps (SNAP) are for food but not alcohol. Medicaid is for healthcare. We use in-kind benefits to prevent money from being spent poorly, such as on alcohol, lottery tickets, or luxury goods. A notable exception is

Temporary Assistance for Needy Families (TANF). This is the signature program that most people think of when they think about welfare. It gives cash directly to single mothers. After the welfare reform act of 1996, the benefits were limited to five years, although states can exempt 20 percent of cases from this limit.

One of the major ideas in the progressive movement over recent decades has been to give cash unconditionally to the poor. This follows basic economics 101 logic. Consumers know what they need better than a bureaucrat working for the government. Maybe a single mother would be better off getting cash so she could get her car fixed, even if it meant having to eat beans and rice for a while. Instead we give her in-kind benefits, and she gets fired from her job because there aren't any bus lines that take her to work.

Direct cash transfers were pioneered in Africa and were supposed to be very successful. "Give a man a fish and he eats for a day. Give a man $1,000 and he buys a fishing boat and eats for a lifetime." I was surprised to find that direct cash transfers don't work very well even in Africa. In the short term they are great, but the effects fade out over time.[399] The hope was that the money would lead to investments and long-term increases in income, but that did not pan out.

There is a deeper problem with direct cash transfers to the poor. In *Foreign Aid and Its Unintended Consequences*, Dirk-Jan Koch points out that direct cash aid results in increased local inflation and documents a 25 percent increase in the price of eggs. So the children of participants in the aid program had a 40 percent reduction in stunted growth because they could afford more food. But the children of non-participants had a 34 percent increase in stunted growth.[400] Injecting Western money into the developing world can easily turn out badly.

Food Sharing Networks

Kill sharing is a common arrangement in hunter-gatherer societies. Hillard Kaplan and Michael Gurven survey these arrangements in *Moral Sentiments and Material Interests*. Large game is shared in many primitive tribes including the Hadza, Dobe, !Kung, Aché, Yanomamö, and Gunwinngu.[401] There are many reasons for people to share kills. Good hunters can use their success to gain social status and advertise themself as an ally or to attract a good mate. But some of the motivation is to reduce the risk of having nothing to eat at all. Kill sharing acts like hunting insurance. If only half the hunters make a kill, but they share their food, the whole tribe eats.

Women in hunter-gatherer tribes also share their food. The difference is that for women, it's not about whether or not they made a kill, since women don't usually hunt, but their stage of life. Women who are nursing or who have small children cut back on their foraging quite a bit, even though they need more calories. However, this loss is offset by food sharing. Aché women shared about 60 percent of their food from extended gathering trips outside their own nuclear family.[402] When a woman is not pregnant or dealing with small children, she gathers more food than she needs and shares it with women who are pregnant or who have small children. Then when she gets pregnant, other women do the same for her. That's textbook social insurance.

One final lesson from primitive tribes is that the best hunters are about five times as good as the worst hunters.[403] This difference means that the best hunters are consistently subsidizing the worst hunters over the span of their entire lives. It isn't that different from the rich and the poor in our society, where the rich pay far more in taxes than the poor.

If I haven't made the connection obvious yet, even primitive tribes have a welfare state. The difference is that it is much easier to detect and punish free riders. When you live in a small, intimate society, everyone knows everyone else's business. One member of the Maimande tribe explained, "If one doesn't give, one doesn't get in return . . . Some people are specifically excluded from most distributions because they never or only rarely give any of their products to us."[404] (I assume this was translated but I'd love for there to be a tribe of hunter-gatherers that speaks like scientists filling out grant applications.) Moral hazard is not a major problem in small tribes.

Ancient Israel

Let's shift from primitive tribes to ancient Israel. They had a number of programs designed to help the poor, immigrants, and the afflicted. Many Christians are familiar with the gleaning laws. These are laws that prohibit landowners from harvesting all the crops on their own land. That way the poor and immigrants could pick the leftover crops (Lev. 19:9-10, Lev. 23:22, Deut. 24:19-21). The Sabbath Laws were similar. Every seventh year the Israelites had to let their fields lie fallow; they could not plant and harvest them. However, whatever grew naturally was left for the poor and wild animals (Ex. 23:10-11, Lev. 25:1-7).

Conservatives have always liked gleaning laws because they force the poor to work for their food. They weren't just given a handout. But not all of Israel's laws had work requirements. You have probably heard that the Israelites were supposed to tithe—to set aside a tenth of their harvest. Well, every third year that tithe was kept in storehouses for the priests, widows, orphans, and immigrants (Deut. 14:28-29). People who needed it could simply claim some grain for themselves without doing any harvesting. Yes, the Israelites had a tax that was at least partially designated for immigrants.

Some parts of ancient Israel's welfare state were even more radical. One provision of the Sabbath Laws was that all debts were forgiven every seven years (Deut. 15:1-6). Every seventh Sabbath year was a special celebration called Jubilee. It was like a regular Sabbath year in that all debts were wiped clean, but it also meant that all land reverted back to its original owners. When the Israelites conquered Canaan, the land was divided up among the tribes, and then each tribe's land was divided up for the families. A family that fell on hard times might sell off some of their land, but when Jubilee arrived it would revert back to them. This made sure that permanent differences in wealth did not arise. Jubilee meant that everyone got a fresh start at least once in their life.

Sometimes liberals use Jubilee as an argument for radical income redistribution. In fact, that was my own interpretation for a while. Imagine if Bernie Sanders and Elizabeth Warren got together and sponsored a Jubilee law. The political optics would be brilliant because how could the Republicans, who have many Christian members, denounce the idea as communism? But that really isn't what Jubilee was about. People in the United States bought their property on the agreement that they would own their land in perpetuity. Jubilee really would be an unfair act of income redistribution in the United States.

In ancient Israel no one would buy land a year before Jubilee for the same price as if it were forty-eight years until Jubilee, let alone the price to own the land forever. The same principle applies to Sabbath laws and the forgiveness of debts. No one is going to offer a thirty-year mortgage knowing that the debt would be cleared after seven years. Unpaid debts were forgiven every Sabbath year, but the Israelites weren't supposed to avoid paying their debts. There are many verses in the Bible that support this. One of them is Psalm 37:21, "The wicked borrow and do not repay, but the righteous give generously;".

The real purpose of the Sabbath and Jubilee laws is much closer to the Hindu religion's belief that cows are sacred. The anthropologist Marvin Harris, who was one of the villains in the saga with Napoleon Chagnon, describes how this works.[405] India is periodically hit with severe famines, and when people are starving, killing the family cow becomes very tempting. But it is also killing the goose that lays the golden egg. As horrible as starving is, starving a little more and saving the family cow is almost always the best choice to make. The cow is a source of wealth, and milk provides valuable calories and animal protein. But the temptation is enormous. Treating the cow as sacred gives the Hindu people an extra guardrail against making a bad decision in times of extreme stress.

The Sabbath and Jubilee laws also act as guardrails. All agricultural societies suffer terribly when droughts, blights, and famines hit, not just India. In non-Israelite cultures, that prosperous yet predatory family in the village will step in and say "Hey, I know you're suffering some hard times. Why don't you sell me that plot of land that's adjacent to my property. The money will keep you and your family on your feet." The poor family sells their land and becomes even poorer. Eventually they struggle to feed their children even in good times.

Libertarians would say these types of sales were mutually beneficial and economically efficient. But unless the subject is prostitution, liberals have always known that poverty forces people into making deals that are against their long-term interests. If the subject is prostitution, then the story changes to "sex work is work", which is why liberal nations like Germany, Switzerland, and New Zealand have legalized prostitution. Belgium just passed a "groundbreaking" law for prostitute "rights." It allows pimps to have government mediators punish prostitutes who refuse sex with a client more than ten times in a six-month period.[406] Apparently women are only allowed to say "no" ten times.

The main lesson is that, just like the Hindus and the cows, it's almost always better to suffer a little more than to give in to the temptation for short-term relief. Think back to the chapter on willpower—our prefrontal cortexes are weak, and the pressure of the moment is enormous. I don't usually manage to pass up ice cream after dinner. How are starving farmers supposed to pass up food and money in times of extreme hunger and deprivation?

That's where Jubilee laws come into play. Struggling farmers could freely sell their land knowing that they're going to get it back some day. The struggling family gets insurance, the wealthy family gets the means to become even wealthier, and no long-term inequalities in Israeli society emerge. That's textbook social insurance.

The temptation to manipulate the system to avoid the Sabbath and Jubilee laws must have been enormous, and the Bible warns specifically about this:

> If anyone is poor among your fellow Israelites in any of the towns of the land the Lord your God is giving you, do not be hardhearted or tightfisted toward them. Rather, be openhanded and freely lend them whatever they need. Be careful not to harbor this wicked thought: "The seventh year, the year for canceling debts, is near,' (Deut. 15:7-9)

Despite this warning, the Israelites never followed the Jubilee and Sabbath laws, so God punished Israel by allowing them to be conquered by the Babylonians. The captivity lasted for seventy years to make up for the seventy missed Sabbath years (2 Chronicles 36:21). The captivity teaches an important lesson, and one that I think conservatives need more than liberals: We are biased towards hardening our hearts even when God tells us to soften them.

Welfare and Moral Hazard

The saddest fact about single motherhood is that it is concentrated at the bottom of the socioeconomic spectrum. Among the group of single mothers, 57 percent were high school dropouts and only 9 percent were college graduates. In terms of income, 80 percent of single mothers made less than $50,000.[407] Even when the poor do marry, they are also more likely to divorce.[408]

These statistics understate the inequality in marriage. When I first became a conservative, I was shocked to find that over 50 percent of Swedish children were born to single mothers.[409] It seemed like Sweden was committing cultural suicide. However, in *The Marriage Go-Round*, Andrew Cherlin points out that unmarried couples in Sweden are less likely to separate than married couples in the United States.[410] Sweden is a small and homogenous nation with a highly cohesive culture. They do not need legal marriage for men and women to make a commitment to each other. For them marriage really is "just a piece of paper."

The middle class in the United States is a bit like Sweden. It's true that 9% of single mothers have a college education, but they are more likely to marry by the birth of their second child.[411] That's because shotgun weddings have fallen out of favor. These days educated couples wait until their baby is born so that they have plenty of time to plan the wedding of their dreams.

There are three main candidates for the rise of single motherhood: welfare, the birth control pill, and culture. Let's begin with welfare. The program began in 1935 but was expanded to include single mothers in 1962. That leads to the obvious moral hazard argument that welfare led to an increase in single motherhood.

Libertarians have two main arguments that welfare causes single motherhood. The first is basic economic reasoning based on moral hazard. People respond to incentives. Hence the economic slogan "You get less of what you tax and more of what you subsidize." Welfare is a subsidy for single motherhood, which means that it will cause single motherhood to increase. The second libertarian argument is that welfare had previously been limited to widows, but in 1962 it was opened to single mothers. Once that happened the rate of single motherhood started to skyrocket.

Progressives make a few arguments against a link between welfare and single motherhood. The first argument is that welfare benefits have been declining relative to inflation even as children born to single mothers have increased. There are two problems with this argument. The first is that welfare is only one type of benefit given to single mothers. There are many others such as food stamps, Section 8 housing, and Medicaid. Once the value of all of the benefits were included, welfare has kept up with inflation.[412] A deeper problem is that even economic determinists don't think that people instantly respond to new incentives. It takes a while for people to change their behavior.

The second argument that progressives make is that some regions pay high welfare benefits but have low rates of single motherhood, whereas other regions pay low benefits and have high rates. In 1997, a three-person family on welfare in Alabama got $164 per month and a similar family in Connecticut got $636, but the rate of single motherhood was higher in Alabama. However, this masks some demographic differences. The rate of children born to single mothers is about three times as high for black women as for white women, and the black population is much higher in Alabama than Connecticut.

Moreover, local cultures have their own norms and values, and Alabama is different from Connecticut in many ways. David Hackett-Fischer points out in *Albion's Seed* that there were four distinct patterns of the initial settlers to the United States. Each pattern of settlement created enduring cultural patterns that remain hundreds of years later. New England was settled by Puritans, and while they have largely secularized, they still retain those internalized Yankee virtues of hard work and self-discipline. (You could plausibly argue that modern liberals are still Puritans at heart. They just traded Jesus for Jean-Jacques Rousseau. I believe the left today would be much healthier if it had a strong counter-culture of devout liberal Christians.)

Most of the South, including Alabama, was settled by the Scots-Irish, who were rowdy and undisciplined. So even if we compare whites in Alabama to whites in Connecticut, we expect Alabama to have more single motherhood. In fact, Thomas Sowell argues in *White Liberals and Black Rednecks* that black people today are the direct cultural inheritors of this rowdy Scots-Irish culture. Many black speech patterns such as saying "ax" instead of "ask," and referring to pig entrails as "chitlins" directly descended from England.[413] Unfortunately blacks also inherited the Scots-Irish penchant for rowdy and undisciplined living, something that the stuffy Puritans of New England did not share.

The next progressive argument is more successful. It comes from research by Robert Moffit. His 1992 research found that welfare had only a minor impact on single motherhood. Other social scientists disagreed. Mark Rosenzweig looked at the data from the National Longitudinal Survey of Youth. He found that a 10 percent increase in welfare benefits resulted in a 12 percent increase in out-of-wedlock childbirths to poor women under age 23.[414] However, this number should trigger your shady science spider sense. Why age 23? Why such an arbitrary cutoff? The 1990s were before the replication crisis so p-hacking used to be common. It still is common, but it used to be common, too.

In response to Rosenzweig's findings, Moffitt revisited the issue in 1998. Moffitt's new analysis showed that welfare caused a slightly larger, but still small, increase in the rate of children born to single mothers. However, it was too small to be the major driver of single motherhood, and there remained no consensus on the size of the effect.[415] Robert Moffitt revisited the issue one more time in 2020. His goal was to study the effects of the 1996 welfare reform act. The key point about the reforms is that they gave block grants to states in the hope that some states would come up with a program that worked. Moffitt looked at the individual state programs and found a few had small effects, but most had no benefit at all.[416] Overall, it seems clear that welfare has a small impact on single motherhood, but it was not a major factor and can't explain the skyrocketing increase in single motherhood that took place in the 1960s.

Culture and The Pill

The birth control pill is the next contender for the rise of single motherhood. The pill was released in 1960, although it wasn't widely available for single women until the 1972 Supreme Court *Eisenstadt v. Baird* decision. This is probably enough to reject the pill theory because single motherhood hit an inflection point ten years earlier. (See Figure 17 from the previous chapter, which graphs the rate of single motherhood over time.) The pill became widely available ten years too late. If it's not welfare, and it's not the pill, then the rise of single motherhood must be from a change in culture.

The first line of evidence for culture comes from the book the *First Measured Century* by Theodore Caplow and colleagues. The title suggests the main goal of the book—to use data to precisely measure how the world changed during the twentieth century. To this end, they gathered data on the many ways that American life changed, including changes towards sex and marriage. In 1900, only 6 percent of women had premarital sex. But the social norm against premarital sex had been steadily eroding over the twentieth century. By 1960, when the Sexual Revolution began, it was already up to 25 percent. By 1991 it was up to 74 percent. See figure 18 below. This suggests that the norms against premarital sex had weakened long before the birth control pill, or changes to welfare.

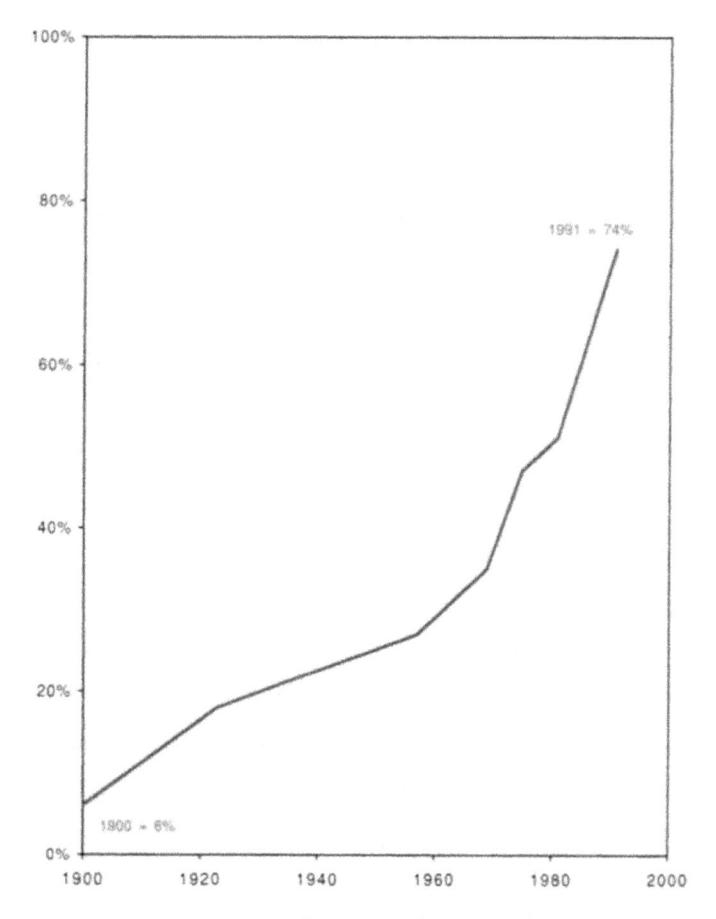

Figure 18: Percentage of unmarried 19-year-old women with sexual experience. From *The First Measured Century*.[417]

You might be skeptical about the reliability of the data in Figure 18. That's a good instinct, but the data is good enough to do the job. In the late 1940s, Alfred Kinsey's research opened the door to studying human sexuality, so we have many surveys covering the second half of the twentieth century. (The fact that human sexuality had become a legitimate research subject also suggests that cultural attitudes towards sex had begun to change long before the 1960s.) The first half of the century is trickier, but we do have interviews of older women, done after the Sexual Revolution, asking them if they had premarital sex. It's not great data, but it's good enough to show the consistent trend of increasing rates of premarital sex starting in 1900, sixty years before the birth control pill or changes in welfare to allow single mothers.[418]

The second line of evidence is more subjective because it comes from literature. It's the closest thing we have to taking a time machine into the distant past. History can tell us the sweeping events, but literature is the best way to put yourself in the hearts and minds of ordinary people. In *Pride and Prejudice*, which is set in the early nineteenth century, the prospect that Lydia Bennet had premarital sex was enough to ruin not just her, but her entire family.

Fast forward a hundred years to *The Great Gatsby*, and we enter the glamorous world of the Roaring Twenties. It's a tale of absurdly rich people leading vacuous lives of alcohol-fueled parties, open adultery, and premarital sex. It is a far cry from the chaperoned balls and intergenerational family-based socializing of Jane Austen's time period.

When I was in high school, *The Great Gatsby* was considered a strong contender for the Great American Novel, but I don't think it has aged well. The core plot line of Gatsby's longing for Daisy still works. That's less true for the broader message that the pursuit of wealth led to licentiousness and moral decline. It wasn't about the money. The wealthy upper class had the social power to openly flout traditional norms of sexual morality and responsible behavior. But they also started a trend that went mainstream and then worked its way down to the poor, at which point it created a far less glamorous underclass of single mothers. Fitzgerald captured a brief snapshot of American history but missed the real lesson.

Jane Austen's books have held up better. Contrary to her reputation, she did not write about anything as trivial as manners. She wrote about social norms—the excellence of an ordinary life well-lived. The insights she drew from her more formal and polite era have only grown in value as the world has coarsened. But she was also a powerful critic of the problems in her own time, and she used Lydia's impending shame to shine a spotlight on them. Austen was criticizing the burden disproportionately placed on women to maintain the family honor; the fact that a cad like Mr. Wickham could get multiple fresh starts after preying on many different women; and that his victims and their family would be ruined forever. The silly and dramatic Mrs. Bennett satirized the way society of her time overreacted to people making forgivable mistakes.

Jesus had at least two encounters with women who violated the ancient world's even more strict norms for sexual morality. The first was the Samaritan woman at the well. She had been married five different times and was currently living with a man to whom she was not married. Yet Jesus treated her with respect and a gentle kindness. His second encounter was when he stopped an adulteress from being stoned to death by telling the crowd, "Let any one of you who is without sin be the first to throw a stone at her." (John 8:7) That made the crowd disperse. "'Then neither do I condemn you," Jesus declared, "'Go now and leave your life of sin.'" (John 8:11)

I'm skeptical that society will successfully steer a middle ground between the Regency era of pre-Victorian England and today. Look at the way norms about racism have changed since the 1980s. Why couldn't we have stopped at "Don't be a racist"? Instead, people don't even have to make a mistake to face the same kind of wrath that Lydia Bennett faced. George Orwell wrote about the role that two minutes of hate played in the fictional totalitarian society of *1984*. We too have our periodic two minutes of hate about people caught on video appearing to be racist. The irony is that it almost invariably turns out that we got the story wrong: Central Park Karen,[419] the MAGA hat Catholic student,[420] and Citi Bike Karen[421] were all cases where we gleefully ruined an innocent person's life so that we could feel the deliciously hot rage of moral superiority and hatred. *1984* was supposed to be a warning, not an instruction manual.

The bright-line rule is a legal principle that good laws should be easy to follow and have simple and objective standards. An example is that the police have to give a Miranda warning after arresting someone. Good social norms should also follow the bright-line rule. Instead, they are vague, ephemeral, and prone to purity spirals. Navigating these norms takes skill, social acumen, and conformity. Once again, I have to revisit my love-hate relationship with postmodernism, because only the postmodernists appreciate the terrifying power of weaponized social norms that evolve too fast for ordinary people to keep up. Creating stable easy-to-follow norms is a hard problem to solve.

Black Single Mothers

The sociologist William Julius Wilson argues that a bad economy explains the rise of single motherhood, at least in the black community. In the 1950s manufacturing industries provided high-quality jobs for relatively unskilled workers. But as roads and transportation improved, many factories moved away from the cities. This left many black men high and dry. They could not get marriage-worthy jobs that would win a woman's approval.

The evidence is against Wilson's disappearing jobs theory. Christopher Jencks found that the marriage rate for black men with steady jobs declined from 80 percent in 1960 to 66 percent in 1980.[422] James Q. Wilson reviews the research in *The Marriage Problem* and finds other issues, such as a comparable drop in the marriage rate of educated black men.[423] Wilson has gotten it backwards: It is the black men who do not want to get married. They have a good thing going.

This is a lesson we've already seen back in the chapter on evolutionary psychology. Studies of the sex ratios on college campuses show that when women have the negotiating power, they demand commitment. When men have the negotiating power, they try to juggle sexual relationships with multiple women.[424] It doesn't matter if the men are inner-city blacks or college-educated whites. If men have the chance to have sex without commitment, they will take it.

The main difference is that college-educated women use birth control because middle-class social norms demand education and marriage before children. By contrast, poor women of all races have far more ambivalent feelings about having children before getting married. This is the main reason why modern birth control hasn't done anything to reduce the rate of single motherhood.

The Stories of Single Mothers

Katherine Edin and Maria Kefalas tell the stories of low-income single mothers in their poignant and sorrowful book, *Promises I Can Keep: Why Poor Women Put Motherhood Before Marriage*. Their goal was to understand the lives of single mothers by getting to know them personally and learning about their lives. They didn't want to treat them like another statistic. So they embedded themselves in Philadelphia and joined churches and volunteer groups to form connections with various local communities. Their book is the result of case studies on the lives of 162 low-income single mothers of different races in various Philadelphia neighborhoods.

The main story that emerges from these young women is that they have a high regard for marriage and longed to form a loving partnership with a man, but their dreams were thwarted before their adult lives truly began. Edin and Kefalas write:

> Trust among residents of poor communities is astonishingly low—so low that most mothers we spoke with said they have no close friends, and many even distrust close kin. The social isolation that is the common experience of those who live in poverty is heightened for adolescents, whose relationships with parents are strained by the developmental need to forge an independent identity. The "relationship poverty" that ensues can create a compelling desire to give and receive love. Who better to do so with, some figure, than a child they can call their own?[425]

Recall the marshmallow test from the chapter on social norms. Two marshmallow children got better grades in school, had fewer problem behaviors, and better social skills.[426] If the latter seems surprising, keep in mind that healthy relationships are a two-way street. We are all biased towards our own needs and interests, so we have to learn to partially repress them in order to form a relationship as an equal. No one is going to want to be a friend or spouse of someone who constantly puts themselves first, or who repeatedly takes out their stresses and frustrations on others.

Isolation from both friends and family causes poor women to choose the next best thing: motherhood. A baby means that there is at least one other person in the world that she can love unconditionally, and who loves her unconditionally in return. And while success stories are few and far between, most young women are optimistic that they will not end up another statistic.

That's because most single mothers are in committed relationships with their child's father when they give birth, and almost half are living together.[427] Moreover, the mother's pregnancy typically causes her partner to shape up, at least initially. But just a year after the birth of their child, half the relationships have ended. By the time the child is three, two-thirds are over. Edin and Kefalas write:

> How does the dream die so quickly? How does a young couple's optimism that they will be the ones to beat the odds turn into the bitter realization that they will not? ...
>
> It is usually the young father's criminal behavior, the spells of incarceration that so often follow, a pattern of intimate violence, his chronic infidelity, and an inability to leave drugs and alcohol alone that cause relationships to falter and die.[428]

Boys are not born as violent and drug-addicted cheats. They are socialized that way. It must be heartbreaking for a mother to watch, powerless, as her son is drawn down the cad path. Her boy was sweet and sensitive as a small child. He loved people and babbled joyfully at strangers. He was expressive and empathetic and had a way of drawing others to him. His sensitivity made him timid and sometimes even fearful, but even that character trait seemed like a positive in a rough neighborhood where wild and aggressive behavior is celebrated. So his mother was sure that his sweetness would protect him from bad role models and lead him to a good life. But she was wrong.

In these impoverished neighborhoods, Judith Rich Harris' observation about the nature of peer socialization becomes a curse: "A child's goal is not to become a successful adult, any more than a prisoner's goal is to become a successful guard. A child's goal is to be a successful child."[429] Her son's sensitivity and empathy made him even more attuned to the unhealthy norms of his neighborhood. It also made him feel like he had something to prove, in a way that the tougher boys did not. Slowly, and by degrees, her sensitive and joyful boy began to change.

He began to harden and grow wild. Sometimes he scared her. No matter what lessons she taught, no matter what life wisdom she tried to impart, she couldn't help him. She knew the exact path he was taking, and how it would end up, but there was nothing she could do to stop him from taking it. This beautiful boy who had once been her heart was now an angry stranger that she could no longer recognize.

When her son's girlfriend became pregnant, she was relieved. A baby was her last hope. A baby would domesticate him. A baby would keep him home instead of out partying and causing trouble with his friends and with the gangs. A baby would make him quit drugs and alcohol. A baby would make him get a job and clean up his act. And for a short period of time, it did.

Then the reality of life as a parent hit. It was different from what he dreamed of when he was lying with his girlfriend in his arms, planning a future where they would take on the world together. He simply did not have the emotional maturity to make the relationship work. He probably couldn't have made it work even without a baby, but with one, the relationship was doomed before it began. He couldn't handle the crying, the sleepless nights, the frazzled nerves, the ever-present money troubles of a young couple, the endless unceasing demands of this tiny little person, and the even more endless and unceasing demands of his overwhelmed and shell-shocked girlfriend. She had long ago stopped being the admiring girl he fell in love with. Now she was an angry and demanding mother that he found impossible to deal with. The constant stress led to constant fighting. When she got angry with him, he would get angry back and lose his temper. He would get mean and sometimes even violent. Escape was easy—go back to his friends, back to drugs and alcohol, back to life on the streets, and back to other women who did not want him to help raise a baby.

Eventually his girlfriend realized that she was wrong—that she was just another statistic after all. She broke off the relationship and reentered the dating world sadder and wiser than before. Now she was more willing to look past beauty and charm to find a man who would bring stability and a steady paycheck. Unfortunately, she was now a single mother without an education, so her value in the dating market had dropped. The only men she could attract were trapped in the same life as her, which meant they would bring the same problems and pathologies as her previous boyfriend.

She picked the best man she could find, and the new couple became pregnant to cement their connection to each other. At that point her first child, let's suppose she is a daughter, became an obstacle to the new couple's happiness. If the daughter was lucky, she would only be pushed aside and neglected in favor of her younger half-sibling. If she was unlucky, she would be abused by her mother's boyfriend, particularly after she developed sexually. The Cinderella Effect means that girls are not always safe around older men, particularly in tough neighborhoods. She learned very early to be wary of her mother's boyfriends.

Her mom didn't have any patience for her either—it's her younger child who attaches her to her boyfriend and his sporadic paycheck. It's the younger child who still has both her hope and her unconditional love. The daughter has been replaced, and she now finds herself facing her mother's frustration and anger instead of her love, particularly if she dares criticize the latest boyfriend. As these habits solidify, her mother's anger can harden into abuse. The daughter wants out. Out of the home where she's not wanted, away from the boyfriend's groping hands, and into a new life.

Then one day she meets a boy who thinks she is beautiful, and they start seeing each other. He tells her that he wants a baby with her eyes and her smile—hers! This beautiful and charming boy chose her out of all the other girls to be united with forever in flesh and blood. Life is finally happening, and this time, it's her chance. She will finally have a baby that she can love unconditionally, and who will love her unconditionally in return. And while success stories are few and far between, she is optimistic that she will not end up another statistic. And so the cycle of poverty continues for another generation.

The stories of single mothers are not tales of empowered feminists living their best lives, or of prodigal daughters who choose to become wild and wanton. Instead, they are stories of loneliness and despair. They are stories of women and girls with a desperate human need for love and connection, but who instead find themselves trapped in growing social isolation—isolation brought on by a lack of basic life skills, and an even greater lack of quality men to build a life with.

This book is a defense of the conservative worldview, and to that end I have criticized liberalism on a variety of fronts. And yet one place where I haven't is the size of the government. I've consistently argued for some type of welfare state throughout this book. I've spent more time on market failure than on what markets do well, to the point that I'm probably doing a minor disservice to readers who aren't economics buffs. I've argued that income taxes do not fit the simple model of "you get less of what you tax." And in this chapter, I've argued that the welfare state is a part of human nature, regardless of how primitive or advanced our society.

This is not about wanting lower taxes, but about doing what it takes to lift up the people who are struggling the most. We can and should find the grace to give money to struggling young mothers, but the government can't give them basic life skills, and it can't socialize their sons to take the dad path. If we want to break the cycle of poverty, then we have to change the culture, and that's something we'll all have to work on together.

These mothers understand, better than most, the battles that are waged within the human heart—that life is beautiful and filled with love, and that human nature is feral and wild and can never be fully tamed, only bent slightly against itself. And so, the world will always be a vale of tears and soul-making—one that brings both heartfelt love and heart-rending despair. But with the faith to carry on, we can cultivate our gardens and nurture the lives that dwell within.

Further Reading

The books mentioned throughout this text are all worth reading, but here is a more curated list. The idea is to give a more intensive pass through the project of building a worldview, starting from the ground and ending with the view from 30,000 feet.

Basic Economics by Thomas Sowell. If you really want to learn economics, you have to study graphs until they become automatic. If you want the next best thing, then read Thomas Sowell. He provides a literary introduction that will get you thinking like an economist. Get an older edition with the subtitle *Citizens Guide* since it's only about half the length. But if you want to read 700 pages, knock yourself out and get the latest edition. An even better idea is to read three or four introductions to economics. Each one is like an introduction to that author's worldview.

Games in Economic Development by Bruce Wydick. Will teach you evolutionary game theory as a way to learn the economics of social norms and cooperation. This book really focuses on cooperation outside of formal contracts and market institutions. It does have some high school level math, but it's confined to the end of each section, so you can easily skip it.

Gut Feelings by Gerd Gigerenzer. A breezy corrective to the abuses of behavioral economics. Does to the rest of behavioral economics (other than a very few areas such as hyperbolic discounting) what the Hawks and Doves did to the endowment effect. His other, more scholarly books are also reasonably accessible and well-written. I particularly liked *Rationality for Mortals*.

The Myth of Monogamy by David Barash. My favorite introduction to evolutionary psychology. Evolutionary psychology is like economics. There are many good introductions, they each have their own flavor, and they tend to be broader introductions to the author's worldview at the same time. So it's worth reading more than one.

Noble Savages by Napoleon Chagnon. It's a great introduction to the Yanomamö, and also a great window into the difficulty of scaling a society up beyond 150 people or so. Chagnon does a great job illustrating the benefits of greater size for security from other villages, but also greater internal conflicts that lead to fissures. It's also a good intellectual history of Marxist cultural anthropology and their favorite shibboleth, the noble savage.

The WEIRDest People in the World by Joseph Henrich. If you liked the chapter on the Hobbesian problem, this book is for you. So many great insights, and yet I only had space for a few. You should read *Noble Savages* first because it will make the more complex anthropology in this book more understandable.

Law's Order by David Friedman. One of the hardest chapters to cut from this book was the chapter on the Coase Theorem and bargaining. It still pains me, but I think it was the right choice because it's even more difficult than the appendix on behavioral genetics. Friedman more than fills in that gap while making the case that common law is both efficient and captures most (all?) of what we mean by fairness. I would say that common law is ecologically rational. This is a hard book so be prepared to read slowly and understand before you move on.

marginalrevolution.com by Tyler Cowen and Alex Tabarrok. The best blog on the internet, but more importantly, a gateway to the world of ideas that you may not know exists. The podcast is also good, but I'm a very infrequent podcast listener, so probably not the best judge.

Herb Gintis Amazon Reviews. You'll probably want to do an internet search for the exact link since it seems to change. Herb Gintis is an ex-Marxist economist who became remarkably centrist and arguably even conservative later in his career. Gintis' book reviews were my real introduction to the world of ideas. His book, *The Bounds of Reason*, is also great, but you'll either have to do a lot of math or skip over it. I opted to skip over most of it.

The Great Courses. This is my heartfelt plea to podcast listeners: Get an Audible or Great Courses subscription. The Great Courses are lectures by college professors known for having an engaging style. I particularly like them for history. You can hear the passion and enthusiasm in the voices of the lecturers, and it's a refreshing contrast to the rich, melodious, and inwardly bored voices of audiobook narrators (apologies to whoever narrates this book!).

The main limitation of the lecture format is that only works for narrative subjects like history, or at least, that's how it is for me. My favorite lecturers are Dorsey Armstrong for medieval history and Elizabeth Vandiver for the ancient Greeks. The course on the Tudors and the Stuarts by Robert Buckholz was how I first heard about the Levellers.

History of Philosophy. If you like politics, you should have a passing familiarity with philosophy. The problem is that there really isn't a "shallow end" of the pool, so it's hard to get started. Your best bet is to begin with the history of philosophy and ignore non-historical books, no matter how catchy and exciting they may appear. There is no mastery method for fuzzy subjects, and historical philosophy is fuzzy, so realize that you need to invest in reading several histories. Most philosophers are atheists, so regardless of whether you are Christian or an atheist, pick up *On Guard* by William Lane Craig and explore the other side of that debate.

@MoleRatCon My handle on Twitter/X.

Appendix: Behavioral Genetics and GWAS

In some ways this appendix only has one goal: to forestall the rebuttal that twin studies have been debunked by genome-wide assessment studies (GWAS). But it will also teach you something about what we used to call "junk" DNA.

Classic Twin Studies

Twin studies are the main workhorse used by behavioral geneticists. Suppose we studied identical twins and found out that a trait had a 64 percent correlation between them. Does this mean the trait is 64 percent genes and 36 percent environment? No, because remember that twins also share the same home and family life. We can't say how much of the 64 percent is from genes and how much is because they live in the same family. We're on the right track, but we need to be a little bit more creative.

What we do is compare identical twins to fraternal twins. Identical twins are genetically identical to each other, but fraternal twins only share half their genes. Once again, let's assume the identical twins are 64 percent correlated. Let's then assume that the fraternal twins are 44 percent correlated. This means that the identical twins are 20 percent "more similar" to each other than the fraternal twins. This extra similarity of 20 percent is because of the extra 50 percent of genes the identical twins share. So the effect of all the genes must be double that, or 40 percent. That means the heritability of this trait is 40 percent.

Now we want to find out how much of the trait is due to the family environment. The identical twins are 64 percent correlated, so subtract the 40 percent due to genes to get 24 percent. That's how much their family life is responsible for. We call this the *shared environment* because it is shared by both twins. Now we've solved the problem of not knowing how much of the 64 percent correlation was genes versus environment.

What about that last 36 percent? That comes from environmental factors that are different between the twins. Even though they are genetically identical, their lives will be at least a little bit different. When they go to school they may be in different classes, participate in different sports, make different friends, and so on. Ronde and Tiki Barber are identical twins who each played in the NFL, but Tiki was a running back and Ronde was a cornerback, so they would be closer friends with players on the offense and defense respectively. We call the environment outside of the family the *nonshared environment* because it is different for each twin.

Criticisms of Twin Studies

A common criticism of twin studies is that they are based on the *equal environments assumption*. That means that the environments of identical and fraternal twins will be equally similar. That assumption may not be true. Think of it this way. If identical twins were separated at birth and raised in different families, then one might play soccer and the other might play football. But if they're raised together, they might both play football because they want to play the same sport as their twin. This would make the influence of genes look larger than they really are. That's a subtle concept so think about it this way: The more similar the environment between two people, the greater the apparent influence of genes. If two people have exactly the same environment, then genes must explain all the differences between them.

There are two lines of evidence that show that the equal environments assumption is reasonable. They both involve replicating the results of twin studies, but without twins. Divorce is one of them. When couples divorce and remarry they may have children in their new marriage. These children will be half-siblings with the children from the previous marriage. This means we can replicate the twin study methodology knowing that half-siblings share 25 percent of genes and full siblings share 50 percent. KS Kendler and colleagues did exactly that and their results agree with the classic twin studies.[430]

Another way to confirm the twin studies is with adoption. A woman who puts one child up for adoption may also put a second child up for adoption later on. Ideally the original adopting family will welcome the second child into their home, but that doesn't always happen. In that case, you have two children who share 50 percent of their genes, but who are raised in different homes. Any correlations between them must be due to their genes, not their environment. This gives a completely different method for estimating the importance of genes. Thomas Bouchard and Matt McGue review the literature and find that the adoption studies broadly agree with the twin studies.[431]

However, twin studies have a different problem: I'm going to call this the *between-group problem*. Twins are members of the same family, so we can't use twin studies to compare rich people to poor people, or black people to white people. We do have adoption studies, but adoptive parents are carefully screened to be good parents and are almost always members of the middle class. So even if a woman puts two children up for adoption and they go to different homes, those homes are going to be very similar to each other. Stephen Pinker explains in his book *The Blank Slate*.

Behavioral genetic methods address variation within the group of the people being examined, not variation between groups of people. If the twins or adoptees in a sample are all middle-class American whites, a heritability estimate can tell us about why middle-class American whites differ from other middle-class American whites, but not why the middle class differs from the lower or upper class, why Americans differ from non-Americans, or why whites differ from Asians or blacks.[432]

A final criticism is that most study designs are based on the assumption that IQ is an *additive* trait. That means there are many genes for intelligence and each one adds a fraction of point of IQ. However, there are *non-additive* factors at work too. That happens because of dominant and recessive traits (one type of gene dominates the other type), or *epigenetics* (environmental factors that regulate genes) or *epistasis* (genes that regulate other genes). However, recent studies suggest that non-additive effects for IQ are small.[433]

Genomics

The world of 2003 was a much simpler and more optimistic place for scientists who study genes. We knew from twin studies that IQ was perhaps 60 percent heritable, and the Human Genome Project had just finished mapping all 25,000 or so genes in humans. It seemed like a simple matter to just give a bunch of people IQ tests and then find out which of these genes contributed to IQ. They did that and found ... essentially nothing.[434] We've identified over a thousand genes associated with intelligence, and yet they explain less than 1 percent of the heritability of IQ. What this meant was that we had to rethink our understanding of genes. You might even call it a paradigm shift.

You have probably heard about junk DNA, either in your high

school science classes or from popular books on evolution. If not, then recall that genes are the part of our DNA that code for proteins. But that's only about 1 or 2 percent of our DNA. The vast majority of our DNA was assumed to be junk that didn't do anything. We now know that junk DNA, which is called *non-coding DNA*, is vital in many ways, such as in regulating gene expression. Here is the new paradigm: Genes are like eggs, flour, and sugar. Non-coding DNA is the chef baking the cake.

Genomics is the science that studies both genes and our non-coding DNA. Humans are about 99.7 percent genetically identical to each other, which means that the interesting bits are the rare places where we find differences. These locations are called *single nucleotide polymorphisms* (SNPs, pronounced "snips"). Humans only have about 25,000 genes but around 15 million SNPs and counting. Another important finding from genomics is that most traits are *polygenic*, which means that they are influenced by many different SNPs. In the case of intelligence there are thousands of SNPs, each of which contributes a small fraction of a point of IQ. Even eye color, which is often taught as being governed by a single gene, is influenced by many SNPs.

The most common way we get data on these SNPs is with a *SNP array*. The way it works is you get a sample of someone's DNA with a cheek swab. Then you fragment it into tiny pieces. Then you put it on a SNP array. The SNP array has a bunch of tiny probes that can bind with different known SNPs. The main limitation of the technique is that most SNP arrays can only identify perhaps a million or so SNPs. Personally, I'm in awe of the fact that we can cheaply identify a million SNPs with a single DNA sample. In some ways that seems more impressive than putting a man on the moon.

With these new tools in place scientists were sure they'd be able to find the basis for traits like intelligence, and once again they were wrong. The estimates for heritability weren't zero, but they were a lot lower than the twin studies.[435] This led to a debate over the *missing heritability problem*. Some scientists thought this was proof that the twin studies were wrong, and others thought that this was because our SNP arrays can only check for the most common SNPs, and that they were missing a lot of rare variants.

The missing heritability problem was solved by using people who are related. There are two main reasons why that helps. The first is that genomics studies are, at heart, a lot like the twin studies. The core insight of the twin studies is that identical twins who share 100 percent of their genes are more strongly correlated for traits like IQ than fraternal twins who only share 50 percent of their genes. However, genomics studies need a lot of subjects and there just aren't enough twins.

That creates a problem. Unrelated people don't share much DNA. So while siblings will share 50 percent of SNPs, two random strangers might only share a fraction of a percent of the SNPs for a given trait. For example, we might have to see if people who share 0.2 percent of SNPs for intelligence are more strongly correlated than people who share 0.1 percent of SNPs for intelligence. That doesn't give us much statistical power. If we could somehow include siblings, then we could check if people who share 50 percent of their SNPs are more strongly correlated than people who share 0.1 percent of their SNPs.[436]

The second reason you want people who are related is because of *linkage disequilibrium*. Here's how it works. If SNP A is close to SNP B on the same chromosome, then a child who gets SNP A from their parent is also very likely to get SNP B too. This is an advantage because our SNP arrays may have only tagged SNP A, but if SNP B is also important for intelligence, then we'll also get SNP B. Using siblings is a great way to include rare variant SNPs even if they haven't been identified and tagged yet.

The problem with including people who are related is that you also introduce the shared environment. Once again, we have the problem of not knowing how much a trait is shared environment and how much is because of the SNPs. If we're going to include people who are related, then we also need to find a way to exclude the shared environment. This is where a technique called GREML-KIN enters the picture. When we use GREML-KIN to crunch the numbers for IQ, we get a heritability of 54 percent.[437] Now that twin studies and genomic studies are in broad agreement, the missing heritability problem is largely solved. The genomics studies end out supporting the twin studies after all.

Every technique has its drawbacks and GREML-KIN is no exception. People with European ethnicity are vastly overrepresented in most of the datasets we have, and even when we do have people from different ethnic groups, they aren't always handled properly.[438] Techniques like GREML-KIN also can't handle *dynastic effects*, which is when the parents' genes, such as for high socioeconomic status, provide their children a more nurturing environment. More importantly, by making use of people who are related, we've reintroduced the between-group problem. If two people are related then they are probably in the same social class and ethnic group, which in turn means they were probably socialized by the same culture.

Acknowledgements

I'd like to thank my wife Kristen and my children Edras and Zemanesh. I was a bright-eyed and bushy-tailed new husband, father, and conservative when I first thought of writing this book. And I did write it, but for some reason I sat on it for almost twenty years. Now I know why. This book is much improved for having twenty years of the joy and the wonder, and the trials and tribulations, of the life of an ordinary husband and father enriching it. Ordinary lives don't make it into the history books, but they are the best lives.

I'd also like to thank my friends Marshall Smith and Daryl Cantrell for their advice and feedback. And finally, I'd like to thank my sister-in-law, Kate Dusel. I tried very hard to bridge the theory-laden gaps between liberals and conservatives and generally failed, but if I succeeded in a few spots, her feedback played a role.

Endnotes

1. Phillips and Loon, "Dietary Protein for Athletes: From Requirements to Optimum Adaptation."

2. Schwarzenegger and Dobbins, *Encyclopedia of Modern Bodybuilding*, 680.

3. Phillips and Loon, "Dietary Protein for Athletes: From Requirements to Optimum Adaptation."

4. Hannam, *The Genesis of Science: How the Christian Middle Ages Launched the Scientific Revolution*.

5. Babie, "Magna Carta and the Forest Charter: Two Stories of Property, What Will You Be Doing in 2017."

6. Rousseau never used the term noble savage, but it's a reasonable characterization and, like many scientific and philosophical ideas, it is associated with someone other than its inventor, John Dryden

7. Russell, *A History of Western Philosophy*, 685.

8. Strathern, *Hume in 90 Minutes*, 45.

9. Burke, *Letter to a Member of the National Assembly*.

10. Sharp, *The English Levellers*, 31.

11. Ashcraft, *Revolutionary Politics and Locke's Two Treatises of Government*.

12. Ferguson, "Has History Got It Wrong About Oliver Cromwell's Persecution of Catholics?"

13. Durant and Durant, *The Story of Civilization: The Age of Voltaire*, 370.

14. Yannelis and Looney, "What Went Wrong with Federal Student Loans?"

15. Gwartney, *Common Sense Economics: What Everyone Should Know About Wealth and Prosperity*, 8.

16. McMillan, *Reinventing the Bazaar: A Natural History of Markets*, 94–110.

17. Acemoglu and Angrist, "Consequences of Employment Protection? The Case of the Americans with Disabilities Act."

18. Doleac and Hansen, "The Unintended Consequences of 'Ban the Box': Statistical Discrimination and Employment Outcomes When Criminal Histories Are Hidden.

19. Williams, "Price Gouging."

20. Suddeth, *USSR: Grocery Store Uncut*.

21. Nodjimbadem, "The Lesser-Known History of African-American Cowboys."

22. King et al., "The Robustness of Bubbles and Crashes in Experimental Stock Markets."

23. Goetze, *Rent Control: Affordable Housing for the Privileged, Not the Poor. A Study of the Impact of Rent Control in Cambridge*.

24. Hakim and Lyles, "For Rangel, Four Rent-Stabilized Apartments."

25. Tucker, *The Excluded Americans: Homelessness and Housing Policies*.

26. Tucker, "How Rent Control Drives Out Affordable Housing."

27. Henderson, "Rent Control."

28. Feldstein, "Tax Rates and Human Behavior."

29. Weisman, "Tax Rates and Unemployment Rates Show Negative Correlation."

30. Eissa and Liebman, "Labor Supply Response to the Earned Income Tax Credit."

31. Keane, "Labor Supply and Taxes: A Survey."

32. Cowen, "What Libertarianism Has Become and Will Become — State Capacity Libertarianism."

33. Miller, Kim, and Roberts, "2021 Index of Economic Freedom."

34. Smith, *The Wealth of Nations*, 1.

35. Gombrich, *A Little History of the World*, 243.

36. Henderson, "Creative Destruction."

37. Henderson.

38. Moore and Simon, "The Greatest Century That Ever Was: 25 Miraculous Trends of the Past 100 Years."

39. Kelley, "Biden Tells Coal Miners to Learn to Code."

40. Gates, "Net Worth."

41. DiLorenzo, *How Capitalism Saved America: The Untold History of Our Country, from the Pilgrims to the Present*, 124.

42. DiLorenzo, 121.

43. DiLorenzo, 125.

44. DiLorenzo, 121.

45. DiLorenzo, "The Origins of Antitrust: An Interest-Group Perspective."

46. Cox, *The Concise Guide to Economics*, 25.

47. Mosendz, "A Complete Timeline of the Donald Sterling Saga."

48. "Walmart Net Profit Margin."

49. "Exxon Profit Margins."

50. Henderson, "Profits."

51. "Microsoft Profit Margins."

52. Gillette and DelMas, "Psycho-Economics: Studies in Decision Making," Classroom Expernomics, Newsletter Published by Department of Economics, Management and Accounting."

53. Smith, "Economics in the Laboratory."

54. David R. Henderson, "Experimental Economics," in *The Concise Encyclopedia of Economics* (2008).

55. Kessel, "A Study of the Effects of Competition in the Tax-Exempt Bond Market."

56. Liebowitz and Margolis, "The Fable of the Keys."

57. Wydick, *Games in Economic Development*, 100.

58. "William Galston's Findings Are Based on a Study by Charles Murray, "According to Age: Longitudinal Profiles of AFDC Recipients and the Poor by Age Group."

59. Caplow, Hicks, and Wattenberg, *The First Measured Century: An Illustrated Guide to Trends in America, 1900-2000*, 87.

60. Osterman et al., "Births: Final Data for 2021."

61. Watts, Duncan, and Quan, "Revisiting the Marshmallow Test: A Conceptual Replication Investigating Links Between Early Delay of Gratification and Later Outcomes."

62. Michaelson and Munakata, "Same Data Set, Different Conclusions: Preschool Delay of Gratification Predicts Later Behavioral Outcomes in a Preregistered Study."

63. Guynet, "Superstimuli."

64. Gwynne and Rentz, "Beetles on the Bottle: Male Buprestids Mistake Stubbies for Females (Coleoptera."

65. Harlow, "Lovin' On Me."

66. Orenstein, "Opinion | The Troubling Trend in Teenage Sex."

67. Bows and Herring, "Getting Away with Murder? A Review of the 'Rough Sex Defence.'"

68. Hume, *A Treatise of Human Nature*.

69. Becker and Murphy, "A Theory of Rational Addiction."

70. Saffer and Chaloupka, "The Demand for Illicit Drugs."

71. Frederick, Loewenstein, and O'Donoghue, "Time Discounting and Time Preference: A Critical Review."

72. Ainslie, *Breakdown of Will*.

73. Gintis, *The Bounds of Reason: Game Theory and the Unification of the Behavioral Sciences*, 11.

74. Burke, *Letter to a Member of the National Assembly*.

75. Fonte, "Liberal Democracy vs. Transnational Progressivism: The Ideological War within the West."

76. Wu, "Illegal Border Crossings, Explained in 7 Charts."

77. Dowden and Schwartz, "Truth."

78. "Munk Debate - Mainstream Media Ft. Douglas Murray, Matt Taibbi, Malcolm Gladwell, Michelle Goldberg."

79. Butler, *Gender Trouble*, 114.

80. Searle, "The Word Turned Upside Down."

81. Sokal, "A Physicist Experiments with Cultural Studies."

82. Pluckrose, Lindsay, and Boghossian, "Academic Grievance Studies and the Corruption of Scholarship."

83. Gross and Levitt, *Higher Superstition: The Academic Left and Its Quarrels with Science*, 209–17.

84. Spiro, *Gender and Culture: Kibbutz Women Revisited*.

85. Chu, *Females*, loc. 740.

86. Andrea Long Chu's Pulitzer was for literary criticism, not his book. But it was awarded after *Females* was published, so clearly it didn't get him into any trouble.

87. "KABC-TV7 (1974) 'Free to Be You & Me!' Original Broadcast!!!!."

88. "The Problem with Jon Stewart."

89. Cantor, "Do Trans Kids Stay Trans When They Grow Up?"

90. Karrington, "Defining Desistance: Exploring Desistance in Transgender and Gender Expansive Youth through Systematic Literature Review."

91. Cass, "Final Report – Cass Review," sec. 76.

92. Sapir, "The Reckoning over Puberty Blockers Has Arrived"; "Why Did Three Journals Reject My Puberty Blocker Study?" UnHerd."

93. David, "European Countries Restrict Trans Health Care for Minors."

94. NHS England, "Clinical Policy: Puberty Suppressing Hormones."

95. Boothman and Puttick, "Puberty Blockers Halted for Children in Scotland after Cass Review."

96. Crisp, "Belgium and Netherlands Call for Puberty Blocker Restrictions Following Cass Review."

97. "WPATH Blocked Publication of Its Own Gender Research."

98. Cass, "Final Report – Cass Review," sec. 9.19.

99. Cass, sec. 9.22.

100. Barnes, "Disturbing Leaks from US Gender Group WPATH Ring Alarm Bells in NHS."

101. Dorwart, "I Am Jazz: Why Did Jazz Jennings Need a Fourth Gender Confirmation Surgery After Complications?"

102. Dhejne et al., "Long-Term Follow-Up of Transsexual Persons Undergoing Sex Reassignment Surgery: Cohort Study in Sweden."

103. Cass, "Final Report – Cass Review," sec. 15.43.

104. Sapir, "Reckless and Irresponsible."

105. Gray, "Dramatic Changes in Teen Suicide Rates over Seven Decades."

106. Barnes, *Time to Think: The Inside Story of the Collapse of the Tavistock's Gender Service for Children*, 12.

107. Barnes, 205.

108. Kenny, "Response to David Shoebridge on Percentage Increases in Young People Presenting to Gender Clinics."

109. Barnes, *Time to Think*, 13.

110. Hardin, "The Tragedy of the Commons."

111. Henderson, "Profits."

112. "Space Launch Market Competition."

113. Urban, "How Much Does It Cost to Launch a Rocket?" Space Impulse."

114. *South Park: Bigger, Longer & Uncut*.

115. Vartabedian, "California High-Speed Rail Politics."

116. Klein, "Opinion | The Story Construction Tells About America's Economy Is Disturbing."

117. Sowell, *A Conflict of Visions: Ideological Origins of Political Struggles*, n. See page 17-Sowell never uses this phrase but it's the clear meaning of that section.

118. "Cape Wind."

119. Hiller and Restuccia, "The U.S. Fast-Tracked a Power Project After 17 Years. It's Nearing Approval."

120. Krugman, *Peddling Prosperity: Economic Sense and Nonsense in the Age of Diminished Expectations*.

121. FitzGibbon and Fanshawe, "Stotting in Thomson's Gazelles: An Honest Signal of Condition."

122. Bucholz and Key, *Early Modern England 1485-1714: A Narrative History*, 350.

123. Johnson, *Lives of the Poets*, vol. 2, chap. Prior.

124. Prendergast, "The Provision of Incentives in Firms."

125. *Big*, n. 29:10.

126. Milgrom and Roberts, "Complementarities and Fit: Strategies, Structure, and Organizational Change in Manufacturing."

127. Brown, "Firms Choice of Method of Pay."

128. Leventis, *Cardiac Surgeons Under the Knife*.

129. Drago and Garvey, "Incentives for Helping on the Job: Theory and Evidence."

130. Gladwell, "The Trouble with College Rankings."

131. Bjerke et al., *Officer Fitness Report Evaluation Study*.

132. "The Devil Wears Prada," n. 1:35:35.

133. Card et al., "Inequality at Work: The Effect of Peer Salaries on Job Satisfaction."

134. Bebchuk, "The Myth That Insulating Boards Serves Long-Term Value."

135. Kastiel, "Lucian Bebchuk and the Study of Corporate Governance."

136. Sonnenfeld, "What Makes Great Boards Great."

137. Friedman, "A Friedman Doctrine: The Social Responsibility of Business Is to Increase Its Profits."

138. Gelles, "Jeff Immelt's Reign at GE: A Look Back."

139. Grossman and Stiglitz, "On the Impossibility of Informationally Efficient Markets."

140. *The Year 2001: Quotes and Quibbles.*

141. Gelles, *The Man Who Broke Capitalism: How Jack Welch Gutted the Heartland and Crushed the Soul of Corporate America—and How to Undo His Legacy.*

142. 142. Robison, Flying Blind: The 737 MAX Tragedy and the Fall of Boeing, 57.

143. Robison, Flying Blind: The 737 MAX Tragedy and the Fall of Boeing, 6.

144. Robison, 105.

145. Contrary to what Coach Beard from Ted Lasso said, Suzanne Simard's research is not that trees share light. They share resources and information over fungal networks that connect their roots, but even that is specific to the Pacific Northwest. Trees in other regions have different arrangements, often less cooperative. Simard's research is revolutionary, but Ted Lasso's writers joined a long list of liberals who overgeneralize the cooperativeness of nature.

146. Chagnon, *Noble Savages: My Life Among Two Dangerous Tribes—the Yanomamö and the Anthropologists*, 277.

147. Keeley, *War Before Civilization.*

148. Gigerenzer, *Gut Feelings: The Intelligence of the Unconscious*, 129.

149. Morrot, Brochet, and Dubourdieu, "The Color of Odors."

150. Hanson, "Near Far Summary."

151. Darwin, "The Descent of Man and Selection in Relation to Sex."

152. Sanger, "My Way to Peace."

153. Birrell, "What Kind of Nation Forcibly Sterilises Girls as Young as 12?"

154. Hayes, "Cast Out: How Knitting Fell into a Purity Spiral."

155. Hayes.

156. Kurilova, "Australian Human Rights Commission Decision Prohibits Female-Only Events for Lesbians."

157.. Olson-Kennedy et al., "Chest Reconstruction and Chest Dysphoria in Transmasculine Minors and Young Adults: Comparisons of Nonsurgical and Postsurgical Cohorts."

158. Luthi, "California's Female Prisoners Feel Threatened by Transgender Inmates. The State Doesn't Care."

159. Gordon, "Fury Erupts Over Video of Little Girl in Miami Led by Strutting Drag Queen with Huge Breasts."

160. Ngo, "Charges Filed Against Sex Offender in Notorious WI Spa Incident."

161. Raymond, "Parents Cannot Challenge School Gender Identity Policy, US Court Rules."

162. Deese, "Indiana Parents Ask Supreme Court to Weigh in on Transgender Child Custody Case."

163. Perry, "Biden Administration Holds School Lunches Hostage to Radical Transgender Agenda."

164. Tackett, *The Coming of the Terror in the French Revolution*, 312.

165. Caplow, Hicks, and Wattenberg, *The First Measured Century: An Illustrated Guide to Trends in America, 1900-2000*, 87.

166. Caplan, "The Myth of the Rational Voter: Why Democracies Choose Bad Policies-New Edition," 8.

167. Stigler, "The Theory of Economic Regulation."

168. Kitroeff, Gelles, and Nicas, "Boeing 737 Max: The FAA Wanted a Safe Plane — but Didn't Want to Hurt America's Biggest Exporter."

169. Kolko, *The Triumph of Conservatism: A Re-Interpretation of American History, 1900-1916*, 98–112.

170. Kolko, chap. 10.

171. Nash, "Jargon Alert/Regulatory Capture."

172. Cox, *The Concise Guide to Economics*, 25.

173. Tabakovic and Wollmann, "From Revolving Doors to Regulatory Capture? Evidence from Patent Examiners."

174. Shuck and Wilson, Understanding America: The Anatomy of an Exceptional Nation, 51–52.

175. Wittman, *The Myth of Democratic Failure: Why Political Institutions Are Efficient*.

176. Surowiecki, *The Wisdom of Crowds: Why the Many Are Smarter Than the Few and How Collective Wisdom Shapes Business, Economies, Societies and Nations*, xv.

177. Ansolabehere, Figueiredo, and Snyder, "Why Is There so Little Money in U.S. Politics?"

178. Caplan, "The Myth of the Rational Voter: Why Democracies Choose Bad Policies-New Edition."

179. Binion, "The Contradictions of 'Queers for Palestine.'"

180. Kruger and Dunning, "Unskilled and Unaware of It: How Difficulties in Recognizing One's Own Incompetence Lead to Inflated Self-Assessments."

181. Simard, *Finding the Mother Tree: Discovering the Wisdom of the Forest*, 2021.

182. Barash and Lipton, *The Myth of Monogamy: Fidelity and Infidelity in Animals and People*, 51–53.

183. Roser and Ritchie, "Maternal Mortality."

184. Goldgeier, "What's the Biggest Challenge Men Face on Dating Apps? A Q&A with Aviv Goldgeier, Junior Growth Engineer."

185. Chagnon, *Noble Savages: My Life Among Two Dangerous Tribes—the Yanomamö and the Anthropologists*, 277.

186. Daly and Wilson, *Homicide*.

187. Wilson, "The Marriage Problem," 169.

188. Barash and Lipton, *The Myth of Monogamy: Fidelity and Infidelity in Animals and People*, 147.

189. Clements, "Can Men Get Pregnant? Outcomes for Transgender and Cisgender Men."

190. Austen, *Persuasion*, chap. 8.

191. Pinker, *The Blank Slate: The Modern Denial of Human Nature*, 345, 436.

192. Pinker, 347.

193. Pinker, 348.

194. Pinker, 350.

195. Hrdy, *Mother Nature*, 48.

196. Hrdy, 90.

197. Russell, "Late Ancient and Medieval Population."

198. Lindsay, *The Ancient World: Manners and Morals*.

199. Durant and Mihell, "The Story of Civilization: Caesar and Christ," 598.

200. Holland, *Dominion: The Making of the Western Mind*, 143–44.

201. Lack, "Ecological Adaptations for Breeding in Birds."

202. Barash and Lipton, *The Myth of Monogamy: Fidelity and Infidelity in Animals and People*, 76.

203. Barash and Lipton, 76.

204. Singh, "Adaptive Significance of Female Physical Attractiveness: Role of Waist-to-Hip Ratio."

205. Barash and Lipton, *The Myth of Monogamy: Fidelity and Infidelity in Animals and People*, 96.

206. Heym et al., "Empathy at the Heart of Darkness: Empathy Deficits That Bind the Dark Triad and Those That Mediate Indirect Relational Aggression"; Jonason and Krause, "The Emotional Deficits Associated with the Dark Triad Traits: Cognitive Empathy, Affective Empathy, and Alexithymia"; Wai and Tiliopoulos, "The Affective and Cognitive Empathic Nature of the Dark Triad of Personality"; Pajevic et al., "The Relationship between the Dark Tetrad and a Two-Dimensional View of Empathy."

207. Jonason et al., "The Dark Triad: Facilitating a Short-Term Mating Strategy in Men."

208. Austen, *Persuasion*, chap. 17.

209. *Kissing Jessica Stein*, n. 1:06:00.

210. Jonason et al., "The Dark Triad: Facilitating a Short-Term Mating Strategy in Men."

211. *Star Wars: Episode V - The Empire Strikes Back*, n. 1:02:50.

212. Twenge, "Egos Inflating Over Time: A Cross-Temporal Meta-Analysis of the Narcissistic Personality Inventory."

213. Falk and Hermle, "Relationship of Gender Differences in Preferences to Economic Development and Gender Equality"; Giolla and Kajonius, "Sex Differences in Personality Are Larger in Gender Equal Countries: Replicating and Extending a Surprising Finding."

214. Wynne-Edwards, *Animal Dispersion in Relation to Social Behavior*.

215. Gagagkar, "Survival Strategies: Cooperation and Conflict in Animal Societies," 26.

216. Pinker, *The Blank Slate: The Modern Denial of Human Nature*, 259.

217. Keeley, *War Before Civilization*, 90.

218. Keeley, 93.

219. Keeley, 100.

220. Keeley, 12, 85, 115.

221. Chagnon, *Noble Savages: My Life Among Two Dangerous Tribes—the Yanomamö and the Anthropologists*, 19.

222. Edgerton, *Sick Societies*, 79–80.

223. Chagnon, *Noble Savages: My Life Among Two Dangerous Tribes—the Yanomamo and the Anthropologists*, 229.

224. Chagnon, 226.

225. Chagnon, 242.

226. That's it for the mole-rat content. My apologies to all conservative mole-rat fans who thought they finally found a book that united their two great interests.

227. Boomsma, "Lifetime Monogamy and the Evolution of Eusociality."

228. Uecker and Regnerus, "Bare Market: Campus Sex Ratios, Romantic Relationships, and Sexual Behavior"; Adkins et al., "Student Bodies: Does the Sex Ratio Matter for Hooking Up and Having Sex at College?"

229. Perry, *The Case Against the Sexual Revolution*, 117.

230. Waal, *Our Inner Ape*, 29.

231. Hrdy, *Mother Nature*, 231.

232. De Waal and Lanting, *Bonobo: The Forgotten Ape*, loc. 1172.

233. De Waal and Lanting, loc. 1798.

234. Henrich, Boyd, and Richerson, "The Puzzle of Monogamous Marriage."

235. Smolin, *The Trouble with Physics: The Rise of String Theory, the Fall of a Science, and What Comes Next*, 64–65.

236. Alexander, "Practically a Book Review: Rootclaim."

237. Technically he calls core beliefs a *hard core*, but unless it involves loud guitars, I'm not going to call it that. Once again, we see that Lakatos was a great philosopher who was bad at naming things. That's ok. In computer programming they say that there are three hard problems: naming things, and off-by-one errors.

238. Wikipedia contributors, "Deferent and Epicycle — Wikipedia, The Free Encyclopedia."

239. Hannam, *The Genesis of Science: How the Christian Middle Ages Launched the Scientific Revolution*, xv.

240. Hannam, 330–31.

241. Rousseau, *A Discourse Upon the Origin and the Foundation of the Inequality Among Mankind*."translator":

242. Chagnon, *Noble Savages: My Life Among Two Dangerous Tribes—the Yanomamo and the Anthropologists*, 26.

243. Tierney, *Darkness in El Dorado: How Scientists and Journalists Devastated the Amazon.*

244. Chagnon, *Noble Savages: My Life Among Two Dangerous Tribes—the Yanomamo and the Anthropologists*, 439.

245. Chagnon, chap. 16.

246. Segerstrale, *Defenders of the Truth: The Battle for Science in the Sociobiology Debate and Beyond.*

247. Lack, "Ecological Adaptations for Breeding in Birds."

248. Alexander, "Practically a Book Review: Rootclaim."

249. Ioannidis, "Why Most Published Research Findings Are False."

250. Open Science Collaboration, "Estimating the Reproducibility of Psychological Science."

251. Camerer et al., "Evaluating the Replicability of Social Science Experiments in Nature and Science between 2010 and 2015"; Camerer et al., "Evaluating Replicability of Laboratory Experiments in Economics"; Klein et al., "Many Labs 2: Investigating Variation in Replicability across Samples and Settings."

252. Begley and Ellis, "Drug Development: Raise Standards for Preclinical Cancer Research"; Errington et al., "Reproducibility in Cancer Biology: Challenges for Assessing Replicability in Preclinical Cancer Biology"; Prinz, Schlange, and Asadullah, "Believe It or Not: How Much Can We Rely on Published Data on Potential Drug Targets?"

253. Turner, "Selective Publication of Antidepressant Trials and Its Influence on Apparent Efficacy."

254. Somerville, "University Blocks Academic from Her Own Gender Wars Research Over 'Dangerous' Data."

255. "Why Did Three Journals Reject My Puberty Blocker Study?" UnHerd."

256. "WPATH Blocked Publication of Its Own Gender Research."

257. Coleman et al., "Standards of Care for the Health of Transgender and Gender Diverse People, Version 8."

258. Simmons, Nelson, and Simonsohn, "False-Positive Psychology: Undisclosed Flexibility in Data Collection and Analysis Allows Presenting Anything as Significant."

259. Alexander, "The Control Group Is Out of Control."

260. Richerson and Boyd, *Not By Genes Alone: How Culture Transformed Human Evolution*, 5.

261. Henrich, *The WEIRDest People in the World: How the West Became Psychologically Peculiar and Particularly Prosperous*, 66.

262. B.I.G, *Things Done Changed*.

263. Golden et al., "What Was a Gap Is Now a Chasm: Remote Schooling, the Digital Divide, and Educational Inequities Resulting from the COVID-19 Pandemic."

264. Weiner, *The Beak of the Finch: A Story of Evolution in Our Time*.

265. Diamond, *Guns, Germs, and Steel*, 312.

266. Chesterton, *The Thing: Why I Am a Catholic*, chap. IV.

267. Koch, *Foreign Aid and Its Unintended Consequences*, 46–48.

268. Koch, 74–76.

269. Koch, 94–98.

270. Koch, 110–16.

271. Willett, "Dietary Fats and Coronary Heart Disease."

272. Enig, "The Tragic Legacy of Center for Science in the Public Interest (CSPI."

273. Clements, "Can Men Get Pregnant? Outcomes for Transgender and Cisgender Men."

274. Makinson, "The Paradox of the Preface."

275. "WPATH Blocked Publication of Its Own Gender Research."

276. Kempf and Tsoutsoura, "Partisan Professionals: Evidence from Credit Rating Analysts."

277. Pinker, *The Blank Slate: The Modern Denial of Human Nature*, 377.

278. Plomin and Deary, "Genetics and Intelligence Differences: Five Special Findings."

279. Strenze, "Intelligence and Socioeconomic Success: A Meta-Analytic Review of Longitudinal Research."

280. Schmidt and Hunter, "The Validity and Utility of Selection Methods in Personnel Psychology: Practical and Theoretical Findings of 85 Years of Research Findings."

281. Bouchard and McGue, "Genetic and Environmental Influences on Human Psychological Differences."

282. Little, Haughbrook, and Hart, "Cross-Study Differences in the Etiology of Reading Comprehension: A Meta-Analytical Review of Twin Studies."

283. Bouchard and McGue, "Genetic and Environmental Influences on Human Psychological Differences."

284. Freese and Jao, "Shared Environment Estimates for Educational Attainment: A Puzzle and Possible Solutions."

285. Bouchard and McGue, "Genetic and Environmental Influences on Human Psychological Differences."

286. Schiffman, "Adventure Playgrounds: A Dying Breed?"

287. Harris, *The Nurture Assumption: Why Children Turn Out the Way They Do, Revised and Updated*, 10.

288. Edin and Kefalas, *Promises I Can Keep: Why Poor Women Put Motherhood Before Marriage*, 74.

289. Lang and Zagorsky, "Does Growing up with a Parent Absent Really Hurt?"

290. "William Galston's Findings Are Based on a Study by Charles Murray, "According to Age: Longitudinal Profiles of AFDC Recipients and the Poor by Age Group."

291. Thornton and Coudert, *The Ditchdigger's Daughters: A Black Family's Astonishing Success Story*.

292. Falk and Hermle, "Relationship of Gender Differences in Preferences to Economic Development and Gender Equality"; Giolla and Kajonius, "Sex Differences in Personality Are Larger in Gender Equal Countries: Replicating and Extending a Surprising Finding."

293. Landman, "How to Talk to Boys so They Grow into Better Men."

294. Harris, *The Nurture Assumption: Why Children Turn Out the Way They Do, Revised and Updated*, 198.

295. Austen, *Pride and Prejudice*.

296. Sibley, Osborne, and Duckitt, "Personality and Political Orientation: Meta-Analysis and Test of a Threat-Constraint Model."

297. Hirsh et al., "Compassionate Liberals and Polite Conservatives: Associations of Agreeableness With Political Ideology and Moral Values."

298. Peterson and Lausten, "Upper-body Strength and Political Egalitarianism: Twelve Conceptual Replications."

299. Kahneman, Knetsch, and Thaler, "Experimental Tests of the Endowment Effect and the Coase Theorem."

300. Thaler and Sunstein, *Nudge: Improving Decisions About Health, Wealth, and Happiness*, 34.

ENDNOTES

301. Smith and Parker, "The Logic of Asymmetric Contests."

302. Gintis, *The Bounds of Reason: Game Theory and the Unification of the Behavioral Sciences*, 205.

303. Bothner, Kang, and Stuart, "Competitive Crowding and Risk Taking in a Tournament: Evidence from NASCAR Racing."

304. Hoffman et al., "Preferences, Property Rights, and Anonymity in Bargaining Games."

305. Hoffman et al.

306. Oxoby and Spraggon, "Mine and Yours: Property Rights in Dictator Games."

307. Henrich, "Cooperation, Reciprocity and Punishment in Fifteen Small-Scale Societies."

308. Martin, "Drafting."

309. Axelrod, *The Evolution of Cooperation*.

310. Ostrom, Gardner, and Walker, *Rules, Games, and Common-Pool Resources*.

311. Gintis, The Bounds of Reason: Game Theory and the Unification of the Behavioral Sciences, Ch. 10.

312. Henrich, *The WEIRDest People in the World: How the West Became Psychologically Peculiar and Particularly Prosperous*, 211.

313. Henrich, 217.

314. Rapaczynski, "The Roles of the State and the Market in Establishing Property Rights," 88.

315. Aginsky, "An Indian's Soliloquy," 43–44.

316. Fukuyama, "Social Capital," 99.

317. Putnam, *Making Democracy Work: Civic Traditions in Modern Italy*, 167.

318. Porta, "Trust in Large Organizations."

319. Gambetta, *The Sicilian Mafia: The Business of Private Protection*, 35.

320. Ostrom, *Understanding Institutional Diversity*.

321. Putnam, "E Pluribus Unum: Diversity and Community in the Twenty-First Century."

322. Ember, "Wanted: An Executive to Repair Boeing."

323. Ostrom, *Understanding Institutional Diversity*, 255.

324. Soto, *The Mystery of Capital*, 169.

325. Soto, 19–20.

326. Soto, 83.

327. Harrison and Huntington, "Culture Matters: How Values Shape Human Progress," 115.

328. Mauro, "The Effects of Corruption on Growth, Investment, and Government Expenditure: A Cross-Country Analysis."

329. Henrich, *The WEIRDest People in the World: How the West Became Psychologically Peculiar and Particularly Prosperous*, chap. 5.

330. Hajnal, "European Marriage Patterns in Perspective," 101–43.

331. Fischer, Albion's Seed: Four British Folkways in America, 76.

332. Henrich, *The WEIRDest People in the World: How the West Became Psychologically Peculiar and Particularly Prosperous*, 225–54.

333. Henrich, 418.

334. Harrison and Huntington, "Culture Matters: How Values Shape Human Progress," 90.

335. Henrich, *The WEIRDest People in the World: How the West Became Psychologically Peculiar and Particularly Prosperous*, 422.

336. Finke and Stark, *The Churching of America, 1776-2005: Winners and Losers in Our Religious Economy*.

337. Henrich, *The WEIRDest People in the World: How the West Became Psychologically Peculiar and Particularly Prosperous*, 14.

338. Clark, *A Farewell to Alms: A Brief Economic History of the World*, 366.

339. Clark, 368.

340. Diamond, *Guns, Germs, and Steel*, 14.

341. Olsson and Hibbs, "Biogeography and Long-Run Economic Development."

342. Pomeranz, *The Great Divergence*.

343. Macfarlane, "Introduction to the Paperback Edition."

344. Maddison, *The World Economy: A Millennial Perspective*, 44.

345. Broadberry and Gupta, "The Early Modern Great Divergence: Wages, Prices, and Economic Development in Europe and Asia, 1500-1800."

346. Lindert, "Preliminary Global Price Comparisons, 1500-1870."

347. Lecky, *History of European Morals: From Augustus to Charlemagne*, 2:69.

348. Lewsey, "Britain Industrialised Much Earlier than History Books Claim."

349. Clark, *A Farewell to Alms: A Brief Economic History of the World*, 261.

350. "The Nation's Report Card", Figures 11, 27; National Assessment of Educational Progress, "Achievement Gaps Dashboard."

351. National Center for Education Statistics, "Table 222.77. Average National Assessment of Educational Progress (NAEP) Mathematics Scale Scores and Achievement-Level Results for Students in Grades 4 and 8, by Selected Student Characteristics: Selected Years, 1990 through 2019."

352. Ferguson, *Toward Excellence with Equity: An Emerging Vision for Closing the Achievement Gap.*

353. Ferguson, 27–30.

354. "Daniel Patrick Moynihan Interview."

355. Caplow, Hicks, and Wattenberg, *The First Measured Century: An Illustrated Guide to Trends in America, 1900-2000*, 87.

356. Osterman et al., "Births: Final Data for 2021."

357. Grogger, "Does School Quality Explain the Recent Black/White Wage Trend?"

358. Peterson, *Generational Change: Closing the Test Score Gap*, 31.

359. Hanushek et al., "School Resources."

360. Chetty, Friedman, and Rockoff, "Measuring the Impacts of Teachers II: Teacher Value-Added and Student Outcomes in Adulthood."

361. Sowell, *Ethnic America: A History*, 201.

362. Peterson, *Generational Change: Closing the Test Score Gap*, 30–31.

363. National Center for Education Statistics, "Table 236.55. Total and Current Expenditures per Pupil in Public Elementary and Secondary Schools: Selected Years, 1919-20 through 2016-17."

364. "The Nation's Report Card.", Figures 11, 27.

365. The Thomas B. Fordham Institute, "Algebra for None: The Effects of San Francisco's De-Tracking Reform."

366. Golden et al., "What Was a Gap Is Now a Chasm: Remote Schooling, the Digital Divide, and Educational Inequities Resulting from the COVID-19 Pandemic."

367. Helland and Tabarrok, *Why Are the Prices So Damn High?*, 36.

368. Scafidi, "Back to the Staffing Surge: The Great Teacher Salary Stagnation and the Decades-Long Employment Growth in American Public Schools."

369. Ferguson, *Toward Excellence with Equity: An Emerging Vision for Closing the Achievement Gap*, 173.

370. Ferguson, 207.

371. Ferguson, 172–75.

372. Ferguson, 180–88.

373. Hanushek, "Evidence, Politics, and the Class Size Debate."

374. Hanushek, "Evidence, Politics, and the Class Size Debate."

375. Hanushek et al.; Chetty, Friedman, and Rockoff, "Measuring the Impacts of Teachers II: Teacher Value-Added and Student Outcomes in Adulthood."

376. Peterson, *Generational Change: Closing the Test Score Gap*, 51–53.

377. Peterson, 51–53.

378. Pianta et al., "The Effects of Preschool Education: What We Know, How Public Policy Is or Is Not Aligned with the Evidence Base, and What We Need to Know."

379. Puma et al., "Head Start Impact Study: Final Report"; Puma et al., "Third Grade Follow-up to the Head Start Impact Study."

380. Bernardy, "Head Start: Assessing Common Explanations for the Apparent Disappearance of Initial Positive Effects."

381. Duncan and Magnuson, "Investing in Preschool Programs."

382. Durkin et al., "Effects of a Statewide Pre-Kindergarten Program on Children's Achievement and Behavior through Sixth Grade."

383. Bedrick and Hroncich, "Pre-K Education & Childcare."

384. Ravitch, *Left Back: A Century of Battles Over School Reform*.

385. Zimmer, "Nearly Three Decades into the Charter School Movement, What Has Research Told Us About Charter Schools?"

386. Cheng, "'No Excuses' Charter Schools: A Meta-Analysis of the Experimental Evidence on Student Achievement."

387. Zimmer, "Nearly Three Decades into the Charter School Movement, What Has Research Told Us About Charter Schools?"

388. Ravitch, *Left Back: A Century of Battles Over School Reform*.

389. Forster, "A Win-Win Solution: The Empirical Evidence on School Choice."

390. Shakeel, Anderson, and Wolf, "The Participant Effects of Private School Vouchers Around the Globe: A Meta-Analytic and Systematic Review."

391. Lubienski, *Review of "A Win-Win Solution" and "The Participant Effects of Private School Vouchers across the Globe."*

392. Bedrich, "Survey Says: African Americans Love School Choice."

393. "National Survey Shows Black Parents Continue to Support Education Choice."

394. "Support for School Choice Remains Strong During Volatile Year."

395. Robinson, *The Best Christmas Pageant Ever.*

396. Zehr, "Obama Administration Targets 'Disparate Impact' of Discipline."

397. Coleman et al., "Equality of Educational Opportunity"; Chetty, Friedman, and Rockoff, "Measuring the Impacts of Teachers II: Teacher Value-Added and Student Outcomes in Adulthood"; Hanushek et al., "School Resources."

398. Summers and Clark, "Labor Market Dynamics and Unemployment: A Reconsideration."

399. Brudevold-Newman et al., "A Firm of One's Own: Experimental Evidence on Credit Constraints and Occupational Choice."

400. Koch, *Foreign Aid and Its Unintended Consequences*, 81.

401. Gintis, *Moral Sentiments and Material Interests*, 6:80.

402. Gintis, 6:92.

403. Gintis, 6:92.

404. Gintis, 6:82.

405. Harris, *Cows, Pigs, Wars, and Witches: The Riddles of Culture.*

406. Crisp, "Belgian Sex Workers to Get Health Insurance, Pensions and Maternity Leave in World First."

407. Solomon-Fears, "Nonmarital Births: An Overview."

408. Härkönen and Dronkers, "Stability and Change in the Educational Gradient of Divorce: A Comparison of Seventeen Countries."

409. "Share of Births Outside of Marriage."

410. Cherlin, *The Marriage-Go-Round: The State of Marriage and the Family in America Today*, 9.

411. Cherlin, "Rising Nonmarital First Childbearing Among College-Educated Women: Evidence from Three National Studies."

412. Wilson, "The Marriage Problem," 145.

413. Sowell, *Black Rednecks & White Liberals*, 28.

414. Rosenzweig, "Welfare, Marital Prospects, and Nonmarital Childbearing."

415. Moffitt, "The Effect of Welfare on Marriage and Fertility."

416. Moffitt, Phelan, and Winkler, "Welfare Rules, Incentives, and Family Structure."

417. Caplow, Hicks, and Wattenberg, *The First Measured Century: An Illustrated Guide to Trends in America, 1900-2000*, 71.

418. Caplow, Hicks, and Wattenberg, 70.

419. Phelps-Roper, "The Real Story of the Central Park Five."

420. Flanagan, "The Media Must Learn from the Covington Catholic Story."

421. "BAR Botched the Citi Bike Karen Story: What They Got Wrong."

422. Jencks, "Is the American Underclass Growing?"

423. Wilson, "The Marriage Problem," 149–50.

424. Uecker and Regnerus, "Bare Market: Campus Sex Ratios, Romantic Relationships, and Sexual Behavior"; Adkins et al., "Student Bodies: Does the Sex Ratio Matter for Hooking Up and Having Sex at College?"

425. Edin and Kefalas, *Promises I Can Keep: Why Poor Women Put Motherhood Before Marriage*, 34.

426. Michaelson and Munakata, "Same Data Set, Different Conclusions: Preschool Delay of Gratification Predicts Later Behavioral Outcomes in a Preregistered Study."

427. Edin and Kefalas, *Promises I Can Keep: Why Poor Women Put Motherhood Before Marriage*, 74.

428. Edin and Kefalas, 75.

429. Harris, *The Nurture Assumption: Why Children Turn Out the Way They Do, Revised and Updated*, 198.

430. Kendler et al., "A Novel Sibling-Based Design to Quantify Genetic and Shared Environmental Effects: Application to Drug Abuse, Alcohol Use Disorder, and Criminal Behavior."

431. Bouchard and McGue, "Genetic and Environmental Influences on Human Psychological Differences."

432. Pinker, *The Blank Slate: The Modern Denial of Human Nature*, 377.

433. Deary, Cox, and Hill, "Genetic Variation, Brain, and Intelligence Differences."

434. Plomin and Stumm, "The New Genetics of Intelligence."

435. Plomin and Stumm.

436. G.C.T.A. and M.-G.C.T.A., "Part 1: Estimating Maternal Genetic Effects on Offspring," 1.

437. Deary, Cox, and Hill, "Genetic Variation, Brain, and Intelligence Differences."

438. Duncan et al., "Analysis of Polygenic Risk Score Usage and Performance in Diverse Human Populations."

Bibliography

Acemoglu, Daron, and Joshua D. Angrist. "Consequences of Employment Protection? The Case of the Americans with Disabilities Act." *Journal of Political Economy* 109, no. 5 (2001): 915–57.

Adkins, Timothy, Paula England, Barbara J. Risman, and Jessie Ford. "Student Bodies: Does the Sex Ratio Matter for Hooking Up and Having Sex at College?" *Social Currents* 2, no. 2 (2015): 144–62.

Aginsky, B.W. "An Indian's Soliloquy." *American Journal of Sociology* 46 (1940): 43–44.

Ainslie, George. *Breakdown of Will*. Cambridge: Cambridge University Press, 2001.

Alexander, Scott. "Practically a Book Review: Rootclaim." *Astral Codex Ten* (blog), March 28, 2024. https://www.astralcodexten.com/p/practically-a-book-review-rootclaim.

———. "The Control Group Is Out of Control." *Slate Star Codex* (blog), April 28, 2014. https://slatestarcodex.com/2014/04/28/the-control-group-is-out-of-control/.

Ansolabehere, Stephen, John M. Figueiredo, and James M. Snyder. "Why Is There so Little Money in U.S. Politics?" *The Journal of Economic Perspectives* 17, no. 1 (2003): 105–30.

Ashcraft, Richard. *Revolutionary Politics and Locke's Two Treatises of Government*. Princeton: Princeton University Press, 1986.

Austen, Jane. *Persuasion*. Project Gutenberg, 1818. https://www.gutenberg.org/ebooks/105.

———. *Pride and Prejudice*. Project Gutenberg Edition. Project Gutenberg, 1813. https://www.gutenberg.org/ebooks/1342.

Axelrod, Robert. *The Evolution of Cooperation*. New York: Basic Books, 1984.

Babie, Paul. "Magna Carta and the Forest Charter: Two Stories of Property, What Will You Be Doing in 2017." *North Carolina Law Review* 94 (2015): 1431.

Barash, David P., and Judith Eve Lipton. *The Myth of Monogamy: Fidelity and Infidelity in Animals and People*. New York: Macmillan, 2002.

Barnes, Hannah. "Disturbing Leaks from US Gender Group WPATH Ring Alarm Bells in NHS." *The Guardian*, March 9, 2024. https://www.theguardian.com/commentisfree/2024/mar/09/disturbing-leaks-from-us-gender-group-wpath-ring-alarm-bells-in-nhs.

———. *Time to Think: The Inside Story of the Collapse of the Tavistock's Gender Service for Children*. Swift Press, 2023.

Bebchuk, Lucian A. "The Myth That Insulating Boards Serves Long-Term Value." *Columbia Law Review* 113 (2013): 1637.

Becker, G.S., and K.M. Murphy. "A Theory of Rational Addiction." *Journal of Political Economy* 96, no. 4 (1988): 675–700.

Bedrich, Jason. "Survey Says: African Americans Love School Choice." *Foundation for Economic Education*, November 19, 2015. https://fee.org/articles/survey-says-african-americans-love-school-choice/.

Bedrick, Jason, and Colleen Hroncich. "Pre-K Education & Childcare," n.d. https://www.cato.org/cato-handbook-policymakers/cato-handbook-policymakers-9th-edition-2022/pre-k-education-childcare.

Begley, C Glenn, and Lee M Ellis. "Drug Development: Raise Standards for Preclinical Cancer Research." *Nature* 483, no. 7391 (2012): 531–33.

Bernardy, Peter M. "Head Start: Assessing Common Explanations for the Apparent Disappearance of Initial Positive Effects." (PhD diss., George Mason University, 2012.

Big, 1988.

B.I.G, The Notorious. *Things Done Changed*. The Notorious B.I.G. Sampler (Teaser. New York: Bad Boy Entertainment, 1994.

Binion, Billy. "The Contradictions of 'Queers for Palestine.'" Reason.com, October 27, 2023. https://reason.com/2023/10/27/the-contradictions-of-queers-for-palestine/.

Birrell, Ian. "What Kind of Nation Forcibly Sterilises Girls as Young as 12?" *Mail Online*, November 11, 2023. https://www.dailymail.co.uk/femail/article-12738369/What-kind-nation-forcibly-sterilises-girls-young-12-cut-welfare-bills-shocking-answer-Denmark-hailed-one-worlds-liberal-nations-recently-2018.html.

Bjerke, David G., Jeanette N. Cleveland, Robert F. Morrison, and William C. Wilson. *Officer Fitness Report Evaluation Study*. NAVY PERSONNEL RESEARCH AND DEVELOPMENT CENTER SAN DIEGO CA, 1987. https://apps.dtic.mil/sti/tr/pdf/ADA189377.pdf.

Boomsma, Jacobus J. "Lifetime Monogamy and the Evolution of Eusociality." *Philosophical Transactions of the Royal Society B: Biological Sciences* 364, no. 1533 (2009): 3191–3207.

Boothman, Helen, and John Puttick. "Puberty Blockers Halted for Children in Scotland after Cass Review." *The Times*, April 2024. https://www.thetimes.co.uk/article/puberty-blockers-paused-for-children-in-scotland-after-cass-review-8j6tkw89t.

Bothner, Matthew S., Jeong-han Kang, and Toby E. Stuart. "Competitive Crowding and Risk Taking in a Tournament: Evidence from NASCAR Racing." *Administrative Science Quarterly* 52, no. 2 (June 2007): 208.

Bouchard, Thomas J., Jr., and Matt McGue. "Genetic and Environmental Influences on Human Psychological Differences." *Journal of Neurobiology* 54, no. 1 (2003): 4–45.

Bows, Hannah, and Jonathan Herring. "Getting Away with Murder? A Review of the 'Rough Sex Defence.'" *The Journal of Criminal Law* 84, no. 6 (2020): 525–38. https://journals.sagepub.com/doi/10.1177/0022018320936777.

Broadberry, Stephen, and Bishnupriya Gupta. "The Early Modern Great Divergence: Wages, Prices, and Economic Development in Europe and Asia, 1500-1800." *Economic History Review* 59 (2006): 2–31.

Brown, Charles. "Firms Choice of Method of Pay." *Industrial and Labor Relations Review* 43, no. 3 (1990): 165–82.

Brudevold-Newman, Andrew Peter, Maddalena Honorati, Pamela Jakiela, and Owen W. Ozier. "A Firm of One's Own: Experimental Evidence on Credit Constraints and Occupational Choice." Policy Research Working Paper. World Bank, 2017.

Bucholz, Robert, and Newton Key. *Early Modern England 1485-1714: A Narrative History*. 2nd ed. Chichester, UK: Wiley-Blackwell, 2009.

Burke, Edmund. *Letter to a Member of the National Assembly*. London: Project Gutenberg, 1791. https://www.gutenberg.org/files/15700/15700-h/15700-h.htm.

———. *Reflections on the Revolution in France*. Project Gutenberg, 2005. https://www.gutenberg.org/ebooks/15679.

Butler, Judith. *Gender Trouble*. New York: Routledge, 2002.

"Californication." Showtime, 2014 2007.

Camerer, Colin F, Anna Dreber, Eskil Forsell, Teck-Hua Ho, Jürgen Huber, Magnus Johannesson, Michael Kirchler, et al. "Evaluating Replicability of Laboratory Experiments in Economics." *Science* 351, no. 6280 (2016): 1433–36.

Camerer, Colin F, Anna Dreber, Felix Holzmeister, Teck-Hua Ho, Jürgen Huber, Magnus Johannesson, Michael Kirchler, et al. "Evaluating the Replicability of Social Science Experiments in Nature and Science between 2010 and 2015." *Nature Human Behaviour* 2, no. 9 (2018): 637–44.

Cantor, James. "Do Trans Kids Stay Trans When They Grow Up?," January 11, 2006. https://archive.is/0tABg. http://www.sexologytoday.org/2016/01/do-trans-kids-stay-trans-when-they-grow_99.html.

"Cape Wind," May 21, 2024. https://en.wikipedia.org/w/index.php?title=Cape_Wind&oldid=1221631679.

Caplan, Bryan. "The Myth of the Rational Voter: Why Democracies Choose Bad Policies-New Edition." In *The Myth of the Rational Voter*. Princeton University Press, 2011.

Caplow, Theodore, Louis Hicks, and Ben J. Wattenberg. *The First Measured Century: An Illustrated Guide to Trends in America, 1900-2000*. American Enterprise Institute, 2001.

Card, David, Alexandre Mas, Enrico Moretti, and Emmanuel Saez. "Inequality at Work: The Effect of Peer Salaries on Job Satisfaction." *NBER Working Paper*, no. 16396 (September 2010).

Cass, Hillary. "Final Report – Cass Review." Cass Independent Review, April 10, 2024. https://cass.independent-review.uk/home/publications/final-report/.

Chagnon, N.A. *Noble Savages: My Life Among Two Dangerous Tribes—the Yanomamo and the Anthropologists*. Simon and Schuster, 2013.

Cheng, Albert. "'No Excuses' Charter Schools: A Meta-Analysis of the Experimental Evidence on Student Achievement." *Journal of School Choice* 11, no. 2 (2017): 209–38.

Cherlin, Andrew J. "Rising Nonmarital First Childbearing Among College-Educated Women: Evidence from Three National Studies." *Proceedings of the National Academy of Sciences 118*, no. 37 (2021).

———. *The Marriage-Go-Round: The State of Marriage and the Family in America Today*. New York: Alfred A. Knopf, 2009.

Chesterton, G.K. *The Thing: Why I Am a Catholic*. London: Sheed & Ward, 1929.

Chetty, Raj, John N. Friedman, and Jonah E. Rockoff. "Measuring the Impacts of Teachers II: Teacher Value-Added and Student Outcomes in Adulthood." *American Economic Review* 104, no. 9 (2014): 2633-2679,. https://doi.org/10.1257/aer.104.9.2633.

Chu, Andrea Long. *Females*. London: Verso Books, 2019.

Clark, Gregory. *A Farewell to Alms: A Brief Economic History of the World*. Princeton, NJ: Princeton University Press, 2007.

Clements, K. C. "Can Men Get Pregnant? Outcomes for Transgender and Cisgender Men," July 12, 2023. https://www.healthline.com/health/transgender/can-men-get-pregnant.

Coffey, Tabatha. "Tabatha's Salon Takeover." United States: Bravo and Reveille Productions, 2008.

Coleman, E., A. E. Radix, W. P. Bouman, G. R. Brown, A. L. C. de Vries, M. B. Deutsch, R. Ettner, et al. "Standards of Care for the Health of Transgender and Gender Diverse People, Version 8." *International Journal of Transgender Health* 23, no. sup1 (2022): S1–259. https://doi.org/10.1080/26895269.2022.2100644.

Coleman, James S., Ernest Q. Campbell, Carol J. Hobson, James McPartland, Alexander M. Mood, Frederic D. Weinfeld, and Robert L. York. "Equality of Educational Opportunity." Washington, DC: U.S. Department of Health, Education, and Welfare, Office of Education, 1966. https://files.eric.ed.gov/fulltext/ED012275.pdf.

Cowen, Tyler. "What Libertarianism Has Become and Will Become — State Capacity Libertarianism," 2020. https://marginalrevolution.com/marginalrevolution/2020/01/what-libertarianism-has-become-and-will-become-state-capacity-libertarianism.html.

Cox, Jim. *The Concise Guide to Economics*. 3rd ed. Auburn, Alabama: Ludwig Von Mises Institute, 2007.

Crisp, James. "Belgian Sex Workers to Get Health Insurance, Pensions and Maternity Leave in World First." *The Telegraph*, May 8, 2024. https://www.telegraph.co.uk/world-news/2024/05/08/belgium-sex-workers-employment-contracts-pensions-maternity/.

———. "Belgium and Netherlands Call for Puberty Blocker Restrictions Following Cass Review." *The Telegraph*, April 2024. https://www.telegraph.co.uk/world-news/2024/04/13/belgium-netherlands-puberty-blocker-restrictions/.

Daly, M., and M. Wilson. *Homicide*. Hawthorne, N.Y: Aldine de Gruyter, 1988.

"Daniel Patrick Moynihan Interview," n.d. https://www.pbs.org/fmc/interviews/moynihan.htm.

Darwin, Charles. "The Descent of Man and Selection in Relation to Sex." *Project Gutenberg*, n.d. https://www.gutenberg.org/cache/epub/2300/pg2300-images.html.

David, Elliot Jr. "European Countries Restrict Trans Health Care for Minors." *US News and World Report*, July 2023. https://www.usnews.com/news/best-countries/articles/2023-07-12/why-european-countries-are-rethinking-gender-affirming-care-for-minors.

De Waal, Frans B. M., and Frans Lanting. *Bonobo: The Forgotten Ape*. Berkeley, CA: University of California Press, 1997.

Deary, Ian J., Simon R. Cox, and W.David Hill. "Genetic Variation, Brain, and Intelligence Differences." *Molecular Psychiatry* 27, no. 1 (2022): 335–53.

Deese, Kaelan. "Indiana Parents Ask Supreme Court to Weigh in on Transgender Child Custody Case." *Washington Examiner*, February 16, 2024. https://www.washingtonexaminer.com/news/2860444/indiana-parents-supreme-court-weigh-transgender-child-custody/.

Dhejne, Cecilia, Paul Lichtenstein, Marcus Boman, Anna L.V. Johansson, Niklas Långström, and Mikael Landén. "Long-Term Follow-Up of Transsexual Persons Undergoing Sex Reassignment Surgery: Cohort Study in Sweden." *PLoS ONE* 6, no. 2 (2011): 16885.

Diamond, Jared. *Guns, Germs, and Steel*. New York: W.W. Norton & Co, 1997.

DiLorenzo, Thomas J. *How Capitalism Saved America: The Untold History of Our Country, from the Pilgrims to the Present*. Forum Books, 2005.

———. "The Origins of Antitrust: An Interest-Group Perspective." *International Review of Law and Economics* 5 (June 1985): 73–90.

Doleac, Jennifer L., and Benjamin Hansen. "The Unintended Consequences of 'Ban the Box': Statistical Discrimination and Employment Outcomes When Criminal Histories Are Hidden." *Journal of Labor Economics* 38, no. 2 (2020): 321–74.

Dorwart, Laura. "I Am Jazz: Why Did Jazz Jennings Need a Fourth Gender Confirmation Surgery After Complications?" In *Cheat Sheet, February 7, 2020*. https://www.cheatsheet.com/entertainment/i-am-jazz-why-did-jazz-jennings-need-a-fourth-gender-confirmation-surgery-after-complications.html/.

Dowden, Bradley, and Norman Swartz. "Truth." In The *Internet Encyclopedia of Philosophy,* 2024. https://iep.utm.edu/truth.

Drago, Robert, and Gerald Garvey. "Incentives for Helping on the Job: Theory and Evidence." *Journal of Labor Economics* 16, no. 1 (1998): 1–25.

Dumas, Alexandre. *The Three Musketeers*. Translated by William Robson. Project Gutenberg, 2004. https://www.gutenberg.org/ebooks/1257.

Duncan, Greg J., and Katherine Magnuson. "Investing in Preschool Programs." *Journal of Economic Perspectives* 27, no. 2 (2013): 109–32.

Duncan, Laramie, Hanyang Shen, J.Meijsen Bizu Gelaye, K. Ressler, M. Feldman, R. Peterson, and Ben Domingue. "Analysis of Polygenic Risk Score Usage and Performance in Diverse Human Populations." *Nature Communications* 10, no. 1 (2019): 3328.

Durant, Will, and Ariel Durant. *The Story of Civilization: The Age of Voltaire.* Simon & Schuster, 1980.

Durant, Will, and Monica Ariel Mihell. "The Story of Civilization: Caesar and Christ," n.d.

Durkin, Kelley, Mark W. Lipsey, Dale C. Farran, and Sarah E. Wiesen. "Effects of a Statewide Pre-Kindergarten Program on Children's Achievement and Behavior through Sixth Grade." *Developmental Psychology* 58, no. 3 (2022): 470.

Edgerton, Robert B. *Sick Societies*. New York: Simon and Schuster, 2010.

Edin, Kathryn, and Maria Kefalas. *Promises I Can Keep: Why Poor Women Put Motherhood Before Marriage*. University of California Press, 2011.

Ehrlich, Paul R. *The Population Bomb*. New York: Ballantine Books, 1968.

Eissa, Nada, and Jeffrey B Liebman. "Labor Supply Response to the Earned Income Tax Credit." *The Quarterly Journal of Economics* 111, no. 2 (1996): 605–37.

Ember, Sydney. "Wanted: An Executive to Repair Boeing." *The New York Times*, April 24, 2024. https://www.nytimes.com/2024/04/24/business/boeing-chief-executive-search.html.

Enig, Mary. "The Tragic Legacy of Center for Science in the Public Interest (CSPI)," n.d. https://www.westonaprice.org/health-topics/know-your-fats/the-tragic-legacy-of-center-for-science-in-the-public-interest-cspi/.

Equiano, Olaudah. "The Interesting Narrative of the Life of Olaudah Equiano, Or Gustavus Vassa, The African," 1789. https://www.gutenberg.org/cache/epub/15399/pg15399-images.html.

Errington, Timothy M, Alexandria Denis, Nicole Perfito, Elizabeth Iorns, and Brian A Nosek. "Reproducibility in Cancer Biology: Challenges for Assessing Replicability in Preclinical Cancer Biology." *Elife* 10 (2021): e67995.

"Euphoria." HBO, 2019.

Falk, Armin, and Johannes Hermle. "Relationship of Gender Differences in Preferences to Economic Development and Gender Equality." *Science* 362, no. 6412 (2018): eaas9899.

February. "Why Did Three Journals Reject My Puberty Blocker Study?" UnHerd." 2024. https://unherd.com/2024/02/why-did-three-journals-reject-my-puberty-blocker-study/

Feldstein, Martin. "Tax Rates and Human Behavior." *Wall Street Journal*, May 7, 1993, 14.

Ferguson, Donna. "Has History Got It Wrong About Oliver Cromwell's Persecution of Catholics?" *The Guardian*, July 31, 2022. https://www.theguardian.com/books/2022/jul/31/has-history-got-it-wrong-about-oliver-cromwells-persecution-of-catholics.

Ferguson, Ronald. *Toward Excellence with Equity: An Emerging Vision for Closing the Achievement Gap*. Cambridge, MA: Harvard Education Press, 2014.

Fifty Shades of Grey. Drama, Romance. Universal Pictures, 2015.

Finke, Roger, and Rodney Stark. *The Churching of America, 1776-2005: Winners and Losers in Our Religious Economy*. New Brunswick, NJ: Rutgers University Press, 2005.

Fischer, David Hackett. *Albion's Seed: Four British Folkways in America*. New York: Oxford University Press, 1989.

FitzGibbon, C.D., and J.H. Fanshawe. "Stotting in Thomson's Gazelles: An Honest Signal of Condition." *Behavioral Ecology and Sociobiology* 23, no. 2 (1988): 69–74.

Flanagan, Caitlyn. "The Media Must Learn from the Covington Catholic Story." *The Atlantic*, January 23, 2019. https://www.theatlantic.com/ideas/archive/2019/01/media-must-learn-covington-catholic-story/581035/.

Fonte, John. "Liberal Democracy vs. Transnational Progressivism: The Ideological War within the West." *Orbis* 46, no. 3 (2002): 449–67. https://doi.org/10.1016/s0030-4387(02)00126-6.

Forster, Greg. "A Win-Win Solution: The Empirical Evidence on School Choice." *Friedman Foundation for Educational Choice*, 2013.

Frederick, Shane, George Loewenstein, and Ted O'Donoghue. "Time Discounting and Time Preference: A Critical Review." *Journal of Economic Literature* 40, no. 2 (June 2002): 351–401. https://doi.org/10.1257/002205102320161311.

Freese, Jeremy, and Yu-Han Jao. "Shared Environment Estimates for Educational Attainment: A Puzzle and Possible Solutions." *Journal of Personality* 85, no. 1 (2017): 79–89.

Friedman, Milton. "A Friedman Doctrine: The Social Responsibility of Business Is to Increase Its Profits." *The New York Times*, September 13, 1970. https://www.nytimes.com/1970/09/13/archives/a-friedman-doctrine-the-social-responsibility-of-business-is-to.html.

Fukuyama, Francis. "Social Capital." In *Culture Matters: How Values Shape Human Progress*, edited by Lawrence E. Harrison and Samuel P. Huntington, 99. New York: Basic Books, 2000.

Gagagkar, Raghavendra. "Survival Strategies: Cooperation and Conflict in Animal Societies," 26.

Gambetta, Diego. *The Sicilian Mafia: The Business of Private Protection*. Cambridge, MA: Harvard University Press, 1993.

Gates, Henry Louis, Jr. "Net Worth." *The New Yorker*, May 25, 1998. https://www.newyorker.com/magazine/1998/06/01/michael-jordans-advertising-empire.

G.C.T.A. and M.-G.C.T.A. "Part 1: Estimating Maternal Genetic Effects on Offspring." *Posted by International Statistical Genetics Workshop* 12, no. 34 (May 30, 2022). https://www.youtube.com/watch?v=l34w7J27M3g.

Gelles, David. "Jeff Immelt's Reign at GE: A Look Back." *The New York Times*, February 5, 2021. https://www.nytimes.com/2021/02/05/business/jeff-immelt-general-electric-corner-office.html.

———. *The Man Who Broke Capitalism: How Jack Welch Gutted the Heartland and Crushed the Soul of Corporate America—and How to Undo His Legacy*. Simon and Schuster, 2022.

Gigerenzer, Gerd. *Gut Feelings: The Intelligence of the Unconscious*. Penguin, 2007.

Gillette, David, and Robert DelMas. "Psycho-Economics: Studies in Decision Making," Classroom Expernomics, Newsletter Published by Department of Economics, Management and Accounting." Marietta College, 1992.

Gintis, Herbert. *Moral Sentiments and Material Interests*. Vol. 6. MIT Press, 2005.

———. *The Bounds of Reason: Game Theory and the Unification of the Behavioral Sciences*. Princeton, NJ: Princeton University Press, 2009.

Giolla, Erik Mac, and Petri J. Kajonius. "Sex Differences in Personality Are Larger in Gender Equal Countries: Replicating and Extending a Surprising Finding." *International Journal of Psychology* 54, no. 6 (2019): 705–11.

Gladwell, Malcolm. "The Trouble with College Rankings." *The New Yorker*, February 6, 2011. https://www.newyorker.com/magazine/2011/02/14/the-order-of-things.

Goetze, Rolfe. *Rent Control: Affordable Housing for the Privileged, Not the Poor. A Study of the Impact of Rent Control in Cambridge*. Cambridge, Massachusetts: GeoData Analysis, 1994.

Golden, Alexandrea R., Emily N. Srisarajivakul, Amanda J. Hasselle, Rory A. Pfund, and Jerica Knox. "What Was a Gap Is Now a Chasm: Remote Schooling, the Digital Divide, and Educational Inequities Resulting from the COVID-19 Pandemic." *Current Opinion in Psychology*, 2023, 101632.

Goldgeier, Aviv. "What's the Biggest Challenge Men Face on Dating Apps? A Q&A with Aviv Goldgeier, Junior Growth Engineer." *Hinge IRL*, n.d. https://hingeirl.com/hinge-reports/whats-the-biggest-challenge-men-face-on-dating-apps-a-qa-with-aviv-goldgeier-junior-growth-engineer/.

Golding, William. *Lord of the Flies*. London: Faber and Faber, 1954.

Gombrich, E.H. *A Little History of the World*. New Haven, CT: Yale University Press, 2008.

Gordon, James. "Fury Erupts Over Video of Little Girl in Miami Led by Strutting Drag Queen with Huge Breasts." *Daily Mail*, July 3, 2022. https://www.dailymail.co.uk/news/article-10979095/Fury-erupts-video-little-girl-R-House-Wynwood-Miami-led-strutting-drag-queen-huge-breasts.html.

Gouges, Olympe de. *The Declaration of the Rights of Woman and of the Female Citizen*. Project Gutenberg Edition. Project Gutenberg, 1791. https://www.gutenberg.org/ebooks/64962.

Gray, Peter. "Dramatic Changes in Teen Suicide Rates over Seven Decades." Psychology Today, September 3, 2023. https://www.psychologytoday.com/us/blog/freedom-to-learn/202309/dramatic-changes-in-teen-suicide-rates-over-seven-decades.

Grogger, Jeff. "Does School Quality Explain the Recent Black/White Wage Trend?" *Journal of Labor Economics* 14, no. 2 (1996): 231–53. https://doi.org/10.1086/209810.

Gross, Paul R., and Norman Levitt. *Higher Superstition: The Academic Left and Its Quarrels with Science*. Baltimore: Johns Hopkins University Press, 1994.

Grossman, Sanford J, and Joseph E Stiglitz. "On the Impossibility of Informationally Efficient Markets." *The American Economic Review* 70, no. 3 (1980): 393–408.

Guynet, Stephen. "Superstimuli." *Whole Health Source* (blog), March 7, 2008. https://wholehealthsource.blogspot.com/2008/03/superstimuli.html.

Gwartney, James D. *Common Sense Economics: What Everyone Should Know About Wealth and Prosperity*. New York: Macmillan, 2016.

Gwynne, Darryl T., and David C.F. Rentz. "Beetles on the Bottle: Male Buprestids Mistake Stubbies for Females (Coleoptera)." *Australian Journal of Entomology* 22, no. 1 (1983): 79–80.

Hajnal, John. "European Marriage Patterns in Perspective." In *Population in History: Essays in Historical Demography*, edited by D. V. Glass and D. E. C. Eversley, 101–43. Edward Arnold, 1965.

Hakim, Danny, and Toby Lyles. "For Rangel, Four Rent-Stabilized Apartments." *The New York Times*, July 11, 2008. http://www.nytimes.com/2008/07/11/nyregion/11rangel.html.

Hannam, James. *The Genesis of Science: How the Christian Middle Ages Launched the Scientific Revolution*. Washington, D.C.: Regnery Publishing, 2011.

Hanson, Robin. "Near Far Summary." *Overcoming Bias* (blog), June 2, 2010. https://www.overcomingbias.com/p/near-far-summaryhtml.

Hanushek, Eric A. "Evidence, Politics, and the Class Size Debate." In *The Class Size Debate*, edited by Lawrence Mishel and Richard Rothstein. Washington, DC: Economic Policy Institute, 2002.

Hanushek, Eric A., Eric A. Hanushek, Eric A. Hanushek, and Steven G. Rivkin. "School Resources." Edited by Eric A. Hanushek, Finis Welch, Eric A. Hanushek, and Finis Welch. *Handbook of the Economics of Education* 113, no. 485 (2006): 865–908.

Hardin, Garrett. "The Tragedy of the Commons." *Science* 162 (1968): 1243–48.

Härkönen, Juho, and Jaap Dronkers. "Stability and Change in the Educational Gradient of Divorce: A Comparison of Seventeen Countries." *European Sociological Review* 22, no. 5 (December 2006): 501–17.

Harlow, Jack. "Lovin' On Me," 2023. https://www.jackharlow.us/.

Harris, Judith Rich. *The Nurture Assumption: Why Children Turn Out the Way They Do, Revised and Updated*. Simon and Schuster, 2009.

Harris, Marvin. *Cows, Pigs, Wars, and Witches: The Riddles of Culture*. Vintage, 2011.

Harrison, Lawrence E., and Samuel P. Huntington, eds. "Culture Matters: How Values Shape Human Progress." New York: Basic Books, 2000.

Hart-Smith, L. John. "Outsourced Profits - The Cornerstone of Successful Subcontracting." Seattle, WA: Boeing Commercial Airplanes, 2001.

Hayes, Gavin. "Cast Out: How Knitting Fell into a Purity Spiral." *UnHerd*, January 2020. https://unherd.com/2020/01/cast-out-how-knitting-fell-into-a-purity-spiral/.

Helland, Eric, and Alexander T. Tabarrok. *Why Are the Prices So Damn High?*, 2019.

Henderson, David R. "Creative Destruction." In *The Concise Encyclopedia of Economics*, 2008.

———. "Profits." In *The Concise Encyclopedia of Economics*, 2008.

———. "Rent Control." In *The Concise Encyclopedia of Economics*, 2008.

Henrich, Joseph. "Cooperation, Reciprocity and Punishment in Fifteen Small-Scale Societies." *American Economic Review* 91 (May 2001): 73–78.

———. *The WEIRDest People in the World: How the West Became Psychologically Peculiar and Particularly Prosperous*. Penguin UK, 2020.

Henrich, Joseph, Robert Boyd, and Peter J. Richerson. "The Puzzle of Monogamous Marriage." *Philosophical Transactions of the Royal Society B: Biological Sciences* 367, no. 1589 (2012): 657–69.

Heym, Nadja, Jennifer Firth, Fiona Kibowski, Alexander Sumich, Vincent Egan, and Claire AJ Bloxsom. "Empathy at the Heart of Darkness: Empathy Deficits That Bind the Dark Triad and Those That Mediate Indirect Relational Aggression." *Frontiers in Psychiatry* 12 (2021): 413.

Hiller, Jennifer, and Andrew Restuccia. "The U.S. Fast-Tracked a Power Project After 17 Years. It's Nearing Approval." *The Wall Street Journal*, May 18, 2023. https://www.wsj.com/articles/the-u-s-fast-tracked-a-power-project-after-17-years-its-nearing-approval-1a7edb86.

Hirsh, J.B., C.G. DeYoung, X. Xu, and J.B. Peterson. "Compassionate Liberals and Polite Conservatives: Associations of Agreeableness With Political Ideology and Moral Values." *Personality and Social Psychology Bulletin* 36, no. 5 (2010): 655–64. Hir.

Hoffman, E., K. McCabe, K. Schachat, and V. Smith. "Preferences, Property Rights, and Anonymity in Bargaining Games." *Games and Economic Behavior* 7, no. 3 (1994): 346–80.

Holland, Tom. *Dominion: The Making of the Western Mind*. Hachette UK, 2019.

Hrdy, Sarah Blaffer. *Mother Nature*. London: Chatto & Windus, 1999.

Hume, David. *A Treatise of Human Nature*. Clarendon Press, 1896.

"I Am Jazz." United States: TLC, 2015.

Ioannidis, John. "Why Most Published Research Findings Are False." *PLoS Medicine* 2 (2005): 124,. https://doi.org/10.1371/journal.pmed.0020124.

Jefferson, Thomas, and Second Continental Congress. "The Declaration of Independence." United States National Archives, July 4, 1776. https://www.archives.gov/founding-docs/declaration-transcript.

Jencks, Christopher. "Is the American Underclass Growing?" In *The Urban Underclass*, edited by Paul E. Peterson and Christopher Jencks, 89. Washington, D.C: Brookings Institution, 1991.

Johnson, Samuel. *Lives of the Poets*. Vol. 2. London: J. Buckland and others, 1781. https://www.gutenberg.org/files/24218/24218-h/24218-h.htm.

Jonason, Peter K, and Laura Krause. "The Emotional Deficits Associated with the Dark Triad Traits: Cognitive Empathy, Affective Empathy, and Alexithymia." *Personality and Individual Differences* 55, no. 5 (2013): 532–37.

Jonason, Peter K., Norman P. Li, Gregory D. Webster, and David P. Schmitt. "The Dark Triad: Facilitating a Short-Term Mating Strategy in Men." *European Journal of Personality* 23 (2009): 5–18.

"KABC-TV7 (1974) 'Free to Be You & Me!' Original Broadcast!!!!." Obsolete Video, July 2021. https://www.youtube.com/watch?v=7PS3nOcLbHI.

Kahneman, Daniel. *Thinking, Fast and Slow*. New York: Farrar, Straus and Giroux, 2011.

Kahneman, Daniel, Jack L. Knetsch, and Richard H. Thaler. "Experimental Tests of the Endowment Effect and the Coase Theorem." *Journal of Political Economy* 98, no. 6 (December 1990): 1325–48.

Karrington, Baer. "Defining Desistance: Exploring Desistance in Transgender and Gender Expansive Youth through Systematic Literature Review." *Transgender Health* 7, no. 3 (2022): 189–212.

Kastiel, Kobi. "Lucian Bebchuk and the Study of Corporate Governance." *The University of Chicago Law Review* 88, no. 7 (2021): 1689–1714.

Keane, Michael P. "Labor Supply and Taxes: A Survey." *Journal of Economic Literature* 49, no. 4 (2011): 961–1075.

Keeley, Lawrence H. *War Before Civilization.* New York: Oxford University Press, 1997.

Kelley, Alexandra. "Biden Tells Coal Miners to Learn to Code." *The Hill*, December 31, 2019. https://thehill.com/changing-america/enrichment/education/476391-biden-tells-coal-miners-to-learn-to-code/.

Kempf, Elisabeth, and Margarita Tsoutsoura. "Partisan Professionals: Evidence from Credit Rating Analysts." *The Journal of Finance* 76, no. 6 (2021): 2805–56. https://doi.org/10.1111/jofi.13042.

Kendler, K.S., H. Ohlsson, A.C. Edwards, P. Lichtenstein, K. Sundquist, and J. Sundquist. "A Novel Sibling-Based Design to Quantify Genetic and Shared Environmental Effects: Application to Drug Abuse, Alcohol Use Disorder, and Criminal Behavior." *Psychological Medicine* 46, no. 8 (2016): 1639–50.

Kenny, Prof Dianna. "Response to David Shoebridge on Percentage Increases in Young People Presenting to Gender Clinics." Parliament of New South Wales, May 3, 2021. https://www.parliament.nsw.gov.au/lcdocs/other/15633/Prof%20Dianna%20Kenny%20-%20received%203%20May%202021.pdf.

Kessel, Reuben. "A Study of the Effects of Competition in the Tax-Exempt Bond Market." *Journal of Political Economy* 79 (August 1971): 706–38.

King, Ronald R., Vernon L. Smith, Arlington W. Williams, and Mark Boening. "The Robustness of Bubbles and Crashes in Experimental Stock Markets." *Nonlinear Dynamics and Evolutionary Economics*, 1993, 183–200.

Kissing Jessica Stein, 2001.

Kitroeff, Natalie, David Gelles, and Jack Nicas. "Boeing 737 Max: The FAA Wanted a Safe Plane — but Didn't Want to Hurt America's Biggest Exporter." *The New York Times*, July 27, 2019. https://www.nytimes.com/2019/07/27/business/boeing-737-max-faa.html.

Klein, Ezra. "Opinion | The Story Construction Tells About America's Economy Is Disturbing." *The New York Times*, February 2023, Opinion.

Klein, Richard A, Michelangelo Vianello, Fred Hasselman, Byron G Adams, Reginald B Adams Jr, Sinan Alper, Mark Aveyard, et al. "Many Labs 2: Investigating Variation in Replicability across Samples and Settings." *Advances in Methods and Practices in Psychological Science* 1, no. 4 (2018): 443–90.

Koch, Dirk-Jan. *Foreign Aid and Its Unintended Consequences*. Rethinking Development. Taylor and Francis, 2023. https://www.routledge.com/Foreign-Aid-and-Its-Unintended-Consequences-1st-Edition/Koch/p/book/9781032412184.

Kolko, Gabriel. *The Triumph of Conservatism: A Re-Interpretation of American History, 1900-1916*. Chicago: Quadrangle, 1967.

Kruger, Justin, and David Dunning. "Unskilled and Unaware of It: How Difficulties in Recognizing One's Own Incompetence Lead to Inflated Self-Assessments." *Journal of Personality and Social Psychology* 77, no. 6 (1999): 1121–34. https://doi.org/10.1037/0022-3514.77.6.1121.

Krugman, Paul R. *Peddling Prosperity: Economic Sense and Nonsense in the Age of Diminished Expectations*. New York: W.W. Norton & Company, 1994.

Kurilova, Eva. "Australian Human Rights Commission Decision Prohibits Female-Only Events for Lesbians." *Reduxx*, September 26, 2023. https://reduxx.info/australian-human-rights-commission-decision-prohibits-female-only-events-for-lesbians/.

Lack, David Lambert. "Ecological Adaptations for Breeding in Birds," 1968.

Landman, Keren. "How to Talk to Boys so They Grow into Better Men." *Vox*, March 2024. https://www.vox.com/even-better/24097641/andrew-tate-masculinity-teens-boys-men-talk-conversations.

Lang, Kevin, and Jay L Zagorsky. "Does Growing up with a Parent Absent Really Hurt?" *Journal of Human Resources*, 2001, 253–73.

Lecky, William Edward Hartpole. *History of European Morals: From Augustus to Charlemagne*. Vol. 2. New York: D. Appleton, 1927.

Leventis, Andrew. *Cardiac Surgeons Under the Knife*. Princeton University, 1997.

Lewsey, Fred. "Britain Industrialised Much Earlier than History Books Claim." University of Cambridge, April 2024. https://www.cam.ac.uk/stories/nation-of-makers-industrial-britain.

Liebowitz, Stan J., and Stephen E. Margolis. "The Fable of the Keys." *The Journal of Law and Economics* 33, no. 1 (1990): 1–25.

Lindert, Peter. "Preliminary Global Price Comparisons, 1500-1870," n.d. http://www.iisg.nl/hpw/conference.html.

Lindsay, Jack. *The Ancient World: Manners and Morals*. Putnam, 1968.

Little, Callie W., Rasheda Haughbrook, and Sara A. Hart. "Cross-Study Differences in the Etiology of Reading Comprehension: A Meta-Analytical Review of Twin Studies." *Behavior Genetics* 47 (2017): 52–76.

Lubienski, Christopher. *Review of "A Win-Win Solution" and "The Participant Effects of Private School Vouchers across the Globe."* Boulder, CO: National Education Policy Center, 2016.

Luthi, Susannah. "California's Female Prisoners Feel Threatened by Transgender Inmates. The State Doesn't Care." *The Free Beacon*, Washington Free Beacon, January 31, 2023. https://freebeacon.com/california/californias-female-prisoners-feel-threatened-by-transgender-inmates-the-state-doesnt-care/.

Macfarlane, Alan. "Introduction to the Paperback Edition." *Savage Wars of Peace*, n.d. http://www.alanmacfarlane.com/TEXTS/savageintropb.pdf.

MacroTrends. "Exxon Profit Margins," n.d. https://www.macrotrends.net/stocks/charts/XOM/exxon/profit-margins.

MacroTrends. "Microsoft Profit Margins," n.d. https://www.macrotrends.net/stocks/charts/MSFT/microsoft/profit-margins.

MacroTrends. "Walmart Net Profit Margin," n.d. https://www.macrotrends.net/stocks/charts/WMT/walmart/net-profit-margin.

Maddison, Angus. *The World Economy: A Millennial Perspective*. Paris: OECD, 2001.

"Magna Carta." British Library, June 15, 1215. https://www.bl.uk/collection-items/magna-carta-1215.

Makinson, David C. "The Paradox of the Preface." *Analysis* 25, no. 6 (1965): 205–7. https://academic.oup.com/analysis/article-abstract/25/6/205/127835?redirectedFrom=fulltext

Martin, Mark. "Drafting." Mark Martin's Racing Tips, n.d. http://www.markmartin.org/drafting.html.

Mauro, Paolo. "The Effects of Corruption on Growth, Investment, and Government Expenditure: A Cross-Country Analysis." In *Corruption and the Global Economy*, edited by Kimberly Ann Elliot, 91. Washington, D.C: Institute for International Economics, 1997.

McMillan, John. *Reinventing the Bazaar: A Natural History of Markets*. New York: Norton, 2002.

Michaelson, Laura E., and Yuko Munakata. "Same Data Set, Different Conclusions: Preschool Delay of Gratification Predicts Later Behavioral Outcomes in a Preregistered Study." *Psychological Science* 31, no. 2 (2020): 193–201.

Milgrom, Paul, and John Roberts. "Complementarities and Fit: Strategies, Structure, and Organizational Change in Manufacturing." *Journal of Accounting and Economics* 19 (1995): 179–208.

Miller, Terry, Anthony B. Kim, and James M. Roberts. "2021 Index of Economic Freedom." The Heritage Foundation, 2021. https://www.heritage.org/index/.

Moffitt, Robert A. "The Effect of Welfare on Marriage and Fertility." In *Welfare, the Family, and Reproductive Behavior*, edited by Robert A. Moffitt, 50–97. Washington, D.C: National Academy Press, 1998.

Moffitt, Robert A., Brian J. Phelan, and Anne E. Winkler. "Welfare Rules, Incentives, and Family Structure." *Journal of Human Resources* 55, no. 1 (2020): 1–42.

Moore, Stephen, and Julian L. Simon. "The Greatest Century That Ever Was: 25 Miraculous Trends of the Past 100 Years." *Cato Policy Analysis*, no. 364 (1999).

Morgan, Edmund S. *The Puritan Family: Religion and Domestic Relations in Seventeenth-Century New England.* Revised. New York: Harper & Row, 1966.

Morrot, Gil, Frédéric Brochet, and Denis Dubourdieu. "The Color of Odors." *Brain and Language* 79, no. 2 (2001): 309–20.

Mosendz, Polly. "A Complete Timeline of the Donald Sterling Saga." *The Atlantic*, 2014. https://www.theatlantic.com/business/archive/2014/05/a-complete-timeline-of-the-donald-sterling-saga/371868/.

"Munk Debate - Mainstream Media Ft. Douglas Murray, Matt Taibbi, Malcolm Gladwell, Michelle Goldberg," November 30, 2022. https://www.youtube.com/watch?v=nvaf7XOOFHc.

Nash, Betty Joyce. "Jargon Alert/Regulatory Capture." *Region Focus* 14, no. 3 (2010): 12.

National Assessment of Educational Progress. "Achievement Gaps Dashboard," 2024. https://www.nationsreportcard.gov/dashboards/achievement_gaps.aspx.

National Center for Education Statistics. "Table 222.77. Average National Assessment of Educational Progress (NAEP) Mathematics Scale Scores and Achievement-Level Results for Students in Grades 4 and 8, by Selected Student Characteristics: Selected Years, 1990 through 2019." *Digest of Education Statistics 2019*, 2019. https://nces.ed.gov/programs/digest/d19/tables/dt19_222.77.asp.

———. "Table 236.55. Total and Current Expenditures per Pupil in Public Elementary and Secondary Schools: Selected Years, 1919-20 through 2016-17." *Digest of Education Statistics 2019*, 2019. https://nces.ed.gov/programs/digest/d19/tables/dt19_236.55.asp?current=yes.

Next Steps Blog. "National Survey Shows Black Parents Continue to Support Education Choice," June 4, 2021. https://nextstepsblog.org/2021/06/national-survey-shows-black-parents-continue-to-support-education-choice/.

Ngo, Andy. "Charges Filed Against Sex Offender in Notorious WI Spa Incident." *New York Post*, September 2, 2021. https://nypost.com/2021/09/02/charges-filed-against-sex-offender-in-wi-spa-casecharges-filed-against-sex-offender-in-notorious-wi-spa-incident/.

NHS England. "Clinical Policy: Puberty Suppressing Hormones," n.d. https://www.england.nhs.uk/publication/clinical-policy-puberty-suppressing-hormones/.

Nodjimbadem, Katie. "The Lesser-Known History of African-American Cowboys." *Smithsonian*, February 13, 2017. https://www.smithsonianmag.com/history/lesser-known-history-african-american-cowboys-180962144/.

Olson-Kennedy, Johanna, Jonathan Warus, Vivian Okonta, Marvin Belzer, and Leslie F. Clark. "Chest Reconstruction and Chest Dysphoria in Transmasculine Minors and Young Adults: Comparisons of Nonsurgical and Postsurgical Cohorts." *JAMA Pediatrics* 172, no. 5 (2018): 431–36.

Olsson, Ola, and Douglas A. Hibbs Jr. "Biogeography and Long-Run Economic Development." *European Economic Review* 49 (2005): 909–38.

Open Science Collaboration. "Estimating the Reproducibility of Psychological Science." *Science* 349, no. 6251 (2015): 4716.

Orenstein, Peggy. "Opinion | The Troubling Trend in Teenage Sex." *The New York Times*, April 12, 2024. https://www.nytimes.com/2024/04/12/opinion/choking-teen-sex-brain-damage.html?unlocked_article_code=1.kk0.1R0X.GaeJGR8jhZlH.

Osterman, Michelle J.K., Brady E. Hamilton, Joyce A. Martin, Anne K. Driscoll, and Carla P. Valenzuela. "Births: Final Data for 2021." *National Vital Statistics Reports* 72, no. 1 (2023). https://doi.org/10.15620/cdc:122047.

Ostrom, Elinor. *Understanding Institutional Diversity*. Princeton University Press, 2009.

Ostrom, Elinor, Roy Gardner, and James Walker. *Rules, Games, and Common-Pool Resources*. Ann Arbor, MI: University of Michigan Press, 1994.

Oxoby, Robert J, and John Spraggon. "Mine and Yours: Property Rights in Dictator Games." *Journal of Economic Behavior & Organization* 65, no. 3–4 (2008): 703–13.

Pajevic, Milica, Tatjana Vukosavljevic-Gvozden, Nevena Stevanovic, and Craig S Neumann. "The Relationship between the Dark Tetrad and a Two-Dimensional View of Empathy." *Personality and Individual Differences* 123 (2018): 125–30.

Parenthood. United States: Universal Pictures, 1989.

Perry, Louise. *The Case Against the Sexual Revolution*. John Wiley & Sons, 2022.

Perry, Sarah Parshall. "Biden Administration Holds School Lunches Hostage to Radical Transgender Agenda," n.d. https://www.heritage.org/gender/commentary/biden-administration-holds-school-lunches-hostage-radical-transgender-agenda.

Peterson, M.B., and L. Lausten. "Upperbody Strength and Political Egalitarianism: Twelve Conceptual Replications." *Political Psychology,* 40 (n.d.): 375–94.

Peterson, Paul E. *Generational Change: Closing the Test Score Gap*. Lanham, MD: Rowman & Littlefield Publishers, 2006.

Phelps-Roper, Megan. "The Real Story of the Central Park Five." *The Free Press.* August 3 (2021). https://www.thefp.com/p/the-real-story-of-the-central-park.

Phillips, Stuart M., and Luc J.C. Loon. "Dietary Protein for Athletes: From Requirements to Optimum Adaptation." In *Food, Nutrition and Sports Performance III*, 29–38, 2013.

Pianta, Robert C., W.Steven Barnett, Margaret Burchinal, and Kathy R. Thornburg. "The Effects of Preschool Education: What We Know, How Public Policy Is or Is Not Aligned with the Evidence Base, and What We Need to Know." *Psychological Science in the Public Interest* 10, no. 2 (2009): 49–88.

Pinker, Steven. *The Blank Slate: The Modern Denial of Human Nature*. Penguin, 2003.

Plomin, Robert, and Ian J. Deary. "Genetics and Intelligence Differences: Five Special Findings." *Molecular Psychiatry* 20, no. 1 (2015): 98–108.

Plomin, Robert, and Sophie Stumm. "The New Genetics of Intelligence." *Nature Reviews Genetics* 19, no. 3 (2018): 148–59.

Pluckrose, Helen, James A. Lindsay, and Peter Boghossian. "Academic Grievance Studies and the Corruption of Scholarship." *Areo Magazine*, October 2018. https://areomagazine.com/2018/10/02/academic-grievance-studies-and-the-corruption-of-scholarship/.

Pomeranz, Kenneth. *The Great Divergence*. Princeton, NJ: Princeton University Press, 2000.

Porta, Rafael. "Trust in Large Organizations." *American Economic Review* 87 (1997): 333–38.

Prendergast, Canice. "The Provision of Incentives in Firms." *Journal of Economic Literature* 37 (1999): 7–63.

Prinz, Florian, Thomas Schlange, and Khusru Asadullah. "Believe It or Not: How Much Can We Rely on Published Data on Potential Drug Targets?" *Nature Reviews Drug Discovery* 10, no. 9 (2011): 712–712.

Puma, Michael, Stephen Bell, Ronna Cook, Camilla Heid, Pam Broene, Frank Jenkins, Andrew Mashburn, and Jason Downer. "Head Start Impact Study: Final Report." Washington, DC: U.S. Department of Health and Human Services, Administration for Children and Families, Office of Planning, Research and Evaluation, January 2010. https://www.acf.hhs.gov/sites/default/files/documents/opre/hs_impact_study_final.pdf.

———. "Third Grade Follow-up to the Head Start Impact Study." OPRE Report. Washington, DC: U.S. Department of Health and Human Services, Administration for Children and Families, Office of Planning, Research and Evaluation, October 2012. https://www.acf.hhs.gov/opre/report/third-grade-follow-head-start-impact-study-final-report.

Putnam, Robert D. "E Pluribus Unum: Diversity and Community in the Twenty-First Century." *Scandinavian Political Studies* 30, no. 2 (2007): 137–74.

———. *Making Democracy Work: Civic Traditions in Modern Italy*. Princeton, NJ: Princeton University Press, 1993.

Ramsay, Gordon. "Gordon Ramsay's Kitchen Nightmares." United Kingdom and United States: Channel 4 and Fox Broadcasting Company, 2004.

Rapaczynski, Andrzej. "The Roles of the State and the Market in Establishing Property Rights." *Journal of Economic Perspectives* 10, no. 2 (1996).

Ravitch, Diane. *Left Back: A Century of Battles Over School Reform*. New York: Simon and Schuster, 2001.

Raymond, Nate. "Parents Cannot Challenge School Gender Identity Policy, US Court Rules." *Reuters*, August 14, 2023. https://www.reuters.com/legal/government/parents-cannot-challenge-school-gender-identity-policy-us-court-rules-2023-08-14/.

Reddit. "BaR Botched the Citi Bike Karen Story: What They Got Wrong." Forum, February 2023. https://www.reddit.com/r/BlockedAndReported/comments/13t7c75/bar_botched_the_citi_bike_karen_story_what_they/.

Richerson, P.J., and R. Boyd. *Not By Genes Alone: How Culture Transformed Human Evolution*. Chicago: University of Chicago Press, 2004.

Robinson, Barbara. *The Best Christmas Pageant Ever*. New York: Harper & Row, 1972.

Robison, Peter. *Flying Blind: The 737 MAX Tragedy and the Fall of Boeing*. Anchor, 2022.

Rosenzweig, Mark R. "Welfare, Marital Prospects, and Nonmarital Childbearing." *Journal of Political Economy* 107, no. S6 (December 1999): 3-32,. https://doi.org/10.1086/250102.

Roser, Max, and Hannah Ritchie. "Maternal Mortality." *Our World in Data*, 2013. https://ourworldindata.org/maternal-mortality.

Rousseau, Jean-Jacques. *A Discourse Upon the Origin and the Foundation of the Inequality Among Mankind*. Translated by G.D.H. Cole. Project Gutenberg, 2004. https://www.gutenberg.org/ebooks/11136.

———. *Discourse on the Origin and Basis of Inequality Among Men*. Project Gutenberg EBook #11136. Project Gutenberg, 1754. https://www.gutenberg.org/cache/epub/11136/pg11136-images.html.

Rubens, Peter Paul. *The Three Graces*. Madrid, Spain, 1635.

Russell, Bertrand. *A History of Western Philosophy*. New York: Simon and Schuster, 1945.

Russell, Josiah Cox. "Late Ancient and Medieval Population." *Transactions of the American Philosophical Society* 48, no. 3 (1958): 1–152.

Saffer, Henry, and Frank Chaloupka. "The Demand for Illicit Drugs." *Economic Inquiry* 37, no. 3 (1999): 401–11.

Sanger, Margaret. "My Way to Peace," January 17, 1932. https://m-sanger.org/items/show/1373.

Sapir, Leor. "Reckless and Irresponsible." *City Journal*, March 17, 2023. https://archive.is/eI4Xt. https://www.city-journal.org/article/reckless-and-irresponsible.

———. "The Reckoning over Puberty Blockers Has Arrived." *The Hill*, April 4, 2024. https://thehill.com/opinion/healthcare/4573662-the-reckoning-over-puberty-blockers-has-arrived/.

Scafidi, Benjamin. "Back to the Staffing Surge: The Great Teacher Salary Stagnation and the Decades-Long Employment Growth in American Public Schools." *EdChoice*, 2017.

Schiffman, Richard. "Adventure Playgrounds: A Dying Breed?" *The New York Times*, May 10, 2019. https://www.nytimes.com/2019/05/10/well/family/adventure-playgrounds-junk-playgrounds.html.

Schmidt, F.L., and J.E. Hunter. "The Validity and Utility of Selection Methods in Personnel Psychology: Practical and Theoretical Findings of 85 Years of Research Findings." *Psychological Bulletin* 124 (1998): 262–74.

Schwarzenegger, Arnold, and Bill Dobbins. *Encyclopedia of Modern Bodybuilding*. New York: Simon and Schuster, 1985.

Searle, John R. "The Word Turned Upside Down." *The New York Review of Books*, n.d. https://www.nybooks.com/articles/1983/10/27/the-word-turned-upside-down/.

Segerstrale, Ullica. *Defenders of the Truth: The Battle for Science in the Sociobiology Debate and Beyond*. Oxford: Oxford University Press, 2000.

Shakeel, Danish M., Kaitlin P. Anderson, and Patrick J. Wolf. "The Participant Effects of Private School Vouchers Around the Globe: A Meta-Analytic and Systematic Review." *School Effectiveness and School Improvement* 32, no. 4 (2021): 509–42.

"Share of Births Outside of Marriage." *OECD Family Database*, n.d. https://www.oecd.org/els/family/SF_2_4_Share_births_outside_marriage.pdf.

Sharp, Andrew. *The English Levellers*. Cambridge, UK: Cambridge University Press, 2002.

Shuck, Peter H., and James Q. Wilson, eds. Understanding America: The Anatomy of an Exceptional Nation. New York, NY: Public Affairs, 2008.

Shyamalan, M.Night. *The Sixth Sense*. United States: Buena Vista Pictures, 1999.

Sibley, C.G., D. Osborne, and J. Duckitt. "Personality and Political Orientation: Meta-Analysis and Test of a Threat-Constraint Model." *Journal of Research in Personality* 46, no. 6 (2012): 664–77. https://doi.org/10.1016/j.jrp.2012.08.002.

Simard, Suzanne. *Finding the Mother Tree: Discovering the Wisdom of the Forest*. New York: Alfred A. Knopf, 2021.

———. *Finding the Mother Tree: Discovering the Wisdom of the Forest*. New York: Alfred A. Knopf, 2021.

Simmons, Joseph P., Leif D. Nelson, and Uri Simonsohn. "False-Positive Psychology: Undisclosed Flexibility in Data Collection and Analysis Allows Presenting Anything as Significant." *Psychological Science* 22, no. 11 (2011): 1359–66.

Singh, Devendra. "Adaptive Significance of Female Physical Attractiveness: Role of Waist-to-Hip Ratio." *Journal of Personality and Social Psychology* 65, no. 2 (1993): 293–307. https://doi.org/10.1037/0022-3514.65.2.293.

Smith, Adam. *The Wealth of Nations*. New York: The Modern Library, 1776.

Smith, J.Maynard, and G.A. Parker. "The Logic of Asymmetric Contests." *Animal Behaviour* 24 (1976): 159–75.

Smith, Vernon L. "Economics in the Laboratory." *Journal of Economic Perspectives* 8, no. 1 (1994): 118.

Smolin, Lee. *The Trouble with Physics: The Rise of String Theory, the Fall of a Science, and What Comes Next*. Boston: Houghton Mifflin Harcourt, 2007.

Sokal, Alan D. "A Physicist Experiments with Cultural Studies." *Lingua Franca* 6, no. 4 (1996): 62–64.

Solomon-Fears, Carmen. "Nonmarital Births: An Overview." *Congressional Research Service*, 2014.

Somerville, Ewan. "University Blocks Academic from Her Own Gender Wars Research Over 'Dangerous' Data." *MSN*, March 15, 2023. https://www.msn.com/en-gb/news/world/university-blocks-academic-from-her-own-gender-wars-research-over-dangerous-data/ar-AA19Uf9Y;

Sonnenfeld, Jeffrey A. "What Makes Great Boards Great." *Harvard Business Review*, September 2002. https://hbr.org/2002/09/what-makes-great-boards-great.

Soto, Hernando. *The Mystery of Capital*. New York, NY: Basic Books, 2000.

South Park: Bigger, Longer & Uncut. Hollywood, CA, 1999.

Sowell, Thomas. *A Conflict of Visions: Ideological Origins of Political Struggles*. Basic Books, 2002.

———. *Black Rednecks & White Liberals*. Encounter Books, 2009.

———. *Ethnic America: A History*. New York: Basic Books, 1981.

"Space Launch Market Competition," n.d. https://en.wikipedia.org/wiki/Space_launch_market_competition.

Spiro, Melford E. *Gender and Culture: Kibbutz Women Revisited*. New Brunswick, NJ: Transaction Publishers, 1979.

Star Wars: Episode V - The Empire Strikes Back. Star Wars, 1980.

Stigler, G.J. "The Theory of Economic Regulation." *The Bell Journal of Economics and Management Science* 2, no. 1 (1971): 3–21. https://doi.org/10.2307/3003160.

Strathern, Paul. *Hume in 90 Minutes*. Philosophers in 90 Minutes Series. Chicago: Ivan R. Dee, 1996.

Strenze, Tarmo. "Intelligence and Socioeconomic Success: A Meta-Analytic Review of Longitudinal Research." *Intelligence* 35, no. 5 (2007): 401–26.

Suddeth, Rick. *USSR: Grocery Store Uncut*. YouTube Video. YouTube, 2015. https://www.youtube.com/watch?v=t8LtQhIQ2AE.

Summers, Lawrence H., and Kim B. Clark. "Labor Market Dynamics and Unemployment: A Reconsideration." *Brookings Papers on Economic Activity* I (1979): 13–60.

"Support for School Choice Remains Strong During Volatile Year." *American Federation for Children*, n.d. https://www.federationforchildren.org.

Surowiecki, James. *The Wisdom of Crowds: Why the Many Are Smarter Than the Few and How Collective Wisdom Shapes Business, Economies, Societies and Nations.* London: Doubleday, 2004.

Tabakovic, Haris, and Thomas G. Wollmann. "From Revolving Doors to Regulatory Capture? Evidence from Patent Examiners." Working Paper. National Bureau of Economic Research, 2018. https://www.nber.org/system/files/working_papers/w24638/w24638.pdf.

Tackett, Timothy. *The Coming of the Terror in the French Revolution.* Cambridge, MA: Belknap Press: An Imprint of Harvard University Press, 2015.

Thaler, Richard H., and Cass R. Sunstein. *Nudge: Improving Decisions About Health, Wealth, and Happiness.* New Haven, CT: Yale University Press, 2008.

The Big Short. Paramount Pictures, 2015.

The Breakfast Club. United States: Universal Pictures, 1985.

"The Devil Wears Prada." United States, 2006.

The Matrix. United States: Warner Bros. Pictures, 1999.

"The Nation's Report Card." National Center for Education Statistics, 2013. https://nces.ed.gov/nationsreportcard/subject/publications/main2012/pdf/2013456.pdf.

"The Problem with Jon Stewart." *The War Over Gender.* Apple, October 6, 2022.

The Thomas B. Fordham Institute. "Algebra for None: The Effects of San Francisco's De-Tracking Reform." Accessed April 9, 2023. https://fordhaminstitute.org/national/commentary/algebra-none-effects-san-franciscos-de-tracking-reform.

The Year 2001: Quotes and Quibbles. Seattle Post-Intelligencer, n.d. https://www.seattlepi.com/local/opinion/article/the-year-2001-quotes-and-quibbles-1076093.php.

Thomas, Marlo, Carole Hart, Mary Rodgers, and Letty Cottin Klagsbrun. "Free to Be... You and Me." ABC, March 11, 1974.

Thornton, Yvonne S., and Jo Coudert. *The Ditchdigger's Daughters: A Black Family's Astonishing Success Story.* New York: Kensington Publishing Corp., 1995.

Tierney, Patrick. *Darkness in El Dorado: How Scientists and Journalists Devastated the Amazon.* New York: W. W. Norton & Company, 2000.

Tolkien, J.R.R. *The Fellowship of the Ring.* Vol. 1. The Lord of the Rings. George Allen & Unwin, 1954.

Tucker, William. "How Rent Control Drives Out Affordable Housing." *Cato Policy Analysis*, May 21, 1997. http://www.cato.org/pubs/pas/pa-274.html.

———. *The Excluded Americans: Homelessness and Housing Policies.* Washington: Regnery Gateway, 1990.

Turner, Erick H. "Selective Publication of Antidepressant Trials and Its Influence on Apparent Efficacy." *New England Journal of Medicine* 358, no. 3 (2008): 252–60.

Twenge, Jean M. "Egos Inflating Over Time: A Cross-Temporal Meta-Analysis of the Narcissistic Personality Inventory." *Journal of Personality* 76, no. 4 (2008): 875–902.

Uecker, Jeremy E., and Mark D. Regnerus. "Bare Market: Campus Sex Ratios, Romantic Relationships, and Sexual Behavior." *The Sociological Quarterly* 51, no. 3 (2010): 408–35.

Urban, Ria. "How Much Does It Cost to Launch a Rocket?" Space Impulse," August 16, 2023. https://spaceimpulse.com/2023/08/16/how-much-does-it-cost-to-launch-a-rocket/.

Vartabedian, Ralph. "California High-Speed Rail Politics." *The New York Times*, October 9, 2022. https://www.nytimes.com/2022/10/09/us/california-high-speed-rail-politics.html.

Voltaire. *Letters on the English*. Project Gutenberg, 2009. https://www.gutenberg.org/ebooks/2445.

Waal, Frans. *Our Inner Ape*. New York: Riverhead Books, 2005.

Wai, Minna, and Niko Tiliopoulos. "The Affective and Cognitive Empathic Nature of the Dark Triad of Personality." *Personality and Individual Differences* 52, no. 7 (2012): 794–99.

Warren, Elizabeth, and Amelia Warren Tyagi. *The Two-Income Trap: Why Middle-Class Parents Are Going Broke*. New York: Basic Books, 2003.

Watts, Tyler W., Greg J. Duncan, and Haonan Quan. "Revisiting the Marshmallow Test: A Conceptual Replication Investigating Links Between Early Delay of Gratification and Later Outcomes." *Psychological Science* 29, no. 7 (2018): 1159–77.

Weiner, Jonathan. *The Beak of the Finch: A Story of Evolution in Our Time*. New York: Alfred A. Knopf, 1994.

Weisman, Jonathan. "Tax Rates and Unemployment Rates Show Negative Correlation." *Washington Post*, March 15, 2004.

Wikipedia contributors. "Deferent and Epicycle — Wikipedia, The Free Encyclopedia," 2024. https://en.wikipedia.org/w/index.php?title=Deferent_and_epicycle&oldid=1224074707.

Willett, Walter C. "Dietary Fats and Coronary Heart Disease." *Journal of Internal Medicine* 272, no. 1 (2012): 13–24.

"William Galston's Findings Are Based on a Study by Charles Murray, "According to Age: Longitudinal Profiles of AFDC Recipients and the Poor by Age Group." In *Working Seminar on the Family and American Welfare Policy*, 89–90. Washington, D.C, 1986.

Williams, Walter. "Price Gouging." *Capitalism Magazine*, March 2004. http://www.capmag.com/article.asp?ID=3578.

Wilson, James Q. "The Marriage Problem," 2002.

Wittman, Donald. *The Myth of Democratic Failure: Why Political Institutions Are Efficient*. Chicago: The University of Chicago Press, 1995.

Womack, James P., Daniel T. Jones, and Daniel Roos. *The Machine That Changed the World: The Story of Lean Production*. New York, NY: Rawson Associates, 1990.

"WPATH Blocked Publication of Its Own Gender Research," n.d. https://unherd.com/breaking_news/wpath-blocked-publication-of-its-own-gender-research/.

Wu, Ashley. "Illegal Border Crossings, Explained in 7 Charts." The New York Times, October 29, 2023. https://www.nytimes.com/interactive/2023/10/29/us/illegal-border-crossings-data.html.

Wydick, Bruce. *Games in Economic Development*. Cambridge: Cambridge University Press, 2007.

Wynne-Edwards, V.C. *Animal Dispersion in Relation to Social Behavior*. New York: Hafner, 1962.

Yannelis, Constantine, and Adam Looney. "What Went Wrong with Federal Student Loans?" *University of Chicago, Becker Friedman Institute for Economics Working Paper* 2024, no. 60 (2024).

Zehr, Mary Ann. "Obama Administration Targets 'Disparate Impact' of Discipline." *Education Week*, October 7, 2010. https://www.edweek.org/leadership/obama-administration-targets-disparate-impact-of-discipline/2010/10.

Zimmer, Ron. "Nearly Three Decades into the Charter School Movement, What Has Research Told Us About Charter Schools?" In *The Routledge Handbook of the Economics of Education*, edited by Steve Bradley and Colin Green, 73–106. New York: Routledge, 2021.